Making Meaning in Popular Song

Also available from Bloomsbury

Andean Aesthetics and Anticolonial Resistance, by Omar Rivera
Philosophy, Literature and Understanding, by Jukka Mikkonen
The Aesthetics of Imperfection in Music and the Arts, edited by Andy Hamilton and Lara Pearson
The Changing Boundaries and Nature of the Modern Art World, by Richard Kalina
The Dialectics of Music, by Joseph Weiss

Making Meaning in Popular Song

Philosophical Essays

Theodore Gracyk

BLOOMSBURY ACADEMIC
LONDON • NEW YORK • OXFORD • NEW DELHI • SYDNEY

BLOOMSBURY ACADEMIC
Bloomsbury Publishing Plc
50 Bedford Square, London, WC1B 3DP, UK
1385 Broadway, New York, NY 10018, USA
29 Earlsfort Terrace, Dublin 2, Ireland

BLOOMSBURY, BLOOMSBURY ACADEMIC and the Diana logo are trademarks of
Bloomsbury Publishing Plc

First published in Great Britain 2022
This paperback edition published 2023

Copyright © Theodore Gracyk, 2022

Theodore Gracyk has asserted his right under the Copyright, Designs
and Patents Act, 1988, to be identified as Author of this work.

For legal purposes the Acknowledgments on pp. viii–ix constitute
an extension of this copyright page.

Cover design by Louise Dugdale
Cover image: Rüdiger Lutz / EyeEm / Getty Images

All rights reserved. No part of this publication may be reproduced or transmitted
in any form or by any means, electronic or mechanical, including photocopying,
recording, or any information storage or retrieval system, without
prior permission in writing from the publishers.

Bloomsbury Publishing Plc does not have any control over, or responsibility for, any
third-party websites referred to or in this book. All internet addresses given in this
book were correct at the time of going to press. The author and publisher regret
any inconvenience caused if addresses have changed or sites have ceased
to exist, but can accept no responsibility for any such changes.

A catalogue record for this book is available from the British Library.

A catalog record for this book is available from the Library of Congress.

ISBN: HB: 978-1-3502-4909-7
PB: 978-1-3502-4913-4
ePDF: 978-1-3502-4910-3
eBook: 978-1-3502-4911-0

Typeset by Integra Software Services Pvt. Ltd.

To find out more about our authors and books visit www.bloomsbury.com
and sign up for our newsletters.

For Robert Stecker and Stephen Davies

Contents

Acknowledgments	viii
Introduction: Key Concepts	1

Part 1 Songs

1	Meanings of Songs and Meanings of Song Performances	21
2	Who Is "You're So Vain" About?	37

Part 2 Performers

3	Performer, Persona, and Musical Performance	55
4	Authenticity in Popular Music	73
5	Pulling Together as a Team: Collective Action and Pink Floyd's Intentions	89

Part 3 Intertextuality

6	Kids're Forming Bands: Making Meaning in Post-Punk	111
7	Allusion and Intention in Popular Song	127
8	Covers and Communicative Intentions	141
9	Listening with Their Eyes: Problems for Radical Intertextuality	157

Conclusion	173
Notes	176
Bibliography	212
Index of Songs Cited	230
General Index	234

Acknowledgments

I have been writing about popular music—initially for college newspapers, later as a scholar—for forty-five years. Thanks to the support and critical feedback of a community of family, friends, and scholars, my thinking about popular music continues to develop. Every chapter of this book has profited from pushback I have received on preliminary versions. I'd like to shout out my thanks to Christopher Bartel, Jeanette Bicknell, Sondra Bacharach, Peg Brand, Lee B. Brown, Franklin Bruno, Ted Cohen, Guy Dammann, Pradeep Dhillon, David Davies, Stephen Davies, A.W. Eaton, John A. Fisher, Michalle Gal, Cynthia Grund, Garry L. Hagberg, Casey Haskins, Kathleen Marie Higgins, William Irwin, Arnold Johanson, Jenny Judge, Jennifer Judkins, Andrew Kania, Joe Kotarba, Serge Lacasse, Justin London, Stefano Marino, Mark Mazullo, Aaron Meskin, Scott Miller, Allan F. Moore, Jonathan Neufeld, Brandon Polite, Bennett Reimer, Michael Rings, Tiger Roholt, Stephanie Ross, Joel Rudinow, Robert Stecker, Jedediah Sklower, Saam Trivedi, Julie Van Camp, Ralf von Appen, and Rachel Zuckert, as well as an anonymous peer reviewer of the manuscript.

The author and publisher gratefully acknowledge the permission granted to reproduce the copyright material in this book. (Every essay has been revised, sometimes very substantially, and each essay has been updated to take account of recent scholarship. As author, I request that future readers ignore the earlier versions in favor of what is presented in this book.) In order of appearance in this book, this material is as follows: "Meanings of Songs and Meanings of Song Performances," *Journal of Aesthetics and Art Criticism*, vol. 71, no. 1 (2013), 23–33, https://doi.org/10.1111/j.1540-6245.2012.01538.x, copyright 2013 by the American Society for Aesthetics; "Who Is 'You're So Vain' About? Reference in Popular Music Lyrics," in *Pop Weiter Denken: Neue Anstöße aus Jazz Studies, Philosophie, Musiktheorie und Geschichte*, edited by Ralf von Appen and André Doehring (transcript Verlag, 2018), copyright 2018 transcript Verlag; "Performer, Persona, and the Evaluation of Musical Performance," in *Contemporary Aesthetics*, vol. 15 (2017), copyright 2017 Theodore Gracyk, published under a Creative Commons Attribution-Noncommercial 3.0 United States License (https://creativecommons.org/licenses/by-nc/3.0/us/); "Authenticity, Creativity, Originality," in *The Bloomsbury Handbook of Rock Music Research*, edited by Allan F. Moore and Paul Carr (2020, Bloomsbury Academic US, an imprint of Bloomsbury Publishing Inc.); "Pulling Together as a Team: Collective Action and Pink Floyd's Intentions," in *Pink Floyd and Philosophy*, edited by George Reisch, copyright 2007 by Carus Publishing; "Kids're Forming Bands: Making Meaning in Post-Punk," in *Punk & Post-Punk*, vol. 1, no. 1 (2012), copyright 2012 Intellect LTD; "Allusions and Intentions in Popular Art," in *Philosophy and the Interpretation of Pop Culture*, William Irwin and Jorge J.E. Gracia, eds. (Rowman & Littlefield: 2007) copyright 2007 by Rowman & Littlefield; "Covers and Communicative Intentions," in *The Journal of Music and Meaning*, vol. 11 (2013), http://www.musicandmeaning.net/articles/JMM11/GracykJMM11.pdf, copyright 2013 by *The Journal of Music and Meaning* and the author; "Listening with Their Eyes: Problems for Radical Intertextuality," in English and French in *Volume! The French Journal of Popular Music Studies* (vol. 10-1, 2013), Editions Mélanie Seteun, France. Every effort has been made to trace copyright holders and to obtain their permission for the use of copyright material. However, if any have been inadvertently overlooked, the publishers will be pleased, if notified of any omissions, to make the necessary arrangement at the first opportunity.

Introduction: Key Concepts

Public Meaning and Song Use

Music is a mode of communication, and songs—music with sung words—are the musical form favored by the majority of people. And in today's world, most song production, performance, and listening fall into the category of popular song. When people refer to "music," they are most often referring to popular song. Granted, some people will listen to Schubert's *lieder* during their morning commute, but—no offense to them—they are a special case, and they constitute a small fraction of the population. Popular songs are the musical *lingua franca* of modern life.

As a philosopher, I find the topic of popular song attractive because it lets us sidestep the longstanding debate about whether music can communicate anything extramusical. That debate is about instrumental music. Because popular songs have words, they are a more straightforward entry into the topic of how music communicates. I leave it to readers to decide whether my position has any implications for "pure" music, that is, music without words.

My approach to this topic is relatively unique in emphasizing pragmatics, which stresses that communication is always grounded in its immediate social context. (Pragmatics, as an area within linguistics and communication studies, should not be confused with pragmatism, the general school of philosophy promoted by William James and John Dewey.) The application of pragmatics to musical meaning is so uncommon that it is never mentioned in the most recent comprehensive survey of philosophy and music, nor in the most comprehensive encyclopedia of aesthetics.[1] Another notable sign of neglect is that music and songs are very rarely discussed in the *Journal of Pragmatics*.[2] The goal of this book is to address this gap in our understanding of how popular songs are used to communicate.

This emphasis differentiates my approach from one that is common in popular music studies: hermeneutics.[3] As developed in popular music scholarship, the hermeneutical approach explores auditors' interpretive responses, explaining how those responses depend on auditor agency: how a listener positions, and differentiates, the music in relation to other music. Very often, hermeneutic analysis concentrates on devoted fans of particular performers. Although my approach is hermeneutical in embracing all such issues as relevant to the communication process, pragmatics insists on a distinction between correct and incorrect interpretations. Where hermeneutics emphasizes auditor *response*, pragmatics emphasizes auditor *uptake*. In the same way that someone misreads a map if they confuse the orientations of north and south, some fans just get it wrong: Charles Manson's infamous readings of what The Beatles were communicating in their music were twisted fantasies.[4]

I also want to acknowledge at the outset that popular music serves many purposes. These include its use as a stimulus for mood regulation (both personal and public), to set the pace while exercising or running, as music for dancing (sometimes for very specific dance routines, such as those for "The Macarena" and "Da Butt"), and even as a way for companies to avoid leaving customers in silence while "on hold" on the telephone. Sometimes, popular music serves an aesthetic function: it's the focus of rapt, open-ended attention, and a source of immediate pleasure.[5] And there is the obvious point that popular music has, for a very long time, served as a profitable commodity within the culture industry. However, this book is not an exhaustive overview of the topic of popular song, and therefore noncommunicative functions will generally be set aside.

My aim, put simply, is to explain the most salient ways that popular songs communicate to audiences by exploiting contexts of presentation. Notice that I say "ways," plural. Consider five examples:

(1) In a tradition that stretches back six decades, 50,000 or more fans of Liverpool Football Club join together in singing "You'll Never Walk Alone" before each home match begins in Anfield Stadium.

(2) It is 1999, and during a commercial break during a televised program, an advertisement begins with a shot of a Volkswagen Cabrio crossing a bridge in the isolated countryside at night. The soundtrack is a strummed acoustic guitar. We follow the car down a country road, its convertible roof down so the twenty-ish passengers can gaze in wonder at the moon. "Pink moon is on its way," sings a wan, gentle voice. The singer, Nick Drake, has been dead for twenty-five years when the commercial first airs.

(3) In September of 2020, Nathan Apodaca posted a self-filmed TikTok video. As with all videos on that mobile app, the video is short, and his is under thirty seconds. On screen, Apodaca chugs juice from a plastic jug while skateboarding to Fleetwood Mac's "Dreams" (1977). In the final seven seconds, he looks into the camera and lip-syncs to Stevie Nicks's vocal line, "It's only right that you should play the way you feel it." By creating and sharing the video clip, Apodaca communicated a laid back "what, me worry?" message about his forbearance in the face of personal adversity. In filing and sharing his spontaneous interaction with the song, he created a meaning that Fleetwood Mac could not have imagined. Yet Mac drummer Mick Fleetwood went on to acknowledge Apodaca by posting his own restaging of the video clip—as did quite a number of other people, some famous, some not. Fleetwood's homage communicates endorsement and thanks (because the band's popularity rose to new levels of streamed popularity due to Apodaca).[6]

(4) One of the most famous speeches in American history is Martin Luther King Jr.'s "I Have a Dream" speech, delivered during the March on Washington gathering

on August 28, 1963. Before the official program started, the crowd heard several musicians associated with the booming "folk" movement. Some of them sang traditional songs such as "We Shall Overcome" and "He's Got the Whole World in His Hands," but at least one song was new and had, just that week, become a million-selling pop hit for Peter, Paul, and Mary. As they sang their hit, "Blowin' in the Wind," its young songwriter, Bob Dylan, stood nearby.

(5) Every year on their wedding anniversary, a couple makes the time to slow-dance to Van Morrison's "Warm Love" (1974). They heard it as background music while they were dining together on what they consider to be their "first date," and they look back on that event as the real start of their relationship. So they play it annually on their anniversary—and embrace and dance—in memory of that event.

Although popular song is used meaningfully in all five of these examples, meaning is generated in distinctly different ways. Those ways, and more, are the subject of this book.

However, only the fourth example satisfies the full range of criteria that are normally associated with music performance, where performers on a stage interpret a piece of music for a listening audience. In the case of Liverpool F.C., the crowd sings, but more for themselves and their team than for an audience listening appreciatively to their ragged, lurching performance.[7] The "Pink Moon" advertisement is very different from the Peter, Paul, and Mary performance, where the singers who popularized the song have selected it as appropriate to the performance context. The advertisement yokes further content to the track without the performer's cooperation or consent. The Volkswagen commercial gave Nick Drake a level of fame he never achieved in his short life. He gave few public performances and sold few recordings; yet, his recording of his song became known to many millions thanks to the repeated broadcasts of the commercial. Among these examples, the advertisement is most similar to Apodaca's recirculation and recontextualization of a recorded track through social media channels that have recently emerged as a major category of making meaning with popular song.

The fifth case is different from the other four in an important way. I have introduced it in order to highlight that difference and then to set such cases to one side. Specifically, the common practice of personal use of popular songs as "our song"— songs that express or symbolize a personal relationship unknown to the song's writers or performers—is an example of assigning an idiosyncratic meaning to it. As Robert Stecker has said about such cases, "the song is special to them because of the occasion on which they heard it and because they found it to express their mood then. That is it. No need to interpret the song for [its] meaning to understand that."[8] In other words, understanding *the song* is one thing, and understanding what it means to the couple is another thing, and the two don't need to have any genuine alignment with one another. My example, "Warm Love," happens to be a good candidate for being "our song" in a relationship, but it might have been a song that has nothing to do with romantic love. A couple might find the same meaning in Hank Williams's "Jambalaya (On the Bayou)" (1952), or Tag Team's "Whoomp! (There It Is)" (1993). Neither of those songs expresses romantic feelings, but both served as background music for countless parties, bar encounters, and other places where couples get together. While a couple can use a song to communicate something personal and idiosyncratic to one another, that's true of almost anything. And while songs may be better suited for this use than most things, the meaning of the song and its meaning to *them* as a couple can be completely independent of one another with no loss of significance to the couple. Since this kind of meaning—personal idiosyncratic meaning—is not something that can be extracted from the song by other listeners, it does not fall within the range of meaning as explored in this book. Like dancing and exercising, it may be a regular use that is made of popular music, but it is based on a chance association rather than the song's meaning, and so it is a kind of meaning that falls outside the scope of this book.

That exclusion may lead some readers to jump to unfounded conclusions about where I locate meaningfulness. By focusing on *communication* of meaning, I am setting aside listeners' idiosyncratic associations as unregulated by pragmatics. By implication, I am also ignoring the "death of the author" movement that sees authorship as an obstacle to understanding how popular texts circulate and function. However, it would be wrong to suppose that I am reinstating a simplistic doctrine about the song's composer or "author" as fully determinative of meaning. In Chapter 2, I explain why a songwriter-based theory of meaning is an obstacle to understanding how popular songs communicate. Performers, not songwriters, are at the center of my account—as are recordings, which complicate the story. And, in the age of social media, nonperformers often take over the role that used to belong to performers.

My general position about song performance and contexts of use should be viewed as an attempt to find the middle path between two extremes. One is the snobbish view that popular songs and their performances are mere entertainments with little value as communication. The other is represented by Allan F. Moore's position that every interpretation stems from an "individual perspective," and therefore "if you encounter claims purporting to identify 'the meaning' of a particular song,... *disbelieve them*."[9] Yes, but my point is that if you shift from songs to particular performances, particular recordings, and particular recontextualizations, then pragmatics provides an account of how these communicative acts (as opposed to bare "songs") convey definite meanings.[10]

It is also important to contrast my appeal to pragmatics with a standard philosophical approach to music performances. Julian Dodd has recently argued that "the point of interpreting a musical work [of Western classical music] in performance is to evince understanding of the performed work" and doing so "is the most fundamental performance value within our practice of work performance."[11] I have my doubts about the plausibility of this claim even when restricted to classical music, but the important point is that performances (and recordings) of popular songs seldom prioritize the performance value cited by Dodd. When the crowd at the March on Washington listened to Peter, Paul, and Mary's performance of "Blowin in the Wind," the performance was a means to an end, which was to support the march's message. Unless one construes "understanding of the performed work" to mean an understanding of the elasticity and pliability of the song that is performed, performers' *understanding* of a popular song is not "the most fundamental performance value" guiding performance and audience response.

For popular songs, a common performance value is that of using it to communicate something (perhaps multiple things) to contextually attuned auditors. Frequently, the point of performing, recording, or sharing a particular song is to communicate meanings generated by doing so. A song's lyrics provide some determinate informational content, and a performer may perform the song in order to communicate that meaning. However, if you think the primary performance value of Taylor Swift doing a cover version of "You're So Vain" in concert is to reveal her understanding of Carly Simon's song, rather than Swift's communicating something to her audience, then we have limited common ground for discussion. Apodaca's TikTok video is another mode of interpretation, but again, I deny that Apodaca's aim was to convey his understanding of "Dreams." My point, therefore, is that standard theories about meaning and value in the realm of Western classical music do not shed much (if any) light on either popular song meaning or the communicative function of song performance in the realm of popular music.

In presenting an alternative approach, I do not mean to downplay the value of work done by the many writers and theorists who have written so much about popular song. Although they adopt very different approaches, I heartily recommend Angela Davis's great book on women blues singers, *Legacies and Black Feminism*, Allan F. Moore's more general tome on popular song, *Song Means*, Philip Auslander's *In Concert: Performing Musical Persona*, and Ted Gioia's trilogy on three broad genres of songs (love songs, work songs, and "healing" or therapeutic songs). In philosophy, Jeanette Bicknell has published important work on songs and singing. And while I have learned an enormous amount from those books and many others, none of them present or defend a general theory of utterance meaning in relation to popular song.

Finally, I must pause to note that personal knowledge about popular music aligns with taste, and so my selection of examples will inevitably reflect my musical tastes. I endorse Jennifer Lena's point that "we must reject the notion that tastes are somehow natural and innate, and instead acknowledge that they are learned and then internalized."[12] Consequently, my examples will not resonate with everyone. If some of my examples are less interesting than others that might have been discussed, the fault lies in the way that my sociocultural position has familiarized me with some genres and artists instead of others. (And, as with all the examples mentioned so far, I use examples with English lyrics.) Nonetheless, the relevant question is not whether my taste prejudices my choice of examples. The issue is whether my tastes lead me to overlook examples that pose problems for my central claims. Are there examples that serve as counterexamples? That's the interesting question to raise against what I've written here.

The remainder of this introduction will outline core background ideas. I address the three main ideas that inform my argument. (1) What is popular music? (2) What is a song, and how does it differ from a recorded song? (3) What do we gain by discussing pragmatics?

I then conclude with an overview of the book's argument.

Popular Music

Popular music is an intrinsically relational, contrastive concept.[13] In this respect, it is like "east" and "public," which are informative only to the degree that one understands that there is an implied opposite. East is the opposite of west, and public is the opposite of private. A more nuanced understanding is that these are not binary opposites, for they admit of degrees. Furthermore, they are social constructs: they are relational concepts that make no sense except in the context of a social structure that gives them a purpose.

So, what is the relational contrast for popular music? Primarily, it is art music: the music that we generally (and very imprecisely) refer to as "classical music."

As such, popular music is a cultural category rather than a natural kind. Music itself is, arguably, a natural kind, because humans are an intrinsically musical species, but by itself that does not imply that every society develops popular music. Instead, popular music is a culturally specific variant of the music impulse, and it has not been present in every human culture. To put it another way, it is like postwar Italian cinema and gothic novels rather than a basic chemical compound like H_2O or a basic element like a charm quark. Since popular music is a cultural kind rather than a naturally occurring thing or category, we can ask when and where the relevant cultural phenomena appeared.

The phrase itself, "popular music," is surprisingly recent. Talk of music that is popular (i.e., widely liked or well known) appears in print in the late eighteenth century. Then, around 1850, there is a widening use of "popular music" to refer to a distinctive field of music, "a category with descriptive content."[14] (I can find no record of the phrase being used in anything like that meaning before the first decade of the nineteenth century.) It is likely, of course, that the gradual social formation that it designates was in place in some form before the designation was adopted. As a cultural kind, we should expect it to have emerged gradually, and for English speakers to coin the descriptive phrase somewhat afterwards.[15] The point of asking when the phrase entered the language is that it identifies a core usage, which in turn may offer criteria for determining where there have been independent (but parallel) developments. Adopting a contrastive or relational definition confirms that a similar cultural dynamic occurred much earlier, in East Asia and in the Mughal Empire, where there was a clear distinction between the learned music of the court and the music of the general population. Similarly, Robert Christgau claims that the concept extends back in time to the commercial music of the urban centers of the Roman Empire.[16] Others equate popular music with the modern products of a commercial music industry.[17] As such, it "is inextricably linked to technology" in both its production and dissemination.[18] All of these claims have some merit. Nonetheless, popular music's fundamental contrast is with the tradition of art music, our so-called "classical" music tradition, which generally upholds the norm that the music composer is the primary communicative agent, rather than the performers. Thus, Ruth Solie thinks that it does not matter if Kathleen Ferrier or Christa Ludwig is singing Robert Schumann's *Frauenliebe* songs: they should be heard as the communication of the two men who co-authored them, rendering each performance by a woman as an "impersonation of a woman."[19] (Granted, some conductors and performers build a fan base that is highly attuned to their performances.[20])

The boundary line between popular and classical music is both fuzzy and porous; yet, there are systematic differences between "high" and "low" music—or, as some describe it, between "art" and "entertainment."[21] What are these differences? Noting that popular *song* is the most common type of popular music, Charles Hamm observes that one of its defining characteristics is that it is "[d]esigned to be performed and listened to by persons of limited musical training and ability."[22] The melodic, rhythmic, and harmonic dimensions of popular songs are selected and combined in ways that keep the music relatively accessible to people who "don't know" music (i.e., who know it through cultural osmosis rather than music education). Accessibility is also facilitated through its comparatively high degrees of standardization and repetition.[23] In contrast, the field of art music encourages compositions that challenge listeners, sometimes with little or no immediate aesthetic reward.[24] Granted, there is a middle ground of cases that might belong to either category. However, there are real musical differences that put the compositions of Irving Berlin and Dolly Parton into the category of popular music while those of Milton Babbitt and Augusta Read Thomas count as art music, and why performances by Mamie Smith and the Velvet Underground are popular music and those by Yuja Wang and Midori Goto are art music.[25] It is also important to stress, up front, that accessible design is frequently combined with more complex, even hermetic, elements, so that it will support a rich interpretation for a more "in the know" or educated audience than for the average listener. (I explore this point in detail in Chapter 7.)

Some writers contend that "the distinction between high and popular culture has no basis in the properties of texts and practices."[26] While this position has been widely endorsed in cultural studies, I think it has been refuted by Derek Scott's historical account of how the idea of popular music developed in the nineteenth century. Scott documents how the two musics—popular and classical—gradually solidified their "own characteristic techniques, forms, and devices," until "popular music had become a different musical language."[27] Furthermore, it wouldn't make sense to talk about cross-pollinations, crossovers, or appropriations unless there were genuine *musical* differences between the two fields. Art music and popular music frequently cross-pollinate, and there are musicians and composers who cross back and forth between these distinctive musical "languages." Scott Joplin and Kurt Weill composed both popular and art music. Listen to one of Joplin's popular piano rags and then the overture to his opera, *Treemonisha*, or listen to one of Weill's Broadway show tunes and then to the Concerto for Violin and Wind Orchestra (Op. 12). I venture that almost anyone who compares them will hear striking compositional differences and basic, genuine "textual" differences. The art music has a marked tendency toward complexity and challenge and the popular music toward simplicity and accessibility. Furthermore, whole schools of music—notably, opera and jazz—have evolved in ways that morphed them from the popular realm to the art field. Although jazz improvisers Sonny Rollins and Branford Marsalis are in the "art" wing of popular culture, both have contributed simple, accessible saxophone solos to mainstream rock music. The changes to jazz that moved it from popular music to art music—it became "complex, dense, and difficult to grasp"[28]—were disturbing to many fans who experienced the transition. Philip Larkin, a jazz critic as well as a poet, hated the incorporation of "art" techniques, after which, he wrote, "it wasn't like listening to jazz at all. Nearly every characteristic of the music had been neatly inverted. [No more] tunes you could whistle."[29] Most popular songs have a steady rhythm and a distinctive melody: a tune you can whistle.

Songs Are Things to Sing

So, what are songs? At the risk of begging the question, let us start from the premise that songs are what we sing when we sing with our voices, for that really is the basic answer. Singing, in turn, is an action—a point that is central to much of what I have to say on the topic of songs.

To understand what popular songs are, it is essential to contrast them with something often confused with them. The following lines from Richard Middleton are a good starting point:

> When Mick Jagger sang ["Street Fighting Man"], the message was inseparable from its musical expression, within the conventions of a specific generic tradition, and this was in turn given its power by the institutional, discursive and ideological contexts that placed its reception.[30]

All true! I became aware of this passage from Sheila Whiteley's discussion of it. She quotes it to make the critical point (endorsed by pragmatics) that, positioned differently in society and in the music industry, women performers were, in the late 1960s, "largely viewed as ineffectual, as entertainment."[31] In 1968, when The Rolling Stones's recording of "Street Fighting Man" was released, there were few women in popular music who could sing that song or a similar one and be taken seriously—Grace Slick being one of the notable exceptions.

However, I have not quoted Middleton to make that point, but for a rather different reason. What's the "it" in the phrase "its musical expression?" The song that Jagger sang, or the recorded track from the *Beggars Banquet al*bum? What he actually sang in the studio, or the full musical expression conveyed to the public in that recorded track? These are two very different things. Singing is an action, something that people *do*, and an action takes places at a specific time and place. Granted, almost anyone who thinks about Jagger singing "Street Fighting Man" is going to think about that specific recorded track by The Rolling Stones. In fact, when Whiteley quotes that passage, she inserts the year that the album was released, 1968, referencing that recording. (If we also stress that it is a Rolling Stones track, and not just Jagger, the communicative act becomes much more complicated. I pursue this point in Chapter 5, where I examine collective action.)

My point is that Middleton's discussion collapses the distinction between the song and a specific recording of the song. The tendency to equate them floods conversations and writing about popular music. I agree that the time the song was written makes a difference, the time it was performed makes a difference, who sings it makes a difference, and how it's arranged stylistically makes a difference (where this last factor seems to be roughly what Middleton means by its "musical expression"). All of these things can be considered in relation to the 1968 recording. However, it is not as if Jagger sang it only once, or could only sing it when it has precisely *that* musical arrangement and sonic profile. After all, the song was part of the band's standard set list when they performed live in the year that followed, and during many subsequent tours. Yet its meaning could (and did) change on different performance occasions. A significant example is that it closed their performance on December 6, 1969, during their infamous appearance at the free Altamont Speedway concert, giving it a peculiar institutional context. The free concert is generally seen as an attempt at a West Coast alternative to Woodstock, the multi-day festival that had made international news the previous August. Audience member Meredith Hunter was murdered in front of the stage during the band's set, and the group's decision to keep performing in the wake of the violence contextualizes the callous privilege of the song's opening line, which discounts social responsibility in favor of "sing[ing] for a rock and roll band."

People speak so loosely when using the word "song" that a streaming series on Netflix is called *Song Exploder*. But the originating podcast and subsequent Netflix series focus on recording practices as well as songwriting. Hosts Hrishikesh Hirway and Thao Nguyen explore the dual topics of how songwriters generate their words and music, and how those songs take on a fixed form in the intricacies of the recording studio. My point is that those are two very different things, collapsed together by the series' emphasis on singer-songwriters and how their songs are shaped in the recording studio. What if, instead of Alicia Keys's "3 Hour Drive" (2020), one of the Netflix episodes examined one of the biggest-selling recordings of the twentieth century, Whitney Houston's cover of "I Will Always Love You" (1992)? Hirway would suddenly have to conduct interviews with different people about two very different things, the song and the recorded track. Dolly Parton would explain how she wrote the song, and producer David Foster would then explain how he spun pop gold for Houston out of that song.[32]

In all that follows, I carefully distinguish between a song and its various performances and recordings. To indicate that I am talking about a sound recording, I will specify that I am doing so by calling it a "track" or "recording." My usage follows John Lennon's distinction between song and track, as in his dismissal of The Beatles's recording of "Lucy in the Sky with Diamonds" (1967): "The track is just terrible. I mean,... a great song, but it isn't a great track because it wasn't made right."[33] The same distinction is conveyed in a different way in Brian Wilson's comment about "Good Vibrations" (1966): "I think it's a good tune, and it's a good record."[34] Songs are merely one ingredient in a recorded track or performance.

The song, then, differs from the totality of sounds one hears when hearing it performed or when playing a recording of it. A song is a template that guides someone who performs (or records) it.[35] Songs are musical-verbal structures that may serve as a template for innumerable and variable sonic events in the world. Thus, I am using "song" as it is used in Hamm's *Yesterdays: Popular Song in America* and in Derek Scott's book on nineteenth-century popular music, *Sounds of the Metropolis*.[36] When Hamm writes about minstrel songs in the 1830s and Stephen Foster songs in the 1840s and 1850s, and when Scott writes about a "music hall Cockney song" in 1885, they are talking about music prior to Thomas Edison's breakthrough on playback of recorded sound. They cannot be talking about the song in its recorded form. Consequently, they cannot commit Middleton's conflation of a "song" and a recording of it.

Returning to "Street Fighting Man," the *song* is credited to the writing team of Jagger and Richards. The recorded *track* opens side two of the vinyl version of the album *Beggars Banquet*, which is instead credited to The Rolling Stones. Different objects, different credit. The track features a wonderful sonic mix of guitar, sitar, and tamboura, as well as a unique drum sound that resulted from the up-close miking of Charlie Watts playing a miniature drum pad rather than his standard drum kit. However, the *song* does not have, as constituent elements, parts for sitar and tamboura. This configuration of instruments has never been employed by the Stones when performing it in concert, and Watts did not bring his miniature drum pad on tour when he played it. And we can, of course, hear others sing it. One can, for example, hear Liam Gallagher steamroll his way through it in Oasis's 1998 cover recording.

The point—seemingly obvious yet too seldom discussed—is that the meaning of a song and the meaning of a recording of the song are not interchangeable or equivalent. As I have just noted, a song can be given diverse musical arrangements, and musical style plays an important role in musical meaning. In this respect, popular songs are very *unlike* the music or "musical works" that get most of the attention in philosophy of music, which is music that is intended to be performed as specified in a musical score. Consider a string quartet by Joseph Haydn. For a string quartet, the score specifies which four instruments are to be used, and it specifies which musical notes are assigned to each of those instruments. If you delete the part for the second violin and assign the part for first violin to a bagpipe, you aren't really playing one of Haydn's string quartets. At best, you're playing a derivative musical work. But if you accompany yourself on ukulele while singing Stephen Foster's "Farewell Mother Dear" (1861), you've simply given it a novel arrangement. You're still performing "Farewell Mother Dear," rather than performing a derivative work. And "Farewell Mother Dear" is what you perform even if Foster neither imagined nor sanctioned playing it on a ukulele, an instrument invented after his death. Except for the special norms for performing "art songs" within the tradition of "art music"—decidedly not the topic of this book—songs have tremendous elasticity. Songs are things that can be arranged and performed in many different ways while still retaining their identity.

Meaningfulness as a Function of Pragmatics

This book explores central ways that pragmatics are exploited in popular song communication. Pragmatics is a branch of philosophy of communication that examines cases where a communication is intended to convey a meaning that is not directly encoded in it according to standard rules for direct communication. To paraphrase a popular example, suppose Blavatsky applies for a job and I ask Blavatsky's employer for a recommendation. In response, I get only the message, "Blavatsky has a very tidy desk."[37] While the message says something positive about the applicant, the *implicature* is that I should not hire the applicant. Trying to grasp how this message addresses the job qualifications, I see that it does not. To make it relevant, I understand it to be the most positive thing that the current employer could say, thus communicating that Blavatsky is not a desirable employee. This inference illustrates the core principle of contemporary pragmatics, the relevance principle: communications are directed at specific people in a specific context, and recipients of the communication will ask how the communication is relevant to the context of its reception, and the message will be designed to exploit the expectation of relevance. The communication succeeds when it yields a contextual implication: "a conclusion deducible from input and context together, but from neither input nor context alone."[38] With popular song, the input will be the song as performed or as presented in mass media, and it will yield relevant implications when "read" in relation to the context of reception.

Rather than discuss verbal and musical semantics and the meaning of songs in the abstract, this book explores pragmatics and the ways that various meanings are implied by specific performances and recordings. Let us consider a relatively straightforward case of song performance: a group of professional popular musicians is on stage, performing a well-known piece of music for a paying audience. However, both input and context make a difference, so details matter. It is April 1971, the musicians are the Grateful Dead, the venue is the Fillmore East concert hall in New York City, they are joined onstage by several vocalists from The Beach Boys, and together they perform Merle Haggard's recent hit song, "Okie from Muskogee" (1969). The performance was recorded and the recording is available to those who seek it out. Despite the prominence of the invited vocalists, fans of the Dead will immediately recognize their rhythm section and Jerry Garcia's distinctive, improvised guitar fills. Without going into great detail about Haggard's song, the central noteworthy point is that it celebrates the values of the white American status quo and it explicitly mocks "the hippies out in San Francisco." It mocks, in other words, the members of the Grateful Dead. Rather than assume that the purpose of the performance was to demonstrate the musicians' understanding of the song composed by Haggard and Roy Burris, my focus is on what the performers *meant* by choosing this song for this audience. The words of the song are clear enough; that is, its semantic content is very straightforward and poses no interpretive challenges. The meaning that interests me is the meaning that emerges from the context of performance (the year, the identity of the musicians, the place, etc.). I propose that the Dead selected the song that night in order to convey irony—something Haggard certainly wasn't communicating with the same song when he recorded it and performed it. And the ironic performance had further implications. The Dead communicated their understanding of how they (and, by extension, how their audience there in that room that night) were viewed by a hostile "silent majority" of Americans, and they further communicated that they celebrated their status. Indeed, they were pleased about society's hostility toward them in a song like "Okie from Muskogee," for it demonstrated mainstream America's awareness of them and, by opposing them, *validated* their alternative "hippie" lifestyle and their repudiation of the status quo. And the presence of The Beach Boys suggests their own desire to be seen as moving to the left of the mainstream.

That's quite a lot to claim for less than four minutes of music. The meaning I've attributed to the performance is quite different from what one would say about it based on its actual semantic content—the basic information encoded in that sequence of words. The semantic content is invariant for anyone who sings all the words to the song. Those words convey clear information concerning intended reference (hippies, the cities of San Francisco and Muskogee) and claims about them (that hippies enjoy LSD and marijuana, but people in Muskogee prefer alcohol). There is some interpretative leeway involved in reading some phrases as meaning something more than what is semantically encoded—for example, we are to take Muskogee as representative of most American towns and "Okies" as representative of a broad class of Americans.[39] Moreover, the *music* falls squarely into the category of country music, which encodes as "white" music. Unless one changes the musical style, those meanings will remain invariant throughout its performances by various musicians. But all the rest that I piled on top of the semantic content—what the Dead were communicating in performing it that night—falls within the pragmatics of meaning.[40]

Three hallmarks of pragmatics are (1) an emphasis on inferential, rather than explicit, communication, and (2) regulation of the inference process by reference to both a communicator's intentions and (3) the context in which communication occurs.

Given the primacy of intentions in pragmatics, I will pause before I say more about context-sensitivity in order to acknowledge and address two closely related issues: the objectivity of meaning and the role of intentions.

When I provide a gloss on the Dead's performance of "Okie from Muskogee," am I imposing a meaning, or am I extracting it? I am proposing that my interpretation is correct, and it is correct because it describes their intentions in performing it. If someone finds no irony in it and says it actually represents a moment of self-reflection in which the Dead communicate their self-loathing, I'm not of the mind to say we happen to differ in our interpretations, *que sera, sera*. Everyone *can* interpret it as they please, but it doesn't follow that every interpretation is equally good.[41] My guiding assumption is that popular musicians are generally trying to communicate, and that when that happens, there is generally a correct interpretation of that communication, which we can approximate through paraphrase.

My approach is consistent with Max Paddison's observation that "interpretation is always provisional and hypothetical."[42] An interpretive paraphrase may be quite complex, and there may be stronger and weaker approximations, but the task is not a free-for-all. The meaning of a communication is something that one can be correct or mistaken about. Consider two examples. When Paul and Linda McCartney wrote "Give Ireland Back to the Irish" (1972) and released it as the first single of their new group, Wings, they meant that the UK should remove its troops from Northern Ireland and give political control of the area to the Republic of Ireland.[43] When Public Enemy recorded "911 Is a Joke" (1990) and released it as a single, they meant that the lack of reliable emergency and paramedic services in predominantly African-American neighborhoods ("in yo[our] town") is racist and unjust. Those are the intended meanings of those recorded tracks. Unlike the Grateful Dead singing "Okie from Muskogee," these messages contain no irony. In making that distinction—in determining whether a *song* is ironic, and whether a *performance* of it or recorded *track* is ironic—we are knee-deep in the realm of pragmatics, and we are asking about the intentions that inform a communicative action.[44]

Because intentions inform actions, a few additional words about intentions are in order. There is a prominent school of thought that avoids referencing intentions when interpreting literature and, by extension, popular music.[45] One common argument says that intentions are hidden, internal states of mind to which others lack access, and therefore referencing them is a doomed attempt to remove obscurity by recourse to something more obscure. However, that is a very narrow idea of what intentions are. Beginning in the 1960s, many philosophers adopted a more complex model, where intentions are related to behaviors: they are conduct-controlling motivational commitments that make sense of those behaviors.[46] To ask about intentions is to regard agents as having reasons for their actions. For example, a sneeze does not arise from a motived commitment to do so, and so counts as a behavior but not an action. However, singing "You'll Never Walk Alone" with all the other fans at Anfield Stadium is not like sneezing, and we can only make sense of it by asking what is intended, that is, what these agents are trying to do by doing it.

A second argument dismissing intentions says that every successful communication will convey its intended meaning, and therefore there is generally no need to ask about intentions. But that is compatible with my view, which is that we are generally so successful in grasping the intentions behind a communication that we effortlessly recognize them. *Conscious* speculation about intentions comes in play when a communication seems unsuccessful, and in such cases it is normal to speculate about the underlying intentions. (Did my friend really mean to call me that in their text, or did their automatic spell-correct function create that insult when they intended something else?) Thinking about a communicator's beliefs and plans is a normal part of interpreting the meaning of a communication. There may be occasions when we set aside specific popular musicians or instances of their work as demonstrating no interest in active communication, but, normally, thinking about intentions is part of thinking about the meaning of any communication.

A third objection to referencing intentions is the fear that doing so implies that the communicator's intentions are only relevant if they conclusively determine the communication's meaning. But then every song just means whatever the songwriter(s) intend it to mean, and perhaps also whatever each performer intends it to mean. This extreme position is sometimes called the Humpty Dumpty view of meaning, where that character (in *Through the Looking-Glass*) maintains, "When I use a word... it means just what I choose it to mean—neither more nor less." However, the objection continues, communication cannot operate if every communication means precisely what the speaker intended it to mean, for the audience would have no public norms to guide their interpretation. While that is correct, it merely redirects us toward a more moderate version of intentionalism. As Alice puts it in her response, "the question is," said Alice, "whether you can make words mean so many different things." The implication, of course, is that you cannot. Semantics are in play, and semantics (established through ongoing social negotiations) limit the range of things an individual can expect to convey to others with any particular communication. Furthermore, the Humpty Dumpty view of meaning treats meanings as context-insensitive (other than intentions), whereas an appeal to the pragmatics of meaning is to assume that some meanings are highly context-sensitive.

Crucially, songs have words. Consequently, the conventional semantic content of the words and their syntactical arrangements contribute a public meaning that prevents a song or song performance's meaning from collapsing into nothing more than a communicator's intended meaning. Semantic conventions are a central *means* of communicating intentions: if I want to communicate something about my dog's behavior and I'm talking to someone who understands English, I will use the expression "my dog" at the start of my sentence, because it's the standard tool for conveying my intention to reference my dog. (If I want to communicate about my dog to a German speaker, I'd select "Mein Hund," and so on for various languages.) There are, of course, communicative tactics within popular music that involve uncoupling phonetic units from established semantics, but, aside from the occasional phrase of nonsense syllables ("Da Doo Ron Ron," "De do do do, de da da da"), *popular* communication generally requires the speaker or singer to work within a framework of established semantic content.[47]

If one then objects that these syntactical rules and semantic conventions are themselves sufficient to produce clear meanings, that point (frequently made about declarative statements in natural languages) does not quite work with popular songs. They are composites of music and words, and their performances seldom function to describe the world. But no one thinks that there is a principle of compositionality for combinations of words and music,[48] such that the meaning of the whole is directly determined by the meaning of the combined parts, as if we somehow know how to compute what meaning is added to "Okie from Muskogee" by each one of Garcia's guitar fills. Although music, qua music, very seldom communicates determinate semantic content, it is governed by musico-cultural conventions and these can be contextually exploited, especially in relation to the song's lyrics and the style of the performance arrangement. (I offer several examples in Chapter 1.) Thus, the musical dimension of song performance also contributes to pragmatic content.[49]

In summary, an appeal to intentions does not mean that intentions are the only player in the game of making meaning. It is, instead, to say that "speakers" in popular music exploit verbal conventions, musical conventions, and performance conventions, all of which contribute to the success of their communicative actions. Performers frequently exploit *and violate* conventions in order to generate novel or additional meanings. If meanings were restricted to what is semantically encoded, then no message could be communicated that was not already encoded through past association of sign and message. However, people are clever, and we constantly use our communication resources in novel ways. Consequently, we must possess a mechanism for understanding at least some communicated meanings despite their departures from fixed associations or established encodings. Pragmatics says that auditors grasp novel and unconventional meanings by engaging in context-sensitive interpretation, including speculation about communicative intentions. In turn, most speakers anticipate these basic auditor strategies when selecting details of their communications.

To complete my introduction to pragmatics, I call attention to two complications. First, pragmatics focuses on speakers' utterances in relation to the context of utterance. This topic is the focus of Chapter 1. However, in the sphere of popular music, "speakers" are not always individuals. They are frequently groups, and I address this phenomenon more directly in Chapter 5.

The second complication requires more explanation. Although I will tend to focus on well-known popular musicians, popular music "amateurs" and fans can also be active, communicating agents, even without performing in the normal sense—a point illustrated by my first and third examples at the start of this introduction, the Liverpool fans and Apodaca's TikTok video. The Liverpool fans communicate by singing the song. But nonprofessionals also construct novel communications without actually performing. Such is the case with Apodaca's appropriation of Fleetwood Mac's "Dreams," where Apodaca adds a visual element that piggybacks on the track's overt meaning. However, Apodaca is not a performer in any usual sense of "performer." At the same time, the video exploits a major element of performativity, gesture.[50] The video weds the recorded track to Apodaca's gestures—how he moves his body, his decision to lip-synch a key bit of the lyric— as it plays. And gesture, added to linguistic communication, places us squarely in the realm of pragmatics.[51]

Where Apodaca's gestures reflect and enhance "Dreams," multimodal recontextualizations of popular songs can also generate meanings that are contrary to the source material's plain meaning. (As should be abundantly clear as my argument unfolds, I am celebrating, not criticizing, such uses.) Here, consider two uses of recordings by the folk-punk Irish band, The Pogues. In 2010, the first two verses of their track "If I Should Fall from Grace with God" (1988) were used as the soundtrack for a television commercial for Subaru Forester. The exuberant music is wedded to visual snippets of a narrative in which a suburban mother takes her three sons to a hockey match and then back home—the music is an inspired match for the controlled chaos of the rough-and-tumble of ice hockey. The track fades out before the third verse, where the song becomes noticeably macabre as singer Shane MacGowan reflects on his own rotting corpse. Most viewers probably missed the fact that the two verses that are included reference death, since MacGowan's singing is often indecipherable except for the rousing chorus of "Let them go, boys," which fits neatly with the commercial's theme of boyhood and sports.

A similar process of excerption obscures the complex messaging of The Pogues's warped Christmas record, "Fairytale of New York" (1987) when it appears on the soundtrack in episode 2 of the streaming series *Dash & Lily* (2020). Here, the track fades after the opening verse, giving the false impression that it is a hopeful, romantic song. A few seconds more and the words would express contempt between the male and female protagonists, something that cannot be allowed to intrude into the love story of *Dash & Lily*. In both cases, the excerpts of the two recordings are exploited for a partial and incomplete meaning, sidestepping the way that The Pogues themselves mixed competing sentiments together to convey the messiness of our emotional lives. Incorporated into narratives constructed by someone else, the tracks contribute to multiply authored messages that diverge from, rather than reinforce, the meanings of the two recordings.

In the car commercial's use of "If I Should Fall from Grace with God," The Pogues's track functions in the way that many popular songs function in daily life. The primary impact is the track's overwhelming *joie de vivre*—that the singer is singing about his death takes a back seat to the lilting rhythm and expressive gestalt. In short, meaning is first registered in the nonpropositional and relatively ineffable realm of musical expression. Since this is the case with most popular song, the Subaru commercial exemplifies the way that the expressive meaning of a song or recording can readily be put to use for communicative purposes that do not necessarily align with the message that is generated by the combination of words and music.[52] Here, again, we are firmly in the realm of pragmatics, for the emotive contribution of nonlinguistic, nonverbal elements of a communication is almost always a major part of the communication, as a "paralanguage" that invites an application of pragmatics.[53] Because popular songs involve music, a "literary" analysis of popular songs is simply not the right method for understanding popular song meaning.

Overview of the Argument

The core idea of this book is explained with Chapter 1, "Meanings of Songs and Meanings of Song Performances," where I explain and endorse a context-sensitive "use" theory of meaning. On that basis I argue that established musical and semantic practices are two among multiple factors contributing to the meaning potential of performing or otherwise sharing any given song. The limited meanings or informational content of a song (as a combination of words and music) underdetermine the possible meanings of its myriad performances and recordings. Many other factors contribute to meaning when a song is put into use, that is, when the song is recorded in a specific way or performed by a particular musician on a particular occasion. Performers' intentions, including intentions about intended audience, play an important role in actualizing a song's meaning potential. In recent years, performer's intentions are conspicuously absent from prevailing theories of meaning in popular music studies. Chapter 2 acknowledges that the intentions of songwriters and performers are relevant to what a performance or recording means. However, those intentions are not fully determinative of popular song meaning. Instead, a use theory of meaning recognizes that songs and recordings create opportunities for multiple communicative uses. They are, to adapt a position articulated by Kendall Walton, "texts for others to use." Carly Simon's "You're So Vain" is offered as a case study, further suggesting that a major use of popular songs is to invite audience make-believe.

The three chapters of Part Two examine how a performer's identity or persona contributes to the context of communication. In Chapter 3, "Performer, Persona, and Musical Performance," I stress the widespread use of popular song to convey ethical and political stances. Messages are frequently conveyed through implicature, often in relation to a performer's persona. Popular music performance norms include the norm that some personae invite auditors to interpret the performer as endorsing the content that is communicated. In such cases, a performer's actual lifestyle, attitudes, and moral character contribute to what is communicated. Consequently, both the performance persona and the personal life of a song's performer can contribute to (or undercut) the ethical and political stance communicated in a performance or recording. Chapter 4 extends this topic by contrasting a sincerity condition rooted in a socio-historical criterion of authenticity with recent theories of auditor authentication. After surveying multiple (sometimes contradictory) notions of authenticity that have been applied to recent popular music, I caution that concepts of authenticity that dominate popular music studies may be less important to the interpretive and evaluative framework employed by fans (especially fans of rock music) than is widely claimed. Chapter 5 corrects the tendency of pervious chapters to emphasize the actions of discrete individuals: singers. In "Pulling Together as a Team: Collective Action and Pink Floyd's Intentions," I address the complication that "the performer" of popular music is frequently a group, not an individual. I address skepticism about the possibility that genuine *group* intentions inform song performances and recordings, a skepticism that reduces them to a singer with musical support. Pink Floyd is discussed as an organizing example, permitting exploration of the related problem of how changing group membership relates to group intentions.

The closing four chapters constitute Part III. They explore several ways that pragmatic implicature generates complex meanings through intentional engagement with various *systems* of communication. The popular arts are highly intertextual. For better or for worse, auditors invariably respond to popular music as organized according to distinct categories of music. There is, obviously, musical style, but there are also stylistically heterogeneous categories. Chapter 6 examines post-punk as an example of how a recording's nonstylistic classification can align popular music with a larger ongoing cultural movement in ways that shape its meaning. Chapter 7 turns to another mode of intertextuality: musical and lyrical allusion. Allusion is intrinsically contextual and relational, and it is widely employed in the popular arts in order to introduce pragmatic implicatures in (seemingly) straightforward and simple recordings and performances. Using a wide range of examples, Chapter 7 maps out a general theory of intention-dependent allusion in popular culture. Chapter 8 then takes up a special type of popular song allusion, "cover" versions. I argue that covers differ from mere remakes in requiring a particular communicative intention within an appropriate cultural context. Unlike remakes, cover recordings belong to the category of extended allusion. I also identify features of different musical cultures that encourage and discourage covers, providing an explanation of why covers are rare in the jazz and classical music traditions. Chapter 9 completes my survey of popular song intertextuality. I outline and defend a relatively modest general theory of intertextuality that emphasizes the centrality of *music* in popular music reception and interpretation. I argue that some common ideas about intertextuality undermine, rather than support, an account of meaning in popular song. While multi-modal intertextuality is the norm for contemporary popular music, we should adopt an account of intertextuality that preserves the idea that popular music is, first and foremost, music.

Part One

Songs

1

Meanings of Songs and Meanings of Song Performances

Distinct performances of the same song can mean very different things. This is because, in the pithy description of Jeanette Bicknell, "meaning is a product of three factors: the song's text, its music, and the performance context."[1] Yet the meaning of the *song* may be fixed. If this sounds paradoxical, my immediate purpose is to show how the interplay of semantics and pragmatics generates different meanings in different performances.[2] The basic idea is that context-dependent aspects of a song's meaning are different from—and supplemented by—context-dependent aspects of a performance's meaning. Popular song performances are rich in meaning because the semantic content of the lyrics is wedded to a very "thin" musical structure. This combination of semantic information, musical flexibility, and shifting performance contexts generates myriad possibilities for generating pragmatic contextual supplementation of the song during its performances.

Sentences and Songs, Utterances and Performances

Pragmatics examines how the meaning of an utterance—one particular communication at a particular moment—depends on the context of utterance. Utterance meaning often diverges from the standard or face-value meaning of a phrase or sentence or larger text. Applied to popular song, it implies that audience interpretation should distinguish meaning-making properties that belong to the song from those that are specific to a particular performance, recording, recontextualization, or some other use of that song.[3]

Consider the following case. Suppose someone utters a sentence and the referring expression of the sentence is a name or description that misdescribes the speaker's intended referent. Is the resulting sentence true or false? In a well-known essay, Saul Kripke discusses cases such as "Her husband is kind to her," erroneously said of a man who is not married to the woman in question.[4] A narrow focus on the semantic content of the sentence tells us that the spoken sentence is false if the woman is unmarried. If the woman is married, the truth of the sentence depends on her husband's behavior. If the actual husband is unkind to her, then (again) the utterance is false. Yet, married or single, the *intended* male referent is the man actually observed being kind to the woman in question. So long as the person to whom the speaker addresses the sentence understands the speaker's *intended* reference, the utterance will successfully refer to that person, and it will succeed even when the intended audience for the sentence recognizes the failure of semantic reference. Thus, a successful understanding of a speaker often requires us to set aside a strict adherence to the semantic reference of the referring expression, and the speaker's utterance can be true even if its proper semantic reference should render it false. Thus, utterance meaning diverges from semantic content.

For my purposes, the important point is one that Kripke mentions in passing, but which is central to pragmatics:

> The notion of what words can mean, in the language, is semantical: it is given by the conventions of our language. What they mean, on a given occasion, is determined, on a given occasion, by these conventions, *together with the intentions of the speaker and various contextual features*... together with various general principles, applicable to all human languages regardless of their special conventions.[5]

In other words, our grasp of the context of utterance can prompt us to amend a sentence's established semantic reference. We do so by distinguishing between the sentence type and its utterance on a particular occasion of use, which allows us to achieve a pragmatically correct understanding of the speaker's reference for that use of that sentence. Correct understanding of "her husband" is not merely a grasp of how context fixes the referent of "her" in the normal way but also of how "husband" operates in an abnormal manner this case.[6]

This distinction between *sentence* reference and *speaker's* reference can be extended to other cases where the meaning of a sentence type diverges from the meaning of a specific utterance. In short, the conventional meaning of a sentence type does not fully determine the meaning of each and every instance (token) of that type.[7] Semantic content is a matter of general conventions, whereas speaker's meaning (utterance meaning) demands sensitivity to context-sensitive pragmatic implicatures.

The implication for songs and song lyrics is straightforward. Because utterance meaning frequently diverges from sentence meaning, song performances frequently communicate context-sensitive meanings that diverge from the semantic content provided by the song's words. The performance context sometimes involves a performer's actual intentions on that occasion. As William Lycan puts it, pragmatics explores how changes in speaker contexts make it possible that "one and the same sentence with an already fixed propositional content can still be used to do interestingly different things in different contexts."[8] Substitute "song lyric" for "sentence" and one and the same song can be used to do interestingly different things in different performance contexts.

In summary, the meaning of a song's words contributes to the meaning of each of its performances, but that is merely one factor among several in generating the meaning of any particular performance. Although our arguments are very different, I am expanding on Stan Godlovitch's general position about the relationship between musical works and their performance: "The fixity of the work must typically be consistent with the opportunities for novelty expected in performance."[9]

Songs as Structural Types

Quite apart from issues of meaning and interpretation, philosophy has long grappled with a fundamental distinction between two basic forms of art. Some arts—most notably painting, drawing, and some forms of sculpture—result in artistic products for which the artistic achievement is identified with a particular physical object. The *Mona Lisa* is painted on a particular wooden panel and Michelangelo's *Pietà* carved into a particular block of marble, and a viewer has only seen the actual artwork if they have been in the physical presence of *that* wooden panel and *that* carved marble. Yet no one seriously extends this "physical object hypothesis" to musical works.[10] When Dolly Parton wrote "Jolene" (1973), she may have written it out on paper, but no one equates the piece of paper with the song. No one thinks that access to the song depends on access to that one piece of paper. It depends, instead, on access to performances and recordings that follow the music-with-words structure that Parton created. Consequently, most philosophers of art endorse the thesis that the products of some art forms are singular (there is only one "original"), but others involve works that are multiple in their instantiation, where none of the instances are more genuine than any others.

I will adopt the standard assumption that songs are structural types and I will concentrate on musical performances and recordings that are instances or tokens of those structures.[11] The present chapter focuses on works for musical performance, namely songs that are meant to be instantiated through the action of performing them, most often for an audience. The audience may be small, as when "Happy Birthday to You" is sung by everyone in the room except grandmother, to whom it is sung because it is her birthday. Or it may be quite large, as when the American national anthem is sung to a crowd of tens of thousands of fans during the opening ceremonies of a university football game.[12] Audience size aside, the cases are alike in that the songs are structures that guide performances. Conversely, their performances are instances or tokens of the structural types.

My analysis of song performance draws on four elaborations of this distinction between types and instances.

First, types place constraints on instances. The act of composing a song includes the songwriter's determination of which features are normative, that is, which ought to be present in performances and other tokens of that type. This point is sometimes made by saying that the musical type is a norm-kind. In the tradition of classical music, the type is usually indicated through the creation and publication of a musical score. In this tradition, scores specify all instrumentation and provide notation and other instructions in order to indicate how the composer's intentions supplement the standard performance conventions of the musico-historical context.[13] However, in the field of popular music, the basic type can be initiated and passed down through oral tradition (as with many "traditional" and folk songs), or generated in the act of recording it, with a minimal score extracted later and published (e.g., much of what we find in *Alicia Keys—Note-for-Note Keyboard Transcriptions*). Because the identity of a popular song is ultimately score-independent, many variants, and many wildly different arrangements of it, will count as instances of the same basic song.

Most scored, classical works are highly prescriptive and constraining, excluding "some sonic possibilities" from their correct performances.[14] The same cannot be said about popular songs. If you add a vibraphone to a string quartet by W.A. Mozart, it's not a performance of Mozart's work. Not so with Kurt Weill's "Mack the Knife" (1928). With lyrics by Bertolt Brecht, the song was written as a musical number for the show *The Threepenny Opera*, a production which Weill and Brecht intentionally undertook as an exercise in popular music theater.[15] While the published score does not indicate use of a vibraphone, no one who has any familiarity with the conventions of popular music would say that a performance cannot be a performance of "Mack the Knife" because it includes vibraphone. And singers often supplement the words of popular songs, as in Ella Fitzgerald's famous 1960 live recording of "Mack the Knife" with extemporaneous lyrics. The Last Town Chorus's mournful interpretation of "Modern Love" (2007) features a crawling tempo and a slide guitar. Sonically, it sounds almost nothing like David Bowie's original, uptempo R&B version (1983). To the casual listener, there is little agreement beyond the lyrics. In this respect, we find that popular song, rather than classical music, exhibits a strong license for meaning alteration by allowing considerable flexibility in the music. With art music, the performance norm is for performers to act in service to the composer and the score.[16]

Second, every type underdetermines the properties of its instances. This relationship generates the one-over-many principle: there are many instances of one and the same type, and each instance will be distinctive in some way. Each instance will have properties associated with the type and consequently shared with other instances; yet, every instance will have more properties than can be specified in the type.[17] If the latter were not so, a performance's meaning would almost always align with the type's meaning as established by its original context. Another way of expressing this point is to say that types are ontologically thinner than their instances, and because types vary in how many performance features are set as invariant in its performances, some types are ontologically thinner (specifying few) or thicker (specifying many) relative to their determinative properties.[18] Popular songs are generally very thin, allowing considerable variation from performance to performance and thus permitting considerable tailoring to the performance context. Whereas it is legitimate to complain that one is not hearing Beethoven's Violin Concerto in D Major (Op. 61) if the first movement cadenza is played on a kazoo, there is no parallel complaint if a chorus of "Happy Birthday to You" is accompanied by kazoos.

Third, the basic properties of a song are determined by the musico-historical context in which it is composed.[19] Every song has meaning established by the time and place of its composition. That meaning is its work-meaning and it is a property of that song. By virtue of the first point, that work-meaning ought to be attributed to all instances of that work. However, any such meaning can be nullified by power of pragmatic implicature. Semantic properties are fixed by a work's musico-historical context. They may inform and contribute to the meaning of subsequent performances, but they do not fully determine the meaning of its performances. The semantic content of the sung words may be exploited in many ways, generating distinct pragmatic supplementation in different performance contexts. In the same way that sentences containing the phrase "her husband" permit use of that phrase to refer to someone who is not married, it is unsurprising when a popular song's semantic content is exploited to communicate meanings that the songwriter would not sanction or endorse for it. Hence, the supposition that all performances will share meanings established by the initial context is not an obstacle to allowing for divergent meanings of different performances. (I discuss this at greater length in Chapter 2.)

Fourth, song instances can count as recognizable instance even when they fail to embody some properties specified by the type. If we do not make this concession, then it would be impossible to have instances/tokens with even a single flubbed note.[20] As I said earlier, the musical type is a norm-kind. It is a pattern that can have better and worse realizations, and so an error-ridden or minimally recognizable performances can be counted as instances. A sloppy, ramshackle, out-of-tune performance of "Happy Birthday to You," or The Replacements performing "Like a Rolling Stone" as "Like a Rolling Pin" (1990), along with other choice word alterations, are nonetheless performances of those two songs.

Ironically, given the variants that arise from contextual supplementation, performance arrangement, and performance style, it is theoretically possible that every performance of a particular popular song might contain enough variation from the composer's expectations and design that every performance of it will fail to convey the composer's intended meanings for it. Unlikely in practice, but a theoretical possibility.[21]

Authorship, Semantic Content, Intentions

This technical overview of ontology has been a prelude to seeing how a single song can communicate many different meanings in its various performances.[22] The key issue is whether, or to what degree, a song (as a type) has invariant meaning.

Normally, semantic properties are independent of any speaker's intentions on any given occasion. Thus, a song's basic semantic properties are determined by prevailing semantic conventions at the time of composition. If a blues fan thinks that Robert Johnson's "Terraplane Blues" (1936) is about some kind of airplane, that interpretation is wrong. But we do not have to peer into Johnson's private thoughts to know this. In the 1930s, "Terraplane" was the name of a brand of automobile, and this bit of public, historical information explains why his lyrics reference the hood, battery, and other car parts, and fails to reference propellors and wings.

Does it follow that a composer's intentions play no role in determining the song's meaning on the grounds that semantic conventions override those intentions? As I explained in the Introduction, the celebration of the "death of the author" and the common prohibition against committing the intentional fallacy have created an environment in which authorial intentions are dismissed as irrelevant to the interpretation of literature and other meaning-structures.[23] However, there has been a counter-movement that explores ways that authorial intention contributes to the context that guides interpretation of composed texts.[24]

Consistent with recourse to pragmatics, I will offer a number of reasons to think that the counter-movement is correct and that performers' intentions play a role in explaining how utterance meanings diverge from semantic meanings. In terms of the pragmatics of popular song performance, the crucial point is that we must distinguish authorial intentions of a song's composer(s) from the supplemental intentions of those who perform them.

So, how does a composer's intentions inform the meaning of the song *qua* abstract structure? A song's meaning might be viewed as the utterance meaning of its composer(s). Robert Stecker offers a robust defense of just such an account of artistic meaning. As such, he is in good company in defending the view that, whether we are interpreting a Shakespearean sonnet or a nineteenth-century opera, the meaning of any work of art is its utterance meaning. Focusing on literary meaning, Stecker proposes that an artwork has whatever meaning that it has due to a combination of "the actual intentions of artists and the conventions in place when the work is created."[25] Therefore any artwork with semantic content, such as a poem or song, has an utterance meaning, which is a function of both semantics and pragmatics.[26] As such, the meaning of any song is a function of the semantic content appropriate to its structure in its original linguistic and art-historical context, together with the composer's intentions for interpreting that structure in that context. Those intentions determine whatever "is pragmatically conveyed" by the song, extending its utterance meaning beyond its semantic content.[27] Consistent with standard pragmatics, contextually informed "work meaning" supplements the meaning of the basic type as determined by prevailing conventions. Thus, work meaning is the meaning of the text as produced in a particular historical context.[28] Stecker concludes that literary and musical works are structures-in-use. They are utterances.[29]

However, what happens when we move from literary texts to performances? Stecker adopts the view that "a performance presents a work." Normally, it does so without adding anything "to the meaning of the work or creating a new work."[30] Stecker is, of course, focusing on traditional high art. However, the norms are different for popular music, where it is not at all unusual for performers to supplement the meaning of the composed song. Thus, the standard analysis goes astray in reserving both semantic and pragmatic properties for the *type*, and then supposing that, at most, pragmatic supplementation generated in a performance will consist of a critical commentary on the work that is being performed.

In the next two sections I offer examples of popular song performances that do something more radical than that. The pragmatic supplementation of their performances is not critical commentaries on the songs that are being performed. They are, instead, full-fledged structures-in-use. In popular music, performances of the songs, not the songs themselves, are the basic structures-in-use that have full-fledged utterance meaning.[31] In popular performance practice, any pragmatic properties intended by lyricist or composer belong to subsequent tokens only if intended as such by the performer who constitutes the "speaker" on the occasion of the performance. (Hence the crucial importance of performers' intentions!)

"The Star-Spangled Banner"

To offer another version of my central point from earlier, "semantics concerns sentences, not utterances."[32] A song, like a sentence, is a type. The semantic content of these types is compatible with an array of utterance meanings. The full meaning of any utterance—meaning as a combination of semantics and pragmatics—depends on the context in which the sentence utterance or song performance, the particular *instance*, is produced. And performance intentions are a key element of the context.

I will illustrate my claim that popular music performances can be vehicles of pragmatic supplementation by focusing on a famous performance, Jimi Hendrix's instrumental performance of "The Star-Spangled Banner" on August 19, 1969 at the Woodstock Festival. Later, I provide a brief gloss on Bob Dylan's performance of "It's Alright, Ma (I'm Only Bleeding)" on February 14, 1974. There is nothing very special about these examples beyond the fact that in each case we know the day of the performance and there is ready access to high-quality, unedited recordings. In both cases, the year of the performance is relevant to grasping the proper context for interpreting it. In Hendrix's case, the performance is an act of political protest, challenging the continuing involvement of the United States in Vietnam. In Dylan's case, the performance calls attention to the congressional impeachment hearings underway for President Richard Nixon. Yet neither *song* does those things. My goal is to explain how the performances mean what they mean without it being the case that the songs have somehow altered their meanings.

Before we turn to the Hendrix performance, consider the reference to the United States that is implicit in all performances of the American national anthem, "The Star-Spangled Banner." Why do performances refer to the United States? No country is named in the song's words. Instead, the words describe a flag. However, the flags of Uzbekistan, New Zealand, and Cape Verde also have both stripes and stars. Taken at face value, Francis Scott Key's referring description refers equally well to those flags, too. However, Key intended the lyrics of "The Star-Spangled Banner" to refer to the flag of the United States, and he further encodes this intention into his lyrics by using the term "our" in two stanzas, as in the line, "Gave proof through the night that our flag was still there." Taking Key to be the speaker of the indexical term "our," prevailing norms tell us that the flag is that of Key's country, the United States. By respecting authorial intention as a relevant part of the originating context, we preserve the idea that original context determines the song's semantic content. Hence, a standard "semantic pragmatics" for indexicals says that the words of the *song* refer to the flag of the United States, no matter how many other flags are equally well described or who sings the words.

However, I deny that Key's authorship is sufficient to establish that "our flag was still there" refers to the United States in every performance. The use of the pronoun has not changed in 200 years, and the literal meaning of this expression is the same today as when he wrote it. Key intended others to sing the song, and he may even have intended all those singers to be Americans. But what if they are not Americans? What happens if a New Zealander sings it while saluting a New Zealand flag? Why should Key's intentions preclude the New Zealander's use of the phrase "our flag" to refer to their own country's flag?

Rather than assume that authorial intentions decisively forbid this use, consider a nonmusical case. Blessed with sudden good fortune, someone might say, "Now is the winter of our discontent made glorious summer." Many lines from Shakespeare are used by people who do not know that he authored them, and this speaker might repeat the line without knowing that its source is Shakespeare's *Richard III*. In its original and intended context (the world of the play), the speaker is King Richard and its semantic reference is Richard (using the royal "we") and, perhaps, the whole house of York. However, there is no reason to suppose that someone who repeats the line out of context, in "real life," thereby refers to Richard and the house of York. In the play and in performances that adhere closely to the script, it means what it does as a result of our standard interpretive norms together with an acknowledgment that the context is theatrical fiction in which the flesh-and-blood actor is playing Richard. Quoted outside a performance of the play, there is no reason to suppose that its origins in Shakespeare's play are relevant to determining its current range of application. The speaker means themselves, and perhaps others who are present, but King Richard drops out of the equation.

In light of this example, reconsider "The Star-Spangled Banner." What happens when Céline Dion, a Canadian citizen, sings it? Why is her performance about the United States (which, I take it, it is), rather than a reference to Canada and to some military event in Canadian history? Two explanations might be offered. At best, "our flag was still there" might be a case where reference has become so habitual in the community that the *phrase* has evolved a special semantic reference.[33] On the other hand, a simpler explanation is that the reference to the Untied States is established pragmatically, by a singer's intentions to honor the composer's intentions.

The latter solution is more plausible for two reasons. First, it parallels the idea that pragmatic meaning can involve consideration of the speaker's intentions. More specifically, I am adapting a standard move in pragmatics: the speaker's intentions are an element of the context that allows "her husband" to refer to someone who is not her husband. Absent this concession about intentions, the phrase's semantic content together with a context of utterance are not jointly sufficient to account for our understanding of the pragmatic content of every use of it. Whenever utterance meaning is unclear, our grasp of the intentions directing the act of producing a particular token of a sentence "picks up the slack" in linking pragmatic content to the utterance.[34] I am proposing that the same holds of song performances construed as utterances. Hence, performer's intentions are analogously relevant to performance meaning. Thus, "our flag" should be interpreted in terms of the singer's intentions, which are, presumably, to refer to the American flag, as did Key. In the Hendrix performance, we take that phrase to be relevant even its absence from the particular, purely instrumental performance.

Second, this approach reaffirms Stephen Davies's proposal that a particular musical performance only counts as a performance of a particular work if they perform it while honoring its composer's work-determinate intentions for it.[35] We consult the speaker's intentions to decide whether a particular use of "Now is the winter of our discontent made glorious summer" is a theatrical use, preserving Shakespeare's intentions, or whether it is a nontheatrical, "real" reference to current circumstances. (Or both, where the former is means to the latter.) Consistent with Davies's proposal, the importance of considering the intention of the performer is already implicit in discussing Hendrix's instrumental performance of "The Star-Spangled Banner" at Woodstock. As an instrumental performance, semantic referential content is present only because of its status as a song in which Key associated particular words with particular musical phrases. Those who know the song will be able to attach particular lines to particular melodic phrases.

However, the mere fact that Hendrix *sounds* as if he's playing "The Star-Spangled Banner" is not sufficient to demonstrate that his performance is an instrumental performance of that work, and that his performance is to be interpreted in light of Key's lyrics. We can ask why Hendrix was giving a performance of *that* song at all, rather than "To Anacreon in Heaven," the earlier English song upon which the American anthem is based. Hendrix's performance of "To Anacreon in Heaven" might be perceptually indiscernible from his performance of "The Star-Spangled Banner." The identity of what Hendrix performed at Woodstock is determined by reference to his performance intention. If we are wrong about his intention, we are not justified in supposing that Hendrix's musical performance makes a statement about the United States.

We want to determine this reference, in part, because at one point Hendrix's guitar pyrotechnics (following what would be the sung line "bombs bursting in air") are then plausibly construed as musical representations of bombs bursting in air. This recognition is facilitated by Hendrix's providing enough of the melody to make it clear that the absent lyric has just referred to bombs. This reading generates new interpretive questions. Who is bombing whom? The British, shelling Fort McHenry in 1814? The consensus is otherwise: Hendrix is calling attention to the ongoing war in Vietnam. He refers to bombs, but not Key's bombs. Where Key's utterance meaning is, broadly, pride in the resilience of the United States, Hendrix is offering a "musical protest against the United States' war in Vietnam."[36]

While there is no lack of discussion of how popular music comments on current society and politics, I am emphasizing the point that Hendrix (the actual person) is protesting the war (an ongoing event).[37] This real-world implication shows that the meaning of his performance is not limited to the presentation of a persona in a virtual, imagined, or fictional world. It cannot be a protest of the ongoing war if its meaning is simply a function of the musician's persona and the performance's mass-art articulation or personic environment.[38] Those things contribute to the meaning of Hendrix's performance, but Hendrix cannot be protesting events in the real world unless audiences (both then, and now) understand how the persona and "virtual" war, present in the music, is meant to relate to a world beyond the stage (and beyond the virtual worlds of the subsequent film and sound recording).

In short, because Hendrix's performance refers to (1) something outside the world of the performance and (2) something that is not referred to by Key's initiated type, Hendrix's utterance meaning involves additional pragmatic considerations arising from the structure-in-use in 1969. The song composed in 1814 is a structure-for-use, not a structure-in-use. This is why performances have pragmatic meanings beyond those anticipated by the songwriter who indicated the type and fixed the semantic content that informs its subsequent use.

Let me take a moment to emphasize that song meaning is not reducible to the meaning of lyrics and other associated texts. Many musical phrases contribute meanings of their own. For example, the melody known as "Taps" is an official American military bugle call that signals the end of the day. However, it is frequently played at military funerals and memorial services, in which context listeners understand the pragmatic implicature that it expresses grief and farewell without understanding that the twenty-four notes have a highly specific communicative function. During his Woodstock performance of the national anthem, Hendrix interrupts the musical melody of the line "Oh, say does that star-spangled banner yet wave" by inserting the opening phrases of "Taps" into the middle of the anthem's melodic line. Hendrix expected his audience to understand this interpolation as a reference to death without their possessing shared knowledge of the official fixed meaning of the bugle call. Thus, Hendrix's arrangement of the music introduces musical material for pragmatic interpretation without relying on audience knowledge of an associated English text. (Historically, the lyrics associated with "Taps" were added many years after its meaning was firmly established.[39]) Independent of words, *musical* details contribute to a performance's pragmatic content through both conventional and unconventional implicature (e.g., "Taps" and the "pictured" bombs, respectively).

In summary, Hendrix's Woodstock performance stands to the song as an utterance of a sentence stands to that sentence. Hence he could exploit the cultural context of 1969 in order to generate pragmatic implications that are not part of the song itself.

Understanding a Song's Music

At this point, some readers may object that, "Taps" aside, song lyrics are doing all the heavy lifting here. Lyrics contribute the semantic content that sets up the pragmatic dimension of the performance. The objection reasons that because the meaning arises from associated words, my discussion of songs does nothing to illuminate the contribution of *music*, where songs are combinations of words and music. In order to counter this objection, let us venture into the topic of musical understanding.

Although vocal music is a human universal, found in every culture, there are few, if any, universal rules governing musical design. A sense of rhythm is essential, but the polyrhythmic patterns of West Africa are very different from a Viennese waltz or a Greek Kalamatianos (7/8 meter) dance rhythm. In much the way that humans effortlessly learn and use the grammatical rules of their first language, through mere exposure, individuals become attuned to the rhythmic approaches that prevail in their own society. The same holds for melodic and harmonic rules or practices of different regions and time periods. And, just as fluency in one natural language does not translate into fluency in unrelated languages, *and may even inhibit subsequent acquisition of it*, understanding of one popular music style may become second nature, inhibiting the understanding and appreciation of others. So, although almost all of the musical features of any example of popular music can be understood effortlessly, based on mere repeated exposure to stylistically similar music, it will not be true that all popular music is equally accessible to everyone.

The analogy between music and natural language is fruitful because there is a sense in which each musical tradition has its own syntactical structure or "grammar."[40] These are patterns of permissible organization of more basic units: just as words and punctuation are grouped into categories that limit or prescribe the order in which they can be arranged, musical tones and beats have their permitted orders. At its most basic level, an understanding of music involves an immediate, unreflective perception of good order, as regulated by the relevant musical style.[41] To offer a simple example, when Thelonious Monk plays the nineteenth-century hymn "Blessed Assurance" in his recording "This Is My Story, This Is My Song," he begins with an extremely straightforward performance of the melody and harmonic progression as composed by Phoebe Knapp.[42] Then, just as he reaches the final notes of the first verse, he begins to embellish the familiar tune with a slight rhythmic disruption and small dissonance. He then plays a second verse, "jazzing" it more and breaking up the rhythm. Suppose we play Monk's recording for a jazz fan and then for a country music fan who never listens to jazz but knows the song through Alan Jackson's version (2006). Although it might take the jazz fan more than forty seconds to do so, it will become evident that the music is jazz—at which point, it may even become apparent that Monk is the pianist. The country fan, hearing the same track, will most likely hear the first moments of "jazzing" the tune as errors. They will literally make no sense—will not fit—within the perceptual gestalt under which the music is being understood. Hearing the second verse, there may be conscious realization that it's jazz, and that the music is meant to sound that way. However, conscious knowledge of this sort does not automatically result in musical understanding of the kind at issue here, which is a matter of the music hanging together in a way that makes sense. To the country music fan, Monk's chord substitutions and timing will sound wrong. Given that Monk's performance choices will make sense to most post-bebop jazz fans, hearing them as wrong is a blameless misunderstanding by someone who does not "know" jazz.

To summarize these very general points, there are two basic competencies involved in understanding the musical component of a song.

First, there is perception of the music's rhythmic, melodic, and harmonic organization and the related ability to anticipate later events based on earlier events (e.g., experiencing the verse as ending and thus expecting a new verse or chorus).[43] In some cases, timbre or tone color is an important aspect of the music's organization. A more advanced level of understanding involves the ability to explain why various organizational choices have been made by the composer and/or performers, relative to the whole piece, but there is no reason to think that level is required in all cases of understanding popular songs.

Second, there is perception of aesthetic and expressive properties of the music as they emerge from the musical organization. Traditionally, aesthetic properties include gestalt properties such as degree of beauty, but it also includes aspects such as balance, originality, and concision. Expressive properties, such as the difference between sad music and peaceful music, are generally classified as a subset of aesthetic properties.[44] There is considerable controversy about how such properties are generated by musical form or organization, but the details of that relationship are not important here.[45]

Given that there is a distinct kind of understanding that characterizes *musical* understanding, we can now defuse the objection that pragmatic considerations stem from words but not music by considering some examples where musical properties make an independent contribution to our understanding of the lyrics of songs and other sung texts. Consider Randy Newman's hit recording of his own song, "Short People" (1977). Lyrics aside, the aggressive staccato lines that dominate the music give way to a gentle, soaring passage in the "bridge" section. Simultaneously, Newman's harsh nasal timbre is smoothed with accompanying vocal harmonies. Not surprisingly, these musical decisions signal a shift in the lyrics, suggesting that the meaning of the previous verses and choruses is not the whole statement. The change in the music communicates that a competing voice has entered into conversation with the dominant one, setting the new lyrics against what has been previously "said."

Furthermore, purely musical humor seems inexplicable unless humorous passages are construed as speech acts.[46] Although jokes can be built into the work itself, as with Mozart's *Ein musikalischer Spaß* (K. 522, "A Musical Joke"), that is not always the case. Performers can interject humor that is not inherent in the type. Frank Zappa often did so with the satirical musical embellishments he supplied when performing music written by others.[47] Hence, my analysis of the legitimate divergence of song meaning and performance meaning extends to cases where pragmatic meaning does not arise from associated language. Lyrics aside, a performance of sad-sounding music can be used to express sadness, given the proper context, and therefore communication can be subject to sincerity conditions even if there is no propositional content that asserts truthfully or falsely. (I explore this point in detail in Chapter 3.) By injecting musical elements that undercut sincerity, Zappa subverted authorial intentions about the song's meaning.

Performances (and Utterances) Are Actions

Despite the various complications that arise when words are combined with music in a song or its performance, two additional parallels are noteworthy in a comparison between language use and song performance.

First, pragmatic content is often difficult to paraphrase. Although it is plausible to seek the pragmatic dimension of every performance or musical utterance, it is unlikely that we are in a position to produce a precise linguistic gloss on Hendrix's intended meaning when performing "The Star-Spangled Banner." Although it is plausible to say that Hendrix's introduction of "Taps" is a reference "the death of American soldiers in Vietnam," there is little reason to regard it as a reference to "the death of the 'American Dream.'"[48] In contrast, a somewhat more determinate interpretation appears to fit parts of Dylan's performance of "It's Alright, Ma (I'm Only Bleeding)" when he sang it on February 14, 1974. Sung at the height of the Watergate scandal and ensuing political crisis, the crowd went wild at the lyric "(E)ven the president... Sometimes must have/ To stand naked." In that context, the referring expression "the president of the United States" called attention to Richard Nixon in a way that it did not call attention to Chester A. Arthur.[49] Taken literally, Dylan's lyric refers to each and every president, and thus to Arthur as much as Nixon. Pragmatically, in the political context of 1974, Dylan singled out Nixon. However, general context always underdetermines pragmatic implications, so it remains possible that Dylan did not emphasize Nixon.[50] Deciding that his performances singled out Nixon requires a decision about his intentions in performing that song on that occasion.

Second, utterances are actions. In ordinary speech, they are "acts of producing tokens of sentences."[51] Song performances are likewise actions. They are, first and foremost, actions of producing tokens or instances of an abstract structure. In each case, these actions generate the pragmatic content.[52] This result might be regarded as a mere elaboration of the point that sensitivity to a speaker's intentions allows us to make sense of an utterance in a context. However, it merits separate attention because it clarifies the point that intentions and pragmatic content are properties of an act of producing an instance of a type. They are never properties of sentences, which is to say that we should not attribute intentions and pragmatic content to the *sentence* that is being uttered. That would be to collapse semantic meaning and pragmatic meaning. Analogously, we should not attribute pragmatic meaning to popular songs *qua* abstract structures. The type has semantic content, which informs yet underdetermines the pragmatic content of any of its utterances/performances.

This second point is a strong reason to reject the position that a popular song is a structure-in-use. Some properties simply cannot be properties of some types. Pragmatic content is such a case. Hence composers' known intentions about *those* meanings are not work-determinative; they do not *determine* anything about performances of their works. For example, Mozart's intentions determine that his Piano Sonata in C Major (K. 545) is to be played in C Major. However, the sonata cannot have the property of being striped teal and mauve. It is impossible for a created sonic type to have this among its normative properties, for these are not sonic properties or relationships among such properties. A wallpaper design might be built around these properties, but not a piano sonata. Hence Mozart's intentions, whatever they were, could not make being striped teal and mauve a property that its tokens ought to have. Likewise, pragmatic content cannot be a property of musical types. But popular song performances have pragmatic content. Consequently, popular songs are not full-fledged types-in-use. Finally, whatever is not an actual property of a work is not normative for its instances. So a composer's intentions about the pragmatic implications of its performances cannot be normative for any of its performances. Mozart's intentions could not give the Piano Sonata in C Major any pragmatic content that its tokens ought to have. At best, the composer can intend a preferred use of the work. But the composer cannot do more than hope that performers will respect and reaffirm those intentions.

To summarize the key argument, a sentence and a song are alike in being types with semantic content governed by shared conventions. Consequently, song performances are like sentence utterances. Both are structures-in-use. Because sentences are not structures-in-use, they lack pragmatic content. Semantic properties belong to sentence types, but both semantic and pragmatic properties belong to utterances.[53] Analogously, *songs* lack pragmatic content but performances possess it.

At best, a song's performances will have the pragmatic content intended by its composer(s), but such content is actualized only when performers choose to respect those intentions.[54] Stecker is right to propose that literary works are contextualized structures-in-use, where that context includes relevant authorial intentions. However, it does not follow that this cultural norm extends to popular songs. Literature and popular music work differently. Relatively few modern literary works are works for performance.[55] In contrast, popular songs are works for performance. Performance practice is at odds with the ideal of each token's having the same pragmatic meanings as the musical work. As we saw with "The Star-Spangled Banner," authorial intentions may guide performers but they do not decisively limit the pragmatic meanings associated with a song's incarnations as a structure-in-use, namely its performances. (I explore this point in greater detail in Chapter 2.)

I am not denying that many or even most performances successfully convey pragmatic meanings that composers hoped would be present. However, when performances *do* carry the pragmatic implications intended by the composer, those implications are not present by virtue of their being among the song's basic properties. They will be there because the work is performed in an appropriate context or with appropriate intentions.

Conversely, a performance can be a sonically correct instance without possessing any of the pragmatic meanings that its composer intended for it. Joseph Haydn's "The Seven Last Words from the Cross" is an instrumental work with an associated religious text. Performed during Lent as part of a religious service, it encourages and guides Christian reflection on Christ's suffering and sacrifices.[56] However, it is not inevitable that, because Haydn designed it to be used in that way, every use will conform to the composer's intended circumstances of presentation, nor that every performance communicates the religious message that he intended for it. Performed in a secular setting without interpolating the intended spoken sermons, a sonically perfect instance of the piece can be appreciated as absolute music, as a set of Classical-era adagios. Despite knowing the work's history, the audience for a secular performance need not construe it as an invitation to reverently reflect on Christ's passion. Although I know of no such case, a particular performance might be used to mock Haydn's intentions for it. Consider, for example, The Roches's performance of G.F. Handel's "Hallelujah Chorus" for the television program *Saturday Night Live* (November 17, 1979). Their performance, arranged for three voices and sung with an over-enunciated New York accent, displays a combination of bravado and disrespect that makes the performance playfully sacrilegious. Given an audience who knew it well enough, the same could be done with Haydn's "The Seven Last Words from the Cross."

Performances, like utterances, are actions. Because the performer's act of generating an instance can occur in a very different context than that which informs the composer's act of creating the type, full understanding of a performance can require attention to two distinct contexts. In the Hendrix case, there is a gap of 150 years; in Dylan's case, a mere decade. Either way, the site of pragmatic meaning is the *action* of performing the song. The *type* contributes semantic but not pragmatic meaning. Even if the same pragmatic content happens to emerge from *every* token of a particular type, it does not follow that the type possesses a corresponding property. Context alone might render a song performance ironic when the song itself is not. As in the Hendrix example, these points explain how a performer can perform a song while simultaneously deviating from its customary pragmatic implications.

Summary and Conclusion

To summarize the argument of this chapter, the semantics/pragmatics distinction maps to the distinction between songs and song performances in the same way that it works for sentences and sentence utterances. Semantics is not concerned with utterance context, whereas pragmatics explains how contexts of utterance affect the meaning of the utterance. On my parallel analysis, popular songs have semantic content because songs have specific linguistic structures as a component of their basic identity. Their musical structures may also function symbolically due to musical conventions. Acts of generating instances of a type generate pragmatic content, but that content should never be counted among the actual properties of the type. Structural types lack pragmatic content. Only specific uses (e.g., particular performances, recordings, and recontextualizations of recordings) have pragmatic content. Hence, accounts of meaning that ascribe pragmatic content to *popular songs* are mistaken in doing so. Consequently, the actual properties of a song will always underdetermine what can be communicated with it in performances. As a result, one and the same song can be used to communicate very different—even unexpected—meanings in different performance contexts.[57] This is enough to permit communication of diverse meanings from any one song without endorsing the more permissive view that the interpretation of each performance is a hermeneutical free-for-all.

2

Who Is "You're So Vain" About?

Speaking with Someone Else's Song

There is a common, perhaps even standard, view of popular songs. It says that songwriters have a specific meaning in mind when they compose their songs, and therefore understanding a popular song performance is primarily a matter of understanding what the songwriter meant to communicate. This common view is a *song-centered* view of popular music. Ironically, it aligns popular music interpretation with the conventions of literary and art interpretation. In contrast, a more accurate description of the norms of popular music is that songwriters bring words and music together, creating works-for-performance, and performers and other subsequent users of the songs have enormous freedom in how they will use them as vehicles for communication. By deploying pragmatics to affirm the context-sensitive generation of meaning, the song-centered view is replaced by a use-centered view. In the last chapter, I defended this proposal by exploring the technical idea that semantic content aligns with songs (types) and pragmatic content is generated in performances. In this chapter, I drop the ontological perspective and stop talking of types and tokens. In Chapter 1, I emphasized that *performance* brings existing songs into new contexts and, through presumption of relevance, generates new content. But pragmatic exploitation of context can also occur through both the creation and subsequent repurposing of a recorded song. The album *Here, My Dear* (1978) is Marvin Gaye's "kiss off" letter addressed to the wife he'd just divorced. Yet its content allowed Brad Pitt to hear it as an expression of his (Pitt's) own situation when he was getting divorced. What Gaye directs to his wife in the 1970s is recontextualized and appropriated, forty years later, as the story of another marriage and its dissolution.[1] Contemporary digital media have made recontextualization so simple that it has become ubiquitous in social media.[2] Nonetheless, the basic conditions for the recontextualization and repurposing of recorded music are inherent in all popular song, and variants of the practice can be traced back as far as we care to look.

I opened the book's Introduction with several examples of recorded music repositioned into new contexts, generating new pragmatic implications—Nick Drake's "Pink Moon," Fleetwood Mac's "Dreams," and two songs by The Pogues. Here is a fresh example. In an iconic scene in the film *Say Anything* (1989), Lloyd Dobler stands outside the bedroom of his former girlfriend and lofts a large boom box above his head. Inside the house, Diane Court recognizes the recording blaring from the boom box: Peter Gabriel's "In Your Eyes" (1986). Lloyd had played it for her once before, shortly after they started to date. To understand the movie, one must understand this scene. To understand the scene, one must understand the song, "In Your Eyes." Above all, one must understand what the character is *doing* with the (recorded) song. Lloyd is not inviting Diane to engage in disinterested, appreciative engagement of a piece of music. Instead, Lloyd is *using* the music to communicate something to Diane. He is using Gabriel's voice, and Gabriel's repeated use of the pronoun "my," to refer to Lloyd, who is appropriating Gabriel's voice in speaking to Diane. The context shifts the referent of the recorded song and Lloyd thereby uses it as his own utterance. He, not Peter Gabriel, is the "speaker" of the utterance, and it is Lloyd's utterance meaning that matters in this communicative act.

As I noted in the Introduction, Nathan Apodaca's TikTok video is similar in repurposing an existing recording. However, it differs because the recorded song is not embedded in a fictional narrative. By filming himself lip-synching to Fleetwood Mac's "Dreams" and then posting it online, Apodaca appropriates Stevie Nicks's voice and words as his own communication. The *Say Anything* and "Dreams" examples exemplify two ways that recordings of popular songs are used to invite auditors to explore what they are about *thematically*, rather than what they are about literally. By connecting the recording's musical and thematic thrust to events and situations different from the ones highlighted by the song's semantic content, recordings are routinely used as open-ended vehicles that can be used to communicate things that the songs themselves do not suggest.

Such cases invite us to extend Chapter 1's initial exploration of *aboutness*—of referentiality, or the activity of referring to one thing rather than another—in popular song use. There are two dimensions to this extension of reference. First, there is reference in the ordinary sense: the communication is about this or that person or situation or thing, and not about these others. Second, the communication conveys some idea, or expresses some emotion, about that referent. In Chapter 1, I discussed how the American national anthem is literally about events in American history; yet, Jimi Hendrix used it to condemn the war in Vietnam. The songwriter could not possibly have intended any such reference to that war, and the *song* makes no such reference. Additionally, what Hendrix is saying is a radical departure from the sentiments encoded in the song.

Another complicating factor is that many popular songs are fictional narratives or portray fictional characters.[3] Yet, thanks to pragmatic implicature, fictional narratives and characters routinely acquire real-world referents. Granted, this practice is not unique to popular song use. It is a staple of popular culture, as when the novel *MASH* (1968) was adapted for film by Robert Altman (*M*A*S*H*, 1970). The novel is about the American experience in the Korean conflict of the early 1950s, and the film does not change the setting. Yet, like Hendrix's use of the national anthem, the film is a statement about the war in Vietnam. Popular culture is swamped with repurposing and pragmatic implicature of this kind, and songs are especially well suited for it. Where literature can communicate ideas to a reading audience apart from any intervening interpretation in performance or adaptation into another medium, songs do not communicate until they receive performance interpretation as an action in a discernible contributing context.[4] A song can be activated in an endless number of new contexts and, thanks to pragmatic implicature, made relevant in a fresh way in any new performance or recording of it.

For example, the song "Tell Me Why You like Roosevelt" was written by Otis Jackson in the 1940s, and it is about Franklin D. Roosevelt. The song was largely forgotten until it was recorded by Jesse Winchester in 1974. His decision to record it raises the question of why he did so. Why sing about Roosevelt some thirty years after his death? How is the communication *relevant*? The basic insight of pragmatics, the relevance principle, tells us that every new occasion of use of a text invites such interrogation.[5] Based on the relevance principle, Winchester's recording should be understood as a fresh use, enmeshed in a new context of utterance. An American draft evader living in Canada, Winchester sang about Roosevelt because he wanted to say something about Canadian politician Pierre Trudeau—he even amends some of Jackson's words to include reference to Trudeau, ensuring that listeners will understand that his performance is an engagement with contemporary politics. By implication, he was also contrasting Trudeau's push for institutional reform with the more reactionary political climate of the United States.

Although it made his message clearer, Winchester did not need to add an explicit reference to Trudeau to generate reference to contemporary events. The invitation to seek relevance affords every song performance with the capacity to refer to events contemporaneous with the performance, referencing people and events over and above any that the song's words are literally about. In recording a forgotten song, Winchester thrusts it into a new political context, inviting auditors to ask how its message remains relevant. Thus, even if he had not inserted Trudeau's name into Jackson's song, the question of relevance generates meaningful implicatures for the recording.

Let us review some other basic points from Chapter 1. Understanding a song—a distinctively identifiable combination of words and music—requires understanding it both musically and verbally, as well as understanding how the two interact. However, neither of these elements are fixed and constant across all renderings of any given song. Consequently, the performance-interpretation of even a relatively simple popular song will contribute features that are not found in other instances, and which may deviate from standard practice (e.g., Hendrix jettisoned the words and gave an instrumental performance of the national anthem at Woodstock). Things become even more complex when the context of performance guides the audience's interpretation. I'll say more about each of the four focal points of interpretation—music, words, their interaction, and their interaction with the performance context—in the course of my argument against the song-centered view.

The Song-Centered View of Meaning

My aim in this chapter is to address, and reject, a common idea about understanding songs. It is the view that the meaning of a song's performance stems from, and is determined by, the meaning of the song. Let's call this the song-centered view. The basic idea of the song-centered view is that any and all information encoded in the *song* determines what both its *performances* and *recordings* communicate.

In contrast, a use-centered approach says that the information encoded in the song contributes to, but does not determine, what it is used to "say" on any particular occasion of use. What it communicates may depart considerably from—and even invert—what is encoded in the song. Every new use invites the question of how the song is being recontextualized. I have mentioned three modes of song recontextualization: performing it, recording it, and appropriating an existing recording. Each of these actions creates new conditions for understanding how the song is being used to communicate. Notice my way of putting that: understanding how the song is being used, not what the song itself means.

Understanding is a goal, and it has success conditions. Consider the following simple example. If someone thinks that Jimi Hendrix's recording of "Purple Haze" (1967) is an early anthem of gay liberation, based on mishearing the lyric "[ex]cuse me while I kiss the sky" as "kiss this guy," then that interpretation is a misunderstanding. The listener misunderstands what Hendrix is communicating. Now consider the more complex case of recontextualizing a recording. Suppose an ophthalmologist says that the boom box scene in *Say Anything* is one of her favorite movie scenes, because the song calls attention to the importance of eyes. Although in a narrow sense it might be a relevant interpretation, that response would also be a profound misunderstanding, for it would also fail to grasp what the song addresses thematically, and therefore also how it is being used by Lloyd in the narrative context.[6]

Granted, some listeners enjoy popular music despite misunderstanding it. Many listeners may even enjoy certain instances of popular song only *because* they misunderstand them. Imagine a socially conservative country music fan purchasing Brandi Carlile's album *By The Way, I Forgive You* (2018) because it won three Grammy awards. Initial enjoyment may give way to annoyance or anger upon realizing that many of the songs critique heteronormality and standard gender roles. From the standpoint of enjoying the album, some people will find that misunderstanding is more satisfying than understanding it. However, I am not endorsing an "anything goes" position toward enjoyment. I am concerned with popular music as communication, and there is no reason to think that the best strategies for *enjoying* the music will align neatly with norms for correctly *understanding* it.[7]

As a theory about the success conditions for understanding popular songs, the song-centered view contains a kernel of good advice: failure to understand the song will normally interfere with understanding its performances. I love the energy of Plastic Bertrand's hit record "Ça Plane pour Moi" (1977). I certainly understand its musical idiom: punkish power pop. However, I have no idea about the meaning of most of its French lyric, and therefore I cannot claim to have more than partial understanding of it. Clearly, the song-centered view is correct insofar one cannot understand a performance if one does not understand how both the music and words contribute to the performance, and how they interact and illuminate one another. A failure to understand either element—or both—is therefore an obstacle to understanding the song and therefore also to understanding its performative uses. However, the song-centered view claims a stronger relationship than a requirement to understand music and words and their interrelationship. It claims that the meaning of the song's performances/recordings is determined by what the song means. On this view, because Neil Young's "Old Man" (1972) was written about the caretaker on his California ranch, The Wailin' Jennys must be singing about this same unnamed man when they recorded a cover version (2004). Young wasn't just singing about a generic old man, but about a specific one, and so The Wailin' Jennys must be singing about that same man, as well.

This song-centered view has the virtue of explaining a particular kind of interest that is frequently directed at popular songs. It focuses attention on why the songwriter chose a specific topic or phrase. Consider the case of "You're So Vain," Carly Simon's hit song of 1972–3. Singing to someone who was (presumably) her former lover, Simon's teasing chorus jokes about her target's vanity: "You probably think this song is about you/Don't you? Don't you?" However, she never names her referent, and for many years interviewers and fans asked about his identity. Then, more than forty years after its release, the song became headline news in major new outlets—one headline reads, "Carly Simon Finally Reveals Who's So Vain."[8] What Simon revealed was long suspected. The second verse of the song describes film star Warren Beatty, how he took advantage of her when she was "naïve," and how he lied to her about his commitment to their relationship.

Although the words do not themselves determine who the song is about, the song-centered view says that, as with Young's "Old Man," Simon's song is about whomever she wrote it about. Therefore, when Marilyn Manson recorded "You're So Vain" for his *Born Villain* album (2012), the song-centered view says the second verse still refers to Beatty. We might modify the standard song-centered account by saying that Manson had the power to avoid such a reference, and could have done so by revising its lyrics (which he did not do). In such cases, it would be plausible to say that a derivative song has been substituted for the original one. However, when the lyrics are not altered, they refer to whoever or whatever they referenced when the song was composed. Because Winchester made changes, it is plausible to say that his performance of "Tell Me Why You Like Roosevelt" involves a derivative song. However, Manson's "You're So Vain" does not.

From the perspective of pragmatics, the song-centered view goes wrong in stressing text-meaning over use-meaning. My primary claim is that the referential meaning of Manson's version does not hinge on Simon's referential intentions, even if Manson sings exactly what Simon wrote. There is no reference to Beatty in the semantic content of the song. Winchester's cover of "Tell Me Why You Like Roosevelt" is plausibly "read" as making reference Roosevelt, because his name is part of the song, but it does not follow that Winchester is communicating something about Roosevelt. As my argument develops, I'll suggest a more radical view: because it is a *song*, the presence of Roosevelt's name is not even a genuine reference to Roosevelt.

Because it ties the determination of meaning to the songwriter(s)'s intentions, the song-centered view does have the virtue of clearing up another mystery about "You're So Vain." An obscure phrase, "they were clouds in my coffee," appears four times. Simon introduces the phrase to characterize her dashed dreams when Beatty "gave [her] away." It seems to be a metaphor, but it lacks the transparency of a classic metaphor like Shakespeare's line given to Romeo, "Juliet is the sun."[9] The song-centered view allows us to cite the author as the authority on what it means. Simon has clarified her meaning in her autobiography, saying that the phrase describes an occasion when the clouds in the sky were reflected in a cup of coffee she was drinking.[10] Understood in this light, saying that her dreams were like the clouds in coffee (i.e., they were a mere reflection) is a relatively straightforward metaphor.[11]

The song-centered view is not simply a default assumption of popular culture. It has been endorsed as a general view of music performance by at least two philosophers, Thomas Carson Mark and Peter Kivy.[12] Technically, Mark concentrates on instrumental music, while Kivy adapts Mark to deal with the question of whether modern performers of Handel's *Messiah* are presenting and endorsing anti-Semitic messages by performing the piece as written. Setting aside this difference in emphasis, they begin with the fact that few performers of composed music restrict themselves to their own compositions. The compositions come to performers with pre-encoded meanings: each musical work "can be likened to statements: works of art can be thought of as entities which are accepted, in certain social or institutional contexts, as making statements."[13] In an important respect, therefore, a performance of a pre-existing composition is socially like the practice of quoting language that another person has put together on some earlier occasion. I have, at various points above, quoted song lyrics. However, to quote is not necessarily to endorse. Therefore, Mark argues, a genuine performance of a musical work must also *assert* whatever the composer intended it to mean.[14] For, otherwise, the performance is a meaningless, empty display of musical talent. I grant that there are such meaningless performances, but these are usually dismissed as defective—as inauthentic, lifeless, "going through the motions," and so on. In effect, the song-centered view tells us that a performance will also be defective whenever a performer is insincere, declining to (personally) assert or endorse whatever the lyric literally asserts.

Before I explain where I part company with this analysis, I want to introduce an important elaboration of the song-centered view. To provide focus, let us set aside, without further concern, examples involving a language barrier, as when I don't understand the line "Une louloute est v'nue chez moi" in "Ça Plane pour Moi." We'll also set aside musical ignorance, as when a country music listener hears a series of musical errors in bop piano. Third, set aside cases where a performer avoids an unwanted meaning by changing or omitting the established text. Although I oppose the song-centered view, I want to acknowledge that its proponents can cite pragmatics in order to allow performers have the power to shift what a performance is about. Its proponents might say that a performance can exploit context so that each performance is necessarily about whatever the song is about; yet, the performance is not *merely* about whatever the song is originally or literally about.

The song-centered view can accommodate context-sensitive shifts of reference in the following way. Consider the first line of Stephen Foster's song "Oh! Susanna" (1848): "I come from Alabama with my banjo on my knee." There is nothing complicated about this lyric. The word "Alabama" refers to the state of Alabama, the words "banjo" and "knee" refer to a stringed musical instrument and a part of the human anatomy, respectively. Those are some things that the song is about. So if I sing "Oh! Susanna," my performance references Alabama, banjos, knees, and so on. Although it is certainly plausible to say that the standard meanings of the song's lyrics contribute to determinate meanings that occur in its various performances, we need to make room for the way that performances generate additional meanings—meanings that cannot be derived from an understanding of the song itself (i.e., the composed combination of text and music). For example, Taj Mahal recorded "Oh! Susanna" for his album *Happy Just to Be like I Am* (Columbia 1971) and he frequently performed it in concerts. We might ask why an African-American singer would give such prominence to a song associated with the minstrel tradition, which did so much to degrade African-Americans.[15] In a verse that is seldom sung, and evidently never sung by Mahal, Foster's lyric includes a racial slur. We might also ask why he sings it in such a joyful, even celebratory, manner. And it might be plausible to answer that the singer is consciously reclaiming his own heritage, ugly as it may be, as an act of self-affirmation and a symbolic rejection of deep-seated racial stereotypes. In short, the performance injects the song's properties into a new context (e.g., the singer's racial identity) and thereby uses the song to generate meanings that are not found in the song itself. This use of Foster's song fits the idea that the musical work (encoded with Foster's meanings) is to be distinguished from its presentation (performance or recording) in a particular social or institutional context.

In short, it is possible to combine the song-centered view with the flexibility of meaning production that comes from context-sensitive pragmatics. The song supplies a specific semantic content, which might be supplemented by the composer's intentions, and then additional meaning is attached to a particular performance through contextual supplementation. The meaning might even be inverted by the performance style, as when a song is performed ironically.[16]

However, things look less rosy when we apply this approach to the example of Lloyd playing the Gabriel song for Diane. The song was (allegedly) written about Rosanna Arquette, with whom Gabriel was involved.[17] Lloyd can take the expression of emotion that Gabriel directed at Arquette, can identify it as his own emotion by his ostentatious act of sharing it, and so can use it to declare his devotion to Diane. However, the song-centered view holds that if Gabriel *did* write it about Arquette, then it is always about her. Therefore "In Your Eyes" was about Arquette when I heard it for the first time, sitting in a movie theater watching *Say Anything*. Presumably, it is about Arquette even in the fictional world where Lloyd dates Diane.

However, I think this approach piles up a load of excess baggage. Reference to Arquette plays no role whatsoever in understanding (1) writer-director Cameron Crowe's selection of this song for two scenes in this movie, (2) the choice made by Lloyd Dobler in world of the film fiction, or (3) my understanding of the scene in the film. On the principle of Occam's Razor, we should toss the excess baggage when a simpler explanation does the job. Returning to Hendrix and "The Star-Spangled Banner," the song-centered view says that he was communicating about *both* the shelling of Fort McHenry in 1814 *and* the American debacle in Vietnam. Occam's Razor suggests that the topic of Fort McHenry is a needless complication.

Taylor Swift sometimes performs "You're So Vain" in concert. When she does, her fans apparently understand her to be (intentionally) making a comment on one or more of her high-profile romances and breakups, and inviting them to treat it as a comment on their own love lives.[18] There is no reason to assume that the song requires Swift to do this by inviting listeners to think about Warren Beatty and then to imaginatively supplement that reference in ways that will allow them to understand a message that is not tied to Beatty. On my view, singers are free to use the song to convey anything that can be communicated given the resources it makes available in its structure of words and music. Simon realized that she could use the same song to make a political statement about the 2016 presidential election. By then she had revealed that Beatty inspired the second verse; yet, there is no reason to suppose that, in 2016, she was making a point about candidate Trump to American voters by making a statement about ex-lover Beatty. In its 2016 use, it is simply about Trump, and it is about Trump even if none of its details are literally true. As such, it makes its point by way of fictional discourse, and this fictional discourse has no need to locate Warren Beatty in the world of the fiction.

In summary, supplementing the song-centered view with context-sensitive pragmatics can get us the results we want, but it turns performance and recontextualization into a complicated and unwieldy communicative act. We can generate context-sensitive implicature, exploiting semantics and pragmatics, while also jettisoning the undesirable assumption that Swift's fans fail to grasp much of what she is communicating when she performs "You're So Vain," or that the crowd at Woodstock was misunderstanding Hendrix's performance if they failed to think about the shelling of Fort McHenry.

Songs as Props in Fiction-Making and Make-Believe

After some howling, the first line of Warren Zevon's original recording of "Werewolves of London" (1978) is "I saw a werewolf with a Chinese menu in his hand." Carly Simon may have seen clouds in her coffee, but I doubt that Warren Zevon ever saw a werewolf prowling London, with or without a Chinese menu. Not to put too fine a point on it, many song lyrics are fictions. On the view that I recommend, fictionality is the default condition for song lyrics in songs written for performance—they are fictions unless there are unusual circumstances that would override this default. Zevon's song is obviously a fiction, given its absurdity. As Is "Oh! Susanna," given its litany of absurdities. It is less obvious that the song "You're So Vain" is a fiction, but there are strong reasons to grant that it is. Here are three arguments in favor of its being a fiction.

First and foremost, fictionality is a matter of social norms and *intended use*, and not, as is sometimes assumed, a question of how much of it is true. Mere assemblage of a set of true statements does not count against the fictionality of the resulting song or performance. As Kendall Walton notes, "fantasy remains fiction even if it happens to correspond to the actual course of events."[19] A statement or group of statements is fictive or fictional by virtue of how it is used: an author, speaker, or performer provides the material with the intention of being recognized as offering it as an occasion for auditor make-believe.[20] Making content fictive through the activity of staging and performing is compatible with the additional goal of pragmatic generation of asserted content—witness, above, Winchester's make-believe that Roosevelt is alive and that he "likes" him, in order to set up the pragmatic implicature of recommending the election of progressive politicians.

To better understand how this works, let us turn to Simon's autobiography. Simon makes it clear that "You're So Vain" is a fantasy: it is an assemblage of incidents involving different men, mixed together with details that were not strictly true. Her description of how she cherry-picked lines that she had written into a notebook at different times and her admission that two key lines of the song were ones she heard others speak indicate that veracity was not the guiding principle in constructing the song's lyric. She set out to write a song about male vanity, and then incorporated a mixture of accurate and fabricated details. Furthermore, it is worth noting that the line that gives the song its title was written long *before* she thought about writing about Warren Beatty.[21] When she originated the line "you're so vain you probably think this song is about you," it was not about Beatty. It appears that, when it written, the line was not about anyone. *It was a line for possible use in a song lyric.*

The key line of "You're So Vain" therefore illustrates my point. One and the same text—understood simply as a particular combination of meaning-bearing symbols—can be false in one use, true in another use, and fictional in yet another use. Simon acknowledges that the song's first verse contains both true and false details.[22] That is, if they were to be taken as assertions, some would be true and others would be false. For performers and auditors, it is less important to decide which details are true or false than it is to understand the intended outcome of Simon's compositional process: the combined lines selected by Simon for her song create an expressively powerful fiction. It would be no less fictional if she had composed it entirely of individually true sentences. The combination would still bear the hallmarks of a work of fiction, which is to say that its function is other than to assert truths about the world.

My second major point is that the very decision to combine words and music in a song for performance gives that construct a default status as fictive.[23] Setting aside the specific semantic content of a song's words, popular music performance encourages adoption of a make-believe identification with the singer or singers in their presentation of that semantic content.[24] (Given the norm of how popular songs are used, our norm is that the songs are fictive, because intended for such use.) Identification moves the auditor beyond mere understanding of what is communicated. Successful song performance makes an auditor internalize the music's expressive properties so that auditors feel some of what the protagonist or subjects would be feeling if it were real and not a prop for make-believe. Here, I am giving partial support to the longstanding tradition that music is expressive by virtue of inculcating or stirring up some degree of emotion in auditors.[25] The main competitor to this "arousal" account of expressivity is the resemblance theory: auditors do not need to feel what it expresses, but must instead recognize that certain features of the musical form are appropriately similar to corresponding features of emotions (or, in an older version, to distinctive features of the human voice betraying a particular emotion). Arousal theory says that Simon's emphatic repetition of "don't you? don't you?" is designed to get us to feel what it's like to spitefully taunt someone, so that we have a first-person engagement and strong imaginative participation in the performance. Resemblance theory says that it succeeds if we can recognize that she sounds like someone who is aggressively taunting, but we can remain in a third-person perspective in our make-believe engagement.

On my view, we should embrace elements of both accounts. We do not grasp the expressivity of a musical performance if we fail to adopt first-person identification. Stephen Davies's version of the resemblance theory emphasizes how music can display elements of "gait, attitude, air, carriage, posture, and comportment of human body" that communicate emotion.[26] But what is the basis of this display? I appeal to meter and rhythm, which are the backbone of song construction, especially in the popular realm. We do not passively perceive meter and tempo: the normal process for perceiving them is to engage in entrainment with rhythmic cues. Basically, auditors perceive rhythm by imaginatively anticipating its unfolding placement of beats and accents. To entrain is to construct an anticipatory schema, which in turn requires a mental representation by each auditor in which they can anticipate rhythm by imaginatively moving their own musculoskeletal system. In short, perception of a beat, a tempo, and a rhythm requires motor planning of bodily action.[27] Foot tapping and head bobbing are the classic displays of entrainment, for they actualize some of that motor planning. The arousal of emotion is a direct effect of entrainment: moving in specific ways disposes us to feel specific emotions, and imagining doing so (representing a movement plan to ourselves) can also generate emotion.

Consequently, lyrics that encourage third-person make-believe will combine with musical features that invite auditors to engage, however minimally, in a first-person perspective. Thus, as it is normally performed, the rhythmic chassis of "Here Comes the Bride" *feels* stately. Entraining to the lilting waltz rhythm of standard performances of "Goodnight, Irene" gives it a markedly dreamy feeling that is unusual for a despairing song of lost love.[28] The Grateful Dead undercut that effect in "The Eleven" (1969), transforming a waltz into 11/8 time by strategically inserting 2/4 after three counts of 3/4, thereby hiking the already "cosmic" lyrics to momentary disruptions and dislocations that feel uncanny in an otherwise joyous affirmation. Because we imaginatively anticipate these movement plans *in relation to ourselves*, there is an important truth in T.S. Eliot's famous line, "you are the music while the music lasts."[29]

Finally, I will point to a third reason why the presence of music directly signals an invitation to make-believe. Music-making satisfies two central criteria that appear to be central to any creative processes that invites make-believe: the creative agent (1) prioritizes factors other than the communication of truth when selecting details and their arrangement and (2) thereby intentionally signals to auditors that the resulting text is a prop for content-oriented make-believe (i.e., it is offered as an occasion for content-guided imaginative engagement).[30] It is obvious that the compositional process of fitting words to the *music* of a song will be informed by the coherence and expressive effect of the music. It is no less true that song composers select and combine words for *their* coherence and expressive effect, including their interaction with the music. As songwriter Jimmy Webb observes, words are combined (or not) with an ear to "the way they can be jammed together in unlikely alliances that delight and entertain ... Which is to say that all great lyrics use the devices of poetry."[31]

When communication is organized by such devices—when it is controlled by cultural devices of "making special," to use Ellen Dissanayake's phrase[32]—and the communication is directed to a general audience rather than specific targeted individuals, the communicative act is an opportunity for make-believe. Now, certainly, aesthetic decisions inform all sorts of nonfiction communications to a general audience (e.g., the cover design of a biography of James Joyce, the design of a restaurant's menu), and there are times when a direct communication is decorated or aesthetically enhanced (e.g., writing a condolence note in a fancy note card rather than on the back of an old envelope). Despite the aesthetic heightening of content in these sorts of cases, we also consider how the communication is meant to function: are we expected to *accept* what is communicated? When information is presented as fictional, the primary function is not assertion of content and audience acceptance of it, but rather presentation of aesthetically heightened content for the purpose of imaginative and empathetic engagement.[33]

Thus, both the actions of *composing a song* and of *singing a song* put the words into the category of presentation of aesthetically heightened content. And, to be clear, aesthetic heightening is not restricted to the pleasant, lovely, graceful, and beautiful. *Unpleasant* music satisfies this criterion, too. But, either way, a song's lyrics become part of a fiction by incorporation into a song for performance, and this status of structure-for-use overrides any assertion of literal truth.

Finally, it is important to note that a communication is no less fictional because it asks us to engage in make-believe about real things. Every fiction must have some toehold in reality in order to provide directions for the imagining. For the sake of argument, let us provisionally assume that the song-centered view is correct and that "Tell Me Why You Like Roosevelt" is always about F.D.R.[34] Anyone who hears Winchester's recording is unlikely to have any feelings one way or another about F.D.R.; yet, the song invites listeners to assume, *imaginatively, of themselves*, that F.D.R. is still alive and the auditor "likes" F.D.R. Similarly, the opening line of The Beatles song "Strawberry Fields Forever" (1967: "Let me take you down, 'cause I'm going to…") invites each listener to imagine going to the Strawberry Field Children's Home, even if the vast majority of listeners never understand that it is a reference to a real place, a Liverpool orphanage. What matters for my argument is that the words provide opportunities for listeners to pretend or imagine they are doing one thing rather than another, where the imagining is directed by the (limited) details of the song. With "Strawberry Fields Forever," the music may provide far more guidance than the words!

A more significant example—and, indirectly, evidence of the predominance of the song-centered view—can be found in American court rooms. Because hip-hop performers included the names of two police officers who had arrested them in their rap "F* the Police" (2012), a judge ruled that they must really be targeting those people by virtue of naming them, and therefore the action of posting it online was a terrorist threat.[35] It is worth noting that there is long litany of American court cases where lyrics are presented as sincere expressions of desire or true declarations of fact when performed by African-American men. In such cases, song lyrics are sometimes treated as confessional evidence leading to imprisonment. However, a closer look makes it clear that the songwriting in these cases is, like most "confessional" songwriting, a fictionalization and amalgamation of reality and make-believe for purposes of dramatic effect.[36]

Emphasizing that fictionality is the default status of songs for performance does not trivialize them. On the contrary, it is a source of their capacity to communicate messages in performance. By engaging in guided imagining, audiences are frequently invited to understand various things about the world.[37] But fictions normally communicate about the world indirectly, by implication. The novels of Charles Dickens called attention to issues of child welfare, bureaucratic incompetence, and systemic injustice, and they were powerful because they personified the issues, rather than through direct assertion ("child labor is bad and should be outlawed") or sloganeering. Famously, Abraham Lincoln is said to have identified the novel *Uncle Tom's Cabin* as the cause of the American civil war.[38] These fictional novels support world-oriented make-believe.[39] Such fictions have potent—but sometimes indeterminate—meanings, and this potency is one of the most valuable—and feared—aspects of popular music.

The same is true of many songs. The songs of Gilbert and Sullivan's *The Mikado* (1885) are nominally about fictitious events in Japan; yet they are, like all of their work together, "engaged with the question of what it meant to be English."[40] Similarly, XTC's "Dear God" (1986) employs fictional address to make a serious point about God's indifference to human suffering or, more likely, it makes the point that "God" refers to a fiction. Granted, some songs are so clearly world-oriented and so specific in their description that we can reasonably hold the songwriter(s) accountable for the claims they make; Bob Dylan took such poetic license with some of the events in the fact-based narrative "Hurricane" (1975) that lawyers convinced him to withdraw his intended recording from the *Desire* album (1976), to rewrite it, and to re-record it.[41] Yet because "Hurricane" is making a general point about systemic racism and injustice, its story and general message can be conveyed to listeners who are indifferent to the truth of its various assertions.

In summary, songs are like novels and other fictional literary works in that both can advance general truths, provide critical commentary, and encourage political action. However, there is an important difference between songs and literature. In the current system of the arts, novels and poems are not normally works for performance. Granted, Dickens made a considerable sum of money by giving public readings of his novels, and *Uncle Tom's Cabin* was almost immediately popularized as a theatrical play. However, in modern times the majority of literary works are not works for performance.[42] Songs essentially are. That difference, I will now argue, combines with fictionality to drain the song-centered view of the explanatory purpose it may seem to serve.

Understanding a Performance

I have raised the concern that the song-centered view of songs wrongly assumes that when song lyrics are worded as assertions about real people, places, and events, it follows that all performances and uses of the song make assertions about those people, places, and events. My alternative is the view that a different operative norm is in place. These references are generally placeholders that invite imaginative engagement with ideas that may depart from what is ostensibly said.

In emphasizing that songs are primarily blueprints for encouraging make-believe, I am also rejecting an aestheticism that regards songs and their performances as primarily of interest as objects of aesthetic attention. As I noted in the book's Introduction, singing is often uncoupled from performing. This is most obvious in the case of work songs. The actual workers who sing them are not singing to please an audience.[43] But even when popular song performances are provided as entertainment and as objects of aesthetic interest, communication may be the performer's primary purpose, with entertainment value and aesthetic attraction a means to this end. To this degree, Mark is correct that we do not generally want a performance that merely "quotes" the musical work: we want the performer to mean something by the performance. As I suggested in the last section of this chapter, the very decision to combine words with music in a song for performance signals that the semantic content is one among several prompts for occasions of make-believe.

My account of how songs are used therefore distinguishes between two things: (1) the person who writes the lyrics draws on biographical and other facts, in which case a particular person or incident *inspired* the song lyric and (2) when sung, the lyric *refers* auditors to those real persons or events in the world. On my view, the writer's inspiration does not automatically equate with the performer's referent. The main reason for distinguishing between inspiration and referent follows from recognition that we should, as a default, regard song lyrics as fictions. As I said in the last section, I do not mean this in the sense that they are false, but instead that they are designed to be opportunities for make-believe and for imaginative simulation.[44]

My point is familiar in philosophy of literature. The fact that there are references to London and Australia in Thomas Hardy's novel *Jude the Obscure* does not mean that the text is making reference to London and Australia as they are in the real world. The novel's many references to the fictional Christminster do not give us a situation in which references to the actual world are mixed together with fictional ones. In the context of the work, the references to London and Australia are references to the "world of the work," rather than the actual world.[45] We know that the references to London and Australia are references to fictional places in *Jude the Obscure*, for one can travel from them to Christminster in this fictional world, which cannot be done from the real London and the real Australia.

This point transfers intact to song lyrics. "Werewolves of London" does not refer to the real London, but rather to a fictional city in which there are werewolves. "You're So Vain" mentions Nova Scotia, but because the text is fictive, the Nova Scotia it references is a location in the fictional world indicated by the song's text. It is, at best, a close counterpart modeled on the real place. And if that is the case for the *places* referenced in songs for performance, then it must also be true of the *people* who are referenced. The degree to which the place or person in the song is like or unlike the real-world counterpart will vary enormously. Evidently, the Alabama of "Oh! Susanna" has magical weather. Simon's reference to an eclipse in Nova Scotia has been used as a clue to dating some of the events of the song, but it is certainly possible that the timing of the eclipse in the world of the song differs from the timing of eclipses in the real world. Returning to this chapter's opening example, "In Your Eyes" might not be a Peter Gabriel song in the fictional world of Lloyd and Diane. However, a presumption of maximum continuity between reality and fiction is the basis for our ability to "know our way around" a fictional world, so we assume that familiar things are direct counterparts of real things until we are offered reasons to think otherwise.[46]

Given that the world-directedness of fictions is only loosely indicated by references to actual places and persons, pragmatics again enter the picture. As I stressed in the previous section, most literature is not created for use in performance, but songs are. Once created, anyone may choose to perform a particular song. As Walton formulates this idea, we should regard songwriters as "thoughtwriters." They produce "texts for others to use in expressing their thoughts (feelings, attitudes)."[47] It is the *performer*, not the songwriter, who uses the song. One of the most frequent uses is to generate a fully realized prop for content-oriented make-believe.[48]

Because songwriters create something that becomes available for use by others, the songwriter's inspiration for the fictional world of the song need not appear in the fictional world conjured up in a particular performance or communicative use. Earlier, I offered the example of Taylor Swift in live performance, singing "You're So Vain" in order to offer herself (fictionalized) to the audience so that they could reflect on their own relationships. It also happens that a parallel shift occurs when a singer-songwriter treats their own prior work as a text-for-use. Brandi Carlile's "The Joke" (2017) contains a line "carrying your baby on your back across the desert." She has explained that when she wrote it, she was responding to the war in Syria and the refugee crisis in the region. Subsequently, harsh American policies against immigrants instigated by President Trump led her to change her view of it when she performs it. In 2019, she said, "It's about our own southern border. When I sing it, that's what I'm thinking of."[49] Same writer, same singer, same song, new context: new meaning. Carlile as songwriter has created a prop for use by Carlile as performer.

The situation is even more complicated than that, for popular music *recordings* also serve as props of this kind. Redirection can occur through recontextualization of an existing recording. As I noted earlier, Simon endorsed the use of her hit recording of "You're So Vain" in a political advertisement ridiculing Donald Trump prior to the 2016 presidential election.[50] The video clip uses the first verse of the original recording, but replaces one word: "scarf" is replaced with "face." The substitution is amusing, but it is so trivial that the result hardly qualifies as a new, derivate musical work. If the song-centered view is correct, then the 2016 video is still about whoever the first verse of the song was about when it was written and recorded by Simon in the 1970s.[51] It is then *additionally* about Trump through contextual supplementation—Simon's approval of the coupling of her recording with images and clips of Trump. But, as I've argued, that is excess baggage: the song's use has parted company from its inspiration.

Simon's 2016 video is hardly a unique case. By extension, *anyone* who recontextualizes a recording may adopt the role of "speaker" who is using the semantic and expressive content to communicate their own meaning. Different playbacks of the same recorded song have always afforded the opportunity to make different statements. This is especially easy with popular songs that omit proper names and use context-sensitive indexical expressions. When someone records themselves (falsely) saying "I can't come to the phone right now, please leave a message," the indexical expression "now" will refer to the present time on each of its playbacks, rather than the time when it was actually spoken.⁵² The indexical "I" can also shift, because the same recording can be used with telephones with different owners. It can be done with recorded songs, too: for years, I used a snippet of Laurie Anderson's "O Superman" (1982) as my own answering machine message ("Hi. I'm not home right now…"), and in its use, each playback meant that I (and not Laurie Anderson) was not available at that time. The same snippet of the same record, on my daughter's phone, tells the world that she (not me, not Anderson) cannot answer the phone right now. Similarly, simply by sharing Thunderclap Newman's "Something in the Air" (1969) on social media late in 2020, I can express my frustrations with the politicization of attempts to control the coronavirus. Without belaboring the point, recordings are *used* in ways that establish world-directed references that the *songs* do not have if taken to be about their semantic content, or if taken to be about whatever the composer intended them to be about.

Conclusion

"The stories behind most songs are less interesting than the songs themselves," Tom Waits told his biographer. "So you tell somebody, 'Hey, this is about Jackie Kennedy.' And they go, 'Oh wow.' Then you say, 'No, I was just kidding, it's about Nancy Reagan.' Well, it's a different song now. In fact, all my songs are about Nancy Reagan."⁵³ That last bit is a joke, of course, but his joke contains a kernel of truth: even if the songs were *inspired* by Nancy Reagan, the inspiration is something *behind* the songs, which are themselves props for us in communicative performance. A song lyric inspired by an actual person does not have to be used to make assertions about that person, and different performances can yield multiple world-directed referents.

The fundamental problem with the song-centered view is that it requires us to think of composed songs as fixed statements by song composers, and then to regard performers as vehicles for the presentation of those statements. This might be a (roughly) useful way to think about art songs in the classical tradition, but even there it is common for performers to append additional meaning to a particular performance through contextual supplementation. But with both art song and popular song, the very decision of what to perform can endow performances with a capacity to make statements about the world. And both art song and popular song normally do so by engaging the audience in make-believe. However, I introduced the philosophical position of Mark and Kivy, two writers on classical music, in order to illustrate the point that this move requires that performers first *endorse* or *assert* the song's meaning. Against this idea I have made the point that popular songs more commonly appear to be occasions for fiction-making, inviting contextually sensitive implicature, rather than direct assertion. (I address the issue of assertion in Chapter 3.)

Because I emphasize that a single song can be used to communicate different things on different occasions of use, my analysis has some overlap with the standard anti-intentionalist idea that a lyric or poem "is detached from the author at birth and goes about the world beyond his power to intend about it or control it. The poem belongs to the public."⁵⁴ However, pragmatics regards intentions as part of the context-of-use.

At best, anti-intentionalism is only plausible about the creative activity that takes place prior to the use of the poem or song in a particular communicative act. It is relevant that poems are not generally created for performance, but songs are, and so we may owe more deference to the intentions of poets than songwriters. Others may note that my analysis resonates with Roland Barthes's idea that authorial intention never constrains interpretation, and that every work is "constitutively ambiguous" and yields multiple texts with distinct interpretations.[55] But, again, I have suggested that there may be important differences between poems and songs. Texts should be interpreted in terms of their use, where a use is a particular act of directing the text to an audience in a particular situation at a particular time. As such, a use reflects intentions, and an audience that is interested in the communicative dimension of a performed song cannot be insensitive to the performer's intentions. The *song* "You're So Vain" may be constitutively ambiguous in reference, but particular performances of it need not suffer that same fate.

Part Two

Performers

3

Performer, Persona, and Musical Performance

The Singer's Persona

There are significant differences between singing a song and performing a song. Whether live or recorded, a performance is directed at an audience. As Paul Thom stresses, a performance is *for* an audience.[1] In contrast, singing in the shower or singing along to the radio is not normally undertaken to entertain or communicate with other people. The relevant point is that performing a popular song is seldom as simple as going before an audience and singing. It would be a rare case where a popular-music performer presents themselves as they are when they sing in the shower or sing along to the radio. Instead, popular songs are channeled through the communicative display of a persona. The persona is a *representation* of self in the performance space, which should be broadly construed to encompass the stage, recordings, videos, marketing, and merchandising.[2]

Stan Hawkins notes that the performance persona is normally structured to convey a personal temperament: Tina Turner's late work conveys both sultriness and personal empowerment, Patti Smith's early work is filled with anger, Kurt Cobain's brief career conveys self-loathing rooted in his rejection of prevailing heteropatriarchy.[3] A performer's persona may be more or less calculated, but it will always differ to some degree from what the person is like when they're not on display in performance. In short, personae communicate information about who is singing to us, and so it plays a major role in the communicative dimension of popular song performance.

However, an established persona may also *interfere* with the communication of emotions, ideas, or values that are encoded in a particular song. Jeanette Bicknell observes that Frank Sinatra's rendition of the George and Ira Gershwin standard "Someone to Watch over Me" (1926) is hard to "take seriously" because it clashes strongly with his adult persona of "a swaggering hipster." Although it is almost certainly the case that Sinatra "experienced... moments of vulnerability" at various times of his life, vulnerability was not an element of his persona, which is a "public display" that informs our sense of who is communicating with us, the audience.[4] This possibility of incongruity is less likely to arise for performers who are one hit wonders, known only for one song and so lacking any comparative basis underwriting the incongruity. The persona of "entertainer" is also quite forgiving, and so "Weird Al" Yankovic can do standard polka tunes alongside satiric covers of rock, grunge, hop-hop, R&B, and country hits. But, as with Sinatra, Yankovic's audience might find it oddly incongruous if he came onstage and tried to perform a straightforward and sincere version of "Someone to Watch over Me."

At this point, I assume that anyone reading this book agrees that popular song performances can be a potent social force.[5] The present chapter examines a risk that singers take when their personae contribute to an ethical or political dimension of their communicated meanings in song performances. My primary point is that some things that are presented as part of a singer's persona may be unacceptable elements of that persona—and so also of their performances—if they are not actually true of that singer. If the persona is an insincere masquerade, then ethical and political stances communicated by the singer are likely to be insincere, as well—even to the point of being reprehensible.

In terms of philosophy of art, my approach puts me at odds with aesthetic autonomism, a traditional position that says that aesthetic value is a distinct and self-standing mode of value. On this view, there cannot be an ethical problem with a work of art. In Oscar Wilde's well-known formulation of autonomism, "there is no such thing as a moral or an immoral book. Books are well written, or badly written. That is all."[6] Thankfully, this view seems to be waning. Consequently, this chapter proceeds on the assumption that autonomism is mistaken. However, I will also explain why the standard formulation of ethicism—autonomism's primary rival—concedes too much to autonomism when applied to musical performance.[7] Contrary to standard ethicism, I propose that the ethical attitudes of *performers* (not merely the attitudes conveyed by their personae) are part of the relevant context for the meanings of song performances.

Before I proceed, I want to stress that the present chapter focuses on one very specific issue. (A wider perspective is adopted in the next chapter, on authenticity.) In keeping with my focus on communication and pragmatics, I focus on what performances communicate, without regard for their social consequences, real or imaginary. Most moralizing about popular music relies on empirically doubtful claims that impressionable listeners will be harmed by its pernicious influence. However, that is not my concern. Nor do I wish to turn back the clock to the era when critics ranked the "relative excellence" of stories, films, and entertainments according to their capacity to positively transform our values and thus behavior.[8] My aim is to advance the claim that ethical attitudes of musicians can be part of the background context of their communicative actions. Some performances move beyond representing an attitude to tacit endorsement of it. Expanding upon an insight supplied by Bicknell,[9] I propose that an expansion of ethicism is particularly apt for evaluating popular music. However, the first step is to align ethicism and contextualism.

Contextualism

Contextualism is well known in contemporary philosophy of art as a result of Arthur Danto's defense of it: "The aesthetic qualities of the work are a function of their own historical identity, so that one may have to revise utterly one's assessment of a work in the light of what one comes to know about it."[10] Above all, we want to understand the context of production, including similarities and divergencies from other works of the same general kind created in the same cultural context. Consider Kendall Walton's well-known example of Pablo Picasso's *Guernica* (1937). Walton argues that its precise expressive character is not self-evident. It is determined by its degrees of similarity and dissimilarity to other cubist paintings, and to its having originated as a painting rather than, say, a sculpture. If an identical image appeared within a tradition of bas-relief sculpture rather than twentieth-century cubism, the artwork would be either very dull or very serene. If that were its generative context, it would certainly be a mistake to perceive it as violent and dynamic—which Picasso's *Guernica* is.[11] Thus, a proper appraisal of *Guernica*'s communicated content also depends, in part, on knowing at least *some* facts about Picasso, the artist. At the very minimum, we should understand that he was, for a time, a cubist painter, and Spanish, and that *Guernica* is his response to a specific, real event in Spain.

Applied to music, contextualism dovetails with a pragmatic account of meaning: both approaches say that any two performances of the same song may communicate very different messages. Part One of this book explained how activation in different contexts can give different meanings to the same song and to recontextualizations of a particular recording. As with the example of Picasso's *Guernica*, contemporary philosophy of art explores contextualism because it shows that auditor knowledge plays a role in the apprehension of aesthetic properties. Aesthetic properties are not just things like beauty and ugliness. They also include expressive properties: the music is happy, or sad, and so on. It should be obvious that contextualism also applies to popular music performances, which are, above all, expressive communications. Thus, expressive aesthetic properties join other context-sensitive meanings of song performances.

What does this mean in practice? The temperament of a performer's persona contributes to its expressivity, as do other facts about the identity of the performer. Listen, for example, to Joni Mitchell's "folkie" original recording of "This Flight Tonight" (1971) and then to the version by the hard rock band Nazareth (1973). Their cover version was a hit record in a number of countries. Setting aside the sense of lightness and heaviness created by the musical instruments employed in the two arrangements, expressive differences emerge when the same lyric and melody is sung by a man rather than a woman. The two versions share the same driving rhythm and approximately the same tempo, but Mitchell sings it in a key that often requires her to use her thin, falsetto soprano voice, creating an urgency that underscores an expression of confusion and regret. Nazareth, in contrast, downplays the confusion and regret (in part, by eliminating the dissonances of the original's guitar part) and, thanks to Dan McCafferty's male voice, conveys a lecherous desire for a woman left behind. Other differences associated with temperament arise from their differing vocal techniques: Mitchell's voice frequently sounds breathless and she rushes some lines, while McCafferty smooths out the melody to create a steadier, and thus stereotypically more masculine, sense of desire.

Here is a slightly different sort of case. A song that is not itself nostalgic and which becomes associated with a singer early in their career can become, over time, nostalgic.

An obvious example is Sinatra's association with "My Way" (1969). It was not nostalgic when he recorded it in his prime, but it certainly was when a visibly aging Sinatra sang it in concerts twenty years later. Likewise, Elvis Presley's mildly countrified take on "My Way" (1973) is all boasting confidence, with no hint of nostalgia. Presley's arrangement is not a great departure from Sinatra's original recording, and Presley briefly reflects aspects of Sinatra's persona. And it is a short step from invoking Sinatra by covering the song to the case of appropriating aspects of Sinatra's persona by simply playing his recording to an audience, as took place on January 20, 2021, when "My Way" was played over loudspeakers to the crowd that assembled to watch Donald Trump fly out of Washington on the last day of his presidency.[12]

In cases like these, where one recording of a song is already established as the standard version, a subsequent cover version by another singer—generally revamped to fit the singer's persona—may be a communication both *to* and *about* the singer of the earlier version. Unlike Presley, Sid Vicious singing "My Way" (1978) is at once both a repudiation of more sophisticated singers like Sinatra and a sardonic modernization of the tough-guy stance of Sinatra's persona.[13] Here, the expressive contrast—Sinatra's "cool" pacing supported by strings and jazzy horn section against Vicious's mock-serious first verse before plunging into a fast, sneering, aggressive, and nearly inarticulate rendition—is essential to the message of Vicious's cover version.

The point to keep in mind is that different performance *personae* contribute to the expressive differences of various performances of the same song. That is, what is expressed is shaped by how performers represent themselves to the audience—vocally, visually, and in many other ways. My goal is to show that we should not draw the line at personae. The ethical stances of *performers* can also contribute to what their performances communicate, and I think this is most easily seen by considering how communication can be sabotaged through incongruity. However, before I defend that idea, I will motivate it by taking a detour into the topic of contextualism as it applies to food consumption.[14] More specifically, I want to connect contextualism and disgust.

Although there may be some people who select food strictly on the basis of its nutritional value, they are certainly not the norm. Most people are strongly influenced by the manifest properties of our food, especially how it looks and tastes. (By "manifest properties" I mean any that are directly apparent in seeing, smelling, tasting, and so on.) Aesthetic responses to food are also strongly influenced by its nonmanifest properties. Although it is a staple source of animal protein, many Americans and Europeans recoil at the thought of eating goat and drinking goat milk. Eel, squirrel, snake, and a host of other tasty creatures are also widely shunned by food consumers who can afford more expensive proteins. Others reject beef, pork, and poultry on the grounds that they are produced under cruel conditions, while others reject pork and octopus on the grounds that the cognitive abilities of these species make them unsuitable for consumption. In short, food choices are guided by a combination of economic, aesthetic, social, and ethical considerations.[15]

Carolyn Korsmeyer is particularly insightful on how contextual factors influence aesthetic responses to food. Here is a morsel of what she says about food and disgust:

Living within a religious milieu that prohibits the eating of pork, for example, inculcates the belief that pork is inappropriate food. The relevant cognitive assessments become exceptionally strong evaluations, such as "pig products are abominable." The assessment also takes a strong visceral form: the smell of bacon is nauseating. ... Upon discovering that one has accidentally eaten pork, perhaps... food believed to have been made of something else, one may feel retrospective nausea and be disgusted by the past event of eating pork.[16]

The lesson here is that the aesthetic response of feeling disgusted can be influenced by a cognitive component, especially beliefs about origins. Although disgust is among our most basic emotions, it is not restricted to an instinctive, noncognitive response to manifest properties. Aesthetic judgments and apprehension of aesthetic properties are not confined to snap judgments about whatever we immediately perceive. They also accrue to complex, ongoing experiences. We also have *retrospective* aesthetic responses that differ from our occurrent responses to what was perceptually apparent to us. Tellingly, Korsmeyer observes that there is "overlap between core [visceral] disgust and moral disgust... when disgust is brought about by human agency with injurious purpose."[17] The same point holds in many cases where there is no injurious purpose. Upon learning that the delicious restaurant meal that I ate the previous evening was prepared in a kitchen where someone on the kitchen staff has hepatitis and poor hygiene, my retrospective disgust is justified even if I believe that exposure to the virus arose from ignorance and laziness rather than bad intentions.[18] Finally, the relevant injury may be to someone or some animal *in the past*, and not an injury or threat for the person making the aesthetic judgment. It is perfectly reasonable to translate ethical sympathy for ducks and geese who are mistreated in the production of foie gras into aesthetic disgust in the stuff itself.

Contextualism buttresses this conclusion about retrospective response by stressing how facts about sources and production should be taken into account when determining what a thing is and what properties it possesses. But sources and production processes are often hidden from users. To the detriment of ducks and geese, modern life puts the early stages of food production out of sight and so encourages an autonomism in which consumers of foie gras ignore its unseen production history when the delicacy arrives at the table. To be clear, contextualism tells us that taste is not just a subjective response—recall the adage, attributed to Otto von Bismarck, that is better not to see laws and sausages being made.

Hence awareness of origins can contribute to both the formation and the justification of disgust, including Korsmeyer's examples of retrospective disgust. But to say that certain foods are disgusting is not merely to say that some people are disgusted by them. It can also mean that those foods can be correctly described as disgusting, with the implication that people *should be* disgusted by them, even when the disgust is kept at bay through ignorance or willful refusal to learn what goes into sausages and foie gras.

Let us switch back from food to other aspects of culture. Historically, aesthetic autonomism was applied to fine art—"art for art's sake"—but its protections were not extended to entertainments that were not regarded as genuine art. Fine art's supposed universality and transcendence of context shielded it from ethical evaluation and censure. No such protection was extended to "low" culture. In practice, one of the most notable examples is the so-called Hays Code, which supported ongoing censorship of Hollywood movies for a significant portion of the twentieth century.[19] Yet during the same period, the legal system of the United States increasingly protected images, language, and narratives that would be prosecuted as obscene in popular culture. The erotic content of James Joyce's *Ulysses* is one among many prominent cases. This differential treatment—ethical autonomism for fine art but not for the popular arts—is increasingly recognized to be an unjustifiable double standard. However, the double standard lingers, and popular music seems to receive a disproportionate share of abuse as a result of this double standard.[20]

But my concern is not scaremongers who worry about the dangers of this or that singer or this or that genre of popular music. If contextualism tells us something useful about fine art, it can also be applied to popular music. Generative context, or provenance, generates aesthetic, expressive, and communicative differences. As such, fans of a particular singer are too often in the position of foodies who see nothing wrong with foie gras and octopus sashimi, that is, reluctant to concede that there is any ethical dimension that arises from thinking about origins.

Which Facts Should Make a Difference?

Contextualists debate whether knowledge of provenance of music requires knowing the identity of the music's composer. It cannot *always* make a difference. There are many musical traditions where sophisticated listeners are not concerned with it. *Time and place* of a song's composition is often more important than *who* originated it. We do not know who composed the traditional fiddle tune "The Soldier's Joy." However, I think a listener's response can go awry if one hears it while under the false impression that it was composed by Gid Tanner, an American, in the late 1920s—based, perhaps, on the fact that Tanner recorded it with The Skillet Lickers in 1929. That recorded performance merits interpretation as a nostalgic and perhaps even reactionary—and thus racist—assertion of Dixie pride. The tune had acquired a Civil War association through the addition of American lyrics about the suffering of soldiers in that war, and the Georgia-based Skillet Lickers must have understood the particular "heritage" it evoked during the late 1920s, a peak period of Ku Klux Klan activity and of southern historical revisionism that would receive widespread legitimacy with the success of the novel *Gone with the Wind* (1936). But that performance context comes late in the tune's history and does not belong to all performances: the tune predates Tanner by centuries. Yet, other than to resist a tight association with the Civil War, how much would it profit us to get the time and place of composition exactly right? It would make little or no difference to learn that it is the only surviving composition by a Scottish Highland fiddler named Gilbert Burns, circa 1642, rather than the only known tune of a fiddler named Patrick Walker, of Stirling, in the Lowlands, and dating from about 1657. Either way, dating the piece back to seventeenth-century Scotland successfully dissociates the music from Tanner's use of it. On the other hand, there are traditions and genres where information about the composer is highly relevant. As Jerrold Levinson observes, had Richard Strauss composed music in 1897 that sounded just like Arnold Schoenberg's *Pierrot Lunaire* (1912), Strauss's music would be expressively very different from Schoenberg's composition.[21] Here, a change of composer and a gap of a mere fifteen years are very significant. These two examples are instrumental compositions, but the point extends to songs and the meaning of their semantic and expressive content.

Because facts about a song's time of composition or the identity of its composer can be semantically and expressively relevant, and because a song's ethical flaws are sometimes aesthetically and informationally relevant, I think the burden of proof falls on those who think that a song's ethical flaws can be relevant and yet a *composer's* or *singer's* ethical flaws remain irrelevant. Tradition aside, why do we think that the moral purposes and moral quality of a cultural artifact can always be determined in the absence of a judgment about the moral character of the artist or artisan? Yet it appears that way to Berys Gaut, who narrows the range of what is ethically relevant to elements within the work: "The artist's attitudes manifested in the work... are a central object of ethical assessment."[22] Elsewhere, he is clear that the attitudes manifested in the work are restricted to "artistic acts performed in the work."[23] Everyone expresses different attitudes on different occasions and in different contexts, and therefore assessment of an artwork should focus on attitudes expressed *in it*.[24]

But why not examine the artist's real-life behavior when it clarifies what is expressed in a particular work? Here, Gaut proposes, "[T]he view also allows that the artist's personality as manifested outside his work *may* be relevant, since it is the same person who acts in both contexts. The test must be whether, in light of one's knowledge of the artist's attitudes outside his work, one can detect in the work traces of these attitudes." For Gaut, the test is whether this knowledge leads us to locate these traces upon further close "inspection" of the work, so that we "see" in a painting something previously overlooked. If we cannot locate any such trace, the standard model of ethicism says that the artist's behaviors and attitudes are ethically and aesthetically irrelevant.[25] That is, nonmanifest factors are relevant if aspects of the work confirm it, but irrelevant if no aspect of the work confirms it. Transferred to our topic, popular song performance, Gaut is proposing that the ethical flaws of performers are irrelevant unless they somehow manifest themselves, however subtly, in the performer's persona.

My central proposal is that this line in the sand is unstable. The relevant ethical merits and flaws are not limited to what can be seen and heard in performances. Consider my earlier example of foie gras production. The mistreatment of the fowl takes place in a context far removed from the consumption of the delicacy, so that it is possible to have eaten it without knowing anything about the animal cruelty involved in its production. When ethically sensitive diners learn of that cruel mistreatment, their ensuing disgust is not based on sudden "detection" of something "in" the food. They do not suddenly become sensitized to a previously unnoticed manifest property. The ethical flaw remains altogether "outside" the aesthetic object. Yet it is relevant to the act of consumption and *should be* taken into account.

Analogously, I recognize that there are cases where an artist's values and attitudes are not reflected in corresponding "traces" in the artwork. Nonetheless, if relevant information about performers' actual values and attitudes would make a difference in audience reception, then it may be ethically relevant.[26] Although worded as a hypothetical, this provides a basic test for determining what counts as a relevant feature of the context of communication—for starters, would this information about the performer make a difference to the audience? This result is a straightforward consequence of contextualism, which tells us that, for any element of a song performance that can be directly perceived, divergent contexts can activate distinct meanings (including the nature of its expressivity), and consequently we should be more context-sensitive about what counts as genuine uptake of anything that is communicated.

Consider the following analogy. Art forgery offers examples in which provenance introduces ethical considerations that ought to be taken into account when determining both meaning and value. Forgery is a category that is concerned with the artist's behavior. More to the point, it is a category where knowledge about the creative process *ought* to influence our response.[27] As I remarked in the book's Introduction, the prevailing hermeneutic model in popular music studies asks us to focus on strategies of reception, especially reception by ardent fans. However, it seems to me that with both foie gras and a popular song performance, some responses are unjustified. A negative response, including, sometimes, disgust, can be warranted through mere knowledge of background context, and there does not have be a discovery of previously overlooked traces in the manifest properties. As Peter Lamarque emphasizes, the forger relies on generating false beliefs about artistic provenance.[28] The artistic failing of a forgery does not depend on the forger's doing a bad job in forging another painter's work or style. A forgery's aesthetic/expressive failure is not always linked to visible traces of being a forgery. A perfect forgery is aesthetically bad because the forger has an unethical stance and constructs a duplicitous communication in relation to the audience. Thus, an ethical flaw in the artist can bequeath an artistic flaw in the artist–audience exchange despite the absence of ethical problems in the attitudes manifested or expressed by, or in, the work. Analogously, a well-crafted persona may disguise the ethical flaws of a song performer.

Performer and Persona

Musical forgery is uncommon. However, it is very similar to artistic insincerity, and at least two noteworthy categories of insincerity arise from a disparity between the artist's persona, the music performed, and, sometimes, the artist's nonperforming life. Both kinds of insincerity are found in popular music. The first category is the more obvious case, where insincerity undercuts the communicative intent. As I explain in the section that follows, the second case is the one where duplicity in the construction of a persona enhances the work ethically and artistically. These contrasting categories are important in popular music because it is dominated by song performance. Consequently, center stage is normally occupied (both literally and metaphorically) by individual singers, rather than the music's composer(s) or its instrumental accompanists. Elaborating on Stan Godlovitch's observation that the visible human agency of musical performance invites the audience to treat "artist and artwork, performance and performer... as inseparable," Jeanette Bicknell observes that every song performance therefore raises the issue of whether the song is appropriate for that particular singer.[29]

Moving beyond the question of failed communication due to incongruity, Bicknell considers the question of whether certain song choices are morally inappropriate for certain singers. She casts the problem as one about singer's need to demonstrate appropriate deference to the social experiences associated with a song. "When a song is valued by a group," she writes, "a morally sensitive singer must try to understand why the song has the significance it does for, and must shape... [the] performance so as to honor or respect that significance."[30] She offers few examples, but the idea is that a socially freighted song such as "We Shall Overcome" should not be sung in a careless manner that conveys a lack of concern for the ideas that are encoded in it. However, this approach restricts her discussion to what can be observed in the performance itself, to the *seeming* appropriateness of a song and singer's approach: does the singer perform a particular song with sufficient sincerity?[31] This narrowing of focus presumes that the popular audience does not care whether that conviction is won through an insincere communication. However, I propose that audiences do care, and, if they do not, they should care. More to the point, insincerity is the most obvious case of a relevant ethical flaw that may reveal no manifest "trace"; the attitudes that are manifested in the song performance are not those of the artist, and yet this disparity is relevant to an ethical appraisal of the communicative action.

Although there are cases where insincerity is ethically innocent, duplicitous insincerity normally merits ethical censure. Misalignment of person and persona can be just as relevant as a misalignment of persona and song selection. Granted, many of these cases will remain invisible to us, for they require supplementing the question of a "fit" between persona and song choice with consideration of relevant real-life behaviors that may never come to the attention of—or which are actively hidden from—the popular audience. However, having granted that an artist's identity can be a relevant aspect of an artwork's provenance, and having agreed with Stan Godlovitch and Bicknell that a performer's persona enters some musical performances as constitutive elements of those performances, we have all the warrant we need to examine any singer's relationship to their persona.

I take it that all stage behavior during performance is part of a singer's persona. Perceived as a "folk" singer in the first half of the 1960s, Bob Dylan's first appearance onstage with an electric guitar (on July 25, 1965) radically redefined his persona. Stage banter can also define and redefine a singer's persona. One of the most famous cases is John Lennon's song introduction when The Beatles performed for British royalty (the Queen Mother and Princess Margaret) in November, 1963, as part of the annual Royal Variety Show. Just about to release their second album, The Beatles were still a young, fresh "boy" band. After performing three of their hits, Lennon spoke to the audience: "Would the people in the cheaper seats clap your hands? And the rest of you, if you'll just rattle your jewelry."[32] The latter, a clear reference to the royals, was perhaps the first time that they had ever been ridiculed to their face in public. For the huge audience watching the television broadcast, it was, however mild, a working-class challenge to the standing political order. With two lines, Lennon moved from hit-making pop singer to a social commentator. But Lennon's subsequent challenges to the status quo were not always welcome. For many fans, especially religious Americans, he harmed his and The Beatles's positive personae with his remark, in an interview, that The Beatles had become "more popular than Jesus."[33]

Consider also the results of a performance by Michelle Shocked on March 17, 2013, where she made derogatory comments about same-sex marriage to a club audience that included a large number of queer fans. Her fans routinely interpreted Shocked's songs and performances in light of a public history that positioned her as a radical feminist lesbian.[34] The 2013 incident quickly led to a cancellation of her current tour of American cities. Due to this change in her persona, we can anticipate that Shocked's longstanding fans will appraise all future performances of her established repertoire differently, on the grounds that it is inappropriate for her to continue to give voice to songs that endorse a degree of personal freedom that the singer's revised persona morally denounces.

Notice, however, how we can view these cases as applications of Bicknell's idea that the problem arises from a discrepancy that arises in public. In contrast, the argument that follows moves beyond cases where changes in a singer's persona can deprive them of what had been, until then, the requisite conviction to perform one or more songs.

I want to focus on cases that are akin to forgery, involving disparities between the singer's persona and the singer's ethical character. For example, early in Dylan's career, journalists discovered that he was supplying a false biography (e.g., his actual name was Robert Zimmerman and he claimed that he was an orphan, when he was not). Some journalists published these discoveries. Others sought to discredit him by relaying the false rumor that he was not the actual songwriter of "Blowin' in the Wind." Most competent listeners can *hear* that the tune is derivate from the African-American spiritual "No More Auction Block," and thus can make an educated guess about its *general* provenance, which connects the song to the civil rights movement. (Lacking this manifest connection to the tradition of African-American spirituals, it is doubtful that the song would have become one of the anthems of the civil rights movement.) Yet the American press was not exploring the song's general provenance when spreading the false claim that Dylan had purchased the words and music from a high school student whom Dylan met while visiting Woody Guthrie in a New Jersey hospital.[35]

Suppose that the rumor had been true rather than false. If true, it would (in 1963 and immediately after) have given good reason to reconsider Dylan's performances of the song. Had Dylan purchased the song instead of composing it, performances of "Blowin' in the Wind" that displayed an emerging talent that rivaled or overshadowed his model, Woody Guthrie, would instead constitute the public actions of a musical charlatan. The fabrications within his Guthrie-like persona are not necessarily a mark against Dylan's performances in the early 1960s, but if it were true that Dylan lied about composing such a significant song, it would be a genuine moral failing of the *singer* that would reduce the conviction and power of his performances at that time. It would certainly be relevant to Dylan's performance for the March on Washington on August 28, 1963, as a featured singer prior to the famous "I Have a Dream" address by Martin Luther King, Jr.[36] Dylan's inclusion in one of the signature events of the American civil rights movement would have been unmerited.

It might be objected that a song's authorship cannot be relevant unless that authorship becomes known, and so it only matters after it is public, again returning us to the fit between song and persona. However, that objection misunderstands the contextualism that frames my argument. The key point is that many facts about provenance are relevant because they are aspects of the generative context (rather than that they are relevant only if we happen to know them). The situation with Dylan's performances of "Blowin' in the Wind" is just as relevant as it is with any other aspect of provenance that makes a difference: the audience's ignorance of relevant facts about provenance can invalidate their endorsement of the performance. Our revised view of Dylan in 1963 upon learning of any such deception would not depend on our suddenly becoming aware of manifest traces of the lie in Dylan's performances of 1963.

I am not, however, advancing a universal principle about song authorship or performance. I am not suggesting that the identity of a songwriter or identity of a performer always makes a relevant difference. Does it really matter that Frank Silver and not Helen Stone wrote the lyrics for "Yes! We Have no Bananas" (1923)? Or could it make an ethical difference, for this particular novelty song, that the singer is Irving Kaufman instead of Billy Jones? But there are times when an aspect of a singer's persona may be unacceptable elements of that persona—and so also of their performances—due to facts about the singer.[37] The relevance of the rumor of Dylan's false claim of authorship is that, had it been true, it would be inconsistent with the ethical dimension of Dylan's persona as it was developing at that time. In sum, the relevance of the rumor about the authorship of "Blowin' in the Wind" illustrates how behaviors that are not incorporated into a singer's persona can be both morally and expressively relevant to a proper evaluation of that singer's performances. In the same way that a persona can deprive a song performance of conviction, facts about the singer's private life can deprive the persona of conviction, too.

Transparency and Opacity

Taking stock, my approach recognizes that there are multiple ways that ethical merits and flaws can matter in a song performance. I agree with Bicknell that one factor is the song selected for performance: the basic lyrical and musical elements of some songs make them potent vehicles for the expression of moral attitudes. Many of Dylan's songs express harsh moral condemnation, including the harsh self-criticism of songs like "Idiot Wind" (1975). Because it is part of the song's design, self-criticism is normally expressed when others sing that song. Second, many songs are designed to solicit particular moral responses from listeners. The solicited response is often, but need not be, identical to what the song expresses. Thus, "Idiot Wind" moves to self-reflection and successful performances of "Idiot Wind" encourage listeners to reflect on their own ignorance and foolishness.

However, talk of what the song expresses must be understood as talk of potentialities encoded in the songs. Recall this chapter's earlier example of Sid Vicious performing "My Way," where performance pragmatics produce unexpected meanings. Where Dylan's performances of "Idiot Wind" convey spite that gives way to self-criticism, successful performances in the genre of National Socialist and fascist black metal express and endorse bigotry, xenophobia, and hate.[38] Alternating between elegiactic and brutal music, Peste Noire's "J'avais rêvé du Nord" (2011) complains that France is being destroyed by immigrants from Africa and sees violence against them as the only solution. The point is not self-reflection but rather to encourage or strengthen corresponding attitudes in auditors. Despite their expressive differences, the Dylan and Peste Noire performances are similar in being expressively direct. In contrast, Randy Newman's "Short People" (1977) is a complex case where the sneering bigotry of the performance is constructed to ridicule the bigotry it espouses. Where "Idiot Wind" and "J'avais rêvé du Nord" employ first-person language encouraging auditors to take their messages at face value, "Short People" uses first-person but encourages auditors to understand that the *character* is a fool and the *singer* is sardonic.

Such examples suggest another path to the conclusion that some performers and performances invite ethical reflection involving facts about the singer's life beyond the persona. Wesley Cray has devised a schema for categorizing the examples I have just introduced. Dylan and Peste Noire employ transparent personae but Newman adopts an opaque one. Setting aside "Idiot Wind," let us consider the two tracks that overtly express bigotry and hate, "J'avais rêvé du Nord" and "Short People." In "J'avais rêvé du Nord," the vocalist begins by reciting the lyrics—talking directly to the listener—before moving to the more guttural singing that is common in black metal. Everything in the singer's performance conveys a sense of transparency, where the listener "sees through" the performance to the views, feelings, and attitude of the person singing the song. In cases of maximum transparency, the performance creates the impression that there is no representation of the person. The singer invites the audience to think that, other than the fact that they are singing, they are simply being themselves.[39] In contrast, Newman tackles "Short People" with an opaque persona: the attentive auditor should quickly understand that the performer cannot be serious and so the words and music express ideas and attitudes that should not be identified with those of the person who is singing. With an opaque persona, a performer intends for the audience to be aware that the performer is performing in the full sense of that word: the persona is a persona, and is to be taken as such.[40] Cray also points out that song construction can contribute to opacity. As I noted in Chapter 1, the "bridge" section of "Short People" is both musically and lyrically incongruous with the rest of it. New voices are both literally and symbolically introduced, indicating that something is amiss.

Crucially, persona is seldom a matter of one performance in isolation. A distinct persona may be adopted just for one song, or for the length of a video, over the course of a tour, or over many years. Over time, a performer's decisions about which kinds of songs to perform add further variables and thus complications. Hearing "Short People" in the context of the album that introduced it (*Little Criminals*, 1977), it would take a dense or inattentive listener to fail to grasp that "Short People" cannot be taken at face value. For those who do not know the album, one of the most striking tracks is "In Germany Before the War," in which Newman's third-person verses ("There was a man... ") describe a child murderer. After two verses, the chorus switches to a first-person, present-tense rumination that has no direct connection to the story of the murder. First person often suggests transparency, but the strange shift to first person makes no sense when treated as a temporary move to a transparent persona. "In Germany before the War" is constructed in a manner that makes any performance of it confusingly opaque. Thus, the use of first-person language—and a corresponding norm that auditors are to imagine *of* the singer that the singer's voice is that of the performed character—does not always align with a transparent persona.[41]

There are other ways that a song's lyrics create opacity, signaling that its performance is fundamentally a prop for make-believe, so that anyone who sings it will convey some distancing from its narrative content. "Long Black Veil" (1959) has been covered by numerous singers and has been a country hit for several. As soon as the performance reaches the second line of the chorus, it is clear that no singer is singing about themselves, for we learn that the narrator of the sad tale is speaking from the grave. But Johnny Cash frequently mixed "opaque" songs like "Long Black Veil" with first-person narratives in his concert performances and on his albums, where the construction of "I Still Miss Someone" (1958) or "Ring of Fire" (1963) could easily be understood as self-expression. Within the course of any two songs Cash might invite listeners to move from some degree of opacity to some degree of transparency. Newman only occasionally suggests transparency, as when as a song like "I'll Be Home" appears on *Little Criminals* or he sings "You've Got a Friend in Me" (1995) in concert.

Cray points out that performers can also stack up opacity upon opacity, as when an opaque, character-driven song is delivered from the stance of an opaque performing persona that does not align with the song. Cray offers some hypothetical cases, but I will pose a real one: Madonna is known for adopting and then abandoning a series of distinct, highly theatrical personae that cumulatively suggest that every popular performer is performing a constructed identity.[42] In the context of her overarching persona, it made no sense in 2000 for Madonna to release a version of Don Mclean's "American Pie" (1971), which is a reactionary, first-person ode to the better times of "them good ol[d] boys" back in the Eisenhower era. (The glossy video she made for it doesn't clarify anything.) Until that point, her career had foregrounded confrontation and provocation, but in this video the audience is served "a simple visual restatement of liberal politics and individualism within the national context."[43] Since it is not satirical, the artistic point is difficult to fathom among the flag waving.

Cray also makes the crucial point that "it is a tacit norm of [popular song] performance practice" that performers will signal when their performance is opaque and when it is transparent.[44] Because the choice between transparency and opacity is something that is signaled by performers, song construction, and performance techniques, the signaling normally occurs within the orbit of the manifest properties of performances. Although many casual listeners may have misunderstood it, the satirical use of "Short People" to ridicule bigotry is generated by artistic acts observable in the performance as presented in the recording. But Newman's opacity is also a general stance—an implication derived from his consistent performance of unsavory characters and narrations of bizarre events. The opacity of "Short People" was reinforced by the way Newman presented himself and his songs—how he constructed an ongoing persona—up to that point in his career.[45]

Cray's point about signaling provides fresh reasons for discussing the real person and not just their persona. If a performer fails to signal whether their performance (or some segment of performance) is transparent or opaque, that failure often muddies the communication process. However, I propose that this performance norm is also an ethical norm. Transparency signals sincerity. The difference between transparent and opaque personae involves a difference in what the audience is invited to believe about the performance in relation to the performer. Understanding the nature of the invitation is part of understanding the communication.[46] Opacity signals an invitation to make-believe that cancels any presumption of the performer's endorsement of the manifest attitudes and ideas embedded in the song or displayed in the performer's role-playing. However, it does not follow that audiences should refrain from evaluating those invitations or opaque personae. Far from it. Returning to Bicknell's case of needing to pay due respect to socially freighted songs, signaling opacity and then performing "Strange Fruit" might be reprehensible. Or maybe not: contextual details matter.

Conversely, a transparent persona invites auditors to regard attitudes and views that appear in the persona as ones that are endorsed by the singer's act of self-expression. Hence, when Dylan is operating with the anti-establishment, truth-in-the-face-of-power persona of the early 1960s, all signals indicate a transparent persona and a tacit pledge of honesty and sincerity. Hence, there are both a communication misfire and a moral failing if the singer is dishonest. I do not mean, of course, that adopting the transparent persona commits the singer to literal truth in every detail of every line of every song. Operating in his transparent, early 1960s mode, Dylan could, by implicature, display concern for miners and their families in northern Minnesota by creating the first-person fictional narrative of "North Country Blues" (1964). As I argued in Chapter 2, every song permits fictionality, and adoption of a transparent persona does not preclude performing songs that portray a character or protagonist who is clearly not the singer.[47]

In summary, a transparent persona *invites* auditors to examine the singer's attitudes and ethical character. In reality, it may be that the singer is insincere, where sincerity and insincerity will be objective features of the communication. If the mismatch between person and persona is great and it concerns a serious matter, auditors have reason to be disturbed about performances where the singer's actual views and attitudes diverge from those communicated by the singer's persona.

Reappraisals: Negative and Positive

Against both autonomism and standard ethicism, I am proposing that a singer's persona-independent attitudes and behaviors can be relevant to a moral evaluation, or reevaluation, of the singer's persona and various performances. Anything we learn about a singer's life—including subsequent events—might be relevant to evaluating that performer's persona and performances during any point in the singer's career. I do not mean that everything is equally relevant. The point should be understood in light of contextualism, which says that different facts relating to provenance are relevant with different artists and artworks. Nor am I saying that we should never trust performers. The transparent persona always carries with it some risk of duplicity and a breach of communication ethics through a misalignment between the singer's own attitudes and values and those expressed in their performances. However, audiences are unlikely to detect, much less confirm, misalignment by suddenly noticing previously overlooked manifest properties within the sphere of performance. Evidence of a duplicitous pretense of transparency generally arises from some other source—perhaps even many years after the fact, or in gossip, a tell-all biography, a lawsuit, or an old social media post that resurfaces. But given such evidence, auditors might justifiably experience retrospective disgust, akin to a diner's retrospective disgust upon learning more about the production of foie gras.

It will be useful to offer an example of subsequent revelations that may justify a moral reevaluation of a popular musician's persona. Just as with an individual singer, a group can have a transparent persona or performance. The Grateful Dead are such a group. They performed an outdoor concert in Toronto, Canada, on June 27, 1970, and some tumultuous events surrounding the concert are presented in the documentary *Festival Express*.[48] Specifically, a crowd of about two thousand protesters gathered at the stadium's entrance and attempted to persuade others not to pay to see the show. Insisting that music should be free, some protesters tried to force their way in, others climbed over the fences, police officers were injured, and there was a concern that rioting would erupt. Jerry Garcia, the Dead's lead guitarist and nominal leader, spoke to the protesters and offered to provide a free show in a nearby park—something the group did from time to time in their home city of San Francisco (and the fact of which was part of their persona, prominently documented in two photographs adorning the *Live/Dead* album of 1969). Garcia pitched the offer of free music as a solution that would avoid violence. The group's persona and Garcia's specific remarks encouraged the gate-crashers to understand that free music was provided in a spirit of generosity and out of concern for everyone's well-being. (Garcia seems sympathetic to the demand for free music when he tells them, "All this is like voluntary in nature." He urges "coolness" while they arrange the "free stage.")

The documentary *Festival Express* shows us these events, but it also provides selections from interviews of key participants filmed more than thirty years later. At best, some members of the group besides Garcia had mixed intentions. Bob Weir, the Dead's second guitarist, emphasizes that he was there "to make a living." He seems to have regarded the protesters as naïve yet dangerous, thereby revealing attitudes that did not enter the Dead's 1970 persona. Festival promoter Ken Walker is also interviewed. Walker makes it clear that the free music was a business decision, provided in order to draw the protesters away from the concert site. In hindsight, it has become apparent that, with the possible exception of Garcia, the Grateful Dead were resourceful and increasingly savvy capitalists. The band was their business, and they protected their interests.[49] Much of the audience for the free concert in Toronto in 1970 might have evaluated the music differently if they could have known that, a few years later, the band would form their own corporation, run their own record company, and introduce innovations in the entertainment business that would generate a comfortable living for them and their employees. Later, the band's business practices would be studied in business schools and serve as a model for twenty-first-century entrepreneurs.[50] If any of the protestors or audience members from the free show saw *Festival Express* and heard Weir and Walker talk about the events of that day, an appropriate response could include some retrospective disgust about the Dead's free performance that day in the park.

However, disparities between musician and persona do not always generate flaws. A reevaluation can go in the other direction and become more favorable. As before, the reevaluation that arises from discovery of duplicity in a persona can be independent of discovery of previously ignored manifest evidence. It can be due to the contrast between what is manifest and what is not. Consider the disco group the Village People. Walter Hughes singles them as a paradigm of disco music's initial relationship to gay culture in the 1970s.[51] They had numerous hit records that combined infectious dance beats with homoerotic innuendo, including "Macho Man," "Y.M.C.A.," and "In the Navy." The potent combination of their songs, music videos, and visual identity (exploiting and exaggerating various male stereotypes) was not without its political edge, for their persona played a role in publicizing gay subcultural identity that had been largely confined to a few urban centers. At the same time that their cartoonish persona supported the gay rights movement, the Village People also became targets of the homophobic backlash to disco.[52]

In this case, dissonance between singer and persona arises from the presumption that the members of the group were, in fact, gay. However, lead singer Victor Willis was not. Yet Willis's voice and stage presence were at the heart of their persona, and he composed the lyrics for several of their major hits. The group's popularity waned significantly after Willis quit in 1979. Within the group's persona, Willis offered himself as an object of gay fantasy and desire. Here, we have a strong parallel to the Michelle Shocked case, but with an important reversal of evaluative valence. As has been said of the revelation that movie star Rock Hudson was homosexual, this revelation of sexual orientation "can alter the dynamics of looking, confirming or bringing out the confusions of the sex comedies... in a way that unsettles their [sexual] affirmations."[53] In my estimation, Willis's presence in The Village People deepens the political dimension of their major hits, for Willis's extended practice of performing as "gay" constitutes a critique of the cultural norms of heterosexual behavior at that time. Minimally, he resisted the deep homophobia of the era in an admirable way. Admittedly, I am assuming that Willis would not have been at the forefront of the group if he was cynically exploiting an emerging music trend. After all, the disco hits of the Bee Gees and other musicians had already demonstrated that men could succeed within disco while endorsing heteronormativity, so Willis's assumption of that persona was not compulsory. To be fully consistent, I have to allow that there may be relevant facts about Willis that remain unknown. However, the point remains that there are performing contexts in which seemingly trivial pop songs are highly politicized social interventions. The Village People are such a case, and consequently an ethical evaluation of the *singer* is relevant to our evaluation of the singer's persona.

Contextualism grants that we don't always know all the important facts, but it reminds us that unknown facts about provenance may be highly relevant.

I have argued that facts about performers' "private" lives can be relevant to the actual character of their performances. I recognize that staunch anti-contextualists have no reason to endorse my argument. Furthermore, I have made no attempt to develop a principled view of where to draw the line between relevant and irrelevant facts. However, I have offered reasons to construe some performances as endorsements of attitudes and views communicated in the performance, and this gives us reason to reconsider how much we should take into account when responding to such performances.

4

Authenticity in Popular Music

Introduction

Authenticity has been identified as "critics' key criterion in assessing the artistic value of new [popular] music."[1] This chapter addresses authenticity as a key aspect of popular music, but not as a "value" in the normative sense, where authentic music is supposed to be better (subject to other qualifications) than inauthentic music. I will examine authenticity as an aspect of popular song communication, both as a background condition and as something communicated.

Whether authenticity is understood as a value-neutral or value-conferring aspect of meaning-making, its presence or absence is widely regarded as more relevant to some genres of popular music than others. There is a prominent school of thought that says it does not apply at all to mainstream "pop" music.[2] However, this ignores the possibility that country music fans are concerned with authenticity in their favored genre, one that is now completely mainstream. Too often, pop music—including mainstream country—is dismissed as entertainment without a serious message. How, then, could fans be concerned with its authenticity? In contrast, it has generally been regarded as of central importance in rock music.[3] For example, when the Sex Pistols sang "We mean it, man, we love the queen" in "God Save the Queen" (1977), did they mean it? Or were they, as most listeners understood, mocking the masses who were enthusiastic about Queen Elizabeth's impending silver jubilee celebrations? As long as their mockery was real and genuinely meant, and not merely an artifice of their punk persona, their signature hit was authentic: they endorsed what they communicated. Or, at any rate, that was how authenticity was formerly understood.

In the first flush of popular music scholarship, authenticity was generally aligned with the expression of the distinctive outlook of either a specific subculture or generation. This approach was challenged by postmodern skepticism, which in turn inspired the strategy of reinterpreting it as audience authentication. It is now common to stress that there are multiple authenticities in popular music, none of which require performer sincerity. Instead, criteria for authenticity change in relation to a multiplicity of local forms of music making and consumption, and it serves as an evolving trope for distinguishing between many different ideas and contrasts.[4] After mapping these major stages in the development of the concept, I will double back and suggest that the initial attempt to align authenticity with less mainstream genres was a term of art that had little connection with ordinary usage: it was *read into* popular culture by music critics and scholars.

Authenticity and Popular Music: The Formative Period

In retrospect, one of the most entertaining milestones of rock criticism is a 1970 review in *Rolling Stone* that opens with the question, "What is this shit?" Primarily authored by Greil Marcus, the target of this long, vitriolic review is Bob Dylan's *Self Portrait* album. The album was savaged as a travesty, based on two criteria. First, Dylan's earlier work is praised for having "changed the world." However, he now "sounded fake" and "routine" rather than "for real."[5] Second, Marcus claimed that the double-LP revealed that Dylan had become an auteur, that is to say a craftsman creating a commercial product instead of an artist motivated by the need to communicate a personal "vision."[6] In a score of different ways, the review accused him of being inauthentic. However, the term "authentic" is never used in the review.

Then, without explanation, Marcus's review shifts from an opposition of the fake and the real—a relationship between musician and the music—and narrows the focus to the musical experience: "It is a matter of the music having power, or not having it."[7] Here, authenticity is restricted to perceivable features of the music. Simon Frith has also endorsed this narrower approach to authenticity, describing it as an "inchoate feature of the music itself, a perceived quality of sincerity and commitment."[8] Lawrence Grossberg agrees that "the authenticity of rock has always been measured by its sound and, most commonly, by its voice."[9] These descriptions of authenticity basically equate it with performing music with a convincing persona.

Marcus's emphasis on "the music itself" contrasts sharply with Joni Mitchell's dismissive evaluation of Dylan's career: "Bob is not authentic at all. ... Everything about Bob is a deception."[10] These are fundamentally different emphases. Marcus, Frith, and Grossberg locate authenticity in what *sounds* real (rather than fake) or what has "believability."[11] In contrast, Mitchell is concerned with authenticity as a relationship between the artist and the audience by means of the music as it relates to the performer's situation in the world. For Mitchell, Dylan's music is inauthentic *despite* the way that it sounds powerful and real.[12]

Consistent with the position I defended in Chapter 3, Mitchell applies a *socio-historical* criterion of authenticity that evaluates the artist's relationship to the community, the audience, or to society at large. In evaluating the music in terms of Dylan's relationship to his sources (including his own biography), Mitchell calls attention to aspects of music making that may not generate sonic traces. Instead, authenticity is grounded in the degree to which the music reflects the socio-historical position of the musician(s) and audience. This, in turn, pivots on the music's relationship to its contributing sources, including community values and traditions.[13] Much like an art historian's authentication of a painting as either genuine or fake relative to alleged origins, this mode of authentication is a source-focused model. Yet there are countless such relationships, ranging from details of musical style to the music's expressive function, and so a socio-historical approach can itself yield many competing standards of authenticity.

Many writers on popular music trace the rise of socio-historical authenticity back to the aesthetics of Romanticism.[14] A more nuanced account is offered by Keir Keightley. Focusing on rock music, he argues that the value structure of rock music pivots on two competing modes of authenticity, Romantic and modernist.[15] Think here of how the modernist prose and narrative style of Gertrude Stein will make little sense when evaluated in terms of a Romantic sensibility that regards the personal self-confessions of John Keats as the ideal of authorship. As Keightley puts it, "where Romanticism believed in an organic, and even traditional, connection between the artist, the material means of expression and the audience, modernism encouraged shock effects and radical experimentation, contending that the relationship between artistic materials and meaning was... arbitrary and therefore open to change and improvement."[16] Where Romanticism favors a community-derived populism (and thus the community-building effects of live music), modernism endorses the experimental and the *avant garde* and thus, in turn, is more invested in the idea of individual artistic genius.[17] For modernism, authenticity requires artistic independence and a rejection of—even an assault on—the mainstream.[18] By way of example, then, the Romantic paradigm of authenticity is Joe Cocker's performance of "With a Little Help from My Friends" at Woodstock (1969), a cover version that overtly united artist and crowd (his "friends").[19] The modernist prefers the studio confection from which the song was drawn, *Sgt. Pepper's Lonely Hearts Club Band* (1967). For subsequent contrasting examples we might compare two eponymous albums from 1982, *The Smiths* and the synthesizer-heavy *Peter Gabriel*, and then fifteen years further on we can oppose Lilith Fair with U2's *Pop* album and subsequent *PopMart Tour*. To bring it to a more recent date, we have the contrast of Beyoncé and Lana Del Rey. In short, Romanticism aligns with transparent personae and modernism with opaque personae as those two approaches were described in Chapter 3.

I do not endorse Keightley's reading of the historical background on authenticity. We should be skeptical of any claim that any particular mode or genre of popular music authenticity—the Delta blues, singer-songwriter confessionals, gangsta rap, music-festival-as-community, or any other—is to be understood in terms of the artistic norms of Romanticism. This may seem a small matter, but the literature is rife with claims that rock authenticity is a vestige of Romanticism.[20] Consider Allan F. Moore's summary of the authenticity of emotionality as a "vision of the musician as explorer, returning to his or her community with the result of [their] inner exploration."[21] Although this is as neat a summary as we might hope to find of Romanticism's defense of the musical avant-garde at the dawn of the nineteenth century,[22] it is precisely what Keightley identifies as modernism, not Romanticism. "Romanticism," I fear, is a signifier cut adrift from actual Romanticism, for no Romantic confused the socio-historical category of the authentic with the doctrine that great art is essentially confessional or revolutionary.[23] Granted, the overarching theme of Romanticism might be summarized as "natural man's conflict with established society,"[24] and so it is relatively easy to argue that critical discourse about late-twentieth-century popular music (broadly construed, as including fan responses) is saturated with the rhetoric of Romanticism. However, it's an anachronistic leap to identify popular music authenticity with the legacy of Romantic metaphysical visions and fantasies about pre-social naturalism, for it is not clear that any popular music styles or genres have much connection with anything called "authenticity" by nineteenth-century Romantic authors.

Setting aside the issue of the accuracy of these claims about larger cultural and historical influences that brought questions of authenticity into the orbit of popular music, what is at stake here? How exactly is authenticity supposed to matter? A number of writers maintain that judgments about authenticity combine a set of artistic norms with aesthetic and ethical evaluation. I have strong reservations about this. Although something like truthful representation is a precondition for some kinds of authenticity, especially emotional authenticity, this criterion is basically a reference to sincerity. Popular musicians frequently emphasize the importance of sincerity, as when John Lennon gave several prominent interviews in which he separated The Beatles's successful songs from the "junk" and "rubbish" that did not arise from the writers' personal feelings or situation. Even a glorious track such as "Sun King" is dismissed as "a piece of garbage," as something akin to musical sound for its own sake.[25]

As I argued in Chapter 3, there is no reason to think that sincerity is relevant with *all* performances in rock music, much less any other genre. An ethical critique—of, say, Paul Simon's appropriation of African music and voices on *Graceland* (1986)—should evaluate the music's relationship to extra-musical factors. After all, "it is," Frith says, "a human as well as a musical judgment."[26] Reverting to the two categories of authenticity I proposed just before my excursion into Romanticism, this calls for a socio-historical criterion of authenticity. However, inconsistencies abound, for Frith also says that sincerity and commitment are "perceived" qualities of the music, and Keightley claims that the ethical dimension is "perceived" by fans. I think otherwise: a judgment that Paul Simon or any other world-music practitioner is genuinely blameworthy in terms of appropriation and cultural plundering would require knowledge of circumstances that are additional to *perceived* qualities of their music.

As I also argued in Chapter 3, background information about the music's generative context can lead listeners to reinterpret and even reject a performance, recording, or artist on the grounds that the performers are not entitled to express what they present in their music. But I also made the point that auditor response is not normally restricted to whatever is directly presented and perceived: the audience (or at least some of the audience) cares about performance pragmatics and its ethical dimension.

My worry, then, is that rejection of the socio-historical or source-focused model is also a rejection of ethical assessment. If we only remain on the level of perceived or manifest features, then the aesthetic/experiential contrast of a committed-sounding performance by Dolly Parton of her song "I Will Always Love You" (1974) and a lame, floundering performance (imagine a bar band doing an impromptu cover of it) provides no warrant for thinking that the committed-sounding performance is *ethically* better, as well. Frith's expansive examination of authenticity routinely restricts it to a music-focused, experiential model of authenticity in which it is merely an *appearance* conveyed through a temporary stylistic investment: "To be authentic and to sound authentic is in the rock context the same thing."[27] Thus, Frith joins Keightley in rejecting socio-historical or source-focused authenticity in favor of the music-focused, *experiential*, or experience-verifying standard. Untethered from facts about genuine social position, the ethical component of authenticity is neutralized. It defeats one of the original purposes of discussing authenticity, which was to provide a hook for exploring ethical aspects of song performance.

Postmodern Reappraisal

Around 1990, music critics and popular music scholars began to embrace skepticism about the possibility of socio-historical authenticity, and did so for either or both of two reasons. First, commodification of music renders authenticity impossible.[28] Second, postmodern values render it meaningless in a world where opaque personae are the norm. Many scholars endorsed the view that authenticity is "nebulous, free-floating… and unanchored."[29] Granted, reference to authenticity has not disappeared, as when it is invoked both to challenge musical appropriation and to affirm boundaries between cultures and subcultures.[30] Conjoined to a growing sense of social instability and recognition that all popular music is commercial product under late capitalism, hindsight reveals that the most prescient album of 1967 was *The Who Sell Out*, where the potential hit singles are sandwiched between fake radio jingles and advertisements. However, this and other early gestures of reflexive self-critique are usually read as mere foreshadowing of a "fundamental rupture" within criticism and theory during the 1980s.[31]

One of the most common markers of this rupture was the shift from discussing criteria of authenticity to the appearance and then ubiquitous repetition of the phrase "the ideology of authenticity."[32] In a move that philosophers call the linguistic turn, attention shifts from discussion of the music to discussion of critical *discourse* about it.[33] Descriptions of the music and its performance norms—by fans, by musicians, by the popular press, by earlier scholars—come to be the main focus of the skeptical interrogation. To oversimplify greatly, the shift parallels the change, in anthropology, from nineteenth-century studies of racial difference to contemporary analyses of the ideology of racial differentiation. In each case, the earlier stance requires a commitment to the existence of some feature of things in the world that can be observed and studied (e.g., authenticity, race). The skeptical, revisionary stance denies that there is any genuine, stable referent for these terms. And just as the ideology of racial identity invents and imposes unreal biological differences, the ideology of authenticity imposes an artistic desideratum that vanishes upon closer inspection of our cultural practices. Because rock music was the primary focus of popular music studies during this period, the key arguments generally proceed by contrasting rock with other genres of popular music.

Discussion of the "ideology" of rock authenticity appears to have originated with Frith, but the phrase and the attendant critique gained traction from the work of Lawrence Grossberg.[34] Rock continues to matter to various people for a variety of reasons, but "the ideology of authenticity [was] becoming irrelevant."[35] Grossberg contends that rock had been important for the way that it "offer[ed] youth places within the transitional spaces of youth where they could find some sense of identification and belonging, where they could invest and empower themselves in specific ways."[36] Rock's authenticity required its differentiation from inauthentic music ("mere entertainment") through an ever-evolving aural and visual stylistic excess that articulated "the experience of postwar youth."[37] In short, authenticity was mainly a smokescreen for boundary-policing rather than a concern for the music as directed communication. However, the transition to postmodernism erased much of that rhetoric, Grossberg says, as it became difficult—perhaps impossible—to think that any music really "matters" in a world where our emotional/affective experiences are unmoored and unrepresentable. The only reasonable response to the contemporary onslaught of movies, television, and music is a sensibility dominated by cynicism, ambivalence, and irreverence.[38] Because a distinctive rock culture can no longer matter in the way it had mattered in the 1960s, questions of authenticity gradually became moot.[39]

In short, Grossberg argues after the late 1970s it became all but impossible to create or listen to popular music as bearing the values that Marcus employed when responding to Dylan at the end of the 1960s.[40] We returned to being a culture where the best of popular music is nothing more than clever entertainment. We no longer look to it to provide insight into our lived conditions. Beginning with punk and disco, the rock formation "renounces" the ideology of authenticity in favor of a stance of ironic nihilism or authentic inauthenticity, which appears in multiple forms, including the excessively sentimental and the grotesque.[41] (Taking a broader perspective, we might say that *fin-de-siècle* aestheticism characterizes Western culture in both the nineteenth and twentieth centuries, except that marketing is more effective the second time around.) Madonna and the Pet Shop Boys are offered as prominent exemplars of authentic inauthenticity: there is no pretense to any meaningfulness or commitment beneath the surface of pleasurable music and image-construction. Style is embraced and enjoyed for what it is.

Grossberg is sparing with details, but on my first reading it puzzled me that *punk* was a harbinger of authentic inauthenticity. Perhaps I'd bought in to the story that they were more authentic than progressive rock? But then it struck me that he might be right: the Ramones never expected the audience to believe that the shared surname of Joey, Dee Dee, Johnny, and Tommy was genuine. It was clearly a joke (about the nature of rock bands?), and their song "Judy is a Punk" (1976) puckishly offers skating in the Ice Capades as the primary example of her punk credentials. Similarly, Johnny Rotten is a "cartoon" version of John Lydon.[42] And who can overlook first-wave punk nomenclature rife with self-conscious inauthenticity, such as Sham 69 and The Adverts? For those persuaded by Grossberg's analysis, it usefully explains why champions of authenticity interpreted David Bowie's signature theatricality as an inauthentic failure of "commitment,"[43] where hindsight reveals a postmodern play with constructed surface, subsequently foregrounded by Madonna.[44]

Numerous writers have endorsed Grossberg's analysis.[45] I grant that the postmodern perspective may be of some use when it comes to thinking about performance and image-construction. But I also have strong reservations about any account of popular music that builds on Grossberg. Looking more closely at his analysis of rock authenticity, neither his evidence nor his argument is specifically about rock: his examples are almost exclusively drawn from discussions of popular movies, not music or music videos. His move from one cultural form to another is unjustified. More to the point, the actual argument emphasizes a loss of investment in rock as a cultural formation, which by no means demonstrates a parallel loss of investment in other genres or particular styles, nor with musicians who remain rock-identified. His focus on rock is also too narrow. The supposed shift away from authenticity occurred at precisely the same time that it seemed to become a major element of hip-hop. Looking back at the significance of Dr. Dre and Snoop Dogg in the 1990s, one scholar remarks that "in gangsta rap, issues of authenticity, credibility, and legitimacy are integrally linked to the streets of the ghetto and their social practices."[46] Furthermore, it begs the question to say that the logic of rock required investment in the whole as a condition of valuing the parts.[47] Instead, the reverse is often the case: suspicion about the integrity of the general enterprise may enhance investment in specific musicians, such as Kurt Cobain and Tom Petty.[48]

Finally, much of the critique of the "ideology" of authenticity has nothing to say about its *ideological* dimension. Other than the problem that rock authenticity is normally gendered as male,[49] relatively little work has been done to show that a concern for authenticity is a cloaked or masked endorsement of established relations of wealth, power, and authority, which is what one expects to see addressed when a cultural practice is ideological. Besides hip-hop, Grossberg's focus on "rock authenticity" also led him to neglect a music genre with a persistent, perhaps even strengthening, ideology of authenticity: American country music. As Aaron Fox observes, country music, especially the dominant strain of working-class country with a "redneck" identity, celebrates "an identity that is canonically bound up with a defensive articulation of whiteness—a particular class-positioned way of being 'white,'" associated with an "ingrained racism."[50] Although a historically informed reading of country recognizes that the genre's conventions can be deconstructed as an "ironic fantasy," the fans regard the music as authentic, "real," and "a basis for sociality in [white, working-class] community."[51] So, while there may be pockets of the audience embracing authentic inauthenticity, an ideology of authenticity still dominates some genres.

Ascribed Authenticities

Earlier in this chapter, I sketched a distinction between source-focused and music-focused (experiential) concepts of authenticity. For reasons summarized in the last section, the source-focused model became unfashionable. Music-focused accounts filled the resulting void and are now the dominant approach for theorizing about authenticity in popular music. Moore, a prominent advocate of music-focused accounts, cautions that "there is no single authenticity"; yet, in paradigm instances it is seen and heard in "[p]articular acts and sonic gestures... made by particular artists."[52] For example, consider the resonance of the moment when, singing "A Hard Rain's a-Gonna Fall" at the 2016 Nobel Prize ceremony for Bob Dylan, Patti Smith fumbles the words, apologizes, and starts the verse over.[53] Who can doubt her investment in this performance and in getting it right?

Moore aims to explain how authenticity is crystalized in the particularity of performance without any commitment to specific modernist or postmodern narratives. He proposes that we can validate a music-focused stance by adopting a hermeneutical framework: as with all other texts that convey meanings to appropriately "literate" audiences, the meaningfulness of a musical performance does not rest on a presumption that performers are communicating fixed or definite messages.[54] Different audiences (and audience members) have diverse and equally legitimate interpretive goals. Furthermore, long-term continuing access to *recorded* music facilitates a proliferation of such goals as the music arrives in unanticipated sites of reception. For example, there is no error on either side when older, "silent majority" Americans experienced Jimi Hendrix's Woodstock performance of their national anthem as disrespectful, akin to flag-burning, while the younger, tuned-in rock audience heard a valid critique of American imperialism. And there is also something to be gained in hearing it—as older ideas about authenticity invite us do—as an African-American lamentation. Or one might see it as a primarily *musical* construct, as Hendrix seemed to do when interviewed about the event: "I thought it was beautiful."[55]

So, what sort of account arises when we reject the idea that authenticity is something mysteriously inscribed in the music based on a musician's relationship to their sources and community, and we refocus on the listener's active role in assigning meaning and relevance to their musical experience? The most notable proposal is Moore's tripartite analysis of authenticity of expression, of experience, and of execution (or first-person, second-person, and third-person authenticity, respectively). Adam Behr usefully supplements this grouping by adding the category of collective, or first-person plural, authenticity.[56] Let me note at the outset that this model rejects the relevance of the "'encoding' and 'decoding'" model that underlies pragmatics and, with it, my own favored approach.[57]

My example of Smith's fumble and apology illustrates Moore's category of first-person authenticity: the audience approvingly authenticates the performance as a genuine communicative act, not as mere show.[58] Watching video of the event, Smith's words, voice, and facial expression invite a judgment of *sincerity*, while her decision to begin over and get it right signals *integrity*.[59] These judgments about performers' actions are the same sorts of judgments that we make about the behaviors of others in everyday social contexts. Observed particulars ground a judgment about this person on this occasion. Such judgments have a social dimension, and they are generally informed by anything else we know about the person we are evaluating. Thus, one may initially attribute expressive authenticity to James Brown's refusal to leave the stage during "Please Please Please" at the T.A.M.I. Show, 1964, but then withdraw the judgment after realizing that it's a rehearsed, staged moment that he'd been performing for years.[60] It remains great theater, but it might not be counted as a sincere gesture any longer.

Much like a listener's judgments that Smith's performance was solemn (rather than, say, playful) and measured (rather than, say, rushed), authenticity is here recast as a response-dependent (rather than inherent) aspect of the performance. And, given that popular music overwhelmingly takes the form of song performance, each audience member responds to a combination of musical features that will be more or less familiar and amendable to them, which in turn will include interpretation of semantic features of lyrics, all of which will be interpreted in various ways. There is nothing surprising, for example, in a glam rock fan's dismissal of The Beach Boys's "Don't Worry Baby" (1964) as insipid but then responding favorably to the Bryan Ferry cover version (1973). Conversely, a fan who's a decade older may find Ferry's singing to be highly artificial and thus fake, where the original is in a more congenial style and is accepted as deeply moving. Both versions articulate the same experience, but they will not resonate with everyone uniformly.

What Moore adds to these basic points about music reception is the key point that each musical event invites the listener to *refer* the experience in one or more of three directions. He proposes that the experience of any musical gesture will be interpreted in terms of various physical vectors that can be followed from the text to different referents: the listener, the musician, and/or the underlying tradition.[61] Another important point is that this includes an *evaluative* response of recipients who "confer"—rather than discover—expressive authenticity. Listeners generally start by evaluating the musician who provides the musical experience, but listeners may also follow a vector back to themselves (second person) or follow a vector out to a broader situation (third person).

It is important to note that when Moore describes following the text to one or more referents, he is not speaking of "reference" in the semantic sense. When Tony Bennett sings his signature song, "I Left My Heart in San Francisco" (1962), the words "San Francisco" semantically refer to that city.[62] But its semantic content does not set up a reference-vector to the listener, nor—as will be apparent in a moment— to Moore's third person. In the model I have been using throughout this book, a consideration of pragmatics will sometimes justify an auditor's interpretation that the performer intends for the first-person language to create these vectors. As I explained in Chapter 2, it is a norm of popular music performance that the performer invites such make-believe, so auditors are justified in looking for indications about which vectors to pursue. However, Moore's first- and second-person authenticities seem to be indifferent to a distinction between semantics, pragmatics, and performance norms. He is emphasizing affordances and downplaying the guidance of encoded communication.[63] From my perspective, Moore's vectors are only present on either of two conditions. First, when they are generated by specific aspects of a particular performance or recording, or, second, the performer adopts a transparent persona and invites first person authentication.

My point is that Moore's account of authentication is not concerned with "decoding" communication so much as with a listener's affective response. When an auditor is moved by a song performance or recording, the experience is frequently interpreted and valued as an illumination and validation of the listener's own experiences. In that case, we have Moore's category of second-person authenticity.[64] It is present when the musical experience "centres the listener" in the face of social change and uncertainty.[65] This mode of authentication often takes on a communal or group element, if only because some level of shared experience is generally a precondition for a listener's capacity for personal resonance.[66] In her autobiographical account of the band Sleater-Kinney, Carrie Brownstein uses the word "authentic" precisely once, and she uses it in a way that illustrates Moore's category. Although she worries that authenticity is an elitist value, she says that "Nirvana had been considered the *cooler*, more authentic band [in grunge].... The songs helped you locate the place where you ached, and in that awareness of your hurting you suddenly knew that the bleakness was collective, not merely your own."[67]

Just as first-person authentication is sometimes negative, so also with second person authentication. To some degree, a negative judgment about authenticity will be directed at music that feels off-putting, unfamiliar, or threatening. Stephen Millar offers a case where a politically progressive audience could not accept the idea that a conservative politician could share their appreciation for The Smiths. This example illustrates that many fans engage in a longitudinal "authentication" of other fans.[68] Based on audience understanding of the constructed identity of an artist, listeners construct a corresponding identity for that artist's audience, so that an active personal appropriation of the music is at the same time an incorporation of one's self into that audience. Upon discovery that the audience contains listeners whose views are abhorrent, or at least contrary to values perceived in the music, both fans (and, sometimes, the musicians) must dismiss the responses of those other listeners as inauthentic. To do otherwise is to unravel the sense of community solidarity that is characteristic of authenticity of experience.

Returning to the James Brown example, reinterpretation might follow the realization that the key gestures—feigning weariness, throwing off the cape, stumbling slowly back to the microphone—are planned and well-rehearsed. As the focal point of his T.A.M.I. performance, this sequence (via film replay) tends to highlight the artificiality of the whole performance, qua performance. And for those listeners who recognize that no performance is entirely spontaneous, unmediated, and communicative *ex nihilo*, there may be an additional step of reflecting on any particular performance's basis in earlier performance practices. Where a listener follows this vector of reference, the evaluation involves an appraisal of authenticity of execution (third-person authenticity). Here, the listener authenticates and endorses the nonliteral presence of an "(absent) other" whose art is in some way preserved and carried forward. This is precisely the stance that Brown's biographer urges us to adopt toward "the cape act": Brown is recreating a tradition of the Black Pentecostal church tradition, conveying the message that he is moved by a force beyond himself.[69] If this vector back to the larger African-American community was lost on the (overwhelmingly) white audience for the T.A.M.I. broadcast, the valuing of a link to that very culture is the key to understanding why white audiences ascribed authenticity to 1960s British appropriations of African-American blues styles.[70] Today, cover bands such as Dark Star Orchestra and Nervana may strike many rock fans as did Sha Na Na in their heyday: nostalgia merchants lacking in originality and so, also, in merit. However, there continue to be fans of many singers and bands whose performing days are done, and these fans often confer a reflected high value on their experience of a cover band when it is heard as preserving the music accurately.[71]

Behr calls attention to an omission in Moore's account as formulated: the first-person vector directs evaluation to an individual, usually the singer: Patti Smith or James Brown.[72] But the cover band phenomenon, just noted, is an evaluation of group identity. A *group* is evaluated in relation to another *group*, generating a fourth category: the first-person plural or collective authenticity. Evaluation of group agency is a common occurrence of everyday life (e.g., "The competing *team* cheated" and "The *bank* overcharged me"). Therefore, there is no special logic involved when we authenticate groups as such, whether in live performance or on record: "I didn't hate it," said Moe Tucker of the Velvet Underground post-Lou Reed, "but it wasn't the Velvets."[73] As with Moore's first person, Behr's category of first-person plural centers on the evaluation of integrity. It opens the door, furthermore, to a fifth category: third-person plural or the nostalgic authentication of an absent (or imagined) nonmusical community. Typically, we may see a version of this in groups associated with American "roots" music as initially exemplified by The Band on their first two albums and then subsequently throughout the general genre of Americana.[74]

Many scholars endorse this general approach because it makes authentication a matter of each auditor's response to whatever is available to them. As Philip Auslander puts it, "the authenticity of a country singer like [Keith] Urban resides not in a match between his biography and what a country musician is supposed to be but rather, in his willingness to perform an identity" in conformity with audience expectations.[75] Robert Walser endorses this authentication model in his account of the malleability of Bon Jovi, a heavy metal band that secured authentication from a broader, nonmetal audience "by wearing jeans, not leather or spandex."[76] Substituting one authentic identity for a different authentic identity is often as simple as changing one's wardrobe—providing one changes one's audience, as well.[77]

However, this approach to authenticity reintroduces the same problem that troubled me in Chapter 3 about the standard position on ethicism. Performers are insulated from any moral responsibility for their constructed identities or for the props for make-believe they deliver in performances. It allows auditors to feel affirmed in their epistemic bubbles, for there is no auditor responsibility to compare appearance and reality. Audience authentication also downplays the degree to which performers negotiate performance norms, especially the norm of signaling the degree of transparency or opacity that holds for their personae. Signals of a transparent persona are active invitations to auditors to treat the attitudes and ideas expressed in a performance as relatively accurate reflections of ones endorsed by the singer as an ordinary person in the world. While I admit that I am engaging in armchair speculation here, I suspect that many fans (and perhaps many casual listeners) engage in second person authenticity because they recognize and accept the implicit invitation of a transparent persona. On this basis, auditors are invited to treat what they are witnessing as subject to a sincerity condition. Although genuine transparency and sincerity are not logically necessary for second person authenticity, there is a psychological investment that encourages a sense of betrayal in response to a change of persona. Many long-time fans of The Smiths find it increasingly difficult to hear their music and the early solo career of hyper-vulnerable singer Morrissey as "offering solidarity to the marginalized" now that he has made it very clear that he feels no sense of solidarity with vulnerable groups who most need such support. As Billy Bragg notes, "he's betraying those fans, betraying his legacy and empowering the very people Smiths fans were brought into being to oppose."[78] However, Morrissey is only betraying them if his early persona was offered as a highly transparent persona. Authentication models of authenticity dodge the question of whether he—or any other performer—has really betrayed anyone.

Concluding Unscientific Postscript

To summarize what I have outlined, many listeners seem to be indifferent to the complex relationship between popular song performers and their personae. At the same time, the scholarship on fandom has generally assumed that fandom involves a "preoccupation with 'authenticity,'"[79] a concept recently recast as fan authentication.

Do any of these accounts of authenticity accurately track popular music practice? I conclude this chapter by wondering out loud about the possibility that authenticity in popular music may be akin to Kudzu vines in the American south—an invasive import that chokes off the local flora. I want to suggest that much of this theorizing about authenticity may obscure actual communication practice by adopting—perhaps even imposing—terminology and related assumptions that misrepresent those practices.

What I have in mind is analogous to a parallel and much-discussed issue in the field of art history. In her pioneering discussion of the effects of sexism on creative practice in the visual arts, Linda Nochlin focuses on the longstanding, distorting ideology of artistic genius. Like authenticity, artistic genius was basically coded as a male prerogative. One engages in wishful thinking, Nochlin cautions, if one assumes that there were "women equivalents for Michelangelo or Rembrandt" in Europe prior to the twentieth century.[80] The search for such women is a Don Quixote quest based on a naïve refusal to understand the prevailing social structures of the artworld. Nochlin issues a caution about combing through art history for examples of genuinely great women artists: doing so is akin to searching through the sporting records for great Inuit tennis players. And pointing to Artemisia Gentileschi's undeniable achievements as evidence of women's creative capacities highlights a token case. Token cases obscure the larger picture, which is that the entire mode of discourse is problematic, for talk of "genius" has systematically misrepresented prevailing art practices back to the Renaissance. Why should we expect to locate exceptional levels of achievements from members of a group who were denied access to the standard means of success?

Looking for authenticity in popular music poses a parallel problem. The idea of authenticity reinforces the centrality of self-presentation—or, more accurately, personae—of popular musicians. However, if authentication accounts are correct, then most fans look no further than the *believability* of a musician's persona, and communicative agency remains with individuals who "front" the music.

A potentially troubling result is that the fan authentication model uses authenticity the way the old system of the arts used genius—as a way to celebrate a select few as special while ignoring the immense collaborative efforts required to make them special. Note the parallel issue in film studies, which examines one of the other principal popular art forms that arose within twentieth-century mass media. Early film scholars quickly understood that a mass media artform is the product of a system of production that is hidden from public view, embedded in an industry that routinely *misrepresents* the creative process of making movies. It does so through its relentless focus on actors and actresses. As Karina Longworth observes about film discourse prior to the arrival of film studies, the most influential messages about classic Hollywood concentrated on "selling regular people the illusion that they were taking them behind the scenes, while really they were reinforcing a system that relied on audiences having no idea how movies were made or what stars were really like."[81] Film scholars recognized these distortions and responded by promoting the idea that movie directors hold primary agency and are primarily responsible for a film's vision and communicative intentions. Change Longworth's "movies" to "popular song performances" and I fear that experiential and experience-verifying models of authenticity tell us that it is irrelevant whether audiences understand how the music is made or what the performers are really like. Not that there have been no efforts to demystify the industry, but they have largely failed to break through to fans.[82] Popular music fandom remains mired in a model of individual achievement, primarily focused on vocalists. Witness, as evidence, the huge success of the recent remake of *A Star Is Born* (2018), which reassures fans that stars succeed due to their innate, individual talent—success merely requires a lucky break so the star can shine, while other careers collapse due to the personal failings of performers.

Granted, Behr takes note of musical groups and fan devotion to groups, but this does not extend to the multiple kinds of musical collaborators shaping the music and its presentation. To take a notable example, there are hundreds of books about The Beatles, including scores of academic studies, but there is basically only one about George Martin (or two, if you count his autobiography), the producer who was instrumental in the development of their music.[83] In keeping with my emphasis on generative contexts, we should also note the general failure to consider the many other modes of creative activity that contribute to song presentation and which complicate and enrich those presentations. Performances and recordings—and the personae they exhibit—most often arise through combined agency and multiple kinds of contributory creative actions. Yet, for example, few music video directors receive the spotlight, and the choreographers for videos and performance tours are largely unknown.[84] In Chapter 5, I will consider general criteria for determining whose agency counts as communicative agency in complex, collaborative music presentation.

Returning to Nochlin, her critical reexamination of the concept of artistic genius offers the potential lesson that a critical examination of popular music authenticity should address the question of when, and with whom, the term "authenticity" entered critical discourse. The next step would be to examine how its use distorts our understanding of creative processes.[85] In this spirit, let me make a modest beginning by returning to an example that opened this chapter, Dylan. Examine any anthology of criticism published about Dylan that spans his long career.[86] It seems that, in the whole of the 1960s, precisely one writer refers to Dylan as either "authentic" or "inauthentic": Ellen Willis remarks that "Dylan's songs bear the stigmata of an authentic middle-class adolescence."[87] Furthermore, the term "authentic" appears in no interview conducted with Dylan in the 1960s and 1970s, which is again odd if it was a central evaluative category.[88] But if the term was not used in contemporaneous evaluation and critical engagement with Dylan, what makes us think that authenticity became a key value in the rock culture of the 1960s, and something that became less important after the 1970s? Perhaps we should rescind an idea introduced at the start of the chapter, which is that the complexity of authenticity derives from its differentiation in local practices. Perhaps other things are mostly at work in local practice, much of it only marginally aligned with anything that should be called "authenticity."[89]

Coming at the same issue from the angle of audience response—"how music is experienced by real people"[90]—we can consult studies of listeners and their evaluative processes. But when we eliminate studies where the researchers set out to learn what fans think about authenticity and examine empirical studies of "everyday" evaluative language about music preferences and uses, something interesting emerges. Authenticity, the "real," and various synonyms are virtually absent from auditors' evaluative vocabulary.[91] Granted, we can easily find fans who dismiss "superficial" musicians who are "selling themselves out."[92] So, while it is possible to find *some* evidence that something like authenticity has been important in the reception and evaluation of popular music, applications of the key concepts are surprisingly absent from what fans actually say in "everyday" discourse about popular music.

It may be, therefore, that influential writers and theorists have overestimated the importance of authenticity. They may have viewed meaning-making in popular music through a lens that was originally devised to privilege art music, literature, and the visual arts at the expense of popular and mass culture. Aiming to elevate some popular music as more serious and art-like than mainstream pop, they adapted the language of art criticism (including the idea of artistic genius) to elevate their favored genres. To be clear, I don't deny that multiple concepts of authenticity have been important to critics, historians, and academic theorists, especially after the mid-1970s. Anne Desler's words, quoted at the start of this chapter, may be all too accurate: authenticity might well be "critics' key criterion in assessing the artistic value of new [popular] music." However, its importance to critics (and theorists) does not show that authenticities have been an equally important touchstone for musicians and fans.[93]

Ironically, it might be the case that popular music scholarship turned against its *own* ideology of authenticity at roughly the time that some "everyday" fans, weaned on popular press reverberations of that discourse, began to accept it, especially in the form of fan authentication. In short, it might be enlightening to find out whether there has been a generational lag between theory and practice, and whether a more comprehensive reexamination of fan discourse supports a revised narrative in which authenticity talk made inroads with fans at about the same time that theorists were announcing its (postmodern) demise.[94]

In conclusion, popular music continues to operate in a cultural space governed by the norm that individual popular music performers are the agents responsible for the content of communications. As such, I think it is appropriate and useful to think about sincerity in relation to popular song performance.[95] As I argued in Chapter 3, some performance norms invite auditors to ask about the sincerity behind personae that are constructed and presented as part of the communicative process. Although *socio-historical* criteria of authenticity would provide guidance in thinking more critically about norms governing performer and performance authenticity, we find limited employment of such criteria in the popular press, fan discourse, and the field of popular music studies. When authenticity is discussed, socio-historical criteria are the exception, not the norm.

5

Pulling Together as a Team: Collective Action and Pink Floyd's Intentions

Introduction

For the sake of theoretical simplicity, my previous chapters have generally proceeded as if popular songs are performed by a lone individual: Nina Simone sings "Mississippi Goddam" (1964) while accompanying herself on piano, or Woody Guthrie strums his guitar and sings about a racist New York real estate mogul, "Old Man Trump" (1954), or Prince, alone in his home studio, multitracks all the parts and vocals of a new composition, "Sign o' the Times" (1987). And even when I've discussed a musical group, I've generally picked out and emphasized one individual, as when I focused on John Lennon in relation to The Beatles in Chapter 3. However, popular song performance is most often conceived, arranged, and performed by musicians working together in groups. For much of the twentieth century, different partners and collectives handled the successive tasks of composing, arranging, performing, and recording. In the 1960s it became increasingly common for all of these tasks to be handled by a set of musicians working together as an ongoing group. In this respect, popular music is very unlike a conversation between one person and another, where successful communication requires auditors to understand one speaker's communicative intentions.[1]

However, if communication with popular song cannot always be modeled on the premise of one speaker whose intentions inform its use, then how do we understand the nature of a group? How do we preserve the insight that intentions underwrite communication? An intention is a willing or a desiring that a result will follow from an action that is being undertaken in the belief that the action will cause that result. (If the final part of that sentence seems redundant, it adds the idea that if I don't believe that a sponge can break a window, I can't intend to break the window by throwing a sponge at it.) When a performer communicates via popular song, they typically desire it to mean one thing rather than another, and they adopt an action plan in light of semantical conventions and musical conventions. But how could a musical group have a desire and thus an intention? Groups seldom have unanimity of purpose, or of belief, or of the other things associated with intentions. So how can there be a group intention to underwrite a group's communication?

I pause to note that this is my third consecutive chapter addressing the issue of fakeness in popular music. However, what "fake" means is different in each case, moving from personal sincerity to lack of proper social grounding to, here, questions about who is communicating. To the extent that there is a shared core to these three aspects of faking it in song performance, it is the shared idea that the auditor is misled about some aspect of the generative context of communication.

To unpack and address this issue, this chapter focuses on one group, Pink Floyd, whose fracture and regrouping throws the question into high relief. By examining one group, we can make better sense how a collective of individuals—whether stable or unstable in membership—can communicate through their joint project of making music together.

Refining the Issue

Overwhelmed by the amount of music that's readily available, students sometimes ask me to recommend music. Suppose a student asked me to recommend some Pink Floyd. What would I say? *Dark Side of the Moon* (1973) is the obvious starting point for any exploration of their music, but I'd probably recommend my personal favorite, *Wish You Were Here* (1975). I'd steer a novice away from *Atom Heart Mother* (1970).

But then what? I see the group's music as dividing into four very distinct eras, and I recognize that there's not much common ground between the Syd Barrett years and the grim concept albums *Animals* (1977), *The Wall* (1979), and *The Final Cut* (1983). Pressed to recommend something, I might point to the two-disc collection *Echoes* (2001), whose generous track list was decided by shared agreement of four individuals who have been members of Pink Floyd: David Gilmour, Roger Waters, Nick Mason, and Rick Wright. It represents each phase of the band. There are five pieces from the Barrett years, five from the albums after Waters quit the band, and two from the period when keyboardist Wright was absent. About half of the album is the music of the quartet of Waters, Gilmour, Mason, and Wright. No member of the band actually appears on every track.

Recommending *Echoes* presents something of a dilemma. To endorse *Echoes* is to endorse a particular history of the band and a particular vision of Pink Floyd. According to Waters, the music recorded and performed by the "so-called Pink Floyd" after 1985 is a fraud, a fake, and a ruse.[2] To endorse *Echoes*, I must treat Waters as mistaken. This chapter begins by examining Waters's claim that Pink Floyd ended when he quit the band on December 12, 1985. I argue that Waters is wrong, and I try to explain why it matters. It isn't just a trivial matter of semantics. This issue bears directly on the merits of Waters's claim that *Pink Floyd* is not communicating with the audience in the post-1985 albums such as *The Division Bell* (1994).

My purpose, of course, is that examining Waters's claims takes us to the heart of what constitutes *group* action and communication.

Waters presented his arguments in a media campaign that followed his 1986 lawsuit to dissolve Pink Floyd. I have nothing to say about the legal issues. (Waters and the other members of the band reached an out-of-court settlement.) What interests me is that Waters made a series of arguments that are independent from—but which seem to have motivated—his lawsuit. His arguments revolve around longstanding philosophical debates on two topics: the nature of identity over time and the possibility of collective responsibility. In turn, those issues are the foundation for understanding and evaluating a body of music made collectively by a group.

I will set the stage with a few points about individual "authorship" and communication. The modern practice of assigning and recognizing artistic authorship underwrites our cultural practice of responding to individual texts and performances in relation to other works by the same artist. As such, imagine the following scenario. Someone has some familiarity with classical music and is familiar with some of Beethoven's symphonies, and then is incredulous when told, of the piano piece *Für Elise*, that it is by Beethoven. Actually, such incredulity might have been quite natural for one of his Viennese contemporaries. His contemporaries had no difficulty accepting that the symphonies were musical communications, and E.T.A. Hoffmann famously defended the symphonies—there were not yet nine—against detractors by articulating the deep significance of what they communicate. Prior to Beethoven, Hoffmann wrote, "poor instrumental composers... laboriously struggle[d]" to represent, musically, our various human emotions. In contrast, "Beethoven's instrumental music unveils before us the realm of the mighty and the immeasurable" and those who immerse themselves in the music and understand it have the honor of becoming "ecstatic visionaries."[3] The symphonies were, at the time, the paradigm of the musical sublime. *Für Elise* is, to use the language of that era, picturesque rather than sublime. So simple that it is commonly assigned to beginning piano students, it communicates little more than the feel of a pleasant few minutes with a charming companion. It certainly does not come across as the music of a prophetic oracle.

For a similar case in the world of popular music, consider Björk's biggest hit, her cover of "It's Oh So Quiet" (1995). In keeping with Betty Hutton's 1951 original recording, Björk delivers one of the most conventional vocal treatments of her career. The musical track is atypical, as well, with jazzy horn charts, tinkling piano, Tin Pan Alley melody and structure, and passages of hushed singing alternating with a boisterous chorus. In short, Björk's version of "It's Oh So Quiet" is the *Für Elise* in the career of one of the quirkiest songwriters and vocalists this side of Captain Beefheart. It's fair to ask, if one knows the body of her work, what she was doing with this one.

My point in offering these examples is that most fans are either puzzled or intrigued by a song or performance that is out of character with the persona, temperament, and musical approach that are characteristic of that musician. However, those two cases pose no obvious philosophical problem. We process *Für Elise* and "It's Oh So Quiet" in terms of the other music of Beethoven and Björk, and we are confident that we know what kinds of things Beethoven and Björk are. They are individual people, and we routinely assign responsibility to individuals. Having determined whose agency is at issue, we can then get on with the business of deciding what *Für Elise* and "It's Oh So Quiet" mean in relation to the larger patterns of activity of each artist.[4] Our attempt to fit each musical product into an artist's larger career trajectory is a standard— sometimes even necessary—step in making sense of what it communicates, and the assemblage of the various items into a larger narrative secures an understanding of an artist's overall vision, which, in turn, we read back into the individual pieces of communication.

Things become more complicated if we shift from individuals to groups. Suppose I want to compare Pink Floyd's *Animals* with the Sex Pistols's "God Save the Queen," as so many in England seemed to want to do back in 1977. At the time, the Pistols seemed fresh and relevant and the Floyd seemed worn out and decadent. While there's not a lot of controversy about how many albums the Sex Pistols recorded (exactly one studio album), Waters disputes whether several studio albums and live albums are actually the work of Pink Floyd. The most prominent studio albums that appeared as Pink Floyd after Waters left the band are *A Momentary Lapse of Reason* (1987) and *The Division Bell* (1994). The live albums include *Delicate Sound of Thunder* (1988) and *Pulse* (1995). If we want to complicate things further, we might question whether *The Final Cut* is a Pink Floyd album. Originally subtitled as "A requiem for the post-war dream by Roger Waters, performed by Pink Floyd," some regard it as a Waters solo album with limited musical participation by Gilmour and Mason. If we decide that none of these five albums are really by Pink Floyd, then nearly a third of the *Echoes* compilation doesn't belong there.

Our overriding philosophical problem, then, is to decide what kind of thing or entity Pink Floyd is, because it isn't, in any ordinary sense, an individual person. On the other hand, there might not seem to be much problem here. Some things, like flocks of birds and schools of fish, are essentially groups of individuals. Obviously, we want to say that Pink Floyd is a group, and the group's music therefore differs in important ways from music created by those individuals when working outside the group. Thus, there are solo projects by Barrett, Wright, Mason, Waters, and Gilmour and none of this music belongs on *Echoes*. But as any Pink Floyd fan knows, some Pink Floyd music was created by individuals in a more or less "solo" fashion—we have, for instance, the four distinct parts of the studio disc of *Ummagumma* (1969). The problem is to determine when these various individuals—acting independently or together in various combinations—constitute the group Pink Floyd.

The issue is sharpened by the way that popular music is almost always collaborative. Many songs are collaborations—a Gershwin tune is, of course, by the two Gershwin brothers—and performances are usually group efforts: Björk did not construct the horn section of "It's Oh So Quiet" by playing each instrument herself and stacking them up with overdubbing. So we should pause to distinguish between cases where (1) music-making is collaborative in a *weak* sense, where others assist without becoming co-authors of the communication and (2) there is collaborative in a *strong* sense, and two or more contributors merit credit as co-authors. We want to "distinguish between mere contributors and genuine coauthors."[5] Thus, Clare Torry's wordless vocal is an important expressive element of *Dark Side of the Moon*'s "The Great Gig in the Sky," but making a vocal contribution as "hired help" does not make one a member of the group, Pink Floyd. But then we see that after 2005, Torry gets songwriting co-credit for that song. Having sued for co-authorship credit and royalties, she is now recognized as a songwriter for that album, elevating her from mere contributor to genuine co-author of that one song.

Torry's struggle for recognition of her contribution is all too common in the "entertainment" or culture industries. However, I am not suggesting that everyone who contributes creatively to a performance or recording is thereby a collaborator in the strong sense. A staggering number of co-writers, co-producers, and musicians are credited as contributors to Beyoncé's *Lemonade* album (2016), but she alone gets credit. *Her* intentions decide what the album means, should these be in question. Similarly, despite the contributions of others as engineers, producers, musicians, plus Torry's co-authorship of a song, Pink Floyd, a quartet of musicians, gets credit for *Dark Side of the Moon*. And they do so even if Waters played a role in it that looks more or less equivalent to Beyoncé's role in the creation of *Lemonade*.

Consequently, the general goal of this chapter is to sketch out some criteria for assigning intentions to a group instead of an individual even though the music is, in both cases, the result of collaboration. When is group attribution warranted? That issue is at the heart of Waters's complaint. Perhaps Waters is right that *Lapse of Reason* is a Gilmour solo project masquerading as Pink Floyd. Given that Waters is the sole songwriter on *The Final Cut* and the other two remaining members are largely absent, many regard it as a Waters solo album passed off as Pink Floyd. Notice, also, that both of those albums have the same number of participating Pink Floyd members as does Syd Barrett's *Barrett* (1970), so member participation is not itself a decisive criterion for its being a group project. If one thinks that either *Lapse of Reason* or *The Final Cut* is not the work of Pink Floyd, then *Ummagumma* and *The Wall* and the rest of the genuine *group* oeuvre are not the primary comparison class for responding to the solo projects and the "fake" Floyd productions. The primary comparison classes are then Gilmour and Waters solo albums. For example, if *The Final Cut* is the last Pink Floyd album, then the group ends its career as a band specializing in concept albums. From 1973 to 1983, they made nothing else, and each album was conceptually unified by the ideas and concerns of Waters, their lyricist. It then makes sense to regard the entire second half of their career as having a unified philosophy or vision.[6] However, if *Lapse of Reason* is a Pink Floyd album, then their later music is no longer so easily pigeonholed. It is not a concept album, Waters contributed nothing to it, and it is no longer true that Pink Floyd's final decade presents a unified vision of the world. In short, the salience of various intertextualities changes according to assignment of authorship.

Waters's Position—Raving and Drooling, or Serious Argument?

Waters offered many reasons why *Lapse of Reason* and the others are not the work of Pink Floyd. Ultimately, there is one basic reason. In 1985, Waters notified the band that he quit the group. In doing so, he terminated their collective project and Pink Floyd ceased to exist. But how does the one fact support the other? Does his argument hang together? Waters offers three reasons why his departure constitutes the end of the band.

First, Waters argues that an album created by only one member of Pink Floyd is a solo album by that musician, so it cannot be a Pink Floyd album. Waters contends that *Lapse of Reason* is almost solely the work of Gilmour, with Mason and Wright in supporting roles that do not constitute genuine membership. *Lapse of Reason* is just a Gilmour solo record relying heavily on hired studio help. Part of Waters's case is that Gilmour hired multiple session musicians and worked with many songwriters besides Mason and Wright, that Wright was on salary and not a co-equal member with Mason and Gilmour, and that Mason was not the primary drummer for any of the actual music. The subsequent tour (documented on *Delicate Sound of Thunder*) also used Mason and Wright as mere sidemen. According to Waters, there was no "functioning" band.[7] Therefore selling it as Pink Floyd is an intentional fraud.

This argument rests on the idea, already mentioned, that Pink Floyd is essentially a group. A group, on this reading, is collaboration in the strong sense, and so lack of genuine musical co-authorship is contrary to the spirit, if not the letter, of the group's implicit agreement about how it operated. Hence music that does not emerge from right kind of ongoing collaboration is not Pink Floyd music.

Second, Waters wrote the words and thus furnished the concepts for Pink Floyd's music after Barrett was booted from the band in 1968. In Timothy White's formulation of this argument, Pink Floyd depended on Waters "lyrically, musically, and conceptually" in their glory years.[8] Even if Mason and Wright had contributed more fully to *Lapse of Reason*, their reliance on multiple lyricists who never joined the group also invalidates the music as a product of the *group* Pink Floyd. The collaborations involve illegitimate assistance.

Third, Waters argues that his leaving is not the end of the band, because "the group disintegrated long ago."[9] His 1986 departure was simply a public admission of what had already taken place—evidently during the recording of *The Final Cut*, if not *The Wall*. Therefore, Gilmour's use of the band's name for *Lapse of Reason* was dishonest.

The third argument is the easiest to dismiss. Unless a group has very well-formalized rules requiring regular periods of activity, as does, for instance, the United States Congress, then the group can very easily exist for long periods of time in a dormant state. In the absence of formal action taken to disband, a group can exist for years without being active, then reactivate, as evidenced by any number of reunion albums and tours.

The second argument is also very weak. As every fan knows, the group's existence cannot depend on Waters's unifying role as lyricist and primary idea guru. Waters had no such role before *Dark Side of the Moon*. Originally, Barrett played that role. Waters's successful accension to the leadership role demonstrates that the continuity of the band did not depend on any particular individual's leadership of the group. Furthermore, there is a significant gap between Barrett's departure and *Dark Side*, during which the four members were perhaps more genuinely collaborative than they were once Waters took the helm for *Dark Side* and made them major rock stars.

Mason and Gilmour independently confirm that the band was relatively adrift after Barrett's firing and remained that way until *Meddle* (1971). That album was the point where Waters became their primary lyricist. Yet, even here, only one of *Meddle*'s six songs is fully Waters's composition where he contributed both the words and music. Furthermore, selecting the lyricist as the guiding force of *Meddle* contradicts musical norms. After all, George Gershwin's songs are primarily attributed to him despite the fact that he wrote none of the lyrics. The opera *The Marriage of Figaro* (1786) is attributed to Mozart despite the fact that he did not write the words. There is no good reason to think that Waters's role as lyricist for the songs on *Meddle* (half the album, since half is instrumentals) makes him its unifying force. *Meddle* is significant because it is their breakthrough to a recognizable "Pink Floyd" *musical* style, which is a collective achievement.

This last point might be taken to support Waters's first argument. If Pink Floyd is a musical collective, then a musical project in which only one member plays a significant part is not the work of a musical *group*, which is what Pink Floyd essentially is. However, this argument then counts against *The Final Cut*. In fact, that very point might be what's behind Waters's claim that the group "disintegrated long ago"—he had become too dominant, and the group had become a weak collaboration. But if that's true, then Waters was himself perpetuating a fraud when the group performed the stage version of *The Wall*.

Personally, I'm not such a Pink Floyd fan that I have any strong feelings about any of this. I have chosen them largely because they serve as a clear, well-documented case study that illustrates the philosophical problem. How can a group that changes its members be *the same group* after the change? If different groups of individuals can be the same group at two different times, then isn't it also equally permissible for the group to operate by different sets of rules at different times? So we must deal with three closely related problems. First, there is the general problem of how anything remains the same thing if it keeps changing. Second, there is the more specific problem of how a shifting aggregate of people preserves group identity. Third, how does this aggregate of individuals possess intentions so that it can have responsibility for communications with genuine utterance meaning and pragmatic implications?

The Same in a Relative Way?

The problem of identifying the feature or features that constitute Pink Floyd—or any other group to which we ascribe collective agency—is an example of the general philosophical problem of identity. This more basic problem arises for everything that exists over a period of time. Seventeenth-century English philosopher John Locke famously captures the problem by citing living organisms:

> In the state of living creatures, their identity depends not on a mass of the same particles, but on something else. For in them the variation of great parcels of matter alters not the identity: an oak growing from a plant to a great tree, and then lopped, is still the same oak; and a colt grown up to a horse, sometimes fat, sometimes lean, is all the while the same horse: though, in both these cases, there may be a manifest change of the parts; so that truly they are not either of them the same masses of matter, though they be truly one of them the same oak, and the other the same horse. The reason whereof is, that, in these two cases—a mass of matter and a living body—identity is not applied to the same thing.[10]

Turning to groups and their identity, one might think of the individual members as analogous to "matter" or material parts. One lesson from Locke is that having stable parts is not necessary to preserve the identity of most things.[11] Putting Barrett in a room with Waters, Mason, and Wright in 1975—as actually happened when the group was working on "Shine on You Crazy Diamond"—does not automatically bring the Pink Floyd of *Piper* back into existence. Hence, assemblage of the same parts or group members is not the principle of organization for a musical group—or, when it is, that would only be for special cases.

For most kinds of things, persistence of constituent materials does not constitute an object's persistence over time. (Yet, where historical or personal significance is of primary concern, perseveration of actual materials may be the key test: one doesn't want to inherit a piece of jewelry because it looks like mother's—one wants the actual one she possessed.[12]) Locke also notes that different kinds of things demand differing principles of organization as criteria of identity over time. Furthermore, matters become more complicated once we see that two or more kinds can coexist in the same object. Many popular music groups are also legally incorporated companies.

While I might have used any number of sources here, Locke is particularly useful because he arrives at the insight that we must distinguish between the continuing existence of the same man and the continuation of the same person. The *man* is the animal. The *person* is the combination of consciousness and memory: "For it is by the consciousness [any intelligent being] has of its present thoughts and actions, that it is self to itself now, and so will be the same self, as far as the same consciousness can extend to actions past or to come."[13] Personal identity requires awareness of one's past and ability to think of oneself in future actions. The *man* Syd Barrett was in Abbey Road Studio Three on June 5, 1975, but it was by virtue of his remembering who Waters and Gilmour were that the *person* Syd Barrett was present there that day.

So why do I endorse Locke's claim that we should distinguish between Barrett the man and Barrett the person? Because the person, not the man, is the locus of responsibility—of punishment and reward, of our praise and blame. Locke's own example is the common case of admitting that someone is "not himself" any longer. If someone is temporarily insane and then reverts to sanity, we should not punish them for what happened during the temporary insanity. Consequently, we allow that two different persons can consecutively or even concurrently share the same "man" or body. As this idea is expressed in *Dark Side*'s "Brain Damage," we want to account for times when "there's someone in my head but it's not me."

However, a musical group isn't a living organism, nor a person with persisting consciousness and memory. Insofar as various members of Pink Floyd can be regarded as its replaceable "parts," these parts possess the group's persisting memory and consciousness. Consequently, many scoff at the idea that the *combination* of the "parts" has its own memory, consciousness, or intentions. Since it is not clear how a group of people can share consciousness and so count as a unified agent responsible for its communications, we need something that functions like—yet which will not be identical with—Locke's criterion of personal identity. The nature of the "kind" that underlies group identity requires patient unpacking.

The Echo of a Distant Time: Identity and Change

As my entry point into the specialized case of group identity, I'll examine one of Waters's arguments and critique its underlying assumptions about identity. In the section following this one, I outline my own criteria for group identity, which sets the stage for an examination of group intentions in the remainder of the chapter.

Consider Waters's observation that earlier versions of Pink Floyd didn't need to hire outsiders to write lyrics. Because the Gilmour-era Floyd of *Lapse of Reason* relies on them following Waters's departure, the band ceased to be Pink Floyd. Like most arguments, this one contains an unstated assumption, which is that we can prove that two things are genuinely different by showing some difference in their properties.

Waters seems to be invoking the principle of the identity of indiscernibles: two things (or what seem to be two things) are indiscernible if there is no feature that distinguishes one from the other. Put another way, two things cannot possess numerical identity unless there are no differences between them. Waters postulates a difference. Hence, no identity.

Unfortunately, Waters employs a strict and therefore dubious version of the principle. He assumes that if there is a property that identifies an object, and then time passes and the object loses that property, then this later object cannot be numerically identical with the earlier object. Unfortunately for Waters, his argument about the Gilmour-era group has the same logic as the following one that employs the principle of the identity of indiscernibles in just the same way.[14] In 1967, the group relied on Barrett as sole lyricist. Assuming that Pink Floyd is the same entity in 1967 and 1975, and applying the strict principle of identity, then having Barrett as sole lyricist in 1967 requires Barrett as sole lyricist in 1975. However, in 1975, Waters was sole lyricist, and the application of the principle yields two sole lyricists in 1975. Because a band can't have two different "sole" lyricists, that last step of the argument is absurd. According to the logic of Waters's argument against Gilmour, we should avoid the absurdity by denying that the band called "Pink Floyd" in 1975 is the band that Barrett founded. The same reasoning that "proves" that Pink Floyd no longer existed after Waters quit can also be used to show that Pink Floyd no longer existed once Gilmour was added to the band, or after Barrett was fired, or after Wright was fired, or because Barrett changed the band's repertoire by teaching them the song "Lucifer Sam." According to this use of the identity of indiscernibles, *any* change demonstrates a lack of numerical identity.

Ironically, if Waters seeks a single person who is there at every stage of the group's development, furnishing intentions, the candidate is not Waters. It would be Nick Mason, who was present at all stages of the group's history and the only individual who participated in the creation of every album. However, no one thinks that Mason is the key to understanding whatever Pink Floyd was communicating. No one answers the question "Which one's Pink?" by pointing to Mason.

Some philosophers agree with Waters's use of the principle and endorse the conclusion that nothing endures change.[15] I don't. More importantly, Waters doesn't—he wants to take credit for keeping the band going after Barrett left.

Therefore, we must reconsider the principle of identity by adjusting it for the presence of contingent, relational, and temporary properties. As originally formulated by W.G. Leibniz, the principle does not take account of these, for Leibniz denied that there are contingencies and regarded every feature of every entity as equally essential. Against Leibniz, I think that actual things have nonessential properties. (After all, this book centers on the idea that songs can support contingent, context-dependent meanings.) Most contingent properties are temporary and therefore time-indexed. Thus, a nonessential contingency placed Barrett together with Pink Floyd at Abbey Road Studio in 1975. But once that happened, Barrett's presence at the June 5 recording session became a feature of Pink Floyd's history, and that entity, Pink Floyd, retained that property (the property of Barrett-having-been-present-06/05/1975). For, once acquired, any time-indexed property remains among an entity's properties. So, likewise, if Barrett was sole-lyricist-in-1967 (time-stamping *when* he was sole lyricist), then it is also true of Pink Floyd in 1975 that the band has the property of having Barrett as sole lyricist in 1967. Time-indexed, the property is a stable property once it is acquired.

But making a list of all such contingent properties does not yet provide any criterion of identity. It merely allows that if we knew all the properties that can be correctly predicated of the band, we'd know which questions to ask in order to differentiate it from others. It does not resolve the dispute about whether responsibility-for-creating-*The-Division-Bell* is among the band's properties. Time-indexing various contingencies shows where Waters's argument goes wrong, but it doesn't settle whether there was a Pink Floyd in any given year.

Let's return to Locke's insight that picking out specific features as a guide to identity makes no sense until we ask, "Same what?" We need to specify what *kind* of thing is involved. Here, the kind is a musical group as an ongoing musical collaboration in the strong sense. Relative to this, Waters is saying that the issue of lyricists has a special status in relation to the identity of thing of this kind—it isn't a coincidence or contingency.

To this extent, Waters is on the right track, for he postulates a principle of group organization. I take it that he is saying that no-outsiders-as-songwriters is an essential aspect of collaboration in the strong sense. However, he fails to explain why it is essential to the organization of that specific band, Pink Floyd, for it would be absurd to postulate it of every musical group. The Andrews Sisters did not disband in 1944 by recording the Cole Porter/Robert Fletcher song "Don't Fence Me In" with Bing Crosby. The Dixie Chicks did not cease to be a group in 2002 because they recorded Fleetwood Mac's "Landslide." Hence Waters's appeal to a nothing-written-by-outsiders rule is only valid if it is a special application of some more general and fundamental criterion for group identity of collective musical action. Waters has not identified a feature of the relevant *kind* (ongoing strong collaboration for creating music) that will settle the issue of when the band ended.

To Join in with the Game

Borrowing from Margaret Gilbert's analysis of joint action by small groups, Sondra Bacharach and Deborah Tollefsen have developed a promising account of artwork co-authorship. They begin with the simple case of co-authorship or co-creation of a specific work or text (e.g., the issue of whether Torry really counts as co-author of "The Great Gig in the Sky"), then build up to a model of co-authorship for groups working together over time. Their account of strong collaboration provides basic identity criteria for small groups like Pink Floyd. Here are the significant criteria:[16]

- Each individual commits to working toward at least one goal as a body.
- Each individual is aware of the joint commitment to work toward the goal.
- Each individual understands and endorses various responsibilities and entitlements associated with their commitment.
- Normally, each individual understands and endorses a division of labor among group members.

For purposes of group agency, a group exists when there is mutual understanding among two or more agents that they share a commitment to jointly pursue at least one general goal together. This commitment differentiates group members from individuals who merely carry out tasks in advancing some particular project. Members must also accept a degree of responsibility for success or (or failure!) in relation to that goal. In practical terms, the members of Pink Floyd had to eat while working in the studio making *Dark Side*, but no one thinks that the on-site canteen of Abbey Road Studio collaborated on that album. The workers of the canteen had no commitment to Pink Floyd's formative goal(s): the canteen staff were engaged in the project of supporting the studio's operation, and only incidentally in supporting Pink Floyd when they booked time there. A similar point arises about Dick Parry's saxophone work on *Dark Side*. He supported the project but it was not through a shared understanding that he was committed to an ongoing, strong musical collaboration.

Notice that a commitment to a *general* goal, with ensuing responsibility, is not yet a commitment to any specific goal.[17] The goal of working as a musical collective might or might not be accompanied by an understanding of what the music will be or which specific tasks will be carried out by a particular person. An oboe player in the Vienna Philharmonic is only responsible for playing the oboe, and someone else will normally decide whether any music by Dmitri Shostakovich will be performed that year. And the oboe player is still, by mutual understanding and agreement, a member of the orchestra when it plays a piece that has no oboe part, such as Shostakovich's Chamber Symphony for Strings in C Minor (1960). The commitment to play oboe for the forthcoming year might lead to disappointment or anger about a lack of oboe parts in the music scheduled for that year; yet, the underutilized group member remains a group member. Similarly, being a member of Pink Floyd at the beginning of 1971 did not entail having a commitment to work, in the coming year, on the development of a twenty-three-minute piece of music ("Echoes," occupying all of side two of *Meddle*). Yet that is what they accomplished as the result of working together in pursuit of their more long-term, indeterminate joint commitment to make music together.

So, what happens when a group member's individual intentions and personal goals are no longer compatible with those of the group to which they belong? Or when an individual acts irresponsibly relative to the group's intentions? Such things happen all the time. I teach at a university. Suppose that I personally reject all of the goals set out in my university's long-range plan. I had my chance to comment on the plan during its drafting, but the time for discussing it is over. The plan is now official policy. Unless I quit my job, my working hours should reflect my acceptance of the official goals by virtue of my position in the organization. As an employee, it's my responsibility to support the collective's plans. Should I act on my individual beliefs and sabotage what the university is trying to accomplish, the university would have just cause for terminating me. On the other hand, I might find it too hard to accept the goals, and I might quit.[18] My department might then hire someone to replace me. These actions of terminating an employee and hiring another would be also actions taken by specific individuals acting on behalf of the institution.

Granted, there are many kinds of collectives. Some are tightly organized, with well-defined rules for membership and formal processes for getting work accomplished. The United States Senate is a good example. Other groups are loosely organized. There are no clear rules about who is or isn't a member, and decision procedures are invented (and discarded) on the fly. Fandom often generates a group of this sort—think here of Beatlemania, Deadheads, and Swifties. University departments and rock bands fall somewhere between these two extremes.

However, whether a group is tightly or loosely organized, two basic principles apply.[19] First, the joint commitment implies that individual members of the group cannot nullify a group intention, decision, or plan. Second, no individual member can unilaterally disband the group. (Normally, if one person has the right to unilaterally suspend a project, it is a solo project and only weakly collaborative.) Sometimes, one person wields enough power or influence that he or she has the practical ability—but not the right—to suspend the group's activities or destroy the group. In response, the group has the right to remove such a person from the group if they act against the interests of the group, as determined by the group. Suppose you belong to a book discussion group and you don't want to read *The Wind in the Willows* when it's chosen as the next book to read. You might try to coerce the group by saying that you can't attend next month's meeting—you're in charge of the refreshments, and you know that everyone else comes for the treats as much as for the book discussion. However, if the group then appoints someone else to bring refreshments and meets without you, you have no grounds for complaint. Nor can you stop them from meeting without you as the same book club by declaring it disbanded.

What is true of a loosely organized book club is—suitably adjusted—also true of most ongoing creative collaborations. Another self-governing enterprise by working musicians, the Vienna Philharmonic, formed in 1842. Scores of musicians have joined and left, but its collective identity is unchanged. In contrast, Pink Floyd has not allowed a new member to join since 1968. Its organizational practices will prevent it from existing for 160 years, like the Vienna Philharmonic, or in the way that the Duke Ellington Orchestra and the Sun Ra Arkestra continued to perform after their founders' deaths, still using their founders' names.

Waters may have had legitimate personal reasons for wanting to leave or even disband Pink Floyd. As the individual who'd guided the band during its greatest successes, he probably believed that a post-Waters group would produce music that would embarrass the Pink Floyd name. However, Waters had no power to disband Pink Floyd, and the other members had every right to replace him in any manner they saw fit. Indeed, once Waters saw that he could no longer function within the Pink Floyd framework, he had a personal duty to leave. Furthermore, in the absence of an explicit, shared agreement about what Pink Floyd was trying to accomplish as an organization and how they would do so, the remaining members were perfectly free to reject the working processes that governed the group when Waters was the dominant voice. Just as Barrett's departure did not automatically disband the group as long as the others wanted to continue, Waters's departure did not spell the end for Pink Floyd.

However, the others were not free to do just *anything* and still claim to be Pink Floyd. From the beginning, the group was a group of musicians. Suppose that Gilmour, Mason, and Wright responded to Waters's departure by quitting music, then using the "Pink Floyd" label as the name for a company that restores vintage aircraft. No one should accept *this* project as a continuation of Pink Floyd. This new project has no continuity with the intentions and general goals previously governing the group's activities. Those commitments are, in retrospect, relatively clear. Pink Floyd was a project for collaboratively creating original music and, in concert, presenting both new and old songs from their repertoire. When Gilmour pushed ahead with *Lapse of Reason* and then a tour in support of it, he was acting in keeping with the group's longstanding formative commitment. Waters had every right to leave, but he had no right to deny Gilmour the opportunity to organize these activities on behalf of the group. The fact that Gilmour had to find an alternative way to make Pink Floyd function (e.g., hiring lyricists) does not undercut Pink Floyd's group identity.

My conclusion, then, is that the *Echoes* compilation is an accurate overview of the real Pink Floyd. In the absence of a special agreement otherwise, group identity is independent of the participation of any specific individual. In the absence of some prior group agreement that Pink Floyd ceased to exist if anyone quit, it only took the joint commitment of two remaining members to preserve group identity. "See Emily Play" (1967) and *A Momentary Lapse of Reason* are both communications by Pink Floyd.

Action Brings Good Fortune: Actions, Intentions, and Responsibility

The remainder of this chapter pursues a technical issue stemming from the point that Pink Floyd was a group committed to expression through the medium of popular music. The four points listed at the start of the preceding section enumerate what individuals must understand and endorse. A group can make commitments by virtue of the commitments of its parts (its members). However, to count as a full-fledged communicative agent, a group must be the kind of thing that can have intentions and be held responsible for actions.[20] As such, my preliminary section's account of how groups form and persist must be supplemented with an account of how commitments to pursue collective action relate to group intentions. To be clear, I am not trying to explain the nuts and bolts of group coordination. I am addressing whether it is coherent to attribute intention-based actions to a group, for that is essential to utterance meaning and I want to attribute utterance meaning to Pink Floyd.

I begin with—and will end with—the standard view of how responsibility depends on intentions. We do not, and should not, assign responsibility to every human behavior. Some behaviors are nonvoluntary and do not accrue responsibility. Suppose a newborn cries because she is hungry, disrupting our activities. We should not interpret the infant's behavior in the same way that we should judge, for example, a disgruntled voter who breaks a window in order to trespass into the US capitol building. Although the baby's crying and the protester's vandalism and trespassing are both disruptive behaviors, the baby does not intend to disrupt anyone. Because the trespassers' behaviors at the US capitol on January 6, 2021, were *intended* to disrupt government business, those individuals bear responsibility—provided, of course, they had basic mental competence, including a capacity for forming intentions and then acting on those intentions.[21] Moving to the next step, can we also make sense of the idea that some responsibility for the violence at the US capitol on that day extends to a group, including people who were not present and who never entered the building? Presumably, we would need to show that those who entered were acting either on behalf of, or in collaboration with, persons not physically present. Many who have examined events of that day think that the group Proud Boys encouraged trespassing and violence, and they did so by pragmatic implicature without directly coordinating the actions of those who were present.[22] If that is correct, then any such communication could count as action taken by that group, on the grounds that group action can include utterances made on its behalf.

Let us backtrack for a moment. In Chapter 1, I stressed that different utterances of the same phrase or sentence will have different meanings when they arise from different intentions relative to different contexts. Philosophers of art have often made the additional point that expressive content is no less sensitive to authorship, intentions, and context. Arthur Danto calls attention to an example in a short story by Jorge Luis Borges in which two authors produce identical texts.[23] The first is a segment of the novel *Don Quixote*, written by Miguel de Cervantes in the early seventeenth century. The second is the same word sequence, but written by Pierre Menard in the twentieth. Cervantes is writing about his own time, but Menard is writing about the past; Cervantes intends to parody contemporary novels of chivalry; Menard has no interest in such novels. Although they appear identical, the two works are different in expression and meaning. They are distinct utterances, with distinct utterance meanings. The implication, applied to our case study, is that *The Final Cut* might mean something different if it is a Waters solo album and not genuinely a Pink Floyd album.

But this takes us to the heart of the matter: is an utterance by *Pink Floyd* really possible? How can groups be responsible for utterance meaning? As I noted at the start of this chapter, an intention includes a desire for something to happen as a result of one's actions. Intentions combine with beliefs and feelings to guide actions, so that voluntary, intention-guided behaviors undertaken to achieve one's goals are behaviors that count as actions. How, then, does a group execute an intention-guided behavior, such as communicating with an audience through a group performance or recording? To make sense of it, we face a choice.

On the one hand, we can endorse the idea that intentions are atomistic in the sense that they always belong to specific individuals. This position is sometimes known as agency individualism and I'll adopt that label. According to agency individualism, only individual people can intend things. Therefore, in the same way that a Spanish text about a deluded *caballero andante* has different meanings depending on individual authorship (Cervantes? Menard?), the overall meaning of the *Wish You Were Here* album depends on the intentions and aims of some among the members of Pink Floyd at that time. Their intentions become the relevant ones in determining the utterance meaning.[24] Thus, agency individualism says that if Barrett is the intended referent of the track "Wish You Were Here," that is because an individual—in this case, Waters—intended it. But if Gilmour's expressive music is the linchpin of the piece, then *his* intentions become the relevant ones. If Gilmour didn't intend to express something about Barrett, then it doesn't. Given how the album *Wish You Were Here* is a patchwork of achievements by various individuals, I draw the conclusion that agency individualism denies that it has a unifying utterance meaning.[25]

On the other hand, we can attribute group intentions and agency to Pink Floyd. To distinguish it from agency individualism, let's call it collective agency. A typical objection to collective agency insists that we must first explain how a group or collective can form intentions that cannot be equated with those of the individuals in the group. A group intention seems to require a group mind. However, there is no overarching mind attached to Pink Floyd, so the group cannot have intentions informing the creation of Pink Floyd albums.[26] Nor is there genuine group agency. In other words, the implausibility of *group* intentions over and above the intentions of distinct individuals supports making peace with agency individualism by picking out just one individual as the creative leader of any group. As such, there must be one such person at each stage of Pink Floyd's history (Barrett, then Waters, then Gilmour). Agency individualism of this sort is a commonplace in film studies, where a film's director is assumed to play the role of agent for communicative purposes.[27] However, if we apply agency individualism to popular music, then we must say that one person must be responsible, and the communication is really theirs. Any musical group is collaborative only in the weak sense, and there are no genuine co-authors of communicative actions. To the degree that any Pink Floyd album is coherent, it is actually a weak collaboration with one person serving as a leader with oversight responsibilities, just like Beyoncé's *Lemonade* album.

I grant that weak collaboration is a satisfactory model for some group communication. Obvious cases are Renaissance workshops where a master painter oversaw multiple apprentices and employees who worked together on a single canvas. More recently, there was Andy Warhol's Factory. It might cover many musical collectives, such as the Count Basie Orchestra, the Miles Davis Quintet, or The Fall. The genuine leader might not even be a performer: think here of Phil Spector's role in many girl-group hits, or the role of Svengali-style management companies in relation to many K-pop groups. However, I am not ready to concede and apply this approach to Pink Floyd and many other musical groups. If Barrett merits responsibility for the communicative act that is *The Piper at the Gates of Dawn*, if Waters merits responsibility for *The Final Cut*, and if Gilmour merits responsibility for *Lapse of Reason*, then these are all solo albums masquerading as something else.[28] However, in the same way that the themes of an early novel can shed light on a later novel by the same author, we ordinarily think that two albums by the same band are two communications from the same source. Hence, we should not give up too quickly on strong collective agency and attendant group intentions.

A Smile from a Veil? Hypothetical and Actual Intentions

There are two philosophical accounts of collective agency that allows us to sidestep agency individualism. I examine one of them in this section and the other in the next.

One approach is to unhook agency from the actual intentions of any specific individual. As such, we might adopt hypothetical intentionalism and extend it to groups. This approach interprets song performances and recordings *as if* all of their features were intended by a hypothetical artist who had complete control over all of its properties. We then assume that each utterance was guided by whichever intentions account for the maximally coherent interpretation of the utterance. (If an utterance seems incoherent, we might assume that it was intended to be that way.) In short, utterance interpretation should be based on hypothetical intentions. Once we adopt a stance that is indifferent to anyone's actual intentions, we can interpret a group's output in relation to the best hypothesis of what it would mean if created as the result of unifying intentions. If it is more fun to hear The Kingsmen's "Louie Louie" (1955) as a smutty sex song, then we are licensed to assume that it was intended as such.[29]

Returning to Pink Floyd, the musical "hook" of "Shine on You Crazy Diamond" is a four-note theme on Gilmour's guitar. In the context of the song, the theme represents the fractured state of Barrett's mind. Gilmour composed it more or less accidentally, while improvising. It was Waters's idea to couple Gilmour's "mournful kind of sound" with lyrics about Barrett's absence.[30] To regard "Shine on You Crazy Diamond" as a highly coherent, unified long-form composition, we might prefer to approach it *as if* Gilmour had the same purpose in mind as did Waters.

Nonetheless, I reject the strategy of hypothetical intentionalism. I think that *actual* intentions provide the proper constraint on utterance meaning. I reviewed reasons to endorse actual intentionalism in my Introduction and in Chapter 1. Given that background, it will be sufficient to provide two reasons why the hypothetical version is unsatisfying in this context.[31]

First, I grant that there are cases where hypothetical intentions will give us a more satisfying interpretation, and thus a more positive evaluation. However, we know perfectly well that we shouldn't interpret and evaluate them in that way. Obvious cases are slips of the tongue and mispronounced words. For example, it's very hard to enunciate some words clearly when singing. Lil Nas X's "Old Town Road" (2019) contains a line about taking his horse to the old town road, but as he actually sings it, listeners frequently hear it as "take my horse to a hotel room." A mistaken interpretation can be more interesting than one that conforms to actual intentions—the hypothesis that "hotel room" was meant is better. His actual line doesn't say much, but the misheard line is funny. Yet the intended words are the words, and they should be the basis for interpretation. Likewise, someone who hears the phrase "ordinary men" in

Pink Floyd's "Us and Them" as "old and hairy men" has just got it wrong, no matter how much they think it improves the song.

Second, hypothetical intentionalism tells us that we gain nothing by consulting interviews with Waters and Gilmour in order to get a better understanding of the music and songs. If actual intentions don't matter, then knowing what the musicians say about their work should not guide our interpretation and evaluation. However, I think that I have a better understanding of *Wish You Were Here* because I've read interviews with Waters in which he clarifies his actual intentions.[32]

Let's take stock. *The Final Cut*, *A Momentary Lapse of Reason*, and several other albums are only relevant to our interpretation of communications by the *group*, Pink Floyd, if they are intended to be treated as such. We should not pick and choose based on the outcome that pleases fans the most, as would be allowed by hypothetical intentionalism. The trick will be how to attribute intentions to the group.

Like a Cardboard Cut-Out Man? Strong Collectives as Individuals

A guiding idea of this book is that there is a close connection between intentions and communication. My initial chapters argued that understanding a communicative action sometimes requires understanding the guiding intentions behind it, for without recourse to these we cannot determine an utterer's meaning for the communication. This will be equally true also when the music is created collaboratively in the strong sense. It seems that Pink Floyd is a good candidate for an ongoing group organized around a commitment to strong collaboration. Consequently, attribution of collective agency directs us to sometimes inquire after the actual intentions of Pink Floyd, and therefore we must agree with Tollefsen that "organizations *really do* have intentional states."[33]

But suppose that "Shine on You Crazy Diamond" was not intended to be about Barrett when Gilmour first came up with the music. Waters added lyrics and he intended those lyrics to be about Barrett. If only one of four members of the group intended "Shine on You Crazy Diamond" to be about Barrett, how can the group, Pink Floyd, intend it? How, then, to attribute actual intentions to a group operating with strong collaboration, rather than reassign such projects to either of two other categories: weak collaboration where one person has leadership and overall control, and those where various contributions are never fully coordinated, and devolve in multiply authored or co-authored constructs?[34]

Recall that the principal argument against genuine joint action is the lack of a group mind to direct such action. However, rather than stress the connection between intentions and mental states, a number of philosophers of action examine the link between intentions and assignment of responsibility for planning and acting.[35] Agency depends on intentions. To postulate responsibility for agency is to postulate intentions, too. The fact that it is sometimes right to direct normative responses toward collectives implies that we think that they collectively display enough coordinated, rational agency to establish that the group possesses group intentions.[36] I take it that Johnny Rotten was engaging in a normative response to Pink Floyd when he walked around London in 1975, wearing a shirt that read "I Hate Pink Floyd." In making a statement about the group—and not "I Hate David Gilmour"—he was expressing the point that his personal world view was at odds with their collective message. As I argued in Chapter 3, normative responses can be relevant as a response to a musical persona. If that is the case for an individual, it is also the case for a group. Responsibility for group action falls on everyone who entered into the joint commitment to pursue collective goals and who has remained with that group as they selected various means to achieve their goals. When those goals include communication with an audience by way of creative agency, as with ongoing music groups, then continuing members give tacit consent to whatever the group communicates and they are jointly responsible for its meaning. In short, a nonsinging member of a group cannot proclaim innocence about its meaning when the group records "Oh! Susanna" (1848) and includes its racist lyrics, nor can they escape some degree of responsibility so long as they continue to be a member.

The upshot is that we do not need to determine whether the individual members of Pink Floyd came to any clear agreement about what they were trying to do with *Wish You Were Here*. Anyone who's familiar with this style of music can tell that the album has an admirable conceptual unity. It is ultimately irrelevant which parts were due to which group members, or whether was internal disagreement about anything that ended up on the album. Discovering, as I recently did, that one of my favorite passages on the album is the work of Wright makes me think better of Wright, but knowing that he contributed that bit is not relevant to my assessment of what the album communicates as a statement by Pink Floyd.

It is easy to become confused about what is being claimed here. After all, I've allowed that the words to "Shine on You Crazy Diamond" are Waters's words, reflecting Waters's intentions. Furthermore, these words have a lot to do with the album's conceptual coherence. So, someone might object, haven't I actually endorsed agency individualism or reverted to a form of hypothetical intentionalism by adopting an "as if one person" stance toward the group?[37]

As Tollefsen emphasizes, assignment of collective responsibility underwrites the claim that the group has a unifying intentional state, which is why I emphasized the link between action, intention, and responsibility in the preceding section. Granted, collective agency is normally accomplished by distributing responsibilities among individuals who are empowered to carry out specific activities on behalf of the group. Collaborative group agency always depends on individual agency, but if it is group agency, the group as a whole and consequently all its members can be held responsible for the actions of some of its members.[38] I think this is particularly true when the members are parties to a joint commitment of the sort outlined in the above section. Every soldier present at the Wounded Knee Massacre (1890) has blood on his hands even if he did not directly kill anyone. How far up the chain of command this goes is a question we need not settle here. Some theorists recognize that the group can be spontaneous and less formally organized, and thus everyone who joined the Tulsa race massacre (1921) bears some responsibility for the deaths and the destruction.[39]

Similarly, normative responses can be directed at Pink Floyd in full knowledge of the fact that different members play different roles in bringing about the results that we admire or criticize. All members have responsibilities to further the goals of the group even when, as individuals, they do not wish to do so. Knowing that *The Wall* had to be finished in time for the Christmas sales period of 1979, Wright should not have made himself unavailable by going to Greece for a vacation.

Because we can criticize individuals for what they do or fail to do within the group, it is tempting to suppose that we must *always* assign praise or blame to specific individuals each time we evaluate group activity. However, there is no reason to think that Johnny Rotten knew how many members were in Pink Floyd, much less who they were, when he wore a shirt that insulted them. A normative response to a group action is not equivalent to a normative response to specific individuals within the collective—witness a 1996 interview where Rotten (that is, John Lydon) said he still hates Pink Floyd, but that doesn't interfere with his ability to "get on well" with David Gilmour.[40] Specific individuals may have carried out actions that elicit positive or negative response, but the normative response can be directed to the group rather than any individual. Because intentions can guide an action without being consciously formalized, Pink Floyd (the strongly collaborative group) can be the communicative agent without internal explicit consensus about what is being communicated on any given occasion.[41] As a communicative agent, the group has group intentions even if some members are unaware of or indifferent about them.

The upshot is that in any case where a group is collaborative in the strong sense and the group commitment is organized around communicative activity, we have collective agency and collective responsibility for the communication. In turn, group intentions inform those communications, and therefore all ongoing members endorse, tacitly if not overtly, the content of any communication for which the group takes credit. It is not a mistake to think about Pink Floyd's communicative intentions in relation to *A Momentary Lapse of Reason*.

Conclusion

This chapter started with the question of whether there is a criterion of identity for Pink Floyd that will settle the question of whether, for example, the Gilmour-era group is "fake" Floyd. To that end, let's retrace our steps. In claiming that *Lapse of Reason* and the ensuing tour is not Pink Floyd, Waters gave flimsy reasons to think Pink Floyd disbanded. However, in doing so he raised the interesting question of the identity of the group that "authored" this body of music. A core premise of pragmatics is that actual intentions inform utterer's meaning, and therefore a proper understanding of a group's meaning in performing or releasing its music also depends on reference to the group's actual intentions. But if we dodge the idea of group intentions by deflecting to the intentions of distinct individuals who participate in the activity, we will replace strong collaboration with either multiple authorship, weak collaboration, or hypothetical authorship. Many philosophers, musicologists, and popular culture scholars will endorse one of those choices. However, I have outlined the case that we give up too much if we deny that Pink Floyd really did have intentional states.

Part Three

Intertextuality

6

Kids're Forming Bands: Making Meaning in Post-Punk

About the best poetry, and not only the best, there floats an atmosphere of infinite suggestion.

—A.C. Bradley

Paradoxically, effective communication arises through both conformity with, and violations of, established conventions. Pattern processing is central to cognition, and therefore successful communication with popular song exploits both affinities and contrasts with other music that the audience is likely to have heard. The present chapter discusses how the unavoidable practice of *grouping* music and musicians with other music and musicians can support complex communication, especially with respect to the music's expressive properties. As such, this chapter broadens the scope of context beyond Chapter 5's narrower focus on a musical group's prior work as providing context for understanding communication in popular song.

In philosophy, the classic essay on this topic is Kendall Walton's discussion of perceptually distinguishable art categories, such as impressionist paintings and Brahmsian music.[1] Music and paintings and other artworks inevitably share features with at least some other works, and these shared perceptual features often constitute a common style. I will supplement this well-known thesis with the point that cultural movements also serve as unifying categories, and they do so despite their lack of stylistic coherence. I discussed art movements of this sort when reviewing the distinction between modernism and Romanticism in Chapter 4, and the present chapter extends that discussion by examining categories that inform musical communication and yet which do not coalesce into perceptually distinguishable categories.

To this end, I will concentrate on post-punk as a distinct category of musical classification, and how that classification is relevant to the meaning of several key examples.[2] As the name implies, post-punk stands in some kind of relationship with punk. If the term "post-punk" is not arbitrary, a distinction between punk and post-punk ought to reflect a difference in the way(s) in which the sounds are organized to facilitate a listener's discovery of meaning in those sounds. However, I will argue, it does not follow that punk and post-punk are contrasting styles of music. The latter is better understood as a relatively short-lived popular music adaptation of a larger cultural movement.[3]

Neighborhoods, Not Essences

The phrase "post-punk" implies a body of music that postdates punk, but its origins were fully contemporaneous with the rise of punk in the 1970s. Describing music as "post-punk" carries the unfortunate implication that it stands to punk as postmodernism stands to modernism, that is, as a repudiating offspring. However, important post-punk bands predate the heyday of punk. The dada-influenced Cabaret Voltaire and Pere Ubu formed in 1973 and 1975, respectively. Consequently, the label does not indicate chronological sequence.

This initial proposal faces the obvious objection that no one talked about "post-punk" until punk became a stable category, and therefore "post-punk" implies chronology. This objection is overturned by observing that every historical phenomenon arises from antecedent preconditions. Following the lead of Clinton Heylin, it is plausible that nascent modes of punk were present as early as 1970.[4] However, this admission allows that post-punk was also in play for some time before punk style coalesced in Great Britain in 1976 and before post-punk was subsequently identified as a related movement. An analogous situation in the visual arts would be the assertion that Paul Cézanne was the first Cubist painter, on the grounds that he produced Cubist paintings long before the work of Georges Braque and Pablo Picasso triggered public recognition of Cubism in 1908. As such, Henri Matisse's Fauve paintings of 1905 and 1906 are a response to Cubism even if most art histories offer a chronology in which Fauvism predates Cubism.[5] Something very similar is true of punk and post-punk.

Ultimately, the issue of chronology is irrelevant unless the two categories differ in some meaningful way. To adopt a philosophical perspective, consider Socrates's foundational question about the problem of classification. Faced with a bewildering list of examples of virtues, he changes the subject and asks, "What is the nature of the bee?... do bees differ as bees...?... tell me what is the quality in which they do not differ, but are all alike."[6] Faced with an astounding range of music that might be classified as post-punk, any inquiry into its nature is question begging if we confine ourselves to cherry-picked examples without articulating an organizing principle. Is there, Socrates asks, a unifying feature in which their manifest diversity does not differ, in which the examples are all alike? Or are they a chronological hodge-podge, grouped according to the simultaneity of their production at a certain time and place? Imagine a classificatory term, Finjav, that covers Finnish and Javanese music for the period 1914 through 2007, and then consider how strange it would be to create an academic department of Finjav Studies. In order to avoid this sort of gerrymandered classification, inquiry into post-punk might *begin* by selecting Gang of Four and The Raincoats (or some other central examples) as paradigm cases of post-punk. The next step is exclusionary: we want to deny the post-punk status of a Rachel Sweet single on Stiff Records in 1978 and Donna Summer's early hits for Casablanca Records (before its purchase by a major conglomerate). These exclusions show that post-punk's emergence on independent record labels is relevant, but not decisive, for a lot of well-known pop and disco was released by independents. Likewise, geography is highly relevant, but not decisive: although both Def Leppard and the core of The Human League formed in Sheffield in 1977, Def Leppard is not post-punk.

However, defending specific groupings is a side issue. My initial goal is to highlight the way that some groupings (e.g., disco and reggae) consist of perceptually distinguishable categories, but some do not. Yet both kinds of categories carry implications for musical communication. Because utterance meaning depends on context, auditors can only recover some meanings by reference to the complex interplay of musical style and the musicians' own understanding of how they position their music in relation to their sociocultural position. By the latter, I do not simply mean their immediate subcultural identity. I also mean their relationship to larger cultural movements that they may join or reject while only marginally aware of the implications for doing so.

Methodologically, I want to stress that all these classifications are moving targets. Musical classifications that are made in hindsight about the 1970s may be out of kilter with some assumptions made by listeners in the 1970s. Today, it is surprising to find that the second edition of *The Rolling Stone Illustrated History of Rock & Roll* identifies Dave Edmunds and Graham Parker as paradigms of British new wave music, as if new wave is an offshoot of pub rock.[7] Three decades after the fact, readers are apt to be surprised by Greil Marcus's idea, in 1981, that Belinda Carlisle's "hardcore credentials" in The Germs are a reason to regard the Go-Go's as a post-punk band, like The Slits and The Raincoats.[8] However, I did not classify Edmunds, Parker, and The Go-Go's as *stylistically* related to Gang of Four and The Human League when I purchased their records when they were first released, and the passage of time has reinforced my resistance to classifying them together. That The Slits, The Raincoats, and The Go-Go's are all feminist bands speaks neither for nor against status as post-punk.

So, do we have anything that serves as an organizing principle for post-punk? That question, which is Socrates's question about bees, unifies this chapter. Unfortunately, citing Socrates invites the objection that the answer will be found in an ahistorical essence, in violation of Stewart Home's observation that the subject is "fluid and its boundaries are subject to ongoing renegotiation."[9] Home's point is important. It reminds us that the very activity of discussing the boundaries contributes toward their renegotiation. Consequently, the following analysis should not be regarded as a description of a fixed essence of the sort Socrates sought, but rather as an attempt to identify relationships among landmarks within a disputed terrain. Above all, the important landmarks ought to relate to what happens musically, or at least they ought to do so when "punk" and "post-punk" serve as *musical* classifications.

With that point in mind, consider a comment that Grateful Dead guitarist and vocalist Jerry Garcia made about new music in 1977. It was becoming apparent that there was a new music movement that was not reducible to punk, and the phrase "New Wave" was gaining currency. That year, Phonogram/Vertigo capitalized on the movement by marketing a compilation album called *New Wave*, which veered away from punk by including The Boomtown Rats, Talking Heads, and New York Dolls.[10] Asked what he thought about the new music in 1977, Garcia answered, "It's nice that kids're forming bands and all that but sooner or later they're gonna wanna hear real music."[11]

Real music? What does Garcia mean, "real music"? Coming from a countercultural icon who should have recognized kindred spirits in the music in question, Garcia's dismissal is simultaneously elitist and hypocritical. Nonetheless, it is interesting because it so perfectly captures a paradox about the process of mapping meanings onto musical phenomena. For if Garcia is correct, the enterprise of finding meaning in post-punk music is a shallow one. Conversely, a philosophical account of this topic might explain how Garcia grasped something important about the new music that was emerging into the commercial mainstream in 1977, and I will offer some thoughts in that direction.

Ironically, Garcia's offhand dismissal might capture something important about post-punk's organizing principle, which is that neither listening nor academic analysis can be motivated by a narrow focus on what post-punk music sounds like. This position is endorsed in the broad methodological recommendation of David Shumway: "I want to say more than merely that rock & roll is an impure musical form; it is not even mainly a musical form."[12] While I will challenge that claim in Chapter 9, he is correct to say that rock is "a historically specific cultural practice" involving a unique combination of specific social conditions and technological developments.[13] Yes, but it is something more. Notice that Garcia's comment is directed at the music, not at the politics or the safety pins or the cultural moment. The members of Gang of Four and The Human League are first and foremost musicians, not agents provocateur, and post-punk is first and foremost a historically localized *musical* practice.[14] There is little reason to examine the past through the prism of a musical movement unless listeners can *audibly* correlate ideas and musical strategies shared by different musicians with shared backgrounds and interests. At the same time, musical groupings are not always stylistic groupings, which necessitate appeal to other kinds of contextualization when thinking about the pragmatics of some instances of popular music.

To deflect a potential misunderstanding, I want to reemphasize that my approach to musical meaning rejects a narrowly formalistic or purely structural methodology. At the risk of becoming repetitious, my view is that music's meaningfulness derives from the fact that musical practices are cultural practices, where the recognition of human-made meaning requires a grasp of cultural context. As with any other utterance, the meaningfulness of a post-punk recording depends on its intertextual connections to other meaningful texts. To paraphrase Paul Ziff, what any given song or recording means depends on what various other songs and recordings in the same language mean.[15] For purposes of the following argument, "the language" will be the broad sweep of popular music, especially during the late twentieth century. To put it another way, the old myth of the autonomy of the musical masterpieces of the classical canon was ultimately a denial of meaningfulness. Nonetheless, it cannot be the case that the scope of the language is a mere idiolect, that is, a mode of making meaning that is unique to a single individual. If composer Daniel Miller were the only one who could ever understand the meaning of The Normal's "T.V.O.D." (1978), then the track would not have a meaning. At the other extreme, if the words are nonsensical placeholders that contribute nothing more for those who know English than for those who do not, then we should doubt that it means anything determinate, at least in the words. In short, some community of shared language users is a prerequisite of song meaning. Semantics and pragmatics are interrelated.

However, languages develop sub-communities. As Ludwig Wittgenstein suggests, a language is like a city with many neighborhoods, and some suburbs are hard to reach from some others.[16] Pursuing this metaphor, this question arises: if Jerry Garcia and Daniel Miller are from different musical boroughs, perhaps even different countries, on what basis do we think that The Normal, The Fall, and Joy Division occupy the same musical neighborhood? Stylistically, The Normal and Cabaret Voltaire are close neighbors on the musical map, but they do not share a musical style with The Raincoats, The Fall, and Joy Division. To group these five bands together is to appeal to a mode of categorization that is not a perceptually distinguishable category.

Style versus Movement

Garcia's dismissal of the music of punk and new wave music reminds us that it is often difficult to *situate* path-breaking music when listeners encounter it in its historical moment. Conversely, categorizing a recording decades after its production usually reflects conscious engagement with its history. The question, then, is whether twenty-first-century listeners are better positioned in relation to this music than Garcia was. But is it really any easier to make sense of post-punk now? Ironically, Garcia may have been gesturing toward something important. The post-punk movement was, *and remains*, difficult to interpret because it lacks stylistic identity. To pursue Wittgenstein's metaphor: the fact that several new suburbs simultaneously develop in one city does not always put them next to one another, and it may be that various strands of post-punk are suburbs on opposite sides of a large city. If it remains difficult to achieve retrospective interpretive agreement, it might be because we are dealing with something that lacks any perceptually distinguishable unification. This point is particularly apt in light of Simon Frith's contemporaneous assessment that post-punk was fundamentally an attempt "to reorganize the meaning of rock devices."[17] Pursuing the map metaphor, Garcia was unable to place them on his mental map of musical language, and so he could not extract meaning from them. Moving beyond Wittgenstein's metaphor, I propose to adopt a familiar distinction from art history, the distinction between art styles and movements.

In the fields of music, literature, and the visual arts, works by artistic contemporaries tend to display stylistic similarities, that is, perceptibly shared characteristic modes of expression.[18] Style, says art critic Meyer Schapiro, "is, above all, a system of forms with a quality and a meaningful expression through which the personality of the artist and the broad outlook of a group are visible."[19] Or audible, as the case may be.

Because it gives us a nice parallel with punk and post-punk, let us expand on Schapiro's point by contrasting impressionist and post-impressionist paintings. Following Roger Fry's lead in selecting painters for two post-impressionism exhibitions in 1910 and 1912, histories of post-impressionism standardly include Paul Cezanne's proto-cubism, Georges Seurat's pointillism, and Henri Matisse's fauvism. Yet these three painters do not share a common style, that is, their work does not belong to a perceptually distinguishable category. To paraphrase Walton, their paintings do not share any immediately perceivable gestalt quality, a quality that will depend on the presence of standard features that can be pointed out to us if we don't understand the basis of the grouping.[20] Post-impressionism is an art movement rather than a style.

Shifting from painting to music, suppose we play the following four songs in some random order for people with a lot of exposure to 1970s popular music: Nina Simone's recording of "Baltimore" (1978), Patti Smith's "Redondo Beach" (1975), the Bee Gees' "Stayin' Alive" (1977), and First Choice's "Love Thang" (1979). Asked to classify the music, our auditors will almost certainly volunteer that the first two are reggae and the second pair are disco. Although the vocals are very different in all four examples, the basic patterns of the first pair clearly embody reggae rhythms, and the second pair disco rhythms. And their characteristic approaches to rhythms—the "replication of patterning" they share with so much other music[21]—provide these tracks with their *general* musical style despite the distinct *individual* or personal styles of the vocalists. Conversely, if we play those four tracks for someone who is *not* familiar with these two musical styles, it may simply be enough to point out which two belong to each pairing for the novice listener to recognize that a common gestalt quality is shared by "Baltimore" and "Redondo Beach" and a different one is shared by the disco tracks.

Although my example emphasizes attention to rhythmic patterns, style differentiation in popular music is not simply a matter of how rhythms are handled. Distinctive strategies of patterning appear in harmony, melody, rhythm, and texture. There is also song form (e.g., strophic or through composed?), lyric structure (e.g., couplets, quatrains, or both?), as well as a track's production style (e.g., Liz Phair's indie low-fi for *Exile in Guyville* (1993) versus the glossy sheen of her eponymous 2003 release). Thus, a musical style is a gestalt emerging from a distinctive combination of several kinds of patterning, and an individual musician or group will develop an individual style by adopting a distinctive method of handling the general style.[22] At the same time, Walton notes, artists gain expressive power by combining contrastandard features with the standard features of an established style. Thus, while the popular music of the past eighty years is overwhelmingly homophonic in texture, with sung melody supported by the other patterns, Simon and Garfunkel stood out within the 1960s "folk" style by highlighting polyphonic texture in "Scarborough Fair/Canticle" (1966).

We are now positioned to see why it is so important to group musical performances and tracks according to style. In Stephanie Ross's succinct summary,

> Knowing the style of a work of art is a prerequisite to correct understanding and appreciation of it. Only after first placing a work in the correct style category can we answer the interpretive questions about its tone, its representational and expressive content, its overall meaning.[23]

In short, situating an artwork within a general style is a necessary step for identifying the context that gives it meaning. In turn, a general style is a precondition for the individual style that fine-tunes the meanings of individuals working within that style.[24]

Thus, style is one of the preconditions for utterance meaning in visual art and music. To illustrate these points, let's consider an example from the art of painting, followed by an example of popular song.

I am hardly the first to borrow E.H. Gombrich's example of Piet Mondrian's *Broadway Boogie Woogie* (1943). The painting is mostly white canvas, intermittently decorated with a grid of thin yellow lines dotted with blue and red. To the uninitiated, it can look stiff, formal, and minimalist, and thus emotionally rather chilly. However, seen as a variant of the abstract style that the Dutch cleverly called De Stijl ("The Style"), it is frenetic, colorful, and joyous—Mondrian's celebration of the city to which he'd recently emigrated, and of its music.[25] The painting's infectious gaiety stems from its contrast with both the general gestalt of De Stijl and the bulk of Mondrian's paintings in that style: much of the meaning of *Broadway Boogie Woogie* emerges through contrast with its more minimalist precursors, many of which feature a grid of black on white with only six or seven isolated patches of color.

Similarly, popular song recordings deliver a parallel emotional punch by adopting a contra-standard arrangement. The Beatles' "Yesterday" (1965) is an obvious example. Featuring only acoustic guitar, a standard string quartet playing with minimal vibrato, and Paul McCartney's voice, it was originally sequenced between the up-tempo rockers "I've Just Seen a Face" and "Dizzy Miss Lizzy" at the end of the *Help!* Album. Heard there, as the Beatles intended, it violates every sonic expectation that an auditor would have had for the music on a Beatles album in 1965. It is subdued, sparse, and elegant. Consequently, it is devastatingly heartbreaking. At the same time, the use of the quartet, rather than massed strings, distances it from the mainstream pop of the era, as well as from the glossy arrangements on Buddy Holly's several tracks with strings (Holly being a major influence on the Beatles). And, of course, the radical arrangement (relative to pop music in 1965) had a nonexpressive implication. The group was musically smarter—perhaps "deeper"—than fans had suspected. And, to be very clear, the point here is to see that deviations from established style contribute to expressivity, and *not* that expressive character is somehow inherent in the music.[26]

Yet, important as it is, style isn't everything when it comes to the production of expressive feature and indirect meaning. Participation in a *movement* contributes, too. As I noted earlier, post-impressionism and post-punk are both stylistically diverse. They are not perceptually distinguishable categories. Walton observes that, stylistically, Cezanne's paintings can be grouped with the impressionists. Why, then, did Fry group his work with van Gogh and Matisse as post-impressionism? My answer is that his organizational category is that of movement, not style, and not every post-impressionist painter made a clean break from the impressionist visual gestalt. However, as the growing movement nudged more painters in the direction of full-blown modernism, it splintered into an array of new styles. For art movements, the Socratic "quality in which they do not differ" is not to be located in shared style.

The lack of a unifying perceptible gestalt for major art movements becomes even more noticeable when we attend to the way that they tend to be multi-modal. Many movements spread across literature, music, and the visual arts. For example, popular music fans do not find it discordant that a musical style aligns with a fashion style, design style, and even a graphic style. However, considered as musical style, punk has no more inherent affinity with its associated visual style than the pairing of Edwardian-style clothing and rockabilly music in the rockabilly revival of the British 1970s. Few if any perceptible cues associate that music with that clothing, so their pairing comes across as arbitrary to American outsiders who did not know that teddy boys were the antecedent historical and cultural basis for the combination. Absent that history, a different cross-modal pairing of sound and fashion might have been equally apt.[27]

I will offer two personal anecdotes to illustrate the relative independence of fashion and sound. Resistance to punk music in the American entertainment media is usually regarded as a historical impetus for the substitution of "New Wave" as a newer, hipper, more accessible category. Personally, I can recall at least three times between 1979 and 1984 when, talking to people who had an interest in music, they professed to never having heard *any* punk music. They all had a very clear idea of what punk *looked* like. They said that they did not know what it *sounded* like. Each time, when I played them something (in at least one case it was the first Clash album), they were quite surprised. While punk visuals struck them as novel, the music struck them as nothing more than ordinary guitar-heavy rock music. Whatever punk was supposed to sound like, recorded punk did not intuitively correlate with visual punk. Similarly, speaking from my own experience, am I the only one to have found the music on David Bowie's *The Rise and Fall of Ziggy Stardust and the Spiders from Mars* (1972) to be disappointingly conventional compared with the visual persona of Ziggy and the Spiders? The music and the visual persona are stylistically linked only through contingent historical association.

Cultural Cues: Audible and Otherwise

Attending to musical style, auditors focus on *audible* cues for making meaning. However, that is precisely what post-punk fails to offer, for it is not a perceptually distinguishable category. Where an informed audience cannot locate audible similarities between Cabaret Voltaire's "Sluggin' for Jesus" (1981) and the Buzzcocks's "Boredom" (1977), these tracks are not united by style. As with Cezanne and impression, "Boredom" is stylistically similar to a number of punk tracks, particularly those of the Sex Pistols.[28] Rather than sounding like the guitar-driven Buzzcocks, the new electronics employed by Cabaret Voltaire are stylistically linked to The Human League and Throbbing Gristle and, on some recordings, to The Associates. Listen, specifically, to the nonvocal musical soundscapes of "Sluggin' for Jesus," The Human League's "Dancevision" (1980), and The Associates's "White Car in Germany" (1981). (If there is a temptation to exclude the Buzzcocks from this sample on the grounds that they count as a punk band, The Fall can be substituted in their place.) Why, apart from the accident of time and place, does anyone group any two or three of these four bands together as post-punk? After all, shared time and place do not encourage us to group together The Human League, Sex Pistols, and Def Leppard beyond the overly broad category of 1970s British rock bands. In seeking something that is audibly common across a range of post-punk, there appears to be no more stylistic agreement than for any three randomly chosen rock bands from the British pop charts of 1978.

Here is another complication, and not simply regarding audible differences between punk, post-punk, and metal. Although the individual style of a musician or band is normally a variant of a more general, shared style, it is often a variant of more than one. There are striking audible similarities, both musically and vocally, between The Associates's "The Affectionate Punch" (1980) and "White Car in Germany" and a number of Talking Heads tracks, particularly from *Fear of Music* (1979). There are some very strong musical similarities (but not vocal) between Talking Heads and the guitar-bass-drums interplay of the instrumental passages in Scritti Politti's "P.A.'s" (1979). With respect to vocal style, however, Green Gartside's singing has more in common with Michael Jackson's voice than with David Byrne's singing. If style is the audible entry point into the ideas informing the music, but post-punk is not a *unified* style, then how does grouping the music together as post-punk help us to interpret that music?

To better understand this point, consider a parallel issue in art history. Art historians distinguish between the art nouveau style and the art deco style. Following exposure to a limited number of examples, most people can readily distinguish art nouveau architectural style from art deco style without any supplementary knowledge about the actual origins of the particular buildings. However, as I noted in Section 2, this usage of the term "style" does not extend to works in distinct perceptual modalities. Thus, although it is commonly said that Claude Debussy composed music in an impressionist style, rather than, say, an art nouveau style, the connection is a historical contingency. The lack of stylistic commonalities between different perceptual modes is one reason that art historians supplement the notion of style with those of genre, movement, and school.[29] Debussy, Maurice Ravel, and Claude Monet were not practitioners of the same style. Instead, they belonged to a common art movement. Approached from another perspective, a historically informed awareness that Stephane Mallarmé influenced Debussy supports classification of both artists as Symbolists; yet, it would be unsound to take another step and to infer that therefore there must be a shared Symbolist style.

Likewise, there is no good reason to expect the Raincoats, The Fall, and Cabaret Voltaire to share a style in the sense of sounding like one another. If it is appropriate to group them together as post-punk, then post-punk is a musical movement. It is a "movement" as that term is used in art history when talking of the Realist movement, the Romantic movement, the Impressionist movement, and so on. Post-punk bands and recordings belong to a nonperceptual category that consists of the sharing of ideas, values, and artistic goals. Once again, I propose that shared intentions matter here.

The phrase "art movement" occurs frequently in overviews of the history of visual art, and my task would be much simpler if I could simply cite a standard analysis of what that means. However, it's a term that has received surprisingly little attention.[30] Returning again to the example of Cezanne and post-impressionism, a recent overview of art jargon observes, of post-impressionism, that it is "largely unified by its rejection of Impressionist ideals while still using some Impressionist techniques."[31] As another such book similarly remarks, "the neo-classical movement of the late eighteenth century was perhaps the first art movement in which general intellectual concerns preceded actual artistic practice."[32] In short, while not every art movement is like Futurism in having a public manifesto, there is a working consensus that art movements are unified by reference to a shared set of general ideals about what sort of art should be produced. (As such, movements are akin to ongoing strong collaborations discussed in Chapter 5, but are more loosely organized.)

If movements are unified more by the "what" than the "how to" of artmaking and music-making, the flexibility of movements is a practical application of another thesis endorsed by most art historians. Specifically, no work of art is to be understood in terms of a "natural" and intuitively unambiguous connection of form and content.[33] Stylistic differences may mislead us into thinking that two painters or musicians have little in common, when in fact they may be using different materials and composition strategies to express the same ideas and values. Caspar David Friedrich and Eugène Delacroix are both Romantic painters, but stylistically they have little or nothing in common. Thus, mere familiarity with style is insufficient to unlock meanings, for style underdetermines meaning. Grasping the Romantic dimensions of Friedrich and Delacroix requires understanding how their symbol systems express a shared worldview. This metacritical perspective explains why it is inherently more difficult to understand music in relation to a broader artistic movement than in relation to a singular musical style. Movements share fewer commonalities to guide the audience, because a single artistic movement may be mediated by many styles. Thus, relevance-groupings that guide interpretation are not always revealed in manifest properties.

To summarize the argument up to this point, styles are recognizable, perceptually manifest entry points into larger social and cultural movements. Yet there are no necessary connections between such movements and their various perceptual manifestations. As with all non-natural meaning, the linkage is ultimately due to shared cultural practices and the intentions of participants in relation to these practices. Different styles can be used to convey common meanings and values, while the multiplication of styles will then tend to obscure the degree of agreement.

I propose that this multiplication of stylistic entry points was unusually rampant in the post-punk movement. Classifying post-punk as a movement directs us to find commonalties in the musicians' aims—a matter both of what they want to achieve, and what they want to avoid—more than in how the music sounds. The pluralism of the music will reflect multiple strategies in achieving common aims.

Modernism on the Jukebox

The immediate relevance of the distinction between style and movement is that any contrast of punk and post-punk will become sidetracked by excessive focus on issues of shared musical style. This point can be illustrated by considering Simon Reynolds's history of post-punk, *Rip It Up and Start Again: Postpunk 1978-1984*.[34] I will endorse some of Reynolds's claims while questioning others.

Reynolds proposes that post-punk is simultaneously "a distinct pop-cultural epoch" and a style.[35] But if post-punk is a movement, then the argument of my last section implies that it should not be expected to display a unified style. Although many styles of music were played and had considerable popularity during the years

1978–84, post-punk was importantly novel within popular music at that time. What happened in post-punk, Reynolds proposes, is that artistic modernism finally became the model for popular music.[36] His characterization of modernism is terse and must be supplemented. Let me expand on Reynold's brief characterization of modernism by citing this one, by David Summers:

> With modernism,... transparency, both of meaning and of pictorial means, began to change. ... The 'usual' [interpretive] expectation lives on, however, animating both 'usual' reaction to works of art and their interpretation, or expectation of interpretability. An unsophisticated viewer might express hostility to a work that seems to block such understanding. Perhaps more frequently, however, this same viewer is intimidated by his or her own puzzlement, and the [interpretive] expectation is exploited to mystify and dignify work, artist, and apparent cognoscenti, at the same time that it stratifies and classifies them relative to the viewer, all because it is assumed by the viewer that there must be some higher meaning he or she is for some reason inadequate to judge.[37]

The important point in this description of modernism is that stylistic experimentation creates an ongoing divide between the means adopted by artists and expectations of their contemporaries. The result is that the modernist musician refuses to spoon-feed listeners with "transparent" meanings. To achieve this end, modernist music is designed to resist the listener's standard expectations of immediate interpretability.

Reynolds's appeal to modernism carries two implications. First, it implies that post-punk is a movement within a larger cultural movement. Second, it implies that the formative goals of post-punk are antithetical to stylistic consistency. If post-punk is an offshoot of artistic modernism, then that does much of the work of explaining its lack of stylistic unity—rather than, for example, endorsing Theodor Adorno's view that popular music succeeds through a constant, albeit trivial, "pseudo-individualization."[38]

These points suggest a methodological problem for Reynolds, who appears to hold that post-punk is a general musical style within modernism. However, *listening* to a range of examples supports the contrary position that post-punk should be organized into several distinct styles within a common movement (if, indeed, there is a single movement). To refresh this argument with a new example, there are audible stylistic similarities between Young Marble Giants and The B52s. However, the inclusion of The Fall, Throbbing Gristle, and Joy Division in the same group either undercuts the claim that post-punk is a style, or makes the notion of style so incoherent that it cannot serve an independent purpose of tethering meaning, for listeners cannot learn to recognize it from a limited number of paradigm examples.

Nonetheless, I endorse Reynolds's general point of assigning a modernist aesthetic to post-punk. It provides us with an important wedge for separating punk from post-punk. Punk is a style within popular music, but under standard interpretations of modernism it is doubtful that punk embraced artistic modernism. Instead, punk was one of the culture's periodic re-investments in the back-to-basics version of Romanticism. Several implications follow from the thesis that punk is a style used to express Romantic ideals and values. Repositioned as post-punk, the same general style might be used to critique Romanticism. Style alone cannot tell us that the Sex Pistols and Stiff Little Fingers were punk but that Howard Devoto's music with the Buzzcocks and then Magazine are post-punk. It is likely, then, that some bands who are considered post-punk by an accident of time and place might not be post-punk at all, for they may not subscribe to the values and goals of the framing movement. Although he does not intend to do so, Reynolds makes a very strong case that Joy Division was not a post-punk band.[39] Reading their songs as Ian Curtis's sincere descriptions of his personal torments, and Curtis's suicide as an act of "commitment" that "confirmed the authenticity of Joy Division's words and music," Reynolds might just as well be discussing John Keats or Lord Byron. Reynolds clearly subsumes them under a Romantic aesthetic.[40] To the extent that the two movements are in binary opposition, there is considerable tension in Reynolds's attribution of Romantic values to a band that he locates within a modernist movement. Joy Division may be no more post-punk than Def Leppard.

The Kantian Thread within Modernism

The proper categorization of Joy Division illustrates another major point. Ian Curtis's sincerity in the expression of personal emotion was, with much of punk, an embrace of nineteenth-century Romantic values. Perversely, post-punk is a throwback, too. Like Reynolds, Bernard Gendron positions it in relation to twentieth-century artistic modernism. While I agree, Gendron's account is narrowly focused on the New York "no wave" scene of the late 1970s as hybrid of popular culture and high art.[41] Expanding our scope of focus, I think an emphasis on twentieth-century modernism misses the connection to the larger historical movement that united post-punk bands on both sides of the Atlantic. My proposal is that post-punk embraces a core value of high art, artistic genius. As I mentioned in Chapter 4, genius rose to prominence in the Renaissance, but it did not emerge as *the* central value of art until the eighteenth century. Although eighteenth-century models of genius are now in disfavor for the way they were so frequently used to uphold exclusionary practices, I do not think the idea is going away any time soon. Furthermore, I think one of the most important eighteenth-century philosophical accounts of genius illuminates the framing artistic value of post-punk and the logic by which it quickly came to embrace so many styles. It also explains Garcia's sense that there was something unmusical about this music.

What I have in mind is a foundational source of modernism, Immanuel Kant's philosophy of art. If this proposal seems far-fetched, it is consistent with Frith's view that, for much of popular music, the goal is originality rather than authenticity.[42] Setting aside Kant's complicated aesthetic theory and its unfortunate associations with formalism and the autonomy of art, there is considerable merit to his proposal that fine art is the art of genius and, as a result, works of art are inherently pulled in competing directions.[43] Kant's account of how they are pulled in competing directions is a surprising accurate description of the values of the music at the core of post-punk.

Making a connection to this larger historical framework has an additional advantage. A full-blown adherence to twentieth-century modernism implies a commitment to sharply reduced accessibility for auditors. But accessibility is a basic feature of popular music. Granted, there are borderline cases where musicians who are normally classified as popular musicians might not be accessible enough to count as such. (I recently had a student tell me he'd rather fail my course than hear Captain Beefheart a second time.) While a lot of post-punk music is less accessible than, say, Fleetwood Mac, it remains relatively accessible. Which is also as it should be according to Kant's theory of genius.

Roughly, Kant's proposal is as follows.[44] Any product of human design is art. Most of it is rule-governed production of useful objects; this is craft.[45] Some is meant merely to entertain. But some is would-be fine art, designed primarily to convey aesthetic ideas.[46] Fine art is not distinguished by the project of expressing emotions. Instead, its unique task is to explore concepts by presenting them in a manner that invites reflection: "It expands the mind by setting the imagination free… [and] connects its presentation with a fullness of thought to which no linguistic expression is fully adequate."[47] However, there are no intrinsic rules for doing this, for rules are contrary to the freedom of the imagination. Hence, fine art is the art of genius; each new production is, at least potentially, a new exemplar or model for bringing together a meaning and a mode of presentation. An original design may be imitated by others, or not. If it does not serve as a model for later designs—if there are no identifiable extensions of the design—then the production is a piece of original nonsense. But if its design strategy directly influences subsequent designs—if others extract a rule from what has been done, but without necessarily having it articulated as a design principle—then it counts as genius rather than nonsense.[48] Thus, one of Kant's most interesting proposals is the idea that the main difference between genius and nonsense is whether, as a matter of historical fact, a design strategy serves a rule, that is, whether it is imitated.

Furthermore, anyone who creates fine art for purposes of communication will want the audience to understand that communication. Consequently, the productive faculty of genius must be tempered by the critical faculty of taste.[49] The genius must balance creativity with concessions to taste, i.e., to some familiar, organizing rule(s) adapted from either previous art or the external subject matter referenced by the piece. The challenge, then, is producing a formal construct "adequate to the thought and yet not detrimental to the freedom in the play of the mental powers" involved in experiencing and interpreting it.[50] One of those mental powers is imagination. If it is lacking, the work may be entertaining and agreeable, but it will be soulless. The soul of a work of art is the presence of an aesthetic idea, which is a "representation of the imagination that occasions much thinking though without it being possible for any determinate thought, i.e., no [determinate] **concept**, to be adequate to it, which, consequently, no language fully attains or can make intelligible."[51]

In short, embodiment of the artist's meaning must be original and not fully subject to verbal paraphrase: it is ineffable and yet not unintelligible. Excessive rule-following produces art with no soul. In the complete absence of rule-following, it is nonsense. Taste must select a structural rule, but it cannot borrow a rule that will render the work completely intelligible through linguistic paraphrase. The trick is to come up with something "original, mind-stretching" and yet "followable."[52]

With this description in hand, let us return to post-punk. Kant's theory elucidates Reynolds's account of The Flying Lizards, another band that predated the stylistic coalescence of punk. Explaining the group's aesthetic, drummer/vocalist Charles Hayward says, "Anything was potentially a source of music."[53] Reynolds then turns to a discussion of San Francisco-based Ralph Records. Echoing Hayward's comment, Tuxedomoon member Steve Brown explains, "The only rule was the tacit understanding that anything that sounded like anyone else was taboo."[54] In short, some post-punk musicians were self-consciously pursuing rule-breaking originality and reduced accessibility. However, post-punk was anchored by a second value, social and political reform. David Hesmondhalgh characterizes post-punk as a mode of media activism intent on democratization.[55] He places the locus of this activism in "the relationship between the commercial company and its creative artists," that is, in direct attempts to reform the record industry. As such, post-punk activism does not necessarily influence the relationship between musicians and their audience.[56] To be *artistically* relevant, the democratization must appear as a conceptual focus of a symbolic exchange, where the idea is explored in a musical product or performance.

Consider two such post-punk gestures. One is The Desperate Bicycles's single, "The Medium was Tedium" (1977), a simple rock tune over which vocalist Danny Wigley berates listeners for not having made their own record; "it was easy, it was cheap, go and do it." The message is reinforced by the back sleeve of the single, which explains that their previous single cost is a mere £153. At the same time, the amateurish design (of both music and sleeve) is perfectly synchronized with the conceptual message of do-it-yourself (DIY); one can both *see* and *hear* that it was easy and cheap. A concept is explored by hitting on a means of expression that itself exemplifies the message. Yet they simultaneously toy with the audience, offering material for imaginative free play—the sleeve mysteriously notes that the recording is "slightly stereo," and that their last amateurish production "subsequently leapt at the throat."

The second example is Gang of Four's "Natural's Not in It" (1979). Although there is no reason to suppose Kant's *Critique of Aesthetic Judgment* was at hand when they wrote the song, it certainly illustrates what Kant describes. Several writers on post-punk mention this track for the lyrics, as though it is simply funky sloganeering about the inability to escape from assigned social positions; Reynolds isolates the line that provides the title "No escape from society/Natural is not in it."[57] Suppose that this line provides the track's organizing concept. Is that the whole message? Or has something been done to express it aesthetically, in Kant's sense, so that the message organizes "freedom in the play of our cognitive powers" and it has an appearance of being "free from all constraint by arbitrary rules?"[58] That is, does the musical construction encourage auditors to reflect on the organizing concept? For if it that is the case, then musical talent, as a natural ability, is present as nature giving a rule to art.[59]

Notice, in that light, the track's opening. Andy Gill's guitar offers four repetitions of a choppy musical phrase; then bass and drums enter and accompany another four repetitions. At the ninth repetition, a geometric rule appears to have been established, at which point the guitar figure changes, violating the rule and providing an immensely pleasurable release. Gill then begins to add the occasional snarl of ornamentation. As vocalist Jon King observes, the typical Gang of Four arrangement conveys democratization by the way that the arrangement gives a distinct place to each of the instruments and the vocal.[60] The music *illustrates* the words—as opposed to expressively supporting them, as is the norm in popular music performance.

In "Natural's Not in It," the verbal dichotomy of nature and society is at odds with the track's own evidence that human dependence on society does not eradicate individuality. Art is a medium in which rules are broken, demonstrating that nature, human nature, is the source of the rules being broken. Gang of Four confirms that rules can be exploited to create a space in which new rules can emerge. None of this is directly *said*, of course. However, to approach these musicians as creative artists is to seek meaning, which can only be rendered through a paraphrase of associations encouraged by the composition *qua* recorded composition. Any interpretation that treats a Gang of Four track as more than sloganeering should provide a paraphrase of what is happening in the verbal-musical interplay. A doctrine of Kantian aesthetic ideas is a surprisingly insightful explanation of what is desirable in a paraphrase of post-punk communication.

In conclusion, post-punk's lack stylistic unity makes sense when we understand it as a movement within a large-scale movement rather than as a style. Specifically, it seems to be an extension of an anti-Romantic strain of artistic modernism. As such, it is strongly characterized by an adherence to experimentation and rule-breaking, both as a strategy for exploring ideas and, providing greater specificity to the movement, as a symbol of political democratization. Because post-punk valued violations of expectations, it was inevitable that particular examples of post-punk struck fans of other music as inept and incoherent and, *qua* music, as unmusical. However, by understanding that anti-Romantic modernism unifies the movement, auditors gain a hermeneutical tool for teasing some meanings from the music while also limiting an expectation to find others.

So Jerry Garcia had it right, in his own way. Embracing the spirit of Kantian genius, post-punk "denies the simple authority of given models," and so the music resisted Garcia's conceptual map.[61] It was a good sign that kids were forming bands. Because early post-punk experimentation furnished sonic strategies for subsequent bands, coalescing into a range of identifiable styles, it eventually led to what Garcia calls "real music." But until others imitated particular cases and, through copying, established a pattern of rules, no one could yet tell what those styles were.

7

Allusion and Intention in Popular Song

The Accessibility Requirement

In the Introduction to the book, I proposed that the "popular" element of popular music is a matter of cultural position and relative accessibility. There is no popular music unless there is a contrasting cultural category of "art" music, and popular music is *comparatively* more accessible to musically unschooled members of the society. In Chapter 6, I discussed post-punk music to show that popular music is not a cultural oasis: it often draws upon larger cultural trends. This chapter shifts focus to allusive reference as another way that popular music communication exploits existing cultural resources.

My overall position is inspired by Noël Carroll's analysis of mass art. Mass art involves artworks that have multiple instances, are produced and distributed by a mass technology, and are intentionally designed to provide accessibility "with minimal effort, virtually on first contact, for the largest number of untutored (or relatively untutored) audiences."[1] Almost everyone with passing familiarity with recent, similar popular music can grasp much of a particular track's meaning without effort on first exposure. But as Carroll observes, this goal of accessibility for "everyone" should not be taken to include those with no knowledge of anything.[2] Communication exploits learned conventions, and knowledge of context makes a difference in auditor understanding. So does other background knowledge.

For example, Beyoncé's "Pretty Hurts" (2013) and Taylor Swift's "Betty" (2020)—together with their official videos—invite sophisticated feminist interpretations. However, only someone who understands feminism will construct such an interpretation. Nonetheless, these are paradigm cases of popular music, and almost everyone can grasp their basic messages.[3] Understanding their shared thematic point that gender stereotypes often hurt women does not require a college course in feminist theory. Yet taking such a course can reveal depths that many auditors will overlook.[4] Such examples illustrate Ted Cohen's thesis of bilateral design, which says we should abandon the common presumption that popular music and art music align with simple and complex communication, respectively. Except for extreme cases, most commercial art (and thus, most popular music) is designed to be of interest to both "low" and "high" audiences, that is, to communicate and appeal in a highly accessible manner to almost everyone, while also having elements that are understood by, and appeal to, a subset of the audience.[5]

In suggesting that the accessibility condition is compatible with the communication of complex ideas, I am not proposing that the presence of complex ideas makes a recording or performance better than a simpler one. As Carroll argues, it is doubtful "that the quality of art varies in proportion to its difficulty."[6] In any case, I am not concerned with value questions here. Instead, I am proposing that, all other things being equal, highly accessible work can communicate relatively complex meanings.

As such, this chapter focuses on the richness of meaning generated by intertextual allusion. Popular songs regularly employ such allusion. Although some allusions are simple and thus highly accessible to almost everyone, many allusions require some degree of critical insight or draw on arcane connections. Consequently, many instances of popular music are only partially understood if the audience does not supply some very specific information that the communication presupposes but does not supply to the audience.[7] While I do not want to overgeneralize, I am proposing that popular music frequently encodes such meanings for a suitably informed audience.

The goal of this chapter, therefore, is to explain how allusion inserts complex messages that require sophisticated interpretation into instances of popular music that are nonetheless designed to be "easily accessible, virtually on first exposure, to mass untutored audiences."[8]

A Paradigm Case: Allusion in *The Matrix*

Examples can be an obstacle as well as help. Before I venture into greater detail about popular music, I want to set the stage with a straightforward, nonmusical example from another popular art, film. Consider *The Matrix* (1999), the first film in a popular series. Recall the scene in which Morpheus offers Neo the choice to learn what the matrix is. "I imagine," says Morpeheus, "that right now you're feeling a bit like Alice, tumbling down the rabbit-hole." Here we have an allusion to the opening chapter of Lewis Carroll's *Alice's Adventures in Wonderland*. The allusion is obvious and signals that something weird is likely to happen. Clearly, we are supposed to understand that Morpheus knows *Alice's Adventures in Wonderland*, and he expects Neo to know it, too. (By implication, the filmmakers must expect many viewers to grasp this allusion, too.) Furthermore, Morpheus's words imply that Lewis Carroll and his books exist in the fictional world of *The Matrix*. While it is fictional that Morpheus alludes to Lewis Carroll, because everything Morpheus does is fictional, the film places that book in the fictional world of that film. Given that audiences approach fictions with a presumption of maximum continuity between reality and fiction, the fact that Carroll's book is present implies that his other books exist in that world, as well.[9]

Thinking about Lewis Carroll then allows us to recognize that Morpheus extends his allusion. He offers Neo two pills. "After this, there is no turning back. You take the blue pill, the story ends. You wake up in your bed and you believe whatever you want to believe. You take the red pill, you stay in Wonderland, and I show you how deep the rabbit-hole goes." This additional allusion to Wonderland and the rabbit-hole adds no new information to the scene. But suppose we pause and ask why the pills are blue and red, and why blue means "stop" and red means "continue." After all, Morpheus and Neo are operating in a simulation of "the end of the twentieth century," where red means "stop" and green means "go." But the film narrative continues past this minor point, never to return to it.[10] The choice of colors for the two pills appears to be arbitrary.

Except that the color choice is not arbitrary, and it deviates from twentieth-century practice because it is an allusion to a nineteenth-century text. It alludes to Chapter 6 of Lewis Carroll's *Sylvie and Bruno*. Sylvie is invited to choose one of two lockets.[11] One locket has a blue gem and the other has a red gem. The blue locket is engraved with the phrase "All–will–love–Sylvie," while the red is engraved with "Sylvie–will–love–all." Seeing the difference, Sylvie selects the red locket. "It's very nice to be loved," she said: "but it's nicer to love other people!" (On a side note, Sylvie never uses the magic locket in *Sylvie and Bruno*. But the locket introduces the theme of love, central to the book and its sequel, for love is the thing that transforms empty ritual into something of genuine significance.) We might also notice that the opening words of *Sylvie and Bruno* are a short poem. It begins, "Is all our Life, then but a dream?"

So Neo's choice parallels Sylvie's in crucial respects. Each is offered something red and something blue, and each chooses the red one. Since it is obvious that this scene in *The Matrix* alludes to one Lewis Carroll novel through its verbal allusion to *Alice's Adventures*, it seems apparent that the same scene contains an equally important, although less obvious, allusion to a second Lewis Carroll novel. However, there is no reason to think that Morpheus (the character in the fictional world) is making an allusion to *Sylvie and Bruno*. That novel is no longer widely read, and there is no reason to suppose, in this fictional world, that Morpheus would know it and would expect Neo to know it, too. So in this case, the *film* makes the allusion without having a character fictionally allude. This subtle allusion to *Sylvie and Bruno* is ingenious, and those who discovered it received a foreshadowing of what was to come at the end of the Matrix Trilogy. In choosing the red pill, Neo would not escape fate. Fate, remember, was what Neo wants to escape by taking the red pill. Despite his rejection of self-sacrifice in *The Matrix Reloaded* (2003), Neo would ultimately be the one to love all. In short, this allusion suggests at the outset that Neo is a Christ-figure who must die for humankind.

So I think that the same scene contains two allusions, one obvious and one subtle. In the vocabulary I'll adopt, the scene with the two pills is the alluding text.[12] The scene intentionally alludes to both *Alice's Adventures* and *Sylvie and Bruno*, which are its two source texts. What analysis of allusion is broad enough to count the references to Alice and to the lockets as allusions despite their differences?

The Three Elements of Allusion

A common kind of allusion in popular song is the "answer" song, in which the full sense of a song presupposes awareness of some earlier song, often by a different musician. One of the first hints of feminism in country-Western music was Kitty Wells's 1952 hit record, "It Wasn't God Who Made Honky Tonk Angels." The phrase "honky tonk angels" had been popularized earlier that year by Hank Thompson's "The Wild Side of Life," a portrait of a heartless woman who hurts men by pursuing the party life of the honky tonk clubs. Wells's answer song was released while Thompson's song was still high in the music charts. Although written by a man, Jay Miller, the answer needed the voice of a woman, and it took Wells from obscurity to fame, making her the first woman to have a number one record on the country charts. In addition to the way the phrase "honky tonk angels" signaled the narrator's motivations, the answer song is melodically similar to Thompson's song. So "It Wasn't God Who Made Honky Tonk Angels" is doubly allusive, linking to "The Wild Side of Life" through the music as well as the words.

Answer songs are merely one of the many modes of allusion in popular song. I am not going to attempt to give a list of types of allusion, but will instead focus on what they have in common. To do so, I will offer a variant of the analysis of allusion developed by William Irwin. Following Irwin, an allusion is an intended reference that calls for associations that go beyond mere substitution of a referent.[13] Breaking this proposal into its constituent parts, there are three necessary conditions for the presence of allusion. The three conditions are jointly sufficient. They are the presence of indirect reference to a specific source text, authorial intention to refer to that text, and a possibility of audience detection of the indirect reference.[14] Since I am sympathetic to Irwin's arguments for these three conditions, I will simply concentrate on extending them beyond Irwin's consciously limited scope of verbal and literary allusion.

On this model, *The Matrix* alludes to *Sylvie and Bruno* in advance of audience recognition of the connection. The audience discovers the allusion (as opposed, say, to creating it through an act of recognition). Although few viewers of the film detect the subtle allusion to *Sylvie and Bruno*, it satisfies the condition that an allusion must offer the audience the possibility of its recognition. Its reference to a source text is established by textual similarity that makes the allusion capable of detection. Citing a verbal joke in a Simpsons episode, Irwin says, "This is clearly intended as an allusion to *Forrest Gump*."[15] Although Irwin does not emphasize the point, the joke alludes to the film as source text, and only secondarily to the fictional character of Forrest. Similarly, the first verse of the David Bowie track "Ashes to Ashes" (1980) is an extended allusion to two different verses of Buddy Holly's "Peggy Sue Got Married" (1959). Bowie alludes to the earlier recording, but he does not allude to the character, Peggy Sue. This is an interesting case, because the lyric also alludes to another track, Bowie's own "Space Oddity" (1969), while "Peggy Sue Got Married" alludes to Holly's early hit, "Peggy Sue" (1957). Thus Bowie suggests an additional allusion, one that arises from his mirroring the allusive technique of the Holly source text. The parallel creates one of the rare cases where allusion is transitive, so that an allusion to a source text that itself alludes carries the allusion back to that earlier source text. It is clear that a transitive allusion is a case of indirect reference, satisfying the first condition for allusion. But such transitive allusions seem the rare exception, not the rule.

Direct reference is another matter. Direct reference in popular song lyrics is common, and it plays no special role in allusion. When Judy Garland performs "On the Atchison, Topeka and the Santa Fe" (1946), she sings about a railroad, and it tells us that it's about that particular railroad by naming it—a clear case of direct reference if there is one.[16] Likewise, Scott McKenzie's song "San Francisco (Be Sure to Wear Some Flowers in your Hair)" (1967) references San Francisco. These are not allusions. Other uses of proper names are less clear, especially when they name fictional characters. For example, Iggy Pop's lyrics for "Lust for Life" (1977) refers to someone named Johnny Yen, who is a character in William S. Burroughs's novel *The Ticket That Exploded* (1962), so it looks like a standard case of direct reference. But is this a way to refer to *other* things in the novel? Are we supposed to derive further meaning from this choice and seek some genuine informational overlap from Burroughs's novel? Only then would the opening line of the song constitute allusion. Thankfully, Pop's lyric clarifies the intention to allude when the end of the second verse concludes with the seemingly out-of-place phrase "hypnotizing chickens." These words are taken from *The Ticket That Exploded*, and they signal that Pop is doing more than simply borrowing a name he saw and liked: he really is inviting us to flesh out the song by looking for resonances in Burroughs's novel. On the other hand, I am uncertain whether the title phrase, "Lust for Life," is another allusion: in this case, to Kirk Douglas's 1956 portrayal of Vincent Van Gogh in the well-known film with that title.

This tendency to worry about the details of lyrics invites a warning. Stephanie Ross reminds us that it is dangerous to treat verbal allusion as typical of all allusion.[17] Our tendency to emphasize literary allusion limits recognition of allusion throughout popular music, where it is frequently visual or aural. "Ashes to Ashes" contains verbal allusion to "Peggy Sue Got Married," but there is no overlap in the *musical* element of Bowie's song. But now we arrive at something very tricky: we have no clear method for identifying musical allusion, for we have no general method for distinguishing between an indirect reference to earlier music and a case of simply copying or varying it.[18] We do not want a simplistic equation of allusion and close musical paraphrase. Although George Harrison was familiar with The Chiffons's "He's So Fine" (1963), he did not intend to reproduce part of it in "My Sweet Lord" (1970), so his song is accidental plagiarism, not allusion. On the other hand, there seem to be some straightforward cases of strictly musical allusion, as when Jimi Hendrix quoted "Taps" while performing the American national anthem—an example I discussed in Chapter 1. Similarly, Frank Zappa introduced brief snatches of highly familiar music into his own. These are often humorous for their incongruity, and they often function as allusion, generally by introducing a satirical edge when the musical theme is associated with lyrics, so that a snatch of "Hail to the Chief" calls attention to the political structures of American life.[19]

Ross also reminds us to look for cross-modal allusion, that is, allusion between two arts that appeal to two sensory modalities. *The Matrix* offers a cross-modal allusion to *Sylvie and Bruno*, taking us from the visual prompt of two colors to the literary text and its verbal description of two lockets. One of my favorite cross-modal allusions is the photograph on the front of The Rolling Stones's album *Get Yer Ya-Ya's Out!* (1970). The photo shows drummer Charlie Watts and a mule. If you look closely at the mule, it has been outfitted to illustrate Bob Dylan's lyric "jewels and binoculars hang from the head of the mule" from "Visions of Johanna" on the *Blonde on Blonde* album (1966). While that allusion is relatively trivial, beyond answering the question of why they procured a mule for the photo, allusions normally enrich the alluding material.

Finally, I want to stress that allusion aligns with the pragmatics of meaning because an allusion *intentionally* refers the audience to another text, an identifiable source text.[20] I will argue that this relationship places normative conditions on audience interpretations of such allusions, limiting the associations that carry from source text to alluding text. If a property cannot be independently assigned to the source text, then associating that property with the alluding text cannot be an association justified by the presence of the allusion. However, if we do not treat the allusion as intentional, then there is no normative force to our recognition that two texts are similar. If we do not treat the allusion as intentional, there is no interpretative error in anachronistically supposing that Buddy Holly alludes to David Bowie, or that the novel *The Ticket That Exploded* alludes to the Iggy Pop song, rather than the other way around.

Moving on from the first of Irvin's three conditions for allusion, the point of the indirect reference goes beyond reminding us of another text. It also refers us to material or ideas in the source text that are beyond the immediate point of overlap between the source and derivative texts.[21] The communicative implication of this indirect reference is to invite a search for salience that enriches the alluding text. In a successful allusion, a different referring expression with equivalent semantic content would not steer us toward the same associations. Allusive associations vary when we substitute different referring terms. Both the Sisters of Mercy song "Amphetamine Logic" (1986) and the Bangles song "Dover Beach" (1984) borrow the same couplet from T.S. Eliot's "The Love Song of J. Alfred Prufrock": "In the room the women come and go/Talking of Michelangelo." In these cases, we are invited to think about the activity of talking about art and about the stifling effect of cultural norms in dictating which art merits attention. A very different set of ideas comes into play when the Grateful Dead song "Dark Star" (1968) paraphrases Eliot's opening of "Prufrock": "Let us go then, you and I, when the evening is spread out against the sky." Lyricist Robert Hunter steers us away from the stifling drawing room toward the wonders of the natural world, and therefore also in the direction of the "overwhelming question" that Prufrock is afraid to say aloud.

Normally, an allusion expands the meaning of the alluding text because it does more than indirectly reference a source text. By choice of the overlap or paraphrase, the alluding text can make some parts of the source text more salient than other parts.

The Importance of Intentions

Some analyses of allusion reject the necessity of citing authorial intention. However, the distinction between genuine and accidental associations is a strong basis for responding to anti-intentionalist analyses. Let us look at another anti-intentionalist argument in greater detail.

Some anti-intentionalists argue that authors cannot intend any "specific interpretation" of the allusion when they introduce one. Authors cannot control the reader's associations, nor can they "direct" or "control" the meaning or interpretation of any allusion they create. Therefore, "no specific interpretation of the allusion can be demonstrated in any convincing way to be intended by the author."[22] An allusion "gains a meaning only through the reader's actualization of it."[23] Each member of the audience "assumes complete interpretive power over the allusive moment."[24] Far from displaying artistic intention, allusion reveals "the transference of meaning's authority from writer to reader."[25]

However, a speaker's lack of control over the associations in the audience's mind is no evidence against the relevance of authorial intentions. In stressing a lack of authorial control, the argument ignores the idea that an allusion is an invitation. By way of analogy, suppose I advise you that the brakes on the car are faulty and warn you against driving it. My words might cause you to think about a near-accident that you had years ago. I didn't intend for you to think about this incident, for I tried to get you to think about the future, not the past. My inability to control the direction of your thoughts is no evidence that you have complete interpretive power over the meaning of my words. If you take my words about the car's brakes to be an invitation to think about earlier events, your "interpretive power" is merely the freedom to free associate and misunderstand. The fact that some associations are subjective, arbitrary, or unexpected does not show that artists cannot intend to suggest one set of associations rather than others.[26]

In brief, I am proposing that giving auditors complete interpretive authority is a recipe for infinite false positives, with allusions everywhere you think you find them, where any similarity counts as allusion if the auditor thinks it is. However, an allusion has auditor-independent features, including reference to an *earlier* text and not just a *similar* text. In order to have reference to the past (and not mere resemblance), the communicating agent must be aware of the earlier text as an earlier, precedent text. For example, Eliot's line in "The Wasteland," "Sweet Thames, run softly till I end my song," alludes to a line in Edmund Spenser's "Prothalamion" (1596). Eliot was writing three hundred years after Spenser. Consequently, if newly discovered letters by T.S. Eliot reveal that "Eliot never read or heard a line of Spenser,"[27] then I would deny that the line alludes to Spenser. Likewise, if the co-directing, co-writing Wachowskis were not aware of *Sylvie and Bruno*, then *The Matrix* does not allude to the two lockets. In that case, my claims about the relevance of the lockets constitute a misunderstanding of the film.

Carroll makes another useful point about the prevalence of resemblance. Many popular films and stories are similar because they recycle the same basic schemas and prototypes—"the sensual woman who loves sex" describes both Samantha in *Sex and the City* and Chaucer's Wife of Bath. But if the similarity ends there, we do not interpret *Sex and the City* as an *invitation* to think of Chaucer.[28] In popular music, the lyric "woke up this morning" appears so frequently in blues songs that it would be absurd to think that B.B. King's "Woke Up This Morning" (1957) and The Doors's "Roadhouse Blues" (1970) both allude to Robert Johnson's "Walking Blues" (1937) simply because they open with similar words. Other earlier songs do, too.

Similarly, allusion is distinct from genre parody, where such parody does not assume audience familiarity with any specific source text. *This Is Spinal Tap* (1984) features songs that lampoon heavy metal music, and while it seems that the idea arose as a spoof of the band Black Sabbath, none of the jokes depend on allusions to that band. In contrast, *The Rutles* film and album (1978) features nongeneric allusions, for each song parodies a specific Beatles song. The song "Ouch" parodies "Help!" (1965), "Piggy in the Middle" parodies the psychedelic style of "I am the Walrus" (1967), the album jacket parodies four different Beatles albums. Some of these jokes rely on aural similarities. Others are visual allusions.

Hence, an intention to allude is realized by proving overlap of highly specific, nongeneric material. When we detect this, we are alerted to intentions advising us to consider the content of the work from a certain perspective.

These intentions are of two kinds. First, the intention to allude is an illocutionary intention: an intention to be understood, and to be understood in a specific way. For an allusion, the illocutionary intention succeeds when the audience recognizes the presence of the intention to allude.[29] Second, artistic allusion involves a perlocutionary intention, that is, an intention to bring about an additional effect beyond mere recognition of the intention to allude. The additional effect is itself twofold: the audience is directed to a specific source text, and by virtue of that, the audience is invited to engage in further interpretation of the alluding text based on salient aspects of the source text. The fact that the audience actively supplies the additional interpretation does not negate the possibility that specific meanings are part of this authorial intention. When you do a crossword puzzle and the clue for 5 across is "feline," the perlocutionary intention is that the reader will fill in the appropriate horizontal spaces with some appropriate word. If there are three spaces and the first two are already filled in with a "c" and an "a," most people will fill in the third space with a "t." And this is the intended perlocutionary effect of the clue. Granted, this effect is not one that the crossword puzzle writer can dictate or fully control. But it does not follow that the author has surrendered all power over meanings in this situation. The author has provided a puzzle and has invited the audience to solve the puzzle. Some clues will be misinterpreted, and some responses to the puzzle will be full of errors and dead ends.[30]

In many ways, the textual similarity that refers the audience to the source text is like a clue in a crossword puzzle. It sends us to one place rather than another, and it also authorizes some associations and proscribes others.[31] I have proposed that this normative aspect of allusion would be absent if allusion did not involve authorial intention. Recognition of allusion requires recognition of an intention to allude, and this recognition is recognition that the author, in alluding, asks us to regard a textual overlap as relevant to the current communication. Again, I stress that the success of the illocutionary act does not guarantee the perlocutionary intention will be realized: understanding a party invitation does not necessitate attendance. The presence of the allusion may be *recognized* (in which case the illocutionary intention succeeds), but the invitation to make associations may be declined. And even if the invitation is accepted, there will be many cases where the clues are not understood. The presence of the perlocutionary intention does not guarantee successful perlocutionary effect.

Finally, a failure of the allusion's perlocutionary intention does not mean that the allusion was wasted on the audience. The most significant feature of allusions in popular music is that they simultaneously present the two illocutionary intentions, only one of which is the perlocutionary intention that the audience should *do something* upon detection of the reference. In popular culture, an artistic allusion authorizes and proscribes various meanings in the alluding text, meanings that are accessible even if some auditors are not aware of the presence of allusion. Almost everyone who hears the Bangles's "Dover Beach" and who knows anything about Michelangelo will understand the plain meaning of the alluding line. In this respect, it is like an audience member's ability to understand Neo's decision (by seeing Neo take the red pill) without having to also recognize the presence of the allusion. But for those who catch the allusion, it authorizes and proscribes additional meanings that arise from associations with the source text. This doubling of illocutionary intention explains how popular songs can satisfy the accessibility condition while simultaneously incorporating references and meanings that are not accessible to much of the audience.

Source Text Salience

When the allusion is recognized and the audience seeks relevant connections under the auspices of a pragmatic relevance principle,[32] two aspects of the allusion will limit the range of associations appropriate to it. An artistic allusion reflects two artistic decisions: the choice of a source text, and the choice of an "echo," quotation, or paraphrase from among the many that might be employed. The two decisions are closely related.

In mass art, a good allusion will serve as a functional element of the alluding text independent of its alluding function. Apart from their indirect reference, the red and blue pills allow us to see Neo's choice without his having to announce it. Two different mass artworks may allude to the same source text, but will choose different allusive elements, ones appropriate to their own direction. When Jefferson Airplane's Grace Slick wrote a song alluding to both of Carroll's Alice books, she chose to mention the rabbit (but not the rabbit hole), Alice, changes in size, the caterpillar with the hookah, the Red Queen, and the pieces on the chessboard coming to life. *The Matrix* mentions Alice and the rabbit-hole but not the rabbit, and I can't recall any references to caterpillars, chess, and hookahs. Viewed in relation to the generative context of San Francisco in 1965, Slick was interested in elements that could serve as drug references in the absence of detailed knowledge of the Alice books. *The Matrix* explores altered realities, but not the sort that comes about by ingesting psychoactive drugs. When the Bangles and Robert Hunter allude to Eliot's "Prufrock," they appropriate from different parts of the poem. The Bangles want to create a positive bond between the song's narrator and the person they address, while Hunter wants a suggestion of the mystical sublimity of the heavens. Each chooses accordingly, and the words contribute sense to the alluding text even in the absence of recognition that it alludes.

This strategy also holds for nonverbal allusion. Irwin mentions the case of the banjo theme from the movie *Deliverance* (1973) appearing in the "Colonel Homer" episode of the Simpsons, humorously foreshadowing danger. This burst of banjo must function even if viewers do not "get" the full allusion. Thanks to prevailing connotations of banjo music, viewers who do not recognize the banjo tune as the theme from *Deliverance* will not laugh, but the mere *sound* of the banjo tells the audience "that Homer has entered a backward, redneck area."[33] In other words, those who fail to catch the allusion can still derive a relevant meaning from its alignment with genre conventions. But when the audience also makes the allusive connection to the film *Deliverance*, there is the possibility of recognition (in principle) that two distinct creative decisions must have been made. A source text was chosen, and an element from that source text was chosen, subject to conventions that allow its integration into the alluding text without diminishing access for those who miss the allusion.

In this way, popular songs gain complexity by employing an integration strategy that is frequently used in the traditional fine arts. It would be silly to suppose that fine art allusions are present solely for the sake of their allusive effects, creating incomprehensible elements for those who do not grasp their reference to a source text. Visually, Edouard Manet's painting *Olympia* (1863) packs its punch independently of its allusion to Titian's *Venus of Urbino* (1538). A quotation of Rossini's *William Tell* (1829) overture in the first movement of Dmitri Shostakovich's Symphony No. 15 (1971) gives the latter a burst of rhythmic drive that can be grasped even if one does not register it as an allusion. While creators of both high and low culture enhance their work with allusion, detecting them is not essential to a baseline understanding of the alluding works or texts. The audience for fine art may be more open to avant-garde techniques and so more tolerant of disruptive allusions, with no function *except* as allusions. Nonetheless, popular music uses a time-tested technique in employing allusions that contribute to the meaning of the alluding work apart from, and prior to, their functions as allusions.

For those who successfully grasp an allusion, the decision to use one element of the source text rather than another provides interpretative direction. It directs the search for relevant associations, suggesting elements of the source text that are to be brought to bear on the alluding text. How and where does the alluding element appear in both texts? *The Matrix* alludes to *Sylvie and Bruno* at the moment of Neo's choice. Any associations that arise should be relevant to his moment of decision making. Morpheus prefaced the allusion with a discussion of fate. It is likely that the associations will tell us about Neo's fate. Subsequent discussions of fate will then invite application of Sylvie's reason for choosing the red locket (e.g., when the Oracle warns Neo that he is fated to sacrifice himself or Morpheus). The Bangles want to play with an ambiguity of gender, which is accomplished by changing Eliot's "women" to "we." Knowledge of Eliot's original line suggests that the narrator is addressing another woman, something that cannot otherwise be determined from the lyric.

However, it is also important to acknowledge that the allusion underdetermines the associations it invokes. A source text normally has many features that are not relevant to the linking of the two texts, and the mechanism by which allusion operates will always leave us with the interpretative problem of which features of each text are relevant when importing associations from one to the other. Hence there is always a possibility that the communicative puzzle will remain unsolved even when the allusion is noticed.

Covert Allusions

The source text for an allusion may be overt (obvious to most of the audience) or covert. We might assume that fine art is more likely to contain covert allusion, and that popular culture is more likely to exploit overt, obvious allusions. But I do not see any reason to generalize in this way. Popular culture is full of covert allusion, too. These are generally cases where the source text is not as well known as the alluding text. Although millions have seen the Foo Fighters video for "Everlong" (1997), relatively few viewers are likely to notice for themselves that it alludes to *Andalusian Dog* (*Le Chien Andalou*) (1929) for the obvious reason that relatively few rock music fans have ever seen the 1929 short film by Luis Buñuel and Salvador Dali. But the visual connections are there in plain sight.

The lesson, of course, is that the distinction between covert and overt will be relative to the audience. Given that the audience for fine art is more homogenous than the audience for popular art, it is even likely that there is more covert allusion in popular music than in art music.

Generational change can rapidly move an allusion from the overt to the covert. The Kinks inserted relatively obvious musical allusions to two other songs about trains, "Smokestack Lightning" (1956) and "Train Kept A Rollin'" (1951), in their recording of "Last of the Steam-Powered Trains" (1968). Today, all three songs are largely forgotten, and I am confident that not many listeners under the age of fifty will now grasp, without outside prompt, that The Kinks's music contains allusions. Another interesting example is pair of songs, "Diana—Part 1" and "Diana—Part 2," featured on the album *Sunfighter* (1971) by Paul Kantner and Grace Slick. As with Nicolas Poussin's seventeenth-century painting *Landscape with Diana and Orion*, the two songs provide a much richer experience for those who grasp their reference to the myth of the Roman goddess Diana. Until recently, that myth was relatively common knowledge in Europe and European-derived cultures, but who today learns the stories of the Roman gods and goddesses? Not many. One generation's common knowledge is another's hermetic specialization. As the audience changes or the culture forgets its past, an obvious allusion can gradually become one for which there is merely the possibility of detection in principle.

A second reason that overt allusions become covert is that popular culture is no longer local or folk culture. The mass distribution of popular music encourages the consumption of music in a vast array of cultural contexts distinct from their origins.[34] Audiences throughout the world see American films. Americans, in turn, have increasing access to mass art that originates throughout the world. Watching a Korean television drama, I was puzzled by one character's (seemingly) random response to another character's words; only later did I understand that the first character was expressing recognition that the other had just made a humorous allusion to one of the most popular television series in recent Korean broadcasting, *Signal* (2016). Virtually every viewer in Korea immediately grasped the allusion as it unfolded in the scene. I did not, and not because of historical distance. Both language barriers and the sheer quantity of mass art ensure that no audience member will grasp all the allusive references that they encounter. I am a great fan of Elvis Costello, but I listened to the *Armed Forces* album (1979) for years before I learned that "Senior Service" (a song title) is a British brand of cigarettes, a nonartistic allusion that greatly enriches the song's theme of youthful dissatisfaction.[35] In popular culture, both overt meanings and allusive implications that are clearly present to their intended audience will fail to register as the art makes its way to new audiences.

Closing Thoughts

I will conclude this chapter by suggesting two additional points about allusion and popular music. One concerns the intention of creating an allusion. The other concerns the possibility of extended allusion.

Irwin proposes that an important aim underwriting allusion "is that is strengthens the connection between the author and the audience, cultivating intimacy and forging a sense of community."[36] While this is certainly important in the case of one-on-one, face-to-face conversation, I am not confident that it is central in the case of recorded music and popular song performance. Irwin is borrowing a page from Ted Cohen's analysis of joke telling. However, Cohen treats joke telling as a direct human encounter, not as one mediated by mass media.[37] When I listen to the Bangles and Grateful Dead and recognize their allusions to T.S. Eliot, the intimacy and community that I share with the musicians are indirect and, consequently, extremely shallow. I would be a fool to think that these musicians have tried to establish an intimacy with me. I would be like Charles Manson, who infamously thought that The Beatles were talking to him through their albums. Reading Christopher Rick's book on Bob Dylan, I recognize scores of allusions to Dylan's lyrics in Rick's prose.[38] But I feel no intimacy with the author, for I know that most readers will be Dylan fans and will recognize them. Furthermore, as I discussed in Chapter 4, a sense of intimacy and community seems to be a widespread effect of popular music fandom.[39] People get the same sense of connection with others by being fans of the same sports team or by finding that they watch the same Korean television dramas on streaming services. There is nothing special about the presence of allusion here.

If the feeling of intimacy and community is neither a major nor a unique dimension of allusion in popular culture, we might shift our focus to other aspects of recognizing and understanding allusions. Irwin proposes that while we do not want allusions to be too obvious, it "should not be a riddle to be pondered for an extended time." We should get it "all at once" by remembering something we already know.[40] Part of his evidence is that this immediacy is essential to the effect of intimacy and community.[41] But since I've cast doubt on *that* purpose, perhaps their game-like quality is more important than Irwin allows. If we admire the wit and skill behind a good allusion, we may think a good deal about the associations that are intended. Many fans of mass-distributed popular music return repeatedly to the same track, listening to the same music again and again. Allusions that were overlooked may suddenly appear, in part because the audience member will have learned new things in the meantime. Rewatching *The Matrix* after learning of the *Sylvie and Bruno* allusion, I became more aware of how the theme of choice and fate was introduced at other points in the plot, and I looked to see how the theme of love might be related to each of them. The allusion's pleasurable prompt of recognition (my awareness that the author intends to allude) is not at odds with its puzzle pleasure.[42] The pleasure of recognition is sometimes an invitation to a puzzle, a puzzle that may be solved over time and after multiple experiences of it.

Finally, I'd like to note that the analysis of allusion that I've endorsed is neutral about the saturation of the alluding text by the source text. Are allusions necessarily local, small-scale aesthetic effects?[43] Is this more likely to be the case with popular music? Allusion is generally viewed as a local event within a text. This view is reinforced by the assumption that allusions please through their immediacy. However, a song or song performance can allude as a whole to another one, as in the relationship of "Peggy Sue Got Married" back to "Peggy Sue," providing saturation of one song with an earlier song. But there is an endless stream of additional cases, because *recordings* frequently allude through saturation. The most common case is the cover version.

Covering, where a new recording is made of an already familiar song, generally satisfies the conditions of allusion. (I explore this phenomenon in great detail in Chapter 8.) For now, consider the phenomenon of tribute albums, in which an assortment of pop musicians contributes "covers" of songs by the same artist. One of my favorites is the British package, *The Last Temptation of Elvis: Songs from His Movies* (1990), in no small part because of the allusion of the title. When Nanci Griffith covers "Wooden Heart" and the Jesus and Mary Chain cover "Guitar Man," each renders the song in their own styles. The musicians intend that we compare what they have done with the "originals," the Elvis Presley versions, and we are invited to interpret each new performance in light of the Elvis source text. But where a tribute album is a collection of related allusive covers, popular music also provides cases of saturated allusion for the length of an entire album. Two notable cases involve Taylor Swift. In 2015, Ryan Adams released *1989*, a track-by-track cover of Swifts's own *1989* album of the previous year. Then, in 2021, Swift released the first of her planned set of remakes of all of her early albums: *Fearless (Taylor's Version)* is an extended remake of *Fearless* (2008*)*. As her fans knew, her re-recording project was undertaken as a response to having lost the legal rights to control of her first six albums. By covering her own records, Swift invites her fans to "simultaneously relive the music as nostalgia and consume it as a vicarious act of empowerment."[44] She invites her fans to look back, but in so doing she invites them to look for the contemporary relevance of what she's doing.

To sum up, allusions involve both illocutionary and perlocutionary intentions, and the pleasure that comes from recognition of an allusion is not always resolved in the immediate recognition of its significance. Many allusions are invisible to much of the audience. Some are puzzles even for those who notice their presence. But a successful allusion in popular music almost always fulfills the accessibility condition—its presence does not disrupt accessibility to the song's basic meaning for those who don't grasp the allusion. For those who "get" an allusion, whether small-scale or saturated, there is a resulting depth of meaning due to the way that the source dovetails into the alluding work.

8

Covers and Communicative Intentions

Covers as a Species of Remakes

Popular music is flooded with songs that have been recorded multiple times: remakes. Many chapters of this book have used remakes to illustrate the relevance of context. Then, at the end of Chapter 7, I noted that there is a special category of such songs: cover versions as extended allusions. This chapter picks up that point and offers an extensive analysis of cover versions.

As an introduction to this phenomenon, consider three recordings of the same song.

(1) Carl Perkins wrote and recorded "Blue Suede Shoes" in 1955, and had a million-selling rhythm and blues hit with it early in 1956. In standard terminology, this is "the original."
(2) Elvis Presley recorded the song and had a hit with it in late 1956. Thanks to general trajectory of their careers, Presley's remake has sold many more copies than Perkin's original.
(3) In 1991, an Elvis Presley tribute album called *The Last Temptation of Elvis* was released in the UK, with all proceeds going to a charity devoted to music therapy. The album has a version of "Blue Suede Shoes" by the band Lemmy and the Upsetters with Mick Green—basically, a group assembled by "Lemmy" Kilmister of the band Motörhead.

The first two communicate roughly the same thing: the joking but defiant assertion of a young man that his "cool cat" persona is more important than anything, implying that, while he knows he lacks power, he has limits and they ought not to be crossed. But neither communicates what the 1991 track additionally conveys: nostalgic fondness for youth, the 1950s, and Elvis.

Popular music is full of remakes like these: recordings of songs that have already been made available on another recording. But this was not always the case. Prior to the twentieth century, popular music was distributed as sheet music or spread by imitation. In this context, the idea of a remake was moot. Yet we were well into the era of recorded music before it became common for multiple musicians to record the same hit song, each of them arranging the same recent hit to appeal to a particular segment of the mass audience.¹ Notoriously, this practice accelerated in the 1950s, when it often took the form of white "rock and roll" singers appropriating from African-American musicians. That practice continued through the 1960s but then became less common due to an increasing preference for hearing new songs from the "original" artists, paving the way for concept of the cover in such phenomena as cover versions and cover bands.

Given the unifying Elvis Presley theme of *The Last Temptation*, the Lemmy remake is clearly packaged as a remake of the Presley recording. However, it is simultaneously a remake of the 1955 Perkins recording even if, by chance, Kilmister and Green did not know the Perkins recording and had only the Elvis version before them as a template for the song. As such, the performer doesn't have to be aware of specific earlier recordings to satisfy the criteria for a remake. All it takes to be a remake is to record a song after someone else has released it as a recording. *Anyone* who records "Blue Suede Shoes" after 1955 is doing a remake—including Perkins's several remakes.

This chapter examines covers, which are remakes that are made *because* the audience is aware that someone else's recording has already popularized the song. Presley did remakes of many songs and didn't care if fans knew the Perkins version. Presley had a new record label and needed a major hit, and the song was tailor-made for that purpose. However, by recording their version for a Presley tribute album, Lemmy and the Upsetters were signaling the connection back to Presley. Recording it for the album clearly communicated the connection, since re-recording songs associated with Presley was the unifying theme of the whole project.

If the musicians know the connection and the musicians want the audience to be aware of it (and even to be aware that they are aware), then the success of their communicative act relies on the audience's grasp of the musician's intentions. This point sets up a significant difference between covers and other remakes. In contrast to remaking, covering is not transitive. The Lemmy and the Upsetters version of "Blue Suede Shoes" is not a cover version of the Perkins recording because they are not referencing that version. However, it is a remake of the Perkins version, even if the musicians did not know so. Remaking is independent of intentions, but covering is not.

This analysis rejects George Plaskete's description of covering as "the musical practice of one artist recording or performing another composer's song."² Collapsing the distinction between a cover and a remake, it treats everyone who is not a singer-songwriter as a cover artist. It ignores Kurt Mosser's crucial insight that a cover differs from a remake in having a relationship to a specific "base" track, which is the best-known prior version, generally taken to be paradigmatic.³ However, as I observed about allusion in Chapter 7, the passage of time and the global distribution of recordings mean that what is paradigmatic in one time and place is not in another. Consequently, I will update Mosser's notion of a base version by relativizing the referent or base of any cover to a paradigmatic version in a particular context of communication. Being a cover is not an intrinsic property of a recording. Instead, it is a contextually contingent status and a byproduct of intentions to create pragmatic implicature. More specifically, I am proposing that the musician anticipates the intended audience's knowledge of the earlier recording. As Deena Weinstein puts it, a... criterion crucial to covers [is] that the listener also knows the original. Otherwise, they are only hearing a recording, not a cover. For example, Elvis' early hit, "Hound Dog," was not a cover song to nearly all who heard it when it topped the charts in 1956, since they were innocent of Willie Mae Thornton's original 1953 release.[4]

In Chapter 5, I briefly discussed Björk's version of "It's Oh So Quiet" (1995). Popularized by a clever Spike Jonze video, it was Björk's biggest hit in much of the world. Originally written in German, Björk knew the English version of it, thanks to Betty Hutton's 1951 recording. But Hutton did not have a hit with it, and there was no reason for any Björk fan to have ever heard it, or even to have heard of Hutton. Björk did a remake, but she did not cover "It's Oh So Quiet."[5]

Notice an important implication of distinguishing covers from other remakes on the basis of an expectation of what music the audience is presumed to know. Two distinct intentions enter into the complex communicative strategy of a cover version. A musician must intend to communicate with a particular audience—many of whom can be expected to recognize its status as a remake—and must intend the target audience to recognize it as referencing and replying to the earlier recorded interpretation.

If I am correct that two intentions differentiate covers from remakes, then we can apply the distinction to the album *Lez Zeppelin I* (2010) by the Led Zeppelin tribute band, Lez Zeppelin.[6] *Lez Zeppelin I* is a song-for-song remake of the more famous band's first album. Here, we have an album that is a cover of another whole album. Furthermore, we get the same complex tangle of relationships that we saw in the three recordings of "Blue Suede Shoes." Led Zeppelin was notorious for appropriating music from folk and blues sources, sometimes without properly crediting them, and this is true of the second and fourth tracks of their debut album, *Led Zeppelin* (1969). Perhaps through ignorance, perhaps for other reasons, Led Zeppelin obscured the origins of "Babe I'm Gonna Leave You" and "Dazed and Confused." When the cover band, Lez Zeppelin, places these same songs as tracks two and four of their album, they are very clearly covering the Led Zeppelin tracks. Yet, in doing so, they are also *remaking* the songs (by Anne Bredon and Jake Holmes, respectively) without necessarily *covering* those antecedent recordings. I propose that they were not covering Bredon and Holmes because they did not intend, by their performances, to invite their audience to hear their work as referencing, reflecting, or deriving from those earlier recorded performances of the same music. Lez Zeppelin is all about their relationship to Led Zeppelin. Nonetheless, the remake relationship carries back through the Led Zeppelin versions to that band's sources Bredon or Holmes. A cover is a version that refers back to a particular performer's arrangement and interpretation of a particular song.[7] As a communication to rock fans, *Lez Zeppelin I* is a communication to Led Zeppelin fans about Led Zeppelin, and not a communication about Bredon or Holmes.

In summary, I propose that covers are important because they contrast with the related categories of remakes, versions, and interpretations, none of which presuppose auditor familiarity with a particular precedent recording. Consistent with the position taken in earlier chapters of this book, the interesting difference arises from artistic intentions in aesthetic communication.[8] In short, I understand the concept of the cover to be a concept that places communicative intentions within the scope of what auditors must consider in order to adequately understand the communicative gesture of that performance or recording.[9] Directing someone to an earlier performance by means of one's own performance is a complex communicative action that invites the audience to "read" the later performance in light of the earlier performance. Consistent with the position on allusion explained in Chapter 7, I am proposing that paradigm cases of "covering" involve an intention that the audience will refer to, and to make a comparison with, an earlier recorded interpretation of the same music.[10]

The success conditions for this communicative action are less likely to arise outside of a musical culture rooted in recorded sound and mass distribution of performances. In theory, it can take place in any musical community where specific compositions are very closely associated with specific performers or contexts, and thus a parallel practice could arise in pre-industrial musical communities. But, for reasons that will become clear, it would be uncommon. Consequently, "covering" in the sense that interests me became a common practice only after the twentieth-century recording industry developed a culture in which recordings became a standard means of access to music, creating the conditions in which large numbers of people associate particular musical works with particular arrangements as interpreted by particular performers. In short, the success conditions for the communicative action of covering only become generally available in mass culture when specific recorded performances can serve as reference points for later performances.[11]

The analysis offered here does not pretend to capture all uses of "cover" in recent popular music. Concepts evolve, and words often develop inconsistent uses, and therefore the early uses of a term are not an infallible guide to its present meaning. Nonetheless, the idea of a "cover" song appears to have arisen within the popular music recording industry, originally only to refer to an attempt by one record label to cannibalize some of the sales of another label's hit recording. This initial usage would suggest that "cover," as noun, is simply an abbreviation of the phrase "cover recording," indicating nothing more than a remake or re-recording. In this context, the category does not extend to live performances. However, my analysis assumes that the concept of a cover has evolved. It is now a species of remake that also extends to live performances. However, I think that the category of the cover does not apply to some cases that are frequently treated as covers. Those cases are merely remakes.

Cover, or Not?

One test of an analysis is the plausibility of its application to borderline and highly similar cases. Consider the following examples.

- "Piece of My Heart" was written by Jerry Ragovoy and Bert Berns. Its first recording was in 1967, when rhythm and blues singer Erma Franklin scored a major hit with it in the R&B charts. The following year, singer Janis Joplin revamped it with Big Brother and the Holding Company's version on the album

Cheap Thrills (1968). Big Brother drops the horns and piano and ramps up the guitars; yet, Joplin's vocal closely follows Franklin's modeling of the melody. In contrast, country-pop singer Faith Hill had never heard either of those recordings when she recorded "Piece of My Heart" in 1993.[12] As a result, her arrangement and interpretation—in the sense explained below—owed no debt to the familiar precedent recordings. Hill's interpretation became a number one country hit in 1994. Not surprisingly, Hill's melody line follows the contours of the well-known melody, but the pauses and inflections are strikingly different from the two 1960s hits.

- Over the course of 1961 and 1962, Herbert von Karajan recorded Beethoven's nine symphonies with the Berlin Philharmonic Orchestra. Their interpretation of Symphony No. 6 is considered the one weak link in the set. In 1977, they recorded the Beethoven symphonies again. The 1977 recording of the sixth symphony is regarded as a great improvement over its predecessor.
- "The Way You Look Tonight" was introduced to the public in the film *Swing Time* (1936), where it is sung by Fred Astaire. He is seen seated alone at the piano, but we hear his voice accompanied by light orchestration, dominated by strings. Reduced to basic melody and support in the two staves of commercial sheet music, it became enormously popular and entered the "Great American Songbook." Further simplified, it appeared in the lead sheets of countless jazz "fake books" that provided melodies for improvisations. Contrasting arrangements became hit records for multiple singers, stretching from Astaire in 1936 to The Lettermen in 1961. I am particularly fond of the instrumental version by Thelonious Monk and Sonny Rollings (1954).
- Released in 1965, "The Last Time" was the first Rolling Stones single that was credited to Mick Jagger and Keith Richards as songwriters. It resurfaced in a major way in 1997 when the underlying music of The Verve's "Bitter Sweet Symphony" looped a short sample of "The Last Time"—not a Stones sample, but as it appeared as an instrumental arrangement by The Andrew Oldham Orchestra (1966).[13] A license for the sample was initially in place, but a lawsuit ensued over the issue of whether the sample exceeded the negotiated length. The Verve lost, and the songwriting credit is now "Jagger/Richards." This event highlights the irony that the chorus of "The Last Time" is itself The Rolling Stones's arrangement of a segment of "This May Be the Last Time," a 1950s gospel recording by the Staple Singers.

My position is that the Joplin recording is a cover.[14] None of the others are covers. Hill's recording is simply a remake, as are all of the various vocal versions of "The Way You Look Tonight" (but not Monk's jazz instrumental). The Verve's "Bitter Sweet Symphony" is neither a cover nor a remake, nor are any of Herbert von Karajan's recordings of Beethoven's sixth symphony.

Hill's remake of "Piece of My Heart" is much like Björk's remake of "It's Oh So Quiet" in that the intended audience would not be expected to know the earlier recording. Yet they differ in that Hill went to lengths to avoid Joplin's influence, whereas Björk appears to have learned the song by listening to Hutton's recording of it, just as The

Rolling Stones learned "The Last Time" from The Staple Singers recording. With The Rolling Stones example, the band was appropriating part of "The Last Time," but it is arguably not a remake on the grounds they used only a portion of the song as the "hook" of their own song. On the other hand, it is much like other remakes before remakes gave way to covering: as in so much of their early career, The Rolling Stones were appropriating music from American culture—especially African-American music—and the source recordings would not have been familiar to a British audience. Similarly, Björk's audience of "arty" pop music fans could not have been expected to know an obscure big band number that had never been a hit. Joplin, in contrast, was American singer remaking a song that had been an American radio hit *in the previous year*. Joplin and her band would have expected many of her listeners to compare their version with Franklin's. Consequently, it was a cover. Lacking this expectation, the Hill and Björk remakes cannot be construed as intended to invite comparison with earlier recordings of the same music. Hence, they are not covers.

Classical Music and Jazz

Why have covers become common in popular music while remaining rare in jazz and, arguably, nonexistent in classical music?[15] In large part, this is because their audience operates with a different understanding of the role of recordings in their respective musical cultures. Jazz and classical recordings continue to be treated as transparent devices for listening to performer's interpretations of works, but at the same time those two audiences have distinct expectations about how performances relate to the musical work that is performed.[16] Jazz and classical performers cannot assume that audiences know particular recordings that serve as common reference points for purposes of comparison.

In classical music, performers normally perform composed works, the essential features of which are conveyed to performers through a score, employing a visual notation. Suppose that a pianist is planning to perform Franz Schubert's Piano Sonata No. 21 in B flat major. The performer interprets the notation and determines what performances of it should sound like. The performer then works out their approach to the piece, and practices that approach.[17] Although one pianist's general way of playing the sonata may be roughly the same as another's (e.g., taking the movements at roughly the same tempo), each will be slightly different if they have developed their approach from personal study of the score. For each pianist, each particular performance will be slightly different from every other; at the same time, two performances by a single pianist will be highly similar if they arise from the same practice regime (e.g., Glenn Gould performing J.S. Bach's Goldberg Variations on different nights during his summer 1959 appearances in Europe).

Consequently, several distinct sets of artistic properties are on display when a classical work is performed. Above all, there is the interplay between the composer and the performer(s). As I noted in this book's Introduction, Julian Dodd has recently argued that "the point of interpreting a musical work [of Western classical music] in performance is to evince understanding of the performed work" and doing so "is the most fundamental performance value within our practice of work performance."[18] A listener can attend to the composed work—as a composition, is Schubert's Piano Sonata No. 21 better or worse than Joseph Haydn's Piano Sonata No. 52 in E flat major? The listener should also focus on the interpretation—is Hélène Boschi's reading of the Haydn a sound one, or is she more astute about the Schubert? Finally, the listener can concentrate on the playing—despite his obvious intelligence, doesn't Gould's audible humming to himself spoil some of his playing? Hopefully, the listener attends to the interplay of all three of these things. However, a positive evaluation of one of the three is never a prerequisite to a positive evaluation of either of the other two. There is the weak work, intelligently interpreted and flawlessly played. There is the great work, given a questionable interpretation, but played with gusto. Finally, Gould is dead and his humming is preserved, even amplified, by its presence on recordings. Humming aside, the 1955 and 1982 studio recordings of Bach's Goldberg Variations can be compared and evaluated *as* recordings, giving us a fourth object of attention.

The key point here is that a composed musical work for performance underdetermines how it is to be performed. (The point does not apply to fully improvised music.) Therefore, a performer's interpretation of the music colors its performance. The classical world is not uniform, of course. Different listeners approach music with different levels of awareness of the work/performance distinction, but someone who took no notice of the distinction would surely not count as understanding what they were hearing. Some composers have attempted to minimize the possibility of performance interpretation, most notably by composing electronic music without the intervention of notation. Other composers push in the opposite direction, maximizing performance variation, as is the case with Julius Eastman's increasingly popular "Femenine" (1974), where a surprisingly short score sets up performances that typically last an hour. While the classical tradition has always included pieces that include performance improvisation, the long tradition of composed music that stretches from, say, Claudio Monteverdi to Steve Reich and John Adams is a tradition of composed works, performer's interpretations, and performances for audiences. In contrast, strong deference to composers' wishes is a relatively minimal constraint on performance practice in popular music and jazz.

Another complication arises when a second layer of interpretation mediates between work and audience, or when the work has multiple versions. Many composed works have both versions and arrangements, which are intermediate between the work and its interpretation. Sophisticated listeners attend to the way that a performer or ensemble is interpreting or navigating a particular *version* or *arrangement* of a work.[19] More often, versions are revisions or alterations made by a work's composer, while arrangements are due to someone else. Versions and arrangements provide competing and/or derivative performance choices for a single work. For example, Anton Bruckner revised his works and thus created multiple versions of them. Reflecting these differences, his symphonies are available in several published editions, including the Haas (1944) and Nowak (1954) editions. These editions give different performing versions. Works also have multiple arrangements. Beethoven prepared an arrangement of his seventh symphony for a wind ensemble. During his lifetime, it was probably performed more frequently in this manner than with a full orchestra.

Most often, arrangements are the work of someone other than the composer. Hanns Eisler contributed two movements to a chamber orchestra arrangement of Bruckner's seventh symphony. Such arrangements can plausibly be regarded as interpretations of works that in turn require interpretation by performers, as when one says, "I don't much care for Bruckner's seventh, but I like what Eisler did with the first movement. Unfortunately, the conductor did not understand Eisler's work and rushed the tempo, which led to a lack of control in the orchestra's playing."[20]

The concept of the work arrangement is also important to my analysis about popular song covers, where audiences are invited to attend closely to differences of meaning that arise from differences in how the song is arranged. I offer an extended example at the end of the chapter.

To orient this in terms of points I introduced in Chapter 1, the gap between features of a particular musical work and features of its performances should take account of whether it is a "thick" or "thin" musical work. Musical works are thin when their "determinative properties are comparatively few in number"—that is, there are relatively few features that must be kept constant in all performances and thick when the determinative properties are relatively high in number, more tightly regulating what performers must do to perform music that counts as an instance of that work.[21] Popular songs, including jazz standards, are relatively thin in their constitutive properties. As long as performers get the words basically right and give listeners a recognizable version of the song's melody, performers can pretty much do whatever else they want to do and it will count as a performance of that song. The Carolina Chocolate Drops do not fail to perform the song "Hit 'Em Up Style (Oops!)" (2001) by dropping Blue Cantrell's original R&B arrangement, eliminating all electronic instruments, and arranging it for fiddle and banjo (2010). In contrast, playing a Haydn string quartet on just fiddle and banjo is not to play it, because performing it with two violins, one cello, and one viola is a work-determinative or necessary property of that work.

Other properties, such as tempo, are also characteristic of thicker works, but that property is more indeterminate than the need for four specific instruments for a Haydn quartet. Where Haydn specifies that the second movement of his Symphony No. 92 is an adagio, conductors understand that it should be performed at a slower tempo than the fourth movement's presto. If it is too slow to recognize as Haydn's music, a performance can be dismissed as not really a performance of Haydn's work. But how slow is too slow? Given that no conductor has ever stretched the Adagio to last more than ten minutes, there seems to be consensus that fifteen minutes is *too* slow. At the same time, this symphony is not in the tradition of musical works for which the precise time length of each movement is a composer-determined feature. Still, in comparison with jazz and popular music, classical works in the mainstream repertoire are relatively thick in their constitutive properties, which is to say that an orchestra does not actually provide an instance of Haydn's Symphony No. 92 if they ignore his detailed normative instructions about the instrumentation, note sequences, tempos, and so on.[22]

As a final point about thicker and thinner works, we may observe that *arrangements* are thicker in constitutive properties than the works they arrange (e.g., compare the three different *styles* of music that guide the distinct arrangements of "Piece of My

Heart" used by Franklin, Joplin, and Hill, where the stylistic differences must be properties additional to the basic words, melody, and so on). However, a music culture centered on recordings encourages auditors to associate each song with a particular arrangement and performance interpretation. When a song is subsequently performed for auditors who can be expected to refer to a base recording, the new interpretation can generate meanings that arise from its degree of similarity to, and degree of departure from, the reference recording. So a cover does more than interpret a song. It also invites auditors to compare the new track with the familiar arrangement and interpretation of that song. Occasionally, but only occasionally, pop covers work by slavishly following the base recording. Two interesting cases are Todd Rundgren's *Faithful* (1976) and Los Lobos's *Native Sons* (2021). Both include sonic recreations of well-known tracks from the 1960s, minimizing the differences.

Although jazz originated as popular music and was popularized through recordings, it has differentiated itself from both popular and classical music by adopting a performance norm of improvisational presentation of thin musical works.[23] Jazz standards were originally popular songs, but vocalists are no longer the norm in jazz groups. Knowledgeable jazz fans did not regard the absence of sung lyrics as a significant interpretive decision when the Bill Evans Trio recorded the Gershwin song "My Man's Gone Now" in 1961, or when Miles Davis recorded "Time after Time" (1985), a song co-written and popularized by Cyndi Lauper (1983). Neither group had a vocalist, and the melody lines were taken over by piano and trumpet, respectively. Some of Davis's audience was aware of Lauper's original version; some probably was not. Here, again, we see the importance of intentions, for if Davis's intention was to treat new pop songs as new standards, rather than a response to Lauper's specific recording, then it was not intended to be heard as a cover.[24]

Granted, someone might say, "I liked the jazz trio last night. They covered Monk and Gershwin." However, I propose that this use of "covered" is synonymous with "performed." Nothing is conveyed by it that would not be present in "They performed Monk and Gershwin." Furthermore, jazz audiences find little value in performances that simply replicate the interpretation of an earlier performer. It might be interesting to hear someone copy Monk's playing for one tune, but a jazz set that consisted of someone other than Monk playing *Solo Monk* (1965) in order, just like the record, will not interest most jazz fans. The jazz audience focuses on real-time interpretation as developed in the particularity of the performance. Because the interpretation is shaped by the performance means available (e.g., which instruments are on the bandstand tonight?), recent jazz offers few opportunities to evaluate a particular performance *as of* a particular arrangement. Today, the jazz audience expects real-time performer interpretation of the work with extensive improvisation.

Consequently, there are three important general contrasts between jazz and popular music. First, jazz celebrates real-time improvisation and spontaneity in performance interpretation. In fact, it does so to such a degree that many or most people find the music hard to follow, even inaccessible. As a general rule, the jazz audience attends to and evaluates each individual performance as a manifestation of the particular players on that occasion. Differences in interpretations of the same work are generally tied to their particular skills. Second, it has largely abandoned the practice of vocal song performance. Third, although recording technology did a great deal to generate the popularity and internal development of jazz, and while certain recordings are regarded as particularly significant by the jazz audience, recordings are not regarded as the primary objects of critical attention except as vehicles for providing access to particular exemplary performances. A jazz fan who does not know Miles Davis's *Kind of Blue* (1959) hardly counts as a jazz fan, but that record is nonetheless treated as a transparent vehicle for hearing stellar performances by a particular group of players. As a result, the arrangements and "original" performances on *Kind of Blue* can serve as a reference point for interpretation of those pieces by subsequent groups. Judging by the number of jazz artists who've recorded it, the most popular piece is probably "So What," but it seems to be stretching the concept to the limits to call those remakes "covers."

This third point is central. Although jazz depends on recordings, jazz is not sufficiently phono-centric to generate a general culture of cover recordings. Popular music operates differently. In jazz, some songs have become "standards," but they are most often performed without the words. In contrast, popular music treats particular recordings as the standards, not just the skeleton of the song.[25] A jazz fan who knows the song "Bye Bye Blackbird" only from Miles Davis recordings, and who consequently does not know the words, would not be regarded as strange—unlike a popular music fan who loves "Dazed and Confused" but knows only the instrumental arrangement on *The String Quartet Tribute to Led Zeppelin* (2007).

Another contributing factor in the culture of covers is the pop music tradition of one-hit wonders: singers and bands who are known for one and only one recording. The performer is not well known and, for most auditors, has no established persona, so the performer's other music is irrelevant to the experience of the recording. Indeed, the one-hit wonder is often of interest *because* it is so unexpected, because the performer is otherwise uninteresting. The focus is the way that a particular song, arrangement, interpretation, and performance come together in a particular recording. The song itself may be of negligible interest. A case in point is Norman Greenbaum's "Spirit in the Sky" (1970) which created a pop hit by appropriating the boogie style of John Lee Hooker (yet without being a cover of any particular song). Ten years later, The Vapors's "Turning Japanese" (1980) was a one-hit wonder of the new wave movement, and ten years after that, Vanilla Ice gave us the multiply derivative "Ice Ice Baby" (1990). In popular music, so many recordings are released each year that having even one successful recording is considered a great success. *Writing* a hit song is not regarded as equally noteworthy.[26] To even know that "Turning Japanese" was written by David Fenton is to qualify oneself as a true aficionado of new wave music.

Taking Stock

To summarize the argument to this point, covering is a complex communicative action. A musical culture founded on mass distribution of recorded music allows musicians to anticipate the audience's facility in comparing their arrangement and interpretation of a particular song with earlier, specific recording of it. To a lesser but not insignificant degree, musicians are expected to write their own material. "It's Oh So Quiet," Björk's biggest hit, is missing from her album *Greatest Hits* (2002) because, she said, she was a "pioneer" within popular music and refused to be defined by someone else's song.[27] The centrality of particular recordings to musical "literacy" and, to a lesser extent, the growing expectation that popular musicians will write their own songs jointly provide the underlying conditions for cover versions.

The Need for a Base Track

I have stressed that a cover is a remake that presupposes audience familiarity with another recording of it, which it thereby "covers." As such, a cover's treatment of the familiar song invites comparison with an established arrangement as interpreted by a particular performer. Where a performer cannot expect the likely audience to have access to or knowledge of an "original" recording as a standard for comparison, there may be a remake but there is no cover. Country music fans of the early 1990s were not, in general, fans of San Francisco blues-based-psychedelia from twenty-five years before, and so Nashville producers knew that the target audience for Faith Hill's debut album would hear "Piece of My Heart" with fresh ears, remaking a proven rock hit to get a new hit record on the country charts.

In the interesting sense of "cover" and "covering" that goes beyond a mere remake, the cover song or cover performance communicates the performer's awareness of, and even attitude toward, a particular recorded fusion of song, arrangement, and musicianship and, frequently, performance persona. General influence is insufficient. Some original songs by popular musicians are derivative without being covers. They adopt the style of another musician or earlier genre, such as Savoy Brown's 1969 single, "Train to Nowhere," a relatively pedestrian original blues song that appropriates several styles without referencing any particular song or musician. It involves appropriation of style without being a cover. The Knickerbockers's top-20 hit "Lies" (1965) is an amazing imitation of The Beatles; yet, it does not imitate or otherwise reference any particular track. Hence, it is not a cover. The requisite level of particularity is at the level of being able to name one particular recording that is being "covered."

As many have emphasized, the first recording of a song is not always the one that serves as the base or "original" for purposes of covering. Kris Kristofferson wrote "Me and Bobby McGee" and "Sunday Morning Coming Down," among many other songs; yet, those two are closely associated with the recorded versions by Janis Joplin (1971) and Johnny Cash (1969, edited for single release 1970), respectively. Both songs had already been recorded and released by other singers in 1969: "Me and Bobby McGee" by Roger Miller and "Sunday Morning Coming Down" by Ray Stevens. Now suppose that a roots-music "Americana" band records its debut album in 2022, and the album features these two songs alongside twelve original songs. I suspect almost everyone who recognizes the songs will regard them as covers of Joplin and Cash—but, absent further specification, not of Kristofferson, even though he has recorded them himself.

"I Think We're Alone Now"

In distinguishing covers from remakes, I have suggested that we must look at precedence, cultural context, performance context, and other variables. Unlike most writers, I see intentions as a key variable. As I explained in Chapter 7, covers are extended allusions to previous works. As such, a cover is an intended reference that is established by intentional textual similarity to a source text, creating an association that goes beyond mere substitution of a referent.[28] Although remakes will always satisfy the requirement of textual similarity, remaking does not require allusion, nor even knowledge of specific earlier recordings. Hence, a mere similarity between versions by different performers is insufficient to establish reference to specific antecedent tracks. Given the guiding role of style norms, any two musicians who perform the same song in the same style might accidentally produce far more similarity than found, for example, between Johnny Cash's famous cover of "Hurt" (2002) and the Nine Inch Nails original (1994).

I have described covers as extended, saturated allusions. Normally, allusion is a local, small-scale aesthetic effect brought about when one text intentionally parallels and thus references another text, a reference intended to be understood in that way by at least some of its audience. It is a means by which accessible works remain accessible while generating indirection and inviting a consequent search for relevance regarding the overlap and, thereby, a richness of meaning. Covers are a mass media application of this familiar technique. Covers are saturated in the sense that every aspect of the performance is to be treated as referencing all aspects of the earlier recording at parallel points in the performance. (Notice that if the expectation of familiarity was simply familiarity with the song, and not a particular recording, then no such comparison could be expected. As thin musical types, popular songs do not have features such as synthesizer squeals, handclaps, and out of tune guitars. These are features of arrangements, performances, and recorded tracks, not songs.)

So how does all of this framework affect utterance meaning? Consider, in this light, two remakes of "I Think We're Alone Now," one by The Rubinoos in 1977 and then the massive hit by the sixteen-year-old Tiffany Darwish in 1987, who performed using only her first name. Tiffany's remake is the more interesting one for multiple reasons. There is nothing in the music or lyric that genders the song. Rather obviously, the original hit by Tommy James and the Shondells (1967) was sung by a man, and the presumption is that the second party of the "we" is female. However, this is an artifact of the performance. Due to her voice, the Tiffany remake of "I Think We're Alone Now" shifts to the perspective of an adolescent girl, and the second party in the "we" is, presumably, male. In the original version, the chorus is followed by three seconds of percussion that mimics a heartbeat, which ties back to the lyric of the chorus. In Tiffany's remake, the breaks after the choruses do not follow the original pattern. The few seconds that lead to the next verse are filled with frenetic electronic percussion and, later, synthesized sound. Because songs are musically "thin," there is no "correct" musical decision here. Yet differences in arrangements drive interpretive differences. Feeling your lover's heartbeat conveys a discovery of intimacy. To drive the point home, Tiffany's remake differs from the original arrangement in another significant way, opening and closing with a new bit of lyric that asserts, with evident pride, "I can change your heartbeat." Despite its lingering veneer of innocence, Tiffany's version is about the manipulation of sexuality. The original hit was about the discovery of it. By contrast, the remake thus makes an assertion about teenage maturity, highlighting female agency.

However, given Tiffany's likely intended audience and the time lag between versions, I suspect that Tiffany's version is more properly a remake than a cover. If we deploy the precise criteria for allusion that I outlined in Chapter 7, where there is an allusion if there is a possibility of audience detection of textual borrowing, then it is an allusion to the Tommy James hit and it is a cover. But this is called into question if we stress, as I did in Chapter 5, that an intention requires a belief that the action informed by the intention will produce the desired result. Did Tiffany and her production team believe that her likely audience of girls her own age (and perhaps younger) would be familiar with that hit record from the 1960s? Once again, context matters.

As Arthur Danto has said, it is hardly possible that those who painted the cave walls at Lascaux intended to make art, for these early "artists" did not have a complex enough culture to have developed the idea that art differs from other cultural activities. Similarly, says Danto, there could not have been flight insurance in the Middle Ages, for there were no airplanes.[29] Cultural achievements and innovations don't just happen because some lone individual initiates them. They can only arise within an appropriate cultural and material context. Covering a pop song might not be as grand as inventing art or even insurance, but audience detection of an allusion cannot occur in a cultural vacuum. Granted, there is a remote possibility that, unprompted, someone who seemingly knows nothing of Chinese culture might understand that I am borrowing from the Chinese *Analects* when I advise them, in response to their bout of writer's block, "the axe handle in your hand is your best model for an axe handle." It is possible, but I wouldn't bet on it. If I have no expectation that my auditor will detect the allusion, it does not really count as an allusion.

Consequently, I think Tiffany and her production team were approaching the song as Hill's production team approached "Piece of My Heart"—a likely hit with a community that would not know the precedent track.

My understanding of the recording would be far richer if I thought that Tiffany's version of "I Think We're Alone Now" is a cover, not just a remake. As a cover, it would allude to the 1960s version and the audience would be invited to hear it as a response. However, remaking a song is insufficient to have it allude to any earlier recording. A cover version differs from a mere remake by responding to, and being about, the song as performed in a certain way by a previous singer or band. As such, if it were a cover, Tiffany's version of "I Think We're Alone Now" would make a comment about differences in attitudes toward teen sexuality in the different decades. As a cover, it would also call attention to the way that 1980s technology and dance beats dominate the arrangement. Beyond the gender change of the main vocal, there would be significance in the alteration of a signature moment of the original hit when the heartbeat percussion is replaced by updated electronic instrumentation. This shift would signal a certain ironic distancing from the relative innocence of the song's overt sentiments. However, this only works if the later combination of arrangement (e.g., the use of synthesizers) and performance interpretation (e.g., Tiffany's oddly slurred vocal at certain points) can be laid against the earlier arrangement (e.g., the use of a "thump thump" heartbeat pattern in the percussion break) and performance (e.g., a vocal that conveys concern and agitation, with occasional interludes of intimacy, but never sexuality). However, in the years before social media and YouTube, Tiffany's target audience was not positioned to make the comparison with a track that was a hit before they were born.

Today, it would be almost impossible to have a hit of that magnitude and not generate a social media firestorm about its borrowed origins. In that sense, the distinction between remake and cover is increasingly erased, and we have entered an age where every remake probably counts as a cover.

In contrast, The Rubinoos's 1977 recording of "I Think We're Alone Now" is almost certainly a cover. It was close enough in time for the pop audience to be aware of the Tommy James hit. It could therefore offer a commentary on teen sexuality by way of allusion and comparison. However, it is less interesting in that it is fairly close to the original hit in its arrangement. Released in the heyday of punk rock, I take it that The Rubinoos were endorsing the value of youthful innocence in response to the cynicism and anger of punk. In the context of their self-titled debut album, that reading of it seems fairly secure.

That I am confident about the cover status of The Rubinoos but not Tiffany is not a problem for my position. Rather, it is the unavoidable result of stressing the covers are *directed*, context-sensitive communications. As such, covers invite reflection on the "speaker's" intentions and beliefs. Was the decision to do a remake based on an expectation that a base version is familiar to the likely audience, or is it based on an expectation of ignorance? If I say that I am uncertain about the beliefs that informed Tiffany's selection and arranging of "I Think We're Alone Now," this is no different from my uncertainty about the beliefs held by others about many things. In the age of social media, I am often uncertain whether people who share certain memes believe the messages they share. (For example, does this person really think that ingesting bleach wards off viral infections, or do they intend to communicate a political stance without actually endorsing the supposed medical benefits of bleach ingestion?) Intentions are enmeshed in beliefs, and beliefs are shaped by cultural position. Most often, the path into a communication that has any complexity is to think about its originating cultural context, and thus the likely beliefs, of the person creating or sharing the communication. As I just suggested about The Rubinoos cover, the relevant cultural context might be a short span of time: 1977, not just the 1970s. The target audience might be local, or very age specific, or established loyal fans.

In conclusion, the alleged simplicity and shallowness of popular music, especially mainstream "pop" hits, is challenged by the existence of covers. As remakes that involve allusions to previously recorded music, covers are rarely present in the classical and jazz traditions. Through interpretive choices, a cover can either endorse the earlier interpretation (by closely following it) or repudiate it (by reworking it stylistically). With mere remakes, an arrangement's differences cannot be taken as commentary on earlier musicians' interpretation and performance choices. With covers, they can. However, as the "wired" world and social media make it effortless to share information, borrowings from older music are more quickly discovered and publicized. In these circumstances the distinction between remake and cover is probably being erased.

9

Listening with Their Eyes: Problems for Radical Intertextuality

Introduction

Every cultural product has antecedents and influences. Consequently, the meaning of an instance of popular music depends on its intertextual connections to other meaningful texts. As such, intertextuality is as indispensable to the meaning of Kitty Wells's hit record "It Wasn't God Who Made Honky Tonk Angels" (1952) as to a high art text such as Richard Wagner's *Parsifal* (1882). Furthermore, intertextuality connects music to many different types of texts, including a wide range of visual texts and material objects. The meaning of Taylor Swift's "Betty" (2020) becomes clearer after relating it to two other songs and attendant videos that were designed to form a trilogy. U2's "The Fly" (1991) became associated with the distinctive wrap-around sunglasses that Bono wore when performing it during the ZOO TV tour. We can generate similar examples until we're exhausted, and the ubiquity of such cases has encouraged the idea that musical and nonmusical texts have equal priority in fixing the meaning of popular songs and performances. The "language" of popular music is dauntingly heterogeneous.

The purpose of this final chapter is to challenge the idea that *aural* intertextuality has no special significance within popular music. Lawrence Grossberg notes that for a broad swath of popular music studies, "it seems to make little or no difference... that we are talking about music."[1] It is a generalization of one critic's claim that "the key to the Pretenders' music has never been their music."[2] As such, *listening* to the music has no special priority as a mode of understanding popular songs in their various uses.

This chapter challenges the idea that listening to popular music's aural properties is incidental to understanding it. As before, my analysis is informed by twentieth-century philosophy of language. However, this chapter shifts focus from intentions and pragmatics to the doctrine of meaning holism.[3] As a generalization from semantic holism, meaning holism underwrites the view that popular music is interesting for everything but the music. Borrowing from Andrew Bennet, I will call this extreme version "radical intertextuality."[4] My goal is to show that this doctrine denies the possibility of meaningful communication. Its adoption—sometimes explicitly but often implicitly—also encourages the view that popular music has social significance while downplaying its capacity to communicate meanings from musicians to the audience. Finally, it often conflates auditor's immediate understanding of a text with a verbal paraphrase of it. However, these are not equivalent as responses.

Radical intertextuality consists of an alignment of three theses. The first thesis is that every text imitates prior texts and is in some sense "about" those texts. Since we will never have access to all of the texts involved, the meaning of any text is fundamentally indeterminate. In Terry Eagleton's influential summary of this idea, the modern text "is plural and diffuse... [and] every word, phrase, or segment is a reworking of other writings... A specific piece of writing thus has no clearly defined boundaries: it spills over constantly into the works clustered around it, generating a hundred different perspectives which dwindle to a vanishing point."[5] Although he is discussing literature, the idea applies to other media. Second, there is the idea that none of the various "works clustered around it" is more relevant than any other in contributing to its meaning. As Eagleton articulates the proposal, there is "no hierarchy of 'textual' levels to tell you what is more or less significant." As such, social media postings about a new music video are not subsidiary or secondary to the video. Third, there is Roland Barthes's frequently cited notion of the death of the author: "There is one place where this multiplicity is focused, and that place is the reader, not, as was hitherto said, the author."[6] Barthes's proclamation is an update of an idea that we have confronted several times already in this book, namely the position that the intentions of songwriters and performers do not matter to the texts they produce. Meanings are produced by readers and auditors, not by authors, speakers, or performers. Within musicology, this view has been strongly defended in recent years by Nicholas Cook, who argues that meaning "is constituted in the experience of hearing and seeing."[7]

I endorse a more moderate model of intertextuality, rejecting the second thesis and modifying the first and third. Recognizing "author" (musician) and "reader" (listener) as joint partners in the production of meaning is both more plausible and pragmatically more desirable.

Radical Intertextuality

Richard Middleton's observes that "cultural studies neglects [music] because of the forbiddingly special character of music."[8] (We might regard this negligence as the theoretical triumph of The Replacements's great line, "I hate music/It's got too many notes.") Unfortunately, when radical intertextuality downplays *musical* intertextuality as of no special importance, it supports the view that fans do not respond to the music *as music*. More specifically, songs and their performances and recordings are only incidentally the bearers of meaning. Such views support the stereotype that popular music is musically trivial.

My interest in this topic stems from my encounter with David Shumway's iconoclastic reading of rock music: "I want to say more than merely that rock and roll is an impure musical form; it is not even mainly a musical form."[9] Obviously, there is no reason to limit this idea to rock and roll. If true, it should also hold for the Delta blues, bluegrass, Finnish death metal—it can be extended to all of popular music. But if audiences are not really responding to a musical form, there is no priority to *listening* for or prioritizing *sonic* intertextual links. We might as well watch music videos with the sound off, a complaint voiced by Chip Z'Nuff of Enuff Z'Nuff: "MTV was only playing big-haired bands, and we wanted to get our stuff accepted... People were listening with their eyes instead of their ears."[10]

Shumway encourages us to approach the music as "a historically specific cultural practice" involving a unique combination of specific social conditions, such as the youth culture of the 1950s and thereafter, and various technological developments.[11] Despite some rather lackluster music and some bad weather, the original Woodstock festival is beloved as a symbol of the end of the sixties (as in "the Woodstock generation"). Shumway recasts it as a complex conjuncture of youth culture and modern technology. I grant that the eternal recurrence of Woodstock in the subsequent documentary film is part of the Woodstock myth, but his stance goes farther in proposing that this amalgamation of music, people, and film constitutes an "instance" of rock and roll. In other words, Woodstock was not a rock festival that happened to get on film. Woodstock is a paradigm case of "rock and roll" precisely because it involves both youth culture and dissemination through film and a soundtrack album. It is also noteworthy for the way it exemplifies the cultural practice of interplay between audience and performers in a participatory event. In Barthes's terms, Woodstock was a writerly text (*scriptible*, challenging the audience to "write" their own text in piecing it together) rather than a readerly text (*lisible*, constructed to lead the audience to concentrate on the writer's intended meanings). It sounds suspiciously as if the festival would not be classified as a rock and roll event if the crowd had been smaller and had been edited out of the documentary film.

I am not rejecting Shumway out of hand. From the start of this book I have argued that the meaning of any particular performance or recording depends on its various relationships within historically contingent cultural practices and events. But I have also aligned meaning with the intentions that inform the actions of real people when they create or share instances of particular songs. Those intentions and actions *constrain* what their agency communicates. My primary goal in this chapter is to demonstrate that these meanings are understood by reference to a more modest network of intertexts and practices than postulated by radical intertextuality.

Treating sound as peripheral also encourages the view that performers themselves are the primary texts or bearers of meaning—rather than songs, videos, recorded tracks, and particular performances. As Shumway puts it, Madonna and R.E.M. are carriers of specific meanings, "distinct from all other bands and performers."[12] However, the artist is never the flesh and blood human. The artist is yet another intertextual construct: "Madonna is... a web of intertextual meanings crossing media boundaries, 'she' is a sign formed by television, film, records, the press, and the publicity industry."[13] Madonna is the intertextual space involving "the aggregate of all [appearances] and an essential part of the reading of any one." A similar stance informs Pamela Wilson's rich analysis of multiple meanings embodied in the persona constructed by Dolly Parton.[14]

While I endorsed the importance of personae in Chapter 3, singing and musicianship are generally central to most popular music personae. Parton became a much-loved singer in Zimbabwe in the pre-internet era when few Zimbabweans had access to her carefully manicured persona. They knew her only from songs on the radio. Unfortunately, Wilson's discussion of Parton concentrates on everything except her singing and songs, the things that come across when access is restricted to songs on the radio.[15] Is Parton (Zimbabwe) different from Parton (USA), or do both count equally as facets of the Parton persona? As a writerly text, radical intertextuality posits as many Partons as there are listeners; there is no stable persona to analyze.

I am also concerned that when general intertextuality takes precedence over *specific* intertextuality, we lose the importance of allusion and cover songs, which are cases of the latter.[16] Although Madonna's video for "Material Girl" (1984) is a hypertext of a famous song and dance number featuring Marilyn Monroe, John Fiske regards that source text as dispensable. The video "refers to our culture's image bank of the sexy blonde star... and upon its intertextuality with all texts that contribute to and draw upon the meaning of 'the blonde' in our culture."[17] However, this emphasis redirects us from textual details to symbolic types. On this approach, one must suppose that a Lenny Kravitz video sets up a dialogue with every text in the image bank featuring "the" Black male. Due to the interracial sexual dynamic generated by the presence of Heather Graham, Kravitz's video for "American Woman" (1999) seems to have as much intertextual play with *The Birth of a Nation* (1915) as with the film *Austin Powers: The Spy Who Shagged Me* (1999: its specific intertextual connection) or the original Guess Who song that Kravitz is covering.

Here we confront the second thesis. Music is merely a staging ground for exploring a range of associated texts, no one among them more relevant than any other for auditor understanding. However, if every intertextual link is of equal importance, then visuals, marketing, and social media comments are more important than the music, for these are more accessible as pathways into intertextuality. Kravitz was covering a song by a musical group from Winnipeg, Canada, which is also the home of film director Guy Maddin, who made the film *My Winnipeg* (2007). Is that film as important to the meaning of the Kravitz video as the song or *Austin Powers*? Evidently so, for radical intertextuality denies that any associations are more important than others. Thus, little or no meaning need be assigned to a listener's sense of the musical gestalt or in the wealth of detail that remains ever ineffable.[18] Meaning is extracted from among an instance's numerous happenstance relationships within a larger cultural apparatus that sustains the ongoing play of texts.

Due to the multitude of texts—swelling each day as new ones are produced, and multiplying each time we notice another intertextual connection—each auditor becomes an idiosyncratic "reader" and the possibility of correct and incorrect interpretation is rendered incoherent. Thus, the third thesis.

Ironically, if some nonmusical "text" or form of discourse had instead become dominant through the same convergence of technology and youth culture in the formative years of rock and roll, then *that* would be fully equivalent to rock and roll. Suppose Elvis had been a professional wrestler, and suppose pro-wrestling played the same role—as a cultural practice disseminated by diverse resources of mass media—historically played by the music that we know as rock and roll and then rock. This "text" would serve as well as rock and roll music, for it would *mean* the same thing. We might therefore say that radical intertextuality treats the actual music as the pretext and not the text.

Global Holism

Music is a cultural universal. Granted, some individuals are unmusical and some even find all musical sounds painful to hear. But those are exceptions. One of the main lessons of ethnomusicology is that music is a meaningful cultural practice because it is a key element "whereby individuals are collectively moved to think and organize themselves."[19] Concerts and clubs are often attended as social arenas, as places to see and be seen, rather than as outlets for music. And this is not a criticism; music played a functional role in human culture for thousands of years before it became "art" in a handful of societies. In many contexts where music is present, music is the sideshow, not the main event.

However, I want to challenge Shumway's hyperbolic claim that rock and roll "is not even mainly a musical form." If it is true of rock and roll that meaning-making depends on almost anything but the music, then it is also true of country music, Gospel music, and every other genre of music.

Earlier, I indicated that the second thesis assumes meaning holism. Holism says that the meaning of any individual utterance or text arises only through its role in the whole language: "The meaning of an expression depends constitutively on its relation to all other expressions in the language."[20] Many global holists also stress interdependencies with nonlinguistic signs and symbols. The essential point is that the *system* is meaningful rather than its basic units.[21] Utterances derive meaning from the system, rather than the other way around.

A holism that will embrace *every* intertextual reference—which does not prioritize sonic elements—erases stylistic boundaries and category placements as trivial. We can discuss "rock music" and point to a "rock formation," but perceptually distinguishable categories are never our referent. "Rock," "heavy metal," and "neo-soul" might designate social practices and relationships, but not differences that are internal to the musical language. Confronted by unfamiliar music, fans would seem to be in the position of being at one of those auctions where the government disposes of sealed boxes whose contents are not open to inspection. The auctioneer can call for bids on "the contents of box 42." We can refer to them successfully under that description, but the success of our reference lies entirely in our singling out the container. Aside from guesses based on the dimensions of the box or its weight when we move it, we don't know what is in the box; the description is without meaning apart from the act of ostension. But an act of ostension that gestures to everything is an empty gesture. An act of ostension is useful only if there are empirical manifestations to which one is specifically directed.

Thus, the most radical version of meaning holism, global holism, underwrites the second thesis of radical intertextuality: it all counts equally. In response, I endorse the moderate position of *local* holism and a correspondingly modest role for intertextuality.²² Local holism says that the meaning of an expression or utterance depends on the meaning of *some* others in the same language.²³ Defending local holism as more plausible than global holism supports the centrality of *musical* intertextuality when it is present.

Entry Points Are Always Local

Readerly texts, ones with definite intended meanings that auditors decode, have long been accused of putting meaning out of reach in an inner, private realm of artistic intention. In earlier chapters, I argued that appeals to artistic intention are not subject to this criticism. However, I fear that accounts that privilege writerly texts might also do so, and therefore we ought not to discount musicians' intentions in an effort to turn Madonna's "Material Girl" video into a writerly text. Radical intertextuality either appeals to the whole system and so renders meaning indeterminate, or it appeals to each reader's "rewriting" to secure a temporary basis for meaning. This emphasis on the audience (the third thesis) generates several well-known problems for global holism and so for radical intertextuality.

Let us return to the idea that differences between *artists* are fundamental, and consider this proposal: "While most listeners to 'Radio Free Europe' haven't any idea what the song is about, they have already come to understand the meaning of R.E.M. as distinct from all other bands and performers of rock & roll."²⁴ Since Michael Stipe's enunciation was so cryptic on early R.E.M. records that the words are anybody's guess, we are invited to conclude that, like opera sung in a foreign language, auditors know that the words have meaning and so seek a "narrative" in the performance. This narrative meaning is supplied, it is generally supposed, by the band's persona. The "meaning" of this persona, in turn, arises only in relation to the whole rock and roll apparatus.

Taking the theory at face value, how could a global holist ever *learn* culturally contingent meanings in the first place? The notion of intertextuality presupposes that audience members find meaning; yet, it also seems to deny the very possibility of ever *entering into* a new or "alien" language. This problem has been raised against W.V. Quine's classic defense of holism, which famously asks us to imagine the case of a linguist cast into an alien culture and assigned the task of producing a translation manual. Quine defends global holism by arguing that two incompatible translation manuals might be equally successful at translating the same language. Considering the case of a field linguistic trying to translate the language of an isolated tribe of people, Quine concludes that there is never any "natural" English expression for any foreign one, so there can be no factual determination that one translation is the "correct" one.²⁵ Therefore, no utterance has a determinate meaning and the whole language is the unit of meaning.

However, Quine's field linguist already knows English and can articulate complex hypotheses in order to evaluate unfamiliar expressions. Ludwig Wittgenstein identifies the same assumption in Augustine's discussion of names and reference, and recognizes that it dodges the question of how we ever got started in the language system.[26] How does the language user acquire the background information to engage in writerly rewriting, much less to engage in readerly interpretation? Yet each language user "entered" a language once, in infancy (one's native language). A one-year-old in an English-speaking household comes to understand an emphatic "No!" in advance of understanding the whole of English grammar and the attendant society. (At the same time, the child is learning the *musical* basics of their society's common music.) Clearly, infants have a method for determining that utterances are meaningful units with relatively stable meanings. And there must be a way to do so without referencing the entire language.[27] If we were free (as "readers" or audience) to "rewrite" every text, then we would never assign consistent meaning to multiple instances of a word or phrase in a way that could guide us in our later, more complex explorations of intertextuality. Paradoxically, if meaning rests with the entirety of the relevant language, the process of grasping the meaning of the simplest texts would be precisely as complex as the meaning of the most complex texts.

In short, if global holism is true, then radical intertextuality cannot explain how anyone could become interested in any area of popular culture in the first place. It must be possible to retrieve *some* meaning from an early R.E.M. song (or an R.E.M. video, a particular book, or episode of a TV show, or whatever) in advance of grasping its place in the whole system. Granted, R.E.M.'s "Losing My Religion" features allusion and complex polysemy, and in actual practice fans do not *begin* by grasping all of the possible meanings of such texts. But to grasp *some* meaning is to grasp something that is not negligible. Understanding may be sufficient without being exhaustive.[28] A modest intertextuality may be sufficient.

Consider the case of Billy Corgan and the Smashing Pumpkins's cover of "Dreaming" (1996). Listening to their early albums, it is safe to say that Corgan listened to The Beatles and Cheap Trick more than The Shaggs, and to Led Zeppelin more than King Crimson and Aretha Franklin. Corgan describes the limited perspective available to him given his Midwestern roots and his initial entry point into rock:

> We didn't grow up hanging out, being cool, going to concerts... our exposure to alternative music was the Smiths, the Cure, and some Bauhaus. We weren't aware of some underground scene, or a punk-rock movement in L.A. We weren't surrounded by a culture that supported experimentation. We were supported by a culture that was like, "I can't come see you play because I've got to be at work at nine in the morning."[29]

Corgan's formative source of music was the radio, so Smashing Pumpkins naturally covers Blondie's "Dreaming" (1979), a radio single, rather than a more obscure album track like "Kidnapper" (1977). The fragmentation of commercial radio, juxtaposing isolated chunks of music, requires listeners to draw meaning from music with few clues as about its place in the rock and roll apparatus. Ignorant of most of the music that led others into alternative music and cut off from the subculture that fostered the music, Corgan nonetheless "got" the core implications of the new wave to which he was exposed. The group's slow, menacing cover version of Blondie's "Dreaming" brings out its dark, neurotic undertones. Ironically, the music is closer to Bauhaus than to Blondie. Corgan caught some of the meaning of both the lighter and heavier sides of new wave through exposure to a very small sample of that larger musical movement. He did not grasp the text's position in relation to every other text in the language. Yet he grasped enough to extract core musical mechanics of expressive communication.

Our capacity to enter into unfamiliar cultural landscapes counts in favor of a more localized holism. As Quine ultimately recognized, meaning arises in relation to "chunks" or relatively small clusters of the language. This is a local holism: meaning depends upon "clusters of sentences just inclusive enough to have critical semantic mass."[30] In this spirit, Corgan's exposure to The Cure and Bauhaus—contrasted with his general exposure to FM radio—was sufficient to provide him with a good idea of their meaning. His understanding of Cure singles and Bauhaus songs did not depend on his ability to distinguish them from the Germs and The Vaselines, nor on his ability to articulate the particular form of rock that they represented.

Deploying the Architextual Apparatus

Radical intertextuality holds that every text presupposes a complex institutional apparatus that supplies its identity and meaning(s). Gérard Genette calls this apparatus the "architextuality of the text" and describes it as "the entire set of general or transcendent categories—types of discourse, modes of enunciation, [relevant] genres—from which emerges each singular text."[31] It includes the sum total of general categories needed to locate any text within the totality of texts.[32] In Vincent Descombes's metaphor, "one must buy the whole... or forgo the purchase."[33] This move clarifies the first thesis. It also bolsters the second thesis' rejection of textual hierarchies: a point I'll explore in detail in the next section.

Because cultural location and textual identity may depend on a vast array of categories, the interpretive framework threatens to become unbounded. Grossberg therefore worries that too much intertextuality "threatens to make all analysis futile," and he endorses a more limited and specific architextual apparatus that downplays some potential intertextual relationships.[34] This appears to be an admission that our interpretive "apparatus" should be some form of local holism. However, I think his version remains insufficiently localized. He says,

> To treat rock and roll as a set of musical texts whose effects can be read off their surface or to be located within the isolated relation between music and fan is already to assume an interpretation of its place within a particular rock and roll apparatus. Instead, the music's effects and identity can only be described within the apparatus which connects particular fragments of heterogeneous domains of social, cultural and material practices.[35]

Grossberg's label for this apparatus is "the rock formation." In Shumway's version, rock is a discursive practice, a cultural practice, and a sign system.[36]

Note Grossberg's proposal that fans cannot "read" from the surface of the music unless it derives is identity and meaning from the cultural apparatus, for no one can read any social implications directly from the music.[37] I agree about social implications, for if we could do so, we would not have to consult contexts of production and intended use to determine those meanings. However, that does nothing to show that fans must be aware of a significant architextual apparatus and cultural formation. Grossberg and Shumway are stressing that social practices, not individual judgment, provide the music's identity, determining whether the Beastie Boys were hip-hop and whether Lil Nas X's "Old Town Road" (2019) is country music. Notice that this point tends to undermine the third thesis, that the audience *constructs* their own text by assigning each instance of the music to a place within the larger web of cultural practices and assumptions.

So just how large is the "web" of intertextuality that confers musical identity? If not the whole language, then what? Do we draw a boundary around the "language" of popular music, or limit it to a particular style or genre? It is not a rhetorical question to ask whether the rock formation is distinct from the hip-hop formation, or the degree to which they intersect: a recent sociological study concludes that popular music currently supports sixteen distinct genres or socio-musical "worlds."[38] The number is not the point. We have a circularity problem in the proposal that interpretation depends on identity, and identity depends on the architextual apparatus or current configuration of domains of practice.

The circularity problem will be familiar to anyone acquainted with a well-known theory in philosophy, the institutional theory of art.[39] Theories of this sort hold that the salience of particular properties of a text derives from identity conferred by a historically contingent cultural "institution" or formation: instances count as instances of the cultural category only if institutionally confirmed as such.[40] As has been noted many times, institutional theories of art must remain mute about the character of the objects it so classifies. Because the institutional theory is meant to affirm creativity and avoid closure on what might become relevant in the future, appeal to the institution can tell us *which* things are included by insiders, but it cannot place limits on why one thing is given that status and others are not.[41] Therefore, the "definition" is hollow insofar as absolutely anything might be admitted as an instance. Music that sounds exactly like classic bluegrass might, in 2030, count as Finnish death metal. At best, limitations may arise because a text's "functions are determined in part by its shape and appearance."[42]

I don't think it helps to say, with Grossberg, that identification of some music as rock and roll (rather than, say, country) "is already to assume an interpretation of its place within a particular rock and roll apparatus." This apparatus is, primarily, a matter of social practices and subcultural identity. But if a text receives a specific classification because the audience already interprets it in light of the whole formation, we arrive at the banal thought that whatever is thus classified by the audience as rock is whatever is thus classified as such by that audience. Auditors must consult other auditors to know what counts as a text within the rock formation. (Granted, some of that must happen in the phase of first learning what belongs in which category.) However, if that formation is a conglomeration of "heterogeneous domains of social, cultural and material practices," then an auditor's primary guidance in classifying unfamiliar instances will be to anticipate the music's social effects on those others in light of prevailing practices. But if *that* is the core of interpretation, then listening attentively and repeatedly to a piece of music becomes a puzzling behavior, as strange as it would be for a motorist to closely study the details of a traffic sign after having already grasped its practical role in the system. Consequently, I think that an excessive emphasis on functionality underestimates the role of aesthetic preference, another point I develop in Section 6.

A better approach is to endorse architextuality as relevant while simultaneously allowing that the myriad details of each text (e.g., song instances)—both standard and nonstandard features—are relevant to its identity and meaning. Although musical kinds are not natural kinds, bluegrass sounds different enough from death metal to support (and also reflect) our socio-musical distinctions. Informed decisions about the presence and absence of these features do not presuppose awareness of the musical text's precise location in the total language. In short, identifiable genres and conventions are normally grounded in manifest musical properties, and yet instances of these local "languages" exemplify standard features in wildly varying degrees.[43]

For example, when The Beatles first appeared on the *Ed Sullivan Show* (February, 1964, and a singular event in rock history if anything was), the audience sat through a lot of non-rock, too. Whole families gathered to watch; kids and parents literally made up a single audience. But in seizing on The Beatles's performance while the older generation made jokes about their hair, the rock audience recognized itself in the performance, just as the members of The Beatles had earlier recognized themselves in the music of Elvis Presley, Chuck Berry, and Little Richard. Few teens and preadolescents recognized themselves in Ed Sullivan's parade of trained animals, Catskill comics, acrobats, and plate jugglers. Did any members of the viewing audience have difficulty separating the rock and roll from the rest? I suspect that virtually everyone could tell that one of these things was not like the others. The discrimination did not rely on the larger rock formation, if only for the reason that many were not aware of it until that evening. Furthermore, the apparatus was incomplete and evolving right before them. If the rock formation is language-like, then we must take account of its capacity to evolve.[44] That evolution must involve deviations from the pre-existing language or formation. To achieve originality, new texts will violate the rules of the pre-existing language.

In sum, we should be very suspicious of any version of intertextuality as *déjà*, in which every text is already written and read.[45] Watching The Beatles on *Ed Sullivan*, the audience recognized that The Beatles were different from the other acts they saw that night, and that The Beatles were very different from American rock and rollers like Elvis Presley. The auditory and visual properties of the performance were more central than any postulated apparatus, for the audience had a direct apprehension of the music in advance of the crystallization of the rock formation. Therefore, a local holism (a level of intertextuality far short of global holism) must sometimes be sufficient to secure considerable meaning for instances of popular music, including "texts" violating the norms of the pre-existing language.

Unlike global and large-scale holisms, local holism assumes that there are incremental limits on what the audience can accept as belonging in a particular genre at any particular time. Think of the scene in the film *Back to the Future* (1985) where Marty, Michael J. Fox's character, starts playing a Chuck Berry tune at a high school prom and then embellishes it with a heavy metal guitar solo. The assembled teens respond as if he were a visitor from Mars, which, in a sense, he is. At least some of the music's own sonic qualities are relevant to its being put forward as a rock text. Handling of tempo and beat was particularly crucial to the music's initial reception as rock and roll.[46] We would be dumbfounded to find Bing Crosby's recording of "Try A Little Tenderness" (1933) *ever* being accepted as indie rock music by Sleater-Kinney fans, and not just for sociological reasons. Fans respond to musical similarities and differences, most of which they work out for themselves—an activity of discovery, not just rewriting.

The upshot is that, as an account of meaning, radical intertextuality offers no reason to refer to sonic differences when explaining what any musical style or genre is, or of its attractions or meanings for its audience.[47] "Rock" and other genre classifications function as proper names for their framing formations rather than as general nouns or kind terms that collect instances based on intrinsic or manifest features. Hence, saying "This is Sinéad O'Connor's reggae album" and "This is where Taylor Swift abandons country for pop" function as acts of ostension directing us away from the details of the instances.

In real life, however, most people can correctly identify the basic genre for any piece of popular music they encounter, and they can do so simply by hearing a tiny snippet of music.[48]

Local Holism and the Immediacy of Meaning

Finally, let us return to the idea that texts have no hierarchical order and so each audience member's interpretive act constrains and constitutes the text, temporarily securing meaning.

Because the rock formation generates too many intertextual relations to permit either musicians or corporations to control the readings given by the audience (the second thesis), we might be tempted to agree that every "reading" must be selectively partial, *constituting* or co-creating the text (the third thesis). The audience's "rewriting" supplants its originating authorship, which was, in any event, a stitching together of many texts. Thus, Fiske emphasizes that younger Madonna fans had never seen Marilyn Monroe movies, so Monroe was irrelevant to their interpretation of Madonna's "Material Girl" video. As I put it in Chapter 7, the allusion was no longer overt. Fiske takes this to mean that young fans must interact with a different text (an "image bank") than do those of us who have seen the film sequence in which Monroe sings "Diamonds Are a Girl's Best Friend" (1953).

This common endorsement of auditor "rewriting" creates a substitution problem. I have repeatedly stressed that auditor rewriting should be understood as indifference to *invitations* issued by performers. Rather than revisit that point, I offer a related criticism: "rewriting" stabilizes nothing. Instead, it substitutes a second "text" for the musical instance. This new text will not be an individualized text (whether artist or song or recording), because locating meaning in the generalized image bank or generalized background refers auditors to abstract *types* rather than instances or tokens of types. Recall Grossberg's emphasis on the goal describing "the specific effects (and popularity) of particular forms of rock and roll."[49] One consequence, for music or for any other system of signs, is that the basic unit of meaning must be an abstraction: we interpret the structure of the general rock formation, not specific recordings, songs, or performances. A search for meaning sends each auditor in search of a text that is different from the particular song instances or utterances we set out to explain. Hence, this approach repudiates most of what I have argued for in this book. Furthermore, prioritizing large-scale architextuality at the expense of special intertextuality seems inconsistent with the anti-hierarchical doctrine of the second thesis. Ironically, it recalls the attention paid to the abstract structural type in classical music: listeners should listen *through* the instances to the abstract work.

The basic problem is that the process of assigning an instance to a location in the larger-scale apparatus generates a theoretically informed interpretation of the instance. Recall Grossberg's words: "A particular music exists as 'rock and roll' for an audience only when it is located in a larger assemblage which I will call 'the rock and roll apparatus.'" However, let us be careful about the relationship between large-scale background conditions for meaningfulness and detection of specific meanings, such as that of the sentence you are reading now. Granted, the words on this page are accessible to readers of the English language only because there is a larger assemblage of the relevant sort. Having the "assemblage" in place is a necessary condition for meaningful communication in English, but *awareness* of that assemblage as such is not a necessary condition for understanding most ordinary utterances.

Tellingly, on those occasions where we do work out a text's position in the architextual apparatus, it "does not mean that the participant natives also read the texts that way."[50] I presume that for rock and roll, participant "natives" would be fans of the music. Popular music is accessible because most of the audience is "at home" with a less complex text than the one emphasized by cultural analysis and radical intertextuality. For example, the fact that low-budget 1950s science fiction films can be read as expressions of cold war hysteria does not mean that their original audiences understood them in that way at that time. Analogously, consider Altamont, the free concert thrown by The Rolling Stones near Livermore, California, on December 9, 1969. It has come to symbolize the collapse of the utopian vision of the Summer of Love and the Woodstock Nation but this does not mean that anyone at the concert understood it as such. I lived in the area at the time and talked to people who were there; they merely regarded it as a lousy show on a cold December day, with limited view of the stage, bad sound, and inadequate parking and toilets. Had it not been for the investigative reporting of *Rolling Stone* and the documentary film shot by David and Albert Maysles, the stabbing death of Meredith Hunter would not have come to symbolize the collapse of the Woodstock dream. Contrary to radical intertextuality's second thesis, I regard the reporting and the film as supplementary, interpretive texts, distinct from the participating audience's text. These are distinct utterances in a language game of explanatory theory.

Let us borrow again from Wittgenstein: "What happens is not that a symbol cannot be further interpreted but: I do no interpreting, because I feel at home in the present picture. When I interpret I step from one level of thought to another."[51] Notice that he is not denying the presence of meaning. Instead, he's noting that experienced language users—or it could be auditors familiar with a musical style—grasp meaning without having to ask themselves what it means, and without attempting to paraphrase what it means. The Olivia Rodriguez fan is interested in the new video. Critical interpretation focuses on the meaning of Olivia Rodriguez.[52] It introduces a different, lager text than the one that ordinarily engages the fan. Both the fan and the theorist will examine what fans are saying about Rodriquez in social media, but the fan and the theorist will process that information with different goals and concepts.

When the audience is at home with the music, most texts yield their meanings directly, without a distinct process of interpretation. If you want "the meaning of R.E.M.," local holism recommends listening to a bunch of R.E.M. But when a music critic or cultural theorist expounds on that meaning, an act of translation is taking place, requiring the mastery of a second "language" and a juggling act between them. (I raised this point in Chapter 4 when I worried that talk of "authenticity" was an interpretive imposition. And, of course, my own contributions here are not neutral, for they attempt to map theoretical philosophy onto popular song meanings.) Empirical studies of audience response introduce yet another interpretive framework. Global holism embraces it all: consideration of the whole apparatus, which includes all the various theories that have been employed by various theorists to make sense of popular music.

In contrast, much of the audience hears music and responds. Cultural theorists observe the web of intertextuality and seek to explain responses or *effects*. But effects are not meanings. A stop sign does not mean "stop" because it causes motorists to stop; motorists stop because they know what the sign means. Recognition of a particular meaning guides action and is logically prior to the "stop" response. To repeat a frequently borrowed quotation that makes the point: "The sadness is to the music rather like the redness to the apple, than it is like the burp to the cider."[53] O.K. Bouwsma's point here is not that the music is inherently sad or meaningful in any other way; Bouwsma argues that it's sad if we have the right kind of musical background and if we know how to use an appropriate range of other sentences about sad things. Much of the audience for popular music is aware of a limited field of intertextualities. Granted, this sometimes results in not understanding it. But misunderstandings also arise from appealing to too much apparatus.

In summary, we will find different levels of competence among participants in any complex system of communication, and the same is true when we paraphrase and translate meanings. The primary thing that must be in place to understand rock music, country music, Gospel music, or any other genre is an appropriately informed *musical understanding*: the audience is "at home" with the way the music is constructed, so that an auditor with the right background experiences will understand it without having to think about how the rest of the audience will respond.[54]

These points invite a final remark about audience entry into an evolving language. There has to be some entry level that does not presuppose any broader meaning, a point at which it is common for the audience to make errors (which can be genuine errors and not necessarily evidence of a writerly text). With music—*especially* music—an initial attempt to comprehend instances as utterances will often fail. However, the auditor may be compensated with aesthetic rewards: "When [readers] do not enjoy the first story in a new genre, they do not read the second."[55] But most people feel excessive disorientation as painful or distressing; in order to become interested, one must at least partially understand. With music, we must (partially) understand the musical contribution *as* a musical contribution. With popular music, most of us acquire the basic requisite skills in early childhood.

Closing Thoughts

I followed the career of R.E.M. for many years after purchasing the *Chronic Town* E.P. (1982) just after its release. I had never read about them or heard of them, but the record store clerk thought I'd like it. So I am alternately puzzled and amused by the idea that there was a text in 1982, "R.E.M.," with a meaning, "the meaning of R.E.M.," and that the latter depended on R.E.M.'s position within the total rock formation. Was this text really intact in 1982, with the release of the "Radio Free Europe" single (1981) and *Chronic Town*? Why did anyone in California (where I was) care about this Georgia-based band if not for their music? The handful who listened between 1982 and their commercial breakthrough at the decade's end heard a strong vocalist, inventive melodies, and an off-kilter rock band. There were also a lot of incomprehensible words. To the extent that R.E.M. had an image, it was generated by the contrast of open music and opaque words, of propulsive, melodic music and moody vocals.

Intertextuality was in play, of course, but it was not simply a matter of recombining elements in a pre-existing musical language. Their gestalt was simultaneously familiar and fresh. (Or does every song necessarily sound fresh to listeners who "rewrite" every text?) We can push the problem of genre-entry back to the roots of rock music. Choose almost any popular music star: Bing Crosby, Elvis Presley, Otis Redding, Dolly Parton, or Olivia Rodriguez. Each was invested in particular kinds of music—and influenced by very specific performers—as a precondition of entering and reshaping a subfield of popular music. If they had not enjoyed particular performers and instances of popular music that they heard, how could they have become its interpreters? The local and the particular are where the action is.

In conclusion, if global holism is correct, then every text that might be relevant to an interaction between audience and music is equally relevant to its meaning. Perhaps global holists desire this consequence, as a corollary of the thesis that audiences rewrite texts. However, I am suggesting that this result does more than destabilize meaning. It implies the text is ultimately always the same text: the whole language, whatever that may be. Similarly, there is a steep price to pay in granting Peter Manuel's assertion that "the holistic interpretation of commercial cultural products lies not in the analysis and reading of reified 'texts,' but in contextualizing such entities in the processes of production, dissemination, consumption, uses, re-uses and varying idiosyncratic popular interpretations."⁵⁶ This interpreted text is not the accessible text that interests most of the audience. Here, I don't mean to be dense, but I see nothing attractive about a theory of meaning that does not elucidate successful, non-idiosyncratic communication (e.g., my understanding of your request to pass the mustard, or my success in understanding directions I find in Google maps, or my understanding of The Ronettes's version of "I Saw Mommy Kissing Santa Claus" [1963]). But if holistic interpretation cannot shed light on mundane interactions of audience and text, then I conclude that the theory is not a theory about the meanings communicated by those texts. Global and large-scale holism sacrifices utterance meanings in the pursuit of richer "texts" (or, more accurately, swaths of culture). However, as I said at the outset of my Introduction, popular songs are the musical *lingua franca* of modern life. As such, there is a danger in invoking too much intertextuality and too much context.

Conclusion

But you do speak of understanding music.... The way music speaks. Do not forget that a poem, even though it is composed in the language of information, is not used in the language-game of giving information.
—Ludwig Wittgenstein

The unifying idea of this book is that popular musicians often want to communicate something to others through their music, and this is most often done with songs. These communications routinely exploit contextual implicature, a communication strategy that is treated within philosophy in the field of pragmatics. The most important implication of this approach is that the overt message that is present in a song's lyrics is not necessarily the message communicated when performed or recorded by a particular musician or band, or when performed in a particular setting, or when repurposed through incorporation in another medium.

To return to an example mentioned in my Introduction, Paul McCartney and Wings's "Give Ireland Back to the Irish" (1972) repeatedly tells someone to give Ireland back, meaning that the UK should no longer govern the six counties of Northern Ireland. Normally, the reasonable addressee for such a message would be the British parliament, not untold thousands of listeners and record-buyers of the general public. However, by entering a political minefield with a pop single, the McCartneys are more clearly addressing ordinary people, not politicians. Since ordinary people lack the power to "give Ireland back," the manifest message is pointless unless we ask about its relevance in 1972 to, say, a twenty-something Beatles fan who remains interested in McCartney. As with so much popular music, the message now appears to be an expressive stance in relation to a situation—in this case, an ongoing political issue. As singer, McCartney expresses his sympathy for the cause of Ireland's reunification, as well as his sympathy for individuals harassed and imprisoned by British troops in Northern Ireland. Furthermore, his expression of sympathy communicates something more, for he is drawing on his status as a former Beatle to recommend to his mass audience that each of them should join him in feeling this way, and should join him in supporting this cause. By further implication, he is communicating to politically indifferent British citizens that they *ought* to be concerned about what their government is doing in their name. He is also suggesting that British voters should support politicians who will change British policy concerning Northern Ireland. Finally, McCartney was also communicating that his persona as the "cute" Beatle required an update: his politics were more aligned with those of John Lennon than might have been apparent. To put it another way, if the McCartneys were *not* communicating all of that, then releasing "Give Ireland Back to the Irish" was a needlessly risky career move, for Wings could have led off with the relatively innocuous "C Moon" (1972).

The implications I have spun from the 1972 release of the track "Give Ireland Back to the Irish" treat it as something meant to be understood within a complex context: a particular high-profile musician with a particular history and persona, including a particular national identity distinct from his ancestry that resonates with that particular political context. I have asked how the track was relevant as a communication, and then interpreted it in light of contextual factors that made it relevant at that time. In short, I extracted multiple nonmanifest meanings by using the principles of communication pragmatics, extending beyond the pragmatic implicature of the words to implicatures generated by other elements of the "utterance."

The upshot of this approach is that neither songs nor performers are the basic units of meaningful communication in popular music. Analogous to the way that the phrase "I'll have what she's having" changes its reference according to speaker and context *on the occasion of a particular utterance* of it, a popular song can function as an utterance with a distinct utterance meaning depending on "speaker" (individual or group) and context of presentation. As popular culture currently functions, there are three primary ways that a song is incorporated into a communicative act that functions as an utterance: (1) a particular musician or group performs it for an audience at a particular time or place, (2) a musician or group releases a recording of it (frequently in tandem with an "official" video), and (3) someone appropriates some or all of an existing recording and reuses it for their own communicative purpose. Appropriation and reuse take many forms, such as licensing it for a movie or commercial, creating a fan video where the track is given a new visual component, having a DJ play it on the radio with a dedication for someone or some cause, or someone sharing it in social media to communicate something about themselves or their views.

Appropriative utterances may seem very different from the case of a musician performing a song or releasing a recording, but I have argued that they share the same logic. Each involves taking a musical type that can be multiply instanced—whether a thin structure of a song or the thick structure of an existing recording of it—and treating it as a structure-for-use in one's own communicative utterance. The logic of these repurposings is no different than when, asked to give a toast at a funeral, I read aloud a poem by the deceased's favorite poet, using the poet's words as my own. And no different than buying a mass-produced greeting card that contains a message of condolences, signing it and mailing it, and thereby making it *my* communication rather than a communication from the Hallmark greeting card company or the design team who "authored" the card. Analogously, I have argued, popular songs frequently enter into performances, recordings, and other modes of sharing that give them specific meanings that are understood—and sometimes misunderstood—by auditors who interpret them in light of communication pragmatics.

None of this is to deny that there are many other ways in which popular music is meaningful and functional. An utterance-meaning analysis is, however, a neglected approach. Pragmatics supplements the many other approaches that are commonly employed.

If I have successfully shown that some song instances are communicative actions with pragmatic content, I will have accomplished three things. First, I have provided a framework for treating song instances—rather than the songs themselves—as utterances with complex, context-sensitive meanings. Second, by doing that, I have challenged the increasingly common view that popular music encodes information; yet, there are nonetheless no "right" and "wrong" ways to respond to it, because it is up to auditors to determine any salience. However, an utterance-meaning account points to a difference between bundling together information (what Chapter 2 recognized as "thoughtwriting") and directing a communication at auditors. In some cases, the act of performing, releasing, or appropriating music is an agent's communication of something very particular. Third, by doing those two things, I have shown that philosophy has a place in the disciplinary matrix that illuminates popular culture. Philosophy can do much more than what philosophers most often do in relation to popular music, which is to provide cultural commentary, most often by explaining ideas and philosophical topics (e.g., the problem of free will, competing conceptions of justice) that appear in some popular song lyrics. Philosophy can shed some additional light on how it all works.

Notes

Introduction

1. They are *The Oxford Handbook of Western Music and Philosophy*, eds. Tomás McAuley, Nanette Nielsen, Jerrold Levinson, and Ariana Phillips-Hutton (Oxford: Oxford University Press, 2020), and *The Encyclopedia of Aesthetics*, 2nd ed., ed. Michael Kelly (Oxford: Oxford University Press, 2014). The topic of pragmatics is also absent from a recent survey of performance philosophy, namely, Laura Cull Ó Maoilearca and Alice Lagaay (eds.), *The Routledge Companion to Performance Philosophy* (New York: Routledge, 2020).
2. A notable example discusses art songs as full-fledged utterances by composers; see Hui-Chieh Hsu and Lily I-wen Su, "Love in Disguise: Incongruity between Text and Music in Song," *Journal of Pragmatics* 62 (2014): 136–50. Similarly, other research ignores the pragmatics of song performance and concentrates on speech acts *represented* in songs and their performances, which is not the same thing (e.g., Elisabeth D. Kuhn, "'I Just Want to Make Love to You': Seductive Strategies in Blues Lyrics," *Journal of Pragmatics* 31 (1999): 525–34). The one essay I can cite as moving us in the right direction is Justin London, "Third-Party Uses of Music and Musical Pragmatics," *Journal of Aesthetics and Art Criticism* 66:3 (2008): 253–64.
3. An excellent introduction is Katherine Reed, "Rock Hermeneutics," in *The Bloomsbury Handbook of Rock Music Research*, eds. Allan F. Moore and Paul Carr (New York and London: Bloomsbury, 2020), 255–68. From the perspective of semiotics, pragmatics is roughly aligned with Ferdinand de Saussure's category of *parole*, or language in use. However, it is remarkable how little attention is directed at *parole* in semiotic accounts of musical meaning. See, for example, Raymond Monelle, *Linguistics and Semiotics in Music* (London and New York: Routledge, 2014) and Kofi Agawa, *Music as Discourse: Semiotic Adventures in Romantic Music* (Oxford: Oxford University Press, 2009). For reasons that will become clear, Agawa's examination of specific Romantic compositions falls sort of discussing *parole* or music in use.
4. See Devin McKinney, *Magic Circles: The Beatles in Dream and History* (Cambridge, MA: Harvard University Press, 2003), chap. 5. Asked if he thought The Beatles *intended* to say what he took them to say, Manson reportedly claimed that they did, but perhaps not consciously (McKinney, *Magic Circles,* 298).
5. For an accessible introduction to this topic, see Bence Nanay, *Aesthetics: A Very Short Introduction* (Oxford: Oxford University Press, 2020).
6. Bobby Allyn, "TikTok Sensation: Meet the Idaho Potato Worker Who Sent Fleetwood Mac Sales Soaring," *NPR*, October 11, 2020, https://www.npr.org/2020/10/11/922554253/tiktok-sensation-meet-the-idaho-potato-worker-who-sent-fleetwood-mac-sales-soari.
7. In part, the fans are singing for each other, a phenomenon with affinities to fans screaming at Beatles concerts; see Philip Auslander, *In Concert: Performing Musical Persona* (Ann Arbor: University of Michigan Press, 2021), 171.

8   Robert Stecker, "Testing Artistic Value: A Reply to Dodd," *Journal of Aesthetics and Art Criticism* 71 (2013): 289. This aligns with Dave Grohl's observation, "You can sing a song to 85,000 people and they'll sing it back for 85,000 different reasons." Quoted in Louis Pattison, "Twenty Years after In Utero, Nirvana's Importance Hasn't Diminished," *The Guardian*, August 31, 2013, https://www.theguardian.com/music/2013/aug/31/nirvana-dave-grohl-krist-novoselic-in-utero. See also Stephen Davies and Constantijn Koopman, "Musical Meaning in a Broader Perspective," in Stephen Davies, *Musical Understanding: And Other Essays on the Philosophy of Music* (Oxford: Oxford University Press, 2011), 81–3.

9   Allan F. Moore, *Song Means: Analysing and Interpreting Recorded Popular Song* (Farnham: Ashgate, 2012), 330. Ironically, Moore's position is otherwise very close to mine. He does not, however, discuss pragmatics as such. The most serious exponent of the first view remains Theodor Adorno, *Essays on Music*, ed. Richard Leppert (Berkeley: University of California Press, 2002).

10 It may appear that I am abandoning a claim that I defended in my early research, which is that contemporary popular music "is not essentially a performing art" (Theodore Gracyk, *Rhythm and Noise: An Aesthetics of Rock* (Durham, NC: Duke University Press, 1996), 75). The current project treats performance as one of several species of communicative action while remaining committed to the view that co-presence of musicians and audience is less significant than media-embedded constructs, such as recordings, videos, and social media shares.

11 Julian Dodd, *Being True to Works of Music* (Oxford: Oxford University Press, 2020), 142. Dodd explicitly restricts his claim to the Western classical tradition, so I am not attacking him. I am simply establishing a contrast.

12 Jennifer C. Lena, *Banding Together: How Communities Create Genres in Popular Music* (Princeton: Princeton University Press, 2012), 168.

13 Here, I follow Gaynor Jones and Jay Rahn, "Definitions of Popular Music: Recycled," *Journal of Aesthetic Education* 11 (1977): 85–6; David Novitz, *The Boundaries of Art* (Philadelphia: Temple University Press, 1992), 29–33; Charles Hamm, *Putting Popular Music in Its Place* (Cambridge: Cambridge University Press, 1995), 3–6. For a more complete account, see Theodore Gracyk, "Popular Music," in *The Oxford Handbook of Western Music and Philosophy*, eds. Tomás McAuley, Nanette Nielsen, Jerrold Levinson, and Ariana Phillips-Hutton (Oxford: Oxford University Press, 2020), 533–53.

14 John Andrew Fisher, "Popular Music," in *The Routledge Companion to Philosophy and Music*, eds. Theodore Gracyk and Andrew Kania (New York: Routledge, 2011), 410. Before 1850, "popular" was used to contrast art music with music subsequently called "folk" music. But with the rise of a commercial, urban music culture, "popular music" came to be viewed as a debased substitute for folk music, the people's true "national music." See Matthew Gelbart, *The Invention of "Folk Music" and "Art Music": Emerging Categories from Ossian to Wagner* (Cambridge: Cambridge University Press, 2007), 256–61.

15 For support, see Richard Middleton, *Voicing the Popular: On the Subjects of Popular Music* (New York: Routledge, 2006), chap. 1. Middleton supports the position that "popular music" is an intrinsically relational concept.

16 Robert Christgau, "Popular Music Colliers Encyclopedia," *Robert Christgau* website, https://www.robertchristgau.com/xg/music/collier.php.

17 For example, Robert Burnett, *The Global Jukebox: The International Music Industry* (New York: Routledge, 1996), and Simon Frith, *Performing Rites: On the Value of Popular Music* (Cambridge, MA: Harvard University Press, 1996).
18 Timothy Warner, *Pop Music—Technology and Creativity: Trevor Horn and the Digital Revolution* (Aldershot: Ashgate, 2003), 11.
19 Ruth A. Solie, "Whose Life? The Gendered Self in Schumann's *Frauenliebe* Songs," in *Music and Text: Critical Inquiries*, ed. Steven Paul Sher (Cambridge: Cambridge University Press, 1992), 220.
20 The rise of fandom directed at celebrity conductors of classical music might be an artworld appropriation of the aesthetic of recorded popular music; see Joseph Horowitz, *Understanding Toscanini: How He Became an American Culture-God and Helped Create a New Audience for Old Music* (New York: Knopf, 1987).
21 This latter contrast is favored by Julian Johnson, *Who Needs Classical Music? Cultural Choice and Musical Value* (Oxford: Oxford University Press, 2002). I agree that these two broad fields of music "are made in different ways and exhibit different properties and characteristics" (ibid., 114).
22 Hamm, *Putting Popular Music in Its Place*, 98.
23 The classic text is Adorno (with George Simpson), "On Popular Music," trans. Susan H. Gillespie, in Adorno, *Essays on Music*, 437–69. Adorno's ideas are updated (but also critiqued) in Alison Stone, *The Value of Popular Music: An Approach from Post-Kantian Aesthetics* (Lancaster: Palgrave-Macmillan, 2016).
24 Discussing mass art, Noël Carroll observes that popular art "is structured in such a way that large numbers of people will be able to understand and appreciate it, virtually without effort.... That is, [it is] comprehensible for untrained audiences, virtually on the first go-around." In contrast, high art, dominated by avant-garde art, "is esoteric." (Noël Carroll, *A Philosophy of Mass Art* (Oxford: Clarendon Press, 1998), 196.) For the view that this difference is functionally valued for aligning "high" and "low" with distinct classes in the social hierarchy, with an attendant social function of reinforcing class divisions, see Pierre Bourdieu, *Distinction: A Social Critique of the Judgement of Taste*, trans. Richard Nice (Cambridge, MA: Harvard University Press, 1984).
25 Again, this tracks Hamm's point about accessibility. Where Babbitt famously renounced any goal of accessibility in classical composition (Milton Babbitt, "Who Cares If You Listen," *High Fidelity* (February 1958): 38–40, 126–7), Parton has a fan base in unexpected corners of the world. See Jonathan Zilberg, "Yes, It's True: Zimbabweans Love Dolly Parton," *Journal of Popular Culture* 29 (1995): 111–25.
26 John Storey, *Inventing Popular Culture: From Folklore to Globalization* (Malden, MA: Blackwell, 2003), 106.
27 Derek B. Scott, *Sounds of the Metropolis: The 19th Century Popular Music Revolution in London, New York, Paris and Vienna* (Oxford: Oxford University Press, 2008), 3, 4.
28 Gary Giddins and Scott DeVeaux, *Jazz* (New York: W. W. Norton, 2009), 296.
29 Philip Larkin, *All What Jazz: A Record Diary 1961–1971* (London: Faber and Faber, 1985), 19.
30 Richard Middleton, quoted in Sheila Whitely, *Women and Popular Music: Sexuality, Identity, and Subjectivity* (London and New York: Routledge, 2000), 27.
31 Whitely, *Women and Popular Music*, 27.
32 When *Song Exploder* devotes an episode (Series 2, episode 3) to Nine Inch Nails's "Hurt" (1994), they acknowledge Johnny Cash's cover version (2002) without providing any comparative analysis. Hirway repeatedly refers to the original "Hurt"

recording as the song, only to have composer Reznor immediately refer to it as a "track."

33 Quoted in David Sheff, *The Playboy Interviews with John Lennon and Yoko Ono* (New York: Playboy Press, 1981), 62.
34 Quoted in Gardiner Harris, "President Obama's Emotional Spotify Playlist Is a Hit," *New York Times*, August 14, 2016, http://www.nytimes.com/2016/08/15/us/politics/president-obama-spotify-playlist.html.
35 I acknowledge that there are also cases where a song performance is improvised and then the template is extracted from what has been improvised.
36 Charles Hamm, *Yesterdays: Popular Song in America* (New York: W. W. Norton, 1979) and Scott, *Sounds of the Metropolis*, 184.
37 My example of damning with faint praise is a variant of a well-known example; see H. P. Grice, "Logic and Conversation," in *Syntax and Semantics, vol. 3, Speech Acts*, eds. Peter Cole and Jerry L. Morgan (New York: Academic Press, 1975), 33.
38 Dierdre Wilson and Dan Sperber, "Relevance Theory," in *The Handbook of Pragmatics*, eds. Laurence R. Horn and Gregory Ward (Malden, MA: Blackwell, 2004), 608.
39 Figurative speech and the use of specific details to convey generalizations are standard, conventionalized modes of implicature. They are so common in song lyrics that I will tend to ignore them as cases that do not illustrate why pragmatics can shed light on meaning production with popular song.
40 There are many good introductions to the semantics-pragmatics distinction, for example, Herman Cappelen, "Semantics and Pragmatics: Some Central Issues," in *Context-Sensitivity and Semantic Minimalism: New Essays on Semantics and Pragmatics*, eds. Gerhard Preyer and Georg Peter (Oxford: Oxford University Press, 2007), 3–24. Capplelen argues that seeking a precise dividing line "is a waste of time" (ibid., 3).
41 Because an incorrect interpretation may be more satisfying aesthetically, reducing popular music to a purely aesthetic function encourages indifference toward the intended communication. See Alan H. Goldman, "Interpreting Art and Literature," *Journal of Aesthetics and Art Criticism* 48 (1990): 205–14. But I neither reduce its function to an aesthetic one nor adopt a sharp distinction between fine art and entertainment.
42 Max Paddison, "Meaning and Autonomy," in *The Oxford Handbook*, eds. McAuley, Nielsen, Levinson, and Phillips-Hutton, 775.
43 For background on the context in which the track was released, see Stephen Millar, *Sounding Dissent: Rebel Songs, Resistance, and Irish Republicanism* (Ann Arbor: University of Michigan Press, 2020), chap. 3.
44 This approach reflects Paul Grice's insight that human communication is meaningful only on the presumption that its goal is to get the auditor to understand the speaker's communicative intentions. The Gricean program is often attacked as downplaying or even rejecting the central role of semantic conventions, but this is simply not true. See Emma Borg, "Intention-Based Semantics," in *The Oxford Handbook of Philosophy of Language*, eds. Ernest Lepore and Barry C. Smith (Oxford: Oxford University Press, 2006), 252–3. However, we need not accept Grice's emphasis on *conversational* implicature and conversational cooperation as our foundation. Recorded songs and most music performances are not conversational, and so are better understood by reference to the neo-Gricean relevance principle than to Grice's own cooperative principle; see Deirdre Wilson and Dan Sperber, *Meaning and Relevance* (Cambridge: Cambridge University Press, 2012), chap. 1. Another

advantage of Wilson and Sperber is their embrace of the idea that communication ranges from precise meanings to vague impressions (ibid., 87): vagueness is common with popular song.

45. For an accessible overview of this topic, see either Noël Carroll, "Interpretation," in *The Routledge Companion to Philosophy of Literature*, eds. Noël Carroll and John Gibson (New York: Routledge, 2016), 302–12, or Robert Stecker, "Interpretation," in *The Routledge Companion to Aesthetics*, 3rd ed., eds. Berys Gaut and Dominic Lopes (New York: Routledge, 2013), 309–19.

46. Michael Bratman, *Intention, Plans, and Practical Reason* (Cambridge: Cambridge University Press, 1999), 16–17, 110. See also G. E. M. Anscombe, *Intention* (Cambridge, MA: Harvard University Press, 1963), 9.

47. Military bugle calls are an example of instrumental music with determinate semantic content.

48. For more on compositionality and semantic value, see Alex Miller, *Philosophy of Language*, 2nd ed. (Milton Park: Routledge, 2007), 25 ff.

49. Mismatch of words and music readily generates issues of relevance and thus pragmatic content; see Hsu and Su, "Love in Disguise."

50. See Philip Auslander, *In Concert: Performing Musical Persona* (Ann Arbor: University of Michigan Press, 2021), chap. 2.

51. See Adam Kendon, *Gesture: Visible Action as Utterance* (Cambridge: Cambridge University Press, 2004).

52. There is evidence that the popular audience derives more meaning, or primary guidance about meaning, from the music, not the words. See Gracyk, *Rhythm and Noise*, 65; James O. Young, *Critique of Pure Music* (Oxford: Oxford University Press, 2014), 137–8; and S. Omar Ali and Zehra F. Peynircioğlu, "Songs and Emotions: Are Lyrics and Melodies Equal Partners?" *Psychology of Music* 34 (2006): 511–34.

53. See Tim Wharton, *Pragmatics and Non-Verbal Communication* (Cambridge: Cambridge University Press, 2009).

Chapter 1

1. Jeanette Bicknell, *Philosophy of Song and Singing: An Introduction* (New York: Routledge, 2015), xi. Bicknell's views are often parallel to mine, but on her view performer's intentions as basically irrelevant (Bicknell, *Philosophy of Song and Singing*, 110), and so the relationship between intentions and the pragmatics of meaning does not enter into her account. For the contrasting position that both intentions and pragmatics are relevant to interpretation, see Robert Stecker, *Interpretation and Construction: Art, Speech, and the Law* (Malden, MA: Blackwell Publishing, 2003), 17–20.

2. To simplify the analysis, this chapter treats recordings as transparent representations of particular performances. However, I have argued that we must be cautious about the metaphor of transparency (e.g., *Rhythm and Noise: An Aesthetics of Rock* (Durham, NC: Duke University Press, 1996), and "Documentation and Transformation in Musical Recordings," in *Recorded Music: Philosophical and Critical Reflections*, ed. Mine Dogantan-Dack (Hedon: Middlesex University Press, 2008), 61–81). Subsequent chapters will adopt a more qualified position.

3 For skepticism about applying the utterance model to popular music, see Jason Toynbee, *Making Popular Music: Musicians, Creativity and Institutions* (London: Arnold, 2000), 43–4.
4 Saul Kripke, "Speaker's Reference and Semantic Reference," in *Midwest Studies in Philosophy 2*, eds. Peter A. French, Theodore E. Uehling, Jr., and Howard K. Wettstein (Morris, MN: University of Minnesota, 1977), 261. Any one of a number of other seminal essays in philosophy of language could take the place of Kripke here.
5 Kripke, "Speaker's Reference," 263, emphasis added.
6 Pronouns normally demand interpretation relative to utterance context. Thus, they call for "semantic pragmatics," whereas standard nouns become contextually sensitive through "pragmatic pragmatics," a distinction emphasized by Max J. Cresswell, *Logic and Languages* (London: Methuen, 1973), 238.
7 I am much influenced by Herman Cappelen and Ernest Lepore, "A Tall Tale: In Defense of Semantic Minimalism and Speech Act Pluralism," in *New Essays in the Philosophy of Language*, eds. Maite Ezcurdia, Robert J. Stainton and Christopher Viger (Calgary: University of Calgary Press, 2004), 3–28.
8 William G. Lycan, *Philosophy of Language: A Contemporary Introduction*, 2nd ed. (London and New York: Routledge, 2008), 142.
9 Stan Godlovitch, *Musical Performance: A Philosophical Study* (New York: Routledge, 1998), 86.
10 The hypothesis is so-called by Richard Wollheim, *Art and Its Objects*, 2nd ed. (Cambridge: Cambridge University Press, 1980), 4.
11 I am excluding consideration of improvised singing in which the singer does not set out to perform any specific song. I also acknowledge that there are interesting alternatives to the basic type-token ontology. This is not the place to review those alternatives, but I see no reason why the position I advance cannot be adapted to fit the major alternatives.
12 The social uses of songs, especially work songs and hymns, generate much of their meaning through the shared activity of advancing some group end. See Nicholas Wolterstorff, *Art Rethought: The Social Practices of Art* (Oxford: Oxford University Press, 2015), chap. 16.
13 "Composers take for granted the musical practices they share with the contemporary musicians to whom they direct their instructions. As a result, they say no more than is necessary." Stephen Davies, *Musical Works and Performances: A Philosophical Exploration* (Oxford: Oxford University Press, 2004), 60.
14 See Stephen Davies, "John Cage's 4'33": Is It Music?" *Australasian Journal of Philosophy* 75 (1997): 458, and Theodore Gracyk, "Misappropriation of Our Musical Past," *Journal of Aesthetic Education* 45:3 (2011): 50–66.
15 A peer reviewer for the manuscript wisely reminds me that many "standards" start out with fixed, notated arrangements for performance in popular theater, only subsequently becoming popularized as simpler, thinner works that are adapted in myriad arrangements.
16 Julian Dodd, *Being True to Works of Music* (Oxford: Oxford University Press, 2020), 142.
17 See Nicholas Wolterstorff, "Toward an Ontology of Art Works," *Noûs* 9 (1975): 115–42. Plausibly, Wolterstorff denies that tokens literally share properties with types. He proposes that they share predicates that direct us to analogous properties ("Toward an Ontology of Art Works," 125–9).

18 A determinative property will be one that, if omitted from an instance, counts against performance accuracy or counts against it being an instance of that work. Stephen Davies, "The Ontology of Musical Works and the Authenticity of Their Performances," *Noûs* 25 (1991): 21–41.
19 See Jerrold Levinson, "What a Musical Work Is," *The Journal of Philosophy* 77 (1980): 5–28. Indexical determination of the original context generates a work's properties without thereby belonging to the resulting set of properties; see Stephen Davies, "Interpreting Contextualities," *Philosophy and Literature* 20 (1996): 22.
20 For a contrasting approach, see Levinson, "What a Musical Work Is." Against Levinson, see Davies, *Musical Works and Performances*, 159–60.
21 "Many sentences are commonly used only to convey something other than their literal content, or would be so used if they were used at all." Nathan Salmon, "Two Conceptions of Semantics," in *Semantics versus Pragmatics*, ed. Zoltán Gendler Szabó (Oxford: Clarendon Press, 2005), 320.
22 An alternative position says that the changes in meaning reflect post-creation changes to the properties of the song. This position is defended by Sondra Bacharach, "Toward a Metaphysical Historicism," *Journal of Aesthetics and Art Criticism* 63 (2005): 165–73. However, I think the argument depends on a failure to keep track of the distinction between structures and their performances.
23 William K. Wimsatt and Monroe C. Beardsley, "The Intentional Fallacy," *Sewanee Review* 54 (1946): 468–88, and Roland Barthes, *Image—Music—Text*, trans. Stephen Heath (New York: Hill and Wang, 1977).
24 For a summary, see Sherri Irvin, "Authors, Intentions and Literary Meaning," *Philosophy Compass* 1 (2006): 114–28.
25 Stecker, *Interpretation and Construction*, 42.
26 Stecker, *Interpretation and Construction*, 17.
27 Stecker, *Interpretation and Construction*, 17.
28 Stecker, *Interpretation and Construction*, 64.
29 Stecker, *Interpretation and Construction*, 88. Important criticisms of Stecker are found in David Davies, "Semantic Intentions, Utterance Meaning, and Work Meaning," in *Contemporary Readings in the Philosophy of Literature: An Analytic Approach*, eds. David Davies and Carl Matheson (Peterborough: Broadview Press, 2008), 167–81. Stecker is in good company, for the view that "the song as a whole is the utterance" is defended by Edward T. Cone, *The Composer's Voice* (Berkeley and Los Angeles: University of California Press, 1974), 18.
30 Stecker, *Interpretation and Construction*, 80.
31 Stecker comes close to this position is in his remarks about works handed down through oral tradition (*Interpretation and Construction*, 199).
32 Kent Bach, "Context ex *Machina*," in *Semantics versus Pragmatics*, ed. Szabó, 22.
33 Kripke, "Speaker's Reference," 271.
34 Bach, "Context ex *Machina*," 38.
35 Davies, *Musical Works and Performances*, 163–75. In terms of Davies's analysis, the relevant intention would be a higher-level rather than a lower-level one, where only the former involves "the intention to perform X's work, where 'X' is a name" (Davies, *Musical Works and Performances*, 171). Given that some works are anonymous, this does not mean that the performers have to actually know who wrote it.
36 Eric F. Clarke, *Ways of Listening: An Ecological Approach to the Perception of Musical Meaning* (Oxford: Oxford University Press, 2005), 46. See also Douglas Dempster, "How Does Debussy's Sea Crash? How Can Jimi's Rocket Red Glare?: Kivy's Account

of Representation in Music," *Journal of Aesthetics and Art Criticism* 52 (1994): 415–28.
37 It is noteworthy that Hendrix played the song repeatedly over a period of two years. See Mark Clague, "'This Is America': Jimi Hendrix's Star Spangled Banner Journey as Psychedelic Citizenship," *Journal for the Society for American Music* 4 (2014): 435–78.
38 The centrality of these factors as meaning-generators is stressed by Allan F. Moore, *Song Means: Analysing and Interpreting Recorded Popular Song* (Farnham: Ashgate, 2012), 188–207. Moore's position is adopted and expanded by Steven Gamble, *How Music Empowers: Listening to Modern Rap and Metal* (New York: Routledge, 2021).
39 Clarke over-emphasizes the role of associated language in interpreting Hendrix's quote from "Taps" (Clarke, *Ways of Listening*, 58).
40 I do not endorse the view that music is an offshoot of language, nor that the "music instinct" derives from the "language instinct."
41 See Jerrold Levinson, *Music in the Moment* (Ithaca, NY: Cornell University Press, 1997). His view is very similar to Francis Wolff's point that "intellectual" understanding—a listener's construction of imaginary causality (*causalit´e imaginaire*) from sound to sound—generates an ideal acousmatic world (*monde idéal*) (Wolff, *Pourquoi la musique?* (Paris: Fayard, 2015), 323).
42 The brief performance was recorded in the 1960s and unreleased until available on an expanded digital reissue of the *Straight, No Chaser* album (Columbia 1996).
43 An excellent short overview is provided by Stephen Davies, "Musical Understanding," in *Musical Understanding: And Other Essays on the Philosophy of Music* (Oxford: Oxford University Press, 2011), 88–99.
44 Alan H. Goldman, "Aesthetic Properties," in *A Companion to Aesthetics*, 2nd ed., eds. Stephen Davies, Kathleen Marie Higgins, Robert Hopkins, Robert Stecker and David E. Cooper (Malden and Oxford: Blackwell, 2009), 124–8.
45 Rafael De Clercq, "Aesthetic Properties," in *The Routledge Companion to Philosophy and Music*, eds. Theodore Gracyk and Andrew Kania (New York: Routledge, 2011), 144–54.
46 Justin London, "Musical and Linguistic Speech Acts," *Journal of Aesthetics and Art Criticism* 54 (1996): 49–64.
47 For example, Frank Zappa, *The Best Band You Never Heard in Your Life* (Barking Pumpkin D2-74233, 1991), recorded in concert, 1988.
48 Clarke, *Ways of Listening*, 57.
49 Lyrics as printed in Bob Dylan, "It's Alright, Ma (I'm Only Bleeding)," *Writings and Drawings by Bob Dylan* (New York: Knopf, 1973), 172; the recorded performance is available on Bob Dylan and the Band, *Before the Flood* (Asylum Records AB-201, 1974), recorded February 14, 1974. Nixon's presidency ended on August 9, 1974.
50 Dylan rejects determinate, "specific" interpretations of his songs and regards them as open to ongoing pragmatic reinterpretation; see Kurt Loder, "Bob Dylan," in *The Rolling Stone Interviews: The 1980s*, ed. Sid Holt (New York: St. Martin's Press, 1989), 96.
51 Bach, "Context ex *Machina*," 18.
52 "The speaker's act … is what brings extralinguistic information into play" (Bach, "Context ex *Machina*," 18).
53 Reasons favoring this characterization of the semantics/pragmatics distinction are summarized by Zoltán Gendler Szabó, "The Distinction between Semantics and Pragmatics," in *The Oxford Handbook of Philosophy of Language*, eds. Ernest LePore and Barry C. Smith (Oxford: Oxford University Press, 2006), 361–89; it corresponds

closely to the view of Robert Stalnaker ("Pragmatics," *Synthese* 22 (1970): 272–89), except that Stalnaker restricts semantics to the study of declarative sentences.

54 This puts popular performance practices sharply at odds with standard assumptions about the relationship between works and their performance in the classical tradition, e.g., Thomas Carson Mark, "Philosophy of Piano Playing: Reflections on the Concept of Performance," *Philosophy and Phenomenological Research* 41 (1981): 299–324.

55 Although I do not find it persuasive, the contrary view is defended by Peter Kivy, *The Performance of Reading: An Essay in the Philosophy of Literature* (Malden, MA: Blackwell, 2006). For compelling arguments against Kivy, see David Davies, "Book Review: *The Performance of Reading: An Essay in the Philosophy of Literature*," *Journal of Aesthetics and Art Criticism* 66 (2008): 89–91.

56 This work falls within the broad category of the characteristic symphony. See Richard Will, *The Characteristic Symphony in the Age of Haydn and Beethoven* (Cambridge: Cambridge University Press, 2002), 83–128.

57 Potentially, this idea can be extended to all music, provided we follow Bach and regard semantics as more than "computational semantics" and as embracing anything communicated as a projection of syntax when interpreted in light of general conventions (Bach, "Context ex *Machina*," 24–5).

Chapter 2

1 Michael Paterniti, "Brad Pitt Talks Divorce, Quitting Drinking, and Becoming a Better Man," *GQ*, May 3, 2017, https://www.gq.com/story/brad-pitt-gq-style-cover-story.

2 Today's open sharing policies are much more liberal than they were in the first decades of the internet, when popular sites such as Facebook and YouTube censored attempts to share copyrighted music. A breakthrough occurred in 2006, leading to a series of copyright payment agreements that continued to unfold for another dozen years. See, for example, Andrew Ross Sorkin and Jeff Leads, "Music Companies Share in YouTube-Google Deal," *New York Times*, October 19, 2006, https://www.nytimes.com/2006/10/19/technology/19iht-youtube.3214225.html, and Amy X. Wang, "Facebook Is Finally Putting Music Back into Social Networking," *Rolling Stone*, June 5, 2018, https://www.rollingstone.com/pro/news/facebook-is-finally-putting-music-back-into-social-networking-629164/.

3 The first lines of "The Star-Spangled Banner" establish a fiction in which listener is asked, in present tense, if they can see something that happened in the past.

4 A more radical view says that literature *always* involves a performative interpretation, including reading a book silently to oneself (e.g., Peter Kivy, *The Performance of Reading: An Essay in the Philosophy of Literature* (Malden, MA: Blackwell, 2006)). For a response, see David Davies, "Book Review: *The Performance of Reading: An Essay in the Philosophy of Literature*," *Journal of Aesthetics and Art Criticism* 66 (2008): 89–91. Either way, I retain my points about song performance, because Kivy's view is that the reader is typically performing the novel for herself, not for others.

5 Dierdre Wilson and Dan Sperber, "Relevance Theory," in *The Handbook of Pragmatics*, eds. Laurence R. Horn and Gregory Ward (Malden, MA: Blackwell,

2004), 607–32. Here, a text is to be understood as a design or structured type with semantic content.

6   This misunderstanding is different from personal association, or so-called "meaning for the subject," which is not a case of misunderstanding at all. See Constantijn Koopman and Stephen Davies, "Musical Meaning in a Broader Perspective," in Stephen Davies, *Musical Understanding: And Other Essays on the Philosophy of Music* (Oxford: Oxford University Press, 2011), 71–87. It also differs from appropriations based on thematic elements that leave the message vague, as when a conservative politician uses a recording to pump up the crowd at a rally despite objections from the musician; see Andrew Solender, "All the Artists Who Have Told Trump to Stop Using Their Songs at His Rallies," *Forbes*, June 28, 2020, https://www.forbes.com/sites/andrewsolender/2020/06/28/all-the-artists-who-have-told-trump-to-stop-using-their-songs-at-his-rallies/.
7   For the argument that the most rewarding interpretation might depart from the correct one, see Stephen Davies, "The Aesthetic Relevance of Authors' and Painters' Intentions," *Journal of Aesthetics and Art Criticism* 41 (1982): 65–76.
8   Christie D'Zurilla. "Carly Simon Finally Reveals Who's So Vain in 'You're So Vain,'" *Los Angeles Times*, November 18, 2015, http://www.latimes.com/entertainment/gossip/la-et-mg-carly-simon-youre-so-vain-about-warren-beatty-partially-20151118-story.html.
9   William Shakespeare, *Romeo and Juliet*, Act 2 Scene 2.
10 Carly Simon, *Boys in the Trees: A Memoir* (New York: Flatiron, 2015), 254.
11 See this book's Introduction for a discussion of anti-intentionalism, which denies that authorial intention at the time of composition contributes to its semantic interpretation, and therefore denies that an author's subsequent clarifications about how to interpret unclear or ambiguous communication determine its correct interpretation.
12 Thomas Carson Mark, "Philosophy of Piano Playing: Reflections on the Concept of Performance," *Philosophy and Phenomenological Research* 41 (1981): 299–324; Peter Kivy, *Authenticities: Philosophical Reflections on Musical Performance* (Ithaca, NY: Cornell University Press, 1995), and "Messiah's Message," in *Sounding Off: Eleven Essays in the Philosophy of Music* (Oxford: Oxford University Press, 2012), 113–30.
13 Mark, "Philosophy of Piano Playing," 319–20. On this model, a work can be composed and then "lost" and never instantiated in performance (Mark, "Philosophy of Piano Playing," 301–2), but the meanings of that unperformed work are no less determinate or real on that account.
14 Mark, "Philosophy of Piano Playing," 307.
15 Eric Lott, *Love and Theft: Blackface Minstrelsy and the American Working Class* (Oxford: Oxford University Press, 1993).
16 Mark, "Philosophy of Piano Playing," 310.
17 Brent Mann, *Blinded by the Lyrics: Behind the Lines of Rock and Roll's Most Baffling Songs* (New York: Citadel, 2005), 90.
18 Randy Lewis, "Carly Simon and Taylor Swift Duet on 'You're So Vain,'" *Los Angeles Times*, August 1, 2013, https://www.latimes.com/entertainment/music/posts/la-et-ms-taylor-swift-carly-simon-duet-youre-so-vain-20130801-story.html.
19 Kendall L. Walton, *Mimesis as Make-Believe: On the Foundations of the Representational Arts* (Cambridge, MA: Harvard University Press, 1990), 74.
20 For a more precise account of this proposal, see Gregory Currie, *The Nature of Fiction* (Cambridge University Press, 1990), 31–3.

21 Simon, *Boys in the Trees*, 254.
22 Simon, *Boys in the Trees*, 254.
23 While allowing that there are exceptions where song lyrics do not function as fictions, the point I am making is a variation on the idea that social institutions, regulated by social norms (including exploitation of nonrepresentational structural features of musical design), create the conditions for the fictionality of an art form. See Catharine Abell, *Fiction: A Philosophical Analysis* (Oxford: Oxford University Press, 2020). While Abell downplays the role of intentions in determining what counts as a fiction, that does not count against the relevance of intentions in using fictions to generate pragmatic implications in relation to performance context.
24 Here, we have a strong difference between hearing a song and reading literature. Derek Matravers notes that many fictions do not have an identifiable narrator. There may be, literally, no one to identify with. See Derek Matravers, *Fiction and Narrative* (Oxford: Oxford University Press, 2014), chap. 9.
25 Although it now has few defenders, this view of expressivity dates back to the Baroque era's *Affektenlehre*. The classic modern account of "arousal" theory is Leo Tolstoy, *What Is Art?* trans. Aylmer Maude (New York: The Liberal Arts Press, 1960).
26 Stephen Davies, "Artistic Expression and the Hard Case of Pure Music," in *Contemporary Debates in Aesthetics and the Philosophy of Art*, ed. Matthew Kieran (Oxford: Oxford University Press, 2006), 182.
27 See N. P. M. Todd, "The Kinematics of Musical Expression," *Journal of the Acoustical Society of America* 97 (1995): 1940–9; N. P. M. Todd, "Sensory-Motor Theory of Rhythm, Time Perception and Beat Induction," *Journal of New Music Research* 28 (1999): 5–28; Justin London, "Metric Entrainment and the Problem(s) of Perception," in *The Philosophy of Rhythm: Aesthetics, Music, Poetics*, eds. Peter Cheyne, Andy Hamilton and Max Paddison (Oxford: Oxford University Press, 2019), 171–82.
28 I discuss this song at greater length in Theodore Gracyk, *I Wanna Be Me: Rock Music and the Politics of Identity* (Philadelphia: Temple University Press, 2001), 84–6.
29 T. S. Eliot, *Four Quartets* (New York: Harcourt, 1943), 20.
30 The former criterion is defended by David Davies, *Aesthetics and Literature* (London: Continuum, 2007), 45–8, the latter by Walton, *Mimesis as Make-Believe*, chap. 2.
31 Jimmy Webb, *Tunesmith: Inside the Art of Songwriting* (New York: Hyperion, 1998), 12.
32 Ellen Dissanayake, *Homo Aestheticus: Where Art Comes From and Why* (Seattle: University of Washington Press, 1992).
33 Nonfiction narrative may also invite imaginative and empathetic engagement, so it is important to keep in mind that those features do not define fiction. Fictionality also involves relaxation of normal standards of fidelity to truth in communication: the audience is not intended to accept or believe the particulars of the communication. Although I am more aligned with David Davies's position on fictive utterance than with Stacie Friend's alternative view, the argument given here is more fully developed in Stacie Friend, "Imagining Fact and Fiction," in *New Waves in Aesthetics*, eds. Kathleen Stock and Katherine Thomson-Jones (Basingstoke: Palgrave, 2008), 150–69, and by Matravers, *Fiction and Narrative*.
34 I will withdraw this concession at a later stage in my argument.
35 Lily E. Hirsch, "Rap as Threat: The Violent Translation of Music in American Law," *Law, Culture and the Humanities* 14 (2014): 1–19.

36 See the case of McKinley Phipps, one of several documented in Andrea L. Dennis and Erik Nielson, *Rap on Trial: Race, Lyrics, and Guilt in America* (New York and London: The New Press, 2019), 4–7.
37 For a survey of some different ways we learn about the world through guided imagining, see Peter Lamarque, *The Philosophy of Literature* (Oxford: Blackwell, 2009), 241–4.
38 Philip F. Gura, *Truth's Ragged Edge: The Rise of the American Novel* (New York: Farrar, Straus and Giroux, 2013), 143.
39 Bradley Armour-Garb and James A. Woodbridge. *Pretense and Pathology: Philosophical Fictionalism and Its Applications* (Cambridge: Cambridge University Press, 2015), 51. However, there are strong reasons to deny that pretense is the key to fiction; see Walton, *Mimesis as Make-Believe*, 81–3.
40 Carolyn Williams, *Gilbert and Sullivan: Gender Genre Parody* (New York: Columbia University Press, 2012), 255.
41 Guido Bieri, *Life on the Tracks: Bob Dylan's Songs* (Basel: Moondance, 2008), 107. "Hurricane" (co-written by Bob Dylan and Jacques Levy) provides considerable detail about a real crime and its aftermath. The lyric deviates from truth in many details, but the lawyers were only concerned about the lyric's description of living individuals who were involved in the case. One of them did sue, but the case was eventually dismissed on the grounds that Dylan and Levy were writing about a public figure, a defense that would not protect them in most countries.
42 Consequently, Currie proposes that reading a fictional story to children "produce[s] no fiction thereby," because the author of the story counts as the speaker who invited make-believe. See Currie, *The Nature of Fiction*, 42.
43 Nicholas Wolterstorff, *Art Rethought: The Social Practices of Art* (Oxford: Oxford University Press, 2015), chap. 16.
44 There is a technical difference between these formulations, but it is not important to my analysis. The key difference is the degree to which simulation theory is indebted to cognitive science.
45 This phrase is found throughout Walton's *Mimesis as Make-Believe*. An alternative view holds that proper nouns must refer to their standard referent, for they have no meaning over and above that function. In that case, fictions invite us to imagine something about or of these real people and places, a position defended by David Davies, "Fictive Utterances and the Fictionality of Narratives and Works," *British Journal of Aesthetics* 55 (2015): 49–55. I strongly doubt that this is the case. I listened to "Werewolves of London" for forty years without knowing that Lee Ho Fooks is a real restaurant in London, and I suspect that most auditors think it's a made-up name. The same for Eleanor Rigby, a name that Paul McCartney believed (mistakenly) he'd invented. Yet there she is, buried very near the spot where he first met John Lennon. Psychologically, I do not see how I was make-believing about the real restaurant or woman while disbelieving in their reality. Instead, I think that auditors who are aware of the reality of London need only imagine the werewolf roaming a London-like city, rather than having to reference the real London restaurant and imagining something about each of them.
46 To put it another way, we incorporate as much of reality into the fiction as the fiction allows. See Stacie Friend, "The Real Foundation of Fictional Worlds," *Australasian Journal of Philosophy* 95 (2017): 29–42.
47 Kendall L. Walton, "Thoughtwriting—In Poetry and Music," in *Other Shoes: Music, Metaphor, Empathy, Existence* (Oxford: Oxford University Press, 2015), 54. A

precursor theory is Peter Jones, "Works of Art and Their Availability-for-Use," *British Journal of Aesthetics* 11 (1971): 115–22. Unfortunately, Jones goes overboard and proposes that no artwork has an utterance meaning: each artwork is a text for use, every interpretive response is a "use" of that artwork, and every interpretation is equally legitimate. For my response, see Chapter 9.

48. Where *publishing* a poem or story constitutes its author's communicative act (understood broadly), publishing a song does not have the same status. In the former cases, the audience has its prop in the published text. With songs, the prop for imaginative engagement is not yet in place.
49. Eve Barlow, "Brandi Carlile on Her Song to Subvert the Grammys: 'It's a Call to Action,'" *The Guardian*, February 8, 2019, https://www.theguardian.com/music/2019/feb/08/brandi-carlile-grammys-country-gay-marriage-cancun.
50. Nerisha Penrose, "Anti-Donald Trump Ad Reworks Carly Simon's 'You're So Vain,'" *Billboard*, October 10, 2016, http://www.billboard.com/articles/news/politics/7534395/donald-trump-ad-carly-simon-youre-so-vain.
51. While Simon has been very clear that the only the second verse was directed at Warren Beatty and the other verses are about two other men, she has not identified them.
52. See Jonathan Cohen, "Indexicality and the Puzzle of the Answering Machine," *Journal of Philosophy* 110 (2013): 5–32.
53. Barney Hoskyns, *Lowside of the Road: A Life of Tom Waits* (London: Faber and Faber, 2009), xix.
54. William K. Wimsatt and Monroe C. Beardsley, "The Intentional Fallacy," *Sewanee Review* 54 (1946): 470.
55. Roland Barthes, *Image—Music—Text*, trans. Stephen Heath (New York: Hill and Wang, 1977), 148.

Chapter 3

1. Paul Thom, *For an Audience: A Philosophy of the Performing Arts* (Philadelphia: Temple University Press, 1993). I offer the following set of features as the necessary and sufficient conditions for being a performance. A performance is (1) an individual or group action, (2) of some particular duration, during which (3) the intention-guided activity aims to generate an observable event, during which (4) the generative activity of framing the focus of appreciation for an audience is itself offered for observation and appreciation for the duration of the generative act, and (5) the observable generative activity exhibits an acquired skill. The point of (4) is to distinguish performers from the many nonperformers who assist a performance and make it possible. In a puppet show, for example, the puppeteer is normally hidden. While the movements of the puppeteer generate the observable show, the puppeteers' own movements are not offered to the audience for observation and appreciation. By extension, live performances of popular music will rely on set designers, clothing designers, lighting designers, and choreographers, but their generative actions are not offered for audience observation. My thinking about this topic is influenced by David Davies, *Philosophy of the Performing Arts* (Oxford: Blackwell, 2011).

2   An excellent introduction to this topic is Philip Auslander, *In Concert: Performing Musical Persona* (Ann Arbor: University of Michigan Press, 2021), chap. 5. The notion of persona discussed here should not be confused with the idea that a piece of instrumental music can have a distinctive persona, e.g., Edward T. Cone, *The Composer's Voice* (Berkeley and Los Angeles: University of California Press, 1974), chap. 1, and Aaron Ridley, "*Persona*, Sometimes *Grata*: On the Appreciation of Expressive Music," in *Philosophers on Music: Experience, Meaning, and Work*, ed. Kathleen Stock (Oxford: Oxford University Press, 2007), 130–46.

3   A good general introduction to the topic is Stan Hawkins, "Personas in Rock," in *The Bloomsbury Handbook of Rock Music Research*, eds. Allan F. Moore and Paul Carr (New York: Bloomsbury Academic, 2020), 242–3.

4   Jeanette Bicknell, *Philosophy of Song and Singing: An Introduction* (New York: Routledge, 2015), 45. A peer reviewer for my manuscript suggests that we also attend to Sinatra's duet with his daughter Nancy on the song "Somethin' Stupid" (1967) as illustrating that audiences must be aware, on some level, that it's a persona, for otherwise this father-duet is incestually creepy.

5   Besides the decades of research in the journal *Popular Music and Society*, see such books as Fernando Orejuela and Stephanie Shonekan (eds.), *Black Lives Matter and Music: Protest, Intervention, Reflection* (Bloomington: Indiana University Press, 2018), and Björn Horgby and Fredrik Nilsson (eds.), *Rockin' the Borders: Rock Music and Social, Cultural and Political Change* (Cambridge).

6   Oscar Wilde, *The Picture of Dorian Gray*, ed. Joseph Bristow (Oxford: Oxford University Press, 2006), 3.

7   For a succinct summary of the positions of autonomism and ethicism, see Berys Gaut, "Art and Ethics," in *The Routledge Companion to Aesthetics*, 3rd ed., eds. Berys Gaut and Dominic McIver Lopes (New York: Routledge, 2013), 395. See also Elisabeth Schellekens, *Aesthetics and Morality* (London: Continuum, 2007), 63–76.

8   Edwin D. Starbuck and Frank K. Shuttleworth, *Guide to Literature for Character Training: Volume 1 Fairy Tale, Myth, and Legend* (New York: Macmillan, 1928), 11.

9   Bicknell, *Philosophy of Song and Singing*, 41.

10 Arthur Danto, *The Transfiguration of the Commonplace: A Philosophy of Art* (Cambridge, MA: Harvard University Press, 1981), 111; see also 154.

11 Kendall L. Walton, "Categories of Art," *Philosophical Review* 79 (1970): 347. For an overview of contextualism, see Theodore Gracyk, "Ontological Contextualism," in *A Companion to Aesthetics*, 2nd ed., eds. David Cooper, Stephen Davies, Kathleen Higgins, Robert Hopkins and Robert Stecker (Oxford: Blackwell, 2009), 449–53.

12 Maggie Haberman, "Trump Departs Vowing, 'We Will Be Back in Some Form,'" *New York Times*, January 20, 2021, https://www.nytimes.com/2021/01/20/us/politics/trump-presidency.html.

13 See Chapter 8 for a detailed analysis of cover versions.

14 An influential formulation of the position that the taste of food and drink is radically different from responses to the cultural world of art and entertainment, see Immanuel Kant, *Critique of the Power of Judgment*, ed. Paul Guyer, trans. Paul Guyer and Eric Matthews (Cambridge: Cambridge University Press, 2000), 165. For further discussion and critique, see Carolyn Korsmeyer, *Making Sense of Taste: Food and Philosophy* (Ithaca and London: Cornell University Press, 1999).

15 See also Jiayang Fan, "Yuck! The World's Most Disgusting Foods," *The New Yorker*, May 17, 2021, 42–9.

16 Carolyn Korsmeyer, *Savoring Disgust: The Foul and the Fair in Aesthetics* (Oxford: Oxford University Press, 2011), 23. An interesting response to Korsmeyer is Shen-Yi Liao and Aaron Meskin, "Morality and Aesthetics of Food," in *The Oxford Handbook of Food Ethics*, eds. Anne Barnhill, Mark Budolfson and Tyler Doggett (Oxford: Oxford University Press, 2018), 658–79. They discuss the case of Japanese ikizukuri, where flesh is sliced from a living fish or octopus, but this example does nothing to challenge what is said here about disgust and retrospective disgust.
17 Korsmeyer, *Savoring Disgust*, 33.
18 Compare this case to the consumption of fugu, a poisonous puffer fish; see Korsmeyer, *Savoring Disgust*, 81.
19 Thomas Doherty, *Hollywood's Censor: Joseph I. Breen and the Production Code Administration* (New York: Columbia University Press, 2009). The standards articulated in the code continued to influence American television even after the code was withdrawn in 1968.
20 The double standard has eroded, but not disappeared; African-American popular music continues to be policed, both literally and figuratively. See Erik Nelson and Andrea L. Dennis, *Rap on Trial: Race, Lyrics, and Guilt in America* (New York and London: The Free Press, 2019).
21 Jerrold Levinson, "What a Musical Work Is," *Journal of Philosophy* 77 (1980): 5–28. For an extended argument that the composer's identity is only sometimes relevant, see Davies, *Musical Works and Performances*, 79–86.
22 Gaut, *Art, Emotion and Ethics*, 108.
23 Gaut, *Art, Emotion and Ethics*, 76.
24 Gaut, *Art, Emotion and Ethics*, 73–4. Although Noël Carroll's moderate moralism differs from Gaut's ethicism, my objections also apply to Carroll's emphasis on works that "fail on their own terms" to secure a desired emotional response due to design failure, generally arising from a narrative's ethical perspective (Carroll, "Moderate Moralism," *The British Journal of Aesthetics* 36 (1996): 223–38).
25 Gaut, *Art, Emotion and Ethics*, 74. Gaut's position parallels the explications of sophisticated aestheticism, moralism, and ethicism provided by Schellekens (*Aesthetics and Morality*, 64–71).
26 I think this was Tolstoy's point in the opening of his book on art, where he explains how the praise lavished on an opera conductor is completely unjustified given his abusive behavior toward the opera company when not performing. Leo Tolstoy, *What Is Art?* trans. Aylmer Maude (New York: The Liberal Arts Press, 1960), chap. 1.
27 Denis Dutton, "Artistic Crimes," *British Journal of Aesthetics* 19 (1979): 302–41.
28 Peter Lamarque, *Work and Object: Explorations in the Metaphysics of Art* (Oxford: Oxford University Press, 2010), 151.
29 Respectively, Stan Godlovitch, *Musical Performance: A Philosophical Study* (New York: Routledge 1998), 139, and Bicknell, Philosophy of Song and Singing, 43. See also Allan F. Moore, *Song Means: Analysing and Interpreting Recorded Popular Song* (Farnham: Ashgate, 2012), 261–71.
30 Bicknell, *Philosophy of Song and Singing*, 83.
31 Bicknell, *Philosophy of Song and Singing*, 88. Earlier in the same book, Bicknell predicts that there would be audience disappointment if it became known that Paul Robeson regarded "Go Down, Moses" as just another song in his repertoire (Bicknell, *Philosophy of Song and Singing*, 41). This concern is about something that cannot be observed in performance, and here Bicknell opens the door to the line of argument that I am advancing. For an extended discussion of this general topic, see Mary Beth

Willard, *Why It's OK to Enjoy the Work of Immoral Artists* (New York: Routledge 2021). Although she rejects a narrowly utilitarian approach, Willard stresses the ethical tradeoffs that arise in commercial transactions. Overall, her conclusions align with Gaut, *Art, Emotion and Ethics*.

32 Martin W. Sandler, *How the Beatles Changed the World* (New York: Bloomsbury, 2014), 50. Unfortunately, Sandler misquotes Lennon.
33 Sandler, *Beatles*, 118.
34 Leah Garchik, "Shocked Show Shut Down over Gay Slur," *SF Gate*, May 18, 2013, http://www.sfgate.com/entertainment/garchik/article/Shocked-show-shut-down-over-gay-slur-4363898.php. Accepting an award in 1989, Michelle Shocked made public remarks that implied that she was a lesbian (Paul Russell, *The Gay 100: A Ranking of the Most Influential Gay Men and Lesbians, Past and Present* (New York: Carol Publishing, 1995), 331), and a few months later she explicitly told an interviewer that another woman was her "lover" (Christie Nordheim, "'Shocking' Revelations from Singer Michelle Shocked," *Outlines* (May 1990): 25).
35 Andrea Svedberg (uncredited), "I Am My Words," *Newsweek* (November 4, 1963): 94–5. The core details of this libelous claim are easily refuted: Dylan had both published and publicly performed it many months prior to the date that the student claimed to have written it. See Bob Dylan, "Blowin' in the Wind," *Broadside*, issue 6, late May 1962, 1. For more on the spread of the false rumor, see Robert Shelton, *No Direction Home: The Life and Music of Bob Dylan* (New York: Beech Tree Books, 1986), 161–2.
36 As I noted in this book's Introduction, Dylan did not perform "Blowin' in the Wind" that day. I wish to be clear here: I am not saying that performers cannot enhance their performance by falsely claiming to have composed something they did not compose. The conceit of doing so could add complexity to what is communicated.
37 Given the complexity of the cases, I will mention but not pursue the examples of R. Kelly and Michael Jackson. However, if accusations about Jackson are correct, then a track like "Childhood" (1995) becomes deeply problematic. For background on the relevant allegations, see Wesley Morris, "Michael Jackson Cast a Spell. 'Leaving Neverland' Breaks It," *New York Times*, February 28, 2019, https://www.nytimes.com/2019/02/28/arts/television/michael-jackson-leaving-neverland.html.
38 See Ryan Buesnel, "National Socialist Black Metal: A Case Study in the Longevity of Far-right Ideologies in Heavy Metal Subcultures," *Patterns of Prejudice* 4 (2020): 393–408.
39 Wesley C. Cray, "Transparent and Opaque Performance Personas," *Journal of Aesthetics of Art Criticism* 77 (2019): 183. The examples are my own and not Cray's. A parallel idea informs Auslander's contrast between modernist authenticity and postmodern pastiche (Auslander, *In Concert*, chap. 9).
40 Cray, "Transparent and Opaque," 184.
41 See also the analysis of Jarvis Cocker in Nicola Dibben, "Vocal Performance and the Projection of Emotional Authenticity," in *The Ashgate Research Companion to Popular Musicology*, ed. Derek Scott (Farnham: Ashgate, 2009), 324–8. Dibben stresses how bodily movement and gesture create distinct implications concerning the performer and the song's fictive narrator, so that auditors are to imagine of Jarvis that he is the character who is "speaking," while simultaneously understanding that Jarvis, the performer, is engaging in a commentary of the process of performing that character.

42 Hans Weisethaunet and Ulf Lindberg "Authenticity Revisited: The Rock Critic and the Changing Real," *Popular Music and Society* 33 (2010): 474. Again, see Dibben, "Vocal Performance," 324–8.
43 Santiago Fouz-Hernández and Freya Jarman-Ivens, *Madonna's Drowned Worlds: New Approaches to Her Cultural Transformations, 1983–2003* (Aldershot: Ashgate, 2004), 130.
44 Cray, "Transparent and Opaque," 188.
45 The communication is more ambiguous if one looks at a live performance of the one song in isolation from a full concert and Newman's developed persona; see Auslander, *In Concert*, 115–17.
46 I thank Cray for stressing this point and getting me to address it more directly.
47 See Auslander, *In Concert*, chap. 5.
48 *Festival Express*, dir. Bob Smeaton, Apollo Films, 2003 (1970 footage dir. Frank Cvitanovich).
49 Following Garcia's death, the band angered many fans by restricting the open circulation of high-quality performance recordings in order to increase their market value; see Jeff Leeds, "Deadheads Outraged Over Web Crackdown," *The New York Times*, November 30, 2005, http://www.nytimes.com/2005/11/30/arts/music/deadheads-outraged-over-web-crackdown.html?mcubz=0.
50 See, for example, Barry Barnes, *Everything I Know about Business I Learned from the Grateful Dead: The Ten Most Innovative Lessons from a Long, Strange Trip* (New York: Business Plus, 2011).
51 Walter Hughes, "In the Empire of the Beat," in *Microphone Fiends: Youth Music and Youth Culture*, eds. Andrew Ross and Tricia Rose (New York: Routledge, 1994), 150.
52 Gillian Frank, "Discophobia: Antigay Prejudice and the 1979 Backlash against Disco," *Journal of the History of Sexuality* 15 (2007): 276–306.
53 Richard Dyer, *The Culture of Queers* (New York: Routledge, 2002), 169. Dyer argues that evidence of Hudson's real-life sexuality cannot be found in his onscreen acting.

Chapter 4

1 Anne Desler, "History without Royalty? Queen and the Strata of the Popular Music Canon," *Popular Music* 32 (2013): 391.
2 Prominent voices aligning it with rock music but not "pop" include Simon Frith, *Taking Popular Music Seriously: Selected Essays* (Aldershot: Ashgate, 2007), 168; Philip Auslander, *Liveness: Performance in a Mediatized Culture* (London and New York: Routledge, 1999), 69; Keir Keightley, "Reconsidering Rock," in *The Cambridge Companion to Pop and Rock*, eds. Simon Frith, Will Straw and John Street (Cambridge: Cambridge University Press, 2001), 131.
3 My early thoughts on this topic are Theodore Gracyk, *Rhythm and Noise: An Aesthetics of Rock* (Durham, NC: Duke University Press), chap. 8.
4 Sarah Thornton, *Club Cultures: Music, Media, and Subcultural Capital* (Cambridge: Polity, 1995), 5–6. See also Ralf von Appen, "Feigning or Feeling? on the Staging of Authenticity on Stage," *Samples* 18 (2020), www.gfpm-samples.de/Samples18/vonappen.pdf.
5 Greil Marcus, *Bob Dylan by Greil Marcus: Writings 1968–2010* (New York: Public Affairs, 2010), 21.

6 The review's use of "auteur" diverges from general usage, but the import is to denigrate commercial motivations.
7 Marcus, *Bob Dylan*, 18.
8 Simon Frith, *Performing Rites: On the Value of Popular Music* (Cambridge, MA: Harvard University Press, 1996), 71.
9 Lawrence Grossberg, "The Media Economy of Rock Culture: Cinema, Postmodernity and Authenticity," in *Sound and Vision: The Music Video Reader*, eds. Simon Frith, Andrew Goodwin and Lawrence Grossberg (London and New York: Routledge, 1993), 204. This standard is applied, for example, to Morrissey, in Stan Hawkins "'You Have Killed Me'—Tropes of Hyperbole and Sentimentality in Morrissey's Musical Expression," in *Morrissey: Fandom, Representations and Identities*, eds. Eoin Devereux, Aileen Dillane and Martin Power (Bristol: Intellect, 2011), 310. For a more nuanced view of rock vocals, see Allan F. Moore, *Song Means: Analysing and Interpreting Recorded Popular Song* (Farnham: Ashgate, 2012), 106–8.
10 Quoted in Katherine Monk, *Joni: The Creative Odyssey of Joni Mitchell* (Vancouver: Greystone Books, 2012), 23.
11 Frith, *Performing Rites*, 19.
12 See Keightley, "Reconsidering Rock," 131.
13 Throughout *Performing Rites*, Frith sees authenticity as a value inherited from folk music and treats it as unrelated to originality, which is valued in the discourse of bourgeois art; rock lays claim to both values in distancing itself from overtly commercial "pop" music. For more details on the "folkloric" conception of authenticity, see Hans Weisethaunet and Ulf Lindberg, "Authenticity Revisited: The Rock Critic and the Changing Real," *Popular Music and Society* 33 (2010): 469–71.
14 An early example is Robert Pattison, *The Triumph of Vulgarity: Rock Music in the Mirror of Romanticism* (Oxford: Oxford University Press, 1986), 96–103.
15 Keightley, "Reconsidering Rock," 135–7.
16 Keightley, "Reconsidering Rock," 136. A similar dichotomy informs Thornton, *Club Cultures*, 30.
17 This concern has been interpreted as an assertion of artistic *autonomy* in an industrial context; see Motti Regev, *Pop-Rock Music: Aesthetic Cosmopolitanism in Late Modernity* (Cambridge: Polity Press, 2011), 72–5.
18 David Hesmondhalgh and Leslie M. Meier, "Popular Music, Independence and the Concept of the Alternative in Contemporary Capitalism," in *Media Independence: Working with Freedom or Working for Free?*, eds. James Bennett and Niki Strange (New York: Routledge, 2014), 97.
19 Louis Menand, *American Studies* (New York: Farrar, Straus and Giroux, 2002), 170.
20 Pattison, *The Triumph of Vulgarity*; Robert Walser, *Running with the Devil: Power, Gender, and Madness in Heavy Metal Music* (Middleton, CT: Wesleyan University Press, 1993); Weisethaunet and Lindberg, "Authenticity Revisited"; Jennifer Otter Bickerdike, *Fandom, Image and Authenticity: Joy Devotion and the Second Lives of Kurt Cobain and Ian Curtis* (Basingstoke: Palgrave Macmillan, 2014).
21 Moore, *Song Means*, 269; see also Walser, *Running with the Devil*, 100.
22 The definitive document is E. T. A. Hoffman, "Beethoven's Instrumental Music," in *E. T. A. Hoffmann's Musical Writings: Kreisleriana, The Poet and the Composer, Music Criticism*, ed. David Charlton, trans. Martyn Clarke (Cambridge: Cambridge University Press, 1989), 96–103.
23 Note, in this regard, that "authenticity" is never mentioned in M. H. Abrams, *The Mirror and the Lamp* (Oxford: Oxford University Press, 1953). Some Romantics were

concerned about some kinds of authenticity, but primarily concerning the distinction between pre-modern, "folk" texts, and those which were fabricated antiquities or, in the case of music, distorted through updating. See Michael Ferber, *Romanticism: A Very Short Introduction* (Oxford: Oxford University Press, 2010), where authenticity is mentioned precisely once, in relation to the "Ossian" hoax.

24 Joanne Schneider, *The Age of Romanticism* (Westport, CT: Greenwood Press, 2007), 4.

25 Barry Golson (ed.), *The Playboy Interviews with John Lennon & Yoko Ono* (New York: Berkley Books, 1982), 214. See also Jann S. Wenner (ed.), *Lennon Remembers* (San Francisco: Straight Arrow Books, 1971).

26 Frith, *Performing Rites*, 71; see also Johan Fornäs, "Moving Rock: Youth and Pop in Late Modernity," *Popular Music* 9 (1990): 302; Keightley, "Reconsidering Rock," 132–3.

27 Simon Frith, *Music for Pleasure: Essays in the Sociology of Pop* (New York: Routledge, 1988), 100. Notice also the lack of interest in the relevance of the music's conditions of origin in Frith, *Taking Popular Music Seriously*, 306.

28 The doctrine of the singular, resistive artist was a supporting pillar of the very system it alleged to challenge; see Jon Stratton, "Capitalism and Romantic Ideology in the Record Business," *Popular Music* 3 (1983): 143–56.

29 Thornton, *Club Cultures*, 34.

30 According to Timothy Taylor, "authenticity" underpins the logic of the rock offshoot of world music, where it is used in relation to musics of indigenous peoples perceived as "real," "pure," and noncommercial, making them valuable as sources for appropriation by rock musicians (*Global Pop: World Music, World Markets* (London and New York: Routledge, 1997), 16–17, 26).

31 Ulf Lindberg, Gestur Guomundsson, Morten Michelsen, and Hans Weisethaunet, *Rock Criticism from the Beginning: Amusers, Bruisers, and Cool-Headed Cruisers* (New York: Peter Lang, 2005), 323.

32 For example, Auslander, *Liveness*, 9, 87, 99; Fornäs, "Moving Rock, 299; Frith, *Taking Popular Music Seriously*, chap. 2; Gracyk, *Rhythm and Noise*, 222; Richard Middleton, *Studying Popular Music* (Milton Keynes: Open University Press, 1990), 140; David Pattie, *Rock Music in Performance* (Basingstoke: Palgrave Macmillan, 2007), 23; Roy Shuker, *Understanding Popular Music*, 2nd ed. (London and New York: Routledge, 2001), 8; Walser, *Running with the Devil*, 100–1.

33 Walser, *Running with the Devil*, chap. 2; Frith, *Performing Rites*, 26, 35.

34 Frith, "The Magic That Can Set You Free"; Lawrence Grossberg, *We Gotta Get Out of This Place: Popular Conservatism and Postmodern Culture* (New York: Routledge, 1992).

35 Grossberg, *We Gotta Get Out*, 236.

36 Grossberg, *We Gotta Get Out*, 205.

37 Grossberg, *We Gotta Get Out*, 206.

38 Grossberg, *We Gotta Get Out*, 217.

39 Auslander usefully expands Grossberg's critique with an account of how a loss of investment in the authenticating function of live performance fueled the "crisis in the ideology of rock authenticity" (*Liveness*, 87).

40 It is unclear whether Grossberg thinks other musical genres operate differently.

41 Grossberg, *We Gotta Get Out*, 224.

42 Hugh Barker and Yuval Taylor, *Faking It: The Quest for Authenticity in Popular Music* (New York: W. W. Norton, 2002), 269.

43 Lester Bangs, "Swan Dive into the Mung," in *The Bowie Companion*, eds. Elizabeth Thomson and David Gutman (New York: Da Capo Press, 1996), 119.
44 Weisethaunet and Lindberg, "Authenticity Revisited," 474. A case can be made that Frank Zappa deserves more credit in this regard; see Kelly Fisher Lowe, *The Words and Music of Frank Zappa* (Westport, CT: Praeger, 2006), 37.
45 For example, Thornton, *Club Cultures*; Philip Auslander, *Performing Glam Rock: Gender and Theatricality in Popular Music* (Ann Arbor: University of Michigan Press, 2006); Adam Behr, "Join Together with the Band: Authenticating Collective Creativity in Bands and the Myth of Rock Authenticity Reappraised," *Rock Music Studies* 2 (2015): 1–21. Behr is another writer who refers to authenticity as an "ideology" (Behr, "Join Together with the Band," 5).
46 David Diallo, "Dr. Dre and Snoop Dogg," in *Icons of Hip Hop" An Encyclopedia of the Movement, Music, and Culture*, ed. Mickey Hess (Westport and London: Greenwood Press, 2007), vol. 2, 318.
47 By analogy, it is as though Grossberg supposes that I must endorse the American medical system as a precondition for respecting my personal physician, when in fact I may respect her because she has integrity *despite* the sorry state of American health care.
48 For example, Petty's death was greeted with a headline of "Tom Petty Stood up for Authentic Rock Music—and He Never Backed Down" (Adam Behr, *The Conversation*, October 4, 2017, https://theconversation.com/tom-petty-stood-up-for-authentic-rock-music-and-he-never-backed-down-85187).
49 For example, Auslander, *Performing Glam Rock*, 204; Kembrew McLeod, "Between Rock and a Hard Place: Gender and Rock Criticism," in *Pop Music and the Press*, ed. Steve Jones (Philadelphia: Temple University Press, 2002), 93–113.
50 Aaron A. Fox, *Real Country: Music and Language in Working-Class Culture* (Durham, NC: Duke University Press, 2004), 25. See also Geoff Mann, "Why Does Country Music Sound White? Race and the Voice of Nostalgia," *Race and Ethnic Studies* 31 (2008): 7–100. In Australia, on the other hand, country music sometimes included hit songs by Aboriginal singers constructing a resistive counter-history to the predominant society; see Toby Martin, "Historical Silences, Musical Noise: Slim Dusty, Country Music and Aboriginal History," *Popular Music History* 12 (2019): 215–36.
51 Fox, *Real Country*, 319, 321.
52 Moore, *Song Means*, 263, 214. Moore challenges the tendency to think that untrained and rough voices are generic signifiers of authenticity in rock, as in Jeremy Gilbert and Ewan Pearson, *Discographies: Dance Music, Culture and the Politics of Sound* (London and New York: Routledge, 1999), 68–9.
53 The source-focused approach might confirm her authenticity by noting, for example, her account of how "a case of nerves" derailed the performance (Patti Smith, "How Does It Feel?" *The New Yorker*, December 14, 2016, https://www.newyorker.com/culture/cultural-comment/patti-smith-on-singing-at-bob-dylans-nobel-prize-ceremony).
54 Moore, *Song Means*, 5–7, 10–13.
55 Michael Ventre, "Hendrix Created Banner Moment at Woodstock," *Today*, August 10, 2009, https://www.today.com/popculture/hendrix-created-banner-moment-woodstock-2D80555766.
56 Behr, "Join Together."

57 This way of putting it is from Allan F. Moore, "Interpretation: So What?" in *The Ashgate Research Companion to Popular Musicology*, ed. Derek Scott (Farnham: Ashgate, 2009), 419.
58 See also Jason Toynbee, *Making Popular Music: Musicians, Creativity and Institutions* (London: Arnold, 2000), 60. Frith comes close to articulating this thesis, but cuts it off to discuss ethical judgment (*Performing Rites*, 71).
59 See Allan F. Moore, "Authenticity as Authentication," *Popular Music* 21 (2002): 214.
60 It had been a part of his act since 1961 (R. J. Smith, *The One: The Life and Music of James Brown* (Garden City, NY: Avery, 2012), 143). The realization example is drawn from the film *The Commitments* (1991, dir. Allan Parker).
61 Moore, "Authenticity as Authentication," 214.
62 For the sake of simplicity, I gloss over Chapter 2's discussion of the make-believe aspect of song performance, where reference to the real San Francisco informs the make-believe of the performance fiction.
63 The same is true of Steven Gamble, *How Music Empowers: Listening to Modern Rap and Metal* (New York: Routledge, 2021).
64 Moore, "Authenticity as Authentication," 220.
65 Moore, "Authenticity as Authentication," 218. See also Frith, "Music and Identity."
66 We cannot predict, in advance, which music will validate which listeners. Despite the general heteronormativity of heavy metal, and Metallica specifically, they have a surprisingly strong following among lesbian-identified fans, for reasons that frequently align with Moore's authenticity of experience. See Amber R. Clifford-Napoleone, *Queerness in Heavy Metal Music: Metal Bent* (New York: Routledge, 2015), 119–20.
67 Carrie Brownstein, *Hunger Makes Me a Modern Girl: A Memoir* (New York: Riverhead Books, 2015), 195.
68 Stephen R. Millar, "'I Forbid You to Like It:' The Smiths, David Cameron, and the Politics of (Mis)appropriating Popular Culture," *Echo*, 2015, http://www.echo.ucla.edu/article-millar-i-forbid-you-to-like-it/#fn-1054-9.
69 Smith, *The One*, 149–50.
70 Moore, "Authenticity as Authentication," 215. In hindsight, many early recordings of The Rolling Stones sound like tepid imitations of Black sources; yet, Brian Jones defended their appropriations: "We haven't adapted our music from a watered down music like white American rock-n-roll. We've adapted our music directly from the early black blues forms." Quoted in Barry Miles, *The British Invasion* (London and New York: Sterling Publishing, 2009), 129–30.
71 Moore, "Authenticity as Authentication," 218.
72 Behr, "Join Together."
73 Quoted in Richie Unterberger, *White Light/White Heat: The Velvet Underground Day by Day* (London: Jawbone Press, 2009), 288.
74 See Barney Hoskyns, *Across the Great Divide: The Band and America* (New York: Hyperion, 1993).
75 Philip Auslander, *In Concert: Performing Musical Persona* (Ann Arbor: University of Michigan Press, 2021), 135.
76 Walser, *Running with the Devil*, 121.
77 The case of Phil Ochs is discussed in Auslander, *In Concert*, 118–19.
78 Tim Jonze, "Bigmouth Strikes Again and Again: Why Morrissey Fans Feel So Betrayed," *The Guardian*, May 30, 2019, https://www.theguardian.com/music/2019/

may/30/bigmouth-strikes-again-morrissey-songs-loneliness-shyness-misfits-far-right-party-tonight-show-jimmy-fallon.
79 Keigthley, "Reconsidering Rock," 131.
80 Linda Nochlin, *Women, Art, and Power and Other Essays* (London and New York: Routledge, 2018), 150.
81 Quoted in Margaret Talbot, "Reach for the Stars: The Secret Hollywood of 'You Must Remember This,'" *The New Yorker*, July 5, 2021, 67–8.
82 One of first attempts to popularize the issue is Geoffrey Stokes, *Star-Making Machinery: Inside the Business of Rock and Roll* (New York: Random House, 1977).
83 Kenneth Womack, *Maximum Volume: The Life of Beatles Producer George Martin, The Early Years, 1926–1966* (Chicago: Chicago Review Press, 2017). I do not mean to discount the existence of writing and scholarship about the production process (e.g., articles and interviews in the *Journal on the Art of Record Production*). For an overview, see Samantha Benner, "Rock Music Engineering and Production," in *The Bloomsbury Handbook of Rock Music Research*, eds. Allan F. Moore and Paul Carr (New York and London: Bloomsbury, 2020), 179–93.
84 I was dismayed to find that a new textbook on popular music video says little about the role of video directors and, instead, routinely assigns agency (and thus intentionality) to the featured musicians, e.g., "Doja Cat keeps the viewer's interest," instead of the *video* doing so (Brad Osborn, *Interpreting Music Video in the Post-MTV Era* (New York: Routledge, 2021), 15). Plausibly, such videos are generally co-authored in the sense explored in Chapter 5. With choreography, consider the role of professional choreographers in shaping Madonna's persona. See Lyndsey Winship, "Into the Groove: How We Taught Madonna to Krump and Thrust," *The Guardian*, November 24, 2015, https://www.theguardian.com/stage/2015/nov/24/into-the-groove-how-we-taught-madonna-to-krump-and-thrust.
85 Two steps in the right direction are Mary Celeste Kearney, *Gender and Rock* (Oxford: Oxford University Press, 2017), chap. 3, and Tom Hennessy, *Beyond Authenticism: New Approaches to Post War Music Culture* (Doctoral thesis, Birkbeck, University of London, 2016). Unfortunately, neither digs into the question of why "authenticity" rose to such prominence when it did; I suspect that the popularization of Sartre's existentialism and the subsequent awareness of Kierkegaard and Heidegger played some role here.
86 For example, Benjamin Hedin (ed.), *Studio A: The Bob Dylan Reader* (New York: W. W. Norton, 2004).
87 Ellen Willis, "Dylan," in *Bob Dylan: A Retrospective*, ed. Craig McGregor (New York: William Morrow, 1972), 220. Her usage does not align very neatly with our issues. I can locate one other case, in the same anthology, but it is used to say that Dylan should be admired as a poet, in the high-art sense of poet.
88 For example, Jonathan Cott (ed.), *Bob Dylan: The Essential Interviews* (New York: Simon and Schuster, 2017).
89 There are strong affinities between the point I make here and David Bordwell's argument that film writing and scholarship was shaped less by the material it studied than by the writers' exposure to doctrines about interpretation they encountered in their university studies; see David Bordwell, *Making Meaning: Inference and Rhetoric in the Interpretation of Cinema* (Cambridge, MA: Harvard University Press, 1989), chap. 2.
90 Tia DeNora, *Music in Everyday Life* (Cambridge: Cambridge University Press, 2000), 23.

91 Susan D. Crafts et al., *My Music: Explorations of Music in Daily Life* (Middletown, CT: Wesleyan University Press, 1993); DeNora, *Music in Everyday Life*. The clearest explicit reference to authenticity is a listener who denigrates recent Dixieland groups as inferior to the "real thing" (Crafts et al., 202).
92 Crafts et al., *My Music*, 61.
93 Hennessey (*Beyond Authenticism*) draws a similar conclusion concerning pre-rock popular music in England.
94 This point originally raised by R. J. Warren Zanes, "Too Much Mead? Under the Influence (of Participant-Observation)," in *Reading Rock and Roll: Authenticity, Appropriation, Aesthetics*, eds. Kevin J. H. Dettmar and William Richey (New York: Columbia University Press, 1999), 60.
95 I suspect that Sheila Whiteley thinks so, too, especially for singer-songwriters; see Whiteley, *Women and Popular Music: Sexuality, Identity, and Subjectivity* (London and New York: Routledge, 2000), 172.

Chapter 5

1   The phenomenon of group-as-speaker is one of several reasons why I favor a version of pragmatics that emphasizes the relevance principle instead of Paul Grice's formulation of pragmatics as governed by conversational implicature. Compare H. P. Grice, "Logic and Conversation," in *Syntax and Semantics, vol. 3, Speech Acts*, eds. Peter Cole and Jerry L. Morgan (New York: Academic Press, 1975), 41–58, and Deirdre Wilson and Dan Sperber, *Meaning and Relevance* (Cambridge: Cambridge University Press, 2012), chap. 1.
2   Timothy White, "Pink Floyd," in *Rock Lives: Profiles and Interviews* (New York: Henry Holt, 1990), 510, 520–1.
3   E. T. A. Hoffmann, "Beethoven's Instrumental Music," in *E. T. A. Hoffmann's Musical Writings: Kreisleriana, The Poet and the Composer, Music Criticism*, ed. David Charlton, trans. Martyn Clarke (Cambridge: Cambridge University Press, 1989), 97.
4   There are also issues with authorship in the classical repertoire. Problems similar to those I'm raising about Pink Floyd are generated by Mozart's *Requiem* and Mahler's Symphony No. 10, both of which were completed in at least two different ways by others after their deaths. Are dual completions distinct musical works due to co-authorship? See, for example, Nemesio García-Carril Puy, "The Ontology of Musical Versions: Introducing the Hypothesis of Nested Types," *Journal of Aesthetics and Art Criticism* 77 (2019): 242.
5   Sondra Bacharach and Deborah Tollefsen, "*We* Did It: From Mere Contributors to Coauthors," *Journal of Aesthetics and Art Criticism* 68 (2010): 23. There is a third approach, perhaps best illustrated by the mash-up track, where a type is multiply authored without collaboration; e.g., see the essays in Stefan Sonvilla-Weiss (ed.), *Mashup Cultures* (Vienna: Springer, 2010).
6   This vision is articulated at length by Phil Rose, *Which One's Pink? An Analysis of the Concept Albums of Roger Waters and Pink Floyd* (Burlington, Ontario: Collector's Guide Publishing, 1998).
7   Waters quoted in White, "Pink Floyd," 519.
8   White, "Pink Floyd," 514.
9   Waters quoted in White, "Pink Floyd," 508.

10 John Locke, *An Essay Concerning Human Understanding*, ed. Peter H. Nidditch (Oxford: Clarendon Press:1975), chap. XXVII.3.
11 The literature on this topic is huge, but those who wish to pursue it might begin with Kit Fine, "The Non-Identity of a Material Thing and Its Matter," *Mind* 112 (2003): 195–234.
12 See Carolyn Korsmeyer, *Things: In Touch with the Past* (Oxford: Oxford University Press, 2019), chap. 1.
13 Locke, *Essay*, chap. XXVII.10.
14 My reconstruction and discussion of this argument is based on a similar argument in Trenton Merricks, "Endurance and Indiscernibility," in *Metaphysics: Contemporary Readings*, ed. Michael J. Loux (New York: Routledge, 2001), 364–5.
15 For an introduction to this doctrine, known as perdurantism, see Michael J. Loux, "Endurantism and Perdurantism," in *Metaphysics*, ed. Loux, 321–7.
16 Bacharach and Tollefsen, "*We* Did It," 29–31.
17 For this reason, I favor the position of Bacharach and Tollefsen ("*We* Did It") over rival accounts that identify any co-authorship with a commitment to very specific goals, e.g., Paisley Livingston, *Art and Intention: A Philosophical Study* (Oxford: Clarendon, 2005), chap. 3.
18 These examples parallel ones in Bacharach and Tollefsen, "*We* Did It," 28–9. To quote drummer Bill Bruford, "collaborative creation is ever full of misunderstandings, communication breakdowns and methodological pitfalls" (Marshall Heiser, "Control, Chaos, Power, and Play: Interview with Dr Bill Bruford," *Journal on the Art of Record Production* (May 2021), https://www.arpjournal.com/asarpwp/control-chaos-power-and-play-interview-with-dr-bill-bruford/).
19 Margaret Gilbert, "Concerning Sociality: The Plural Subject as Paradigm," in *The Mark of the Social: Discovery or Invention?* ed. John Greenwood (Lanham, MD: Rowman and Littlefield, 1997), 17–36.
20 For the parallel problem in relation to film production (but with a compressed and slightly different explanation of the solution), see C. Paul Sellors, "Collective Authorship in Film," *Journal of Aesthetics and Art Criticism* 65 (2007): 263–71.
21 For background on why those who merely walked around the building interior might also bear some responsibility for more egregious actions that day, see the essays in Saba Bazargan-Forward and Deborah Tollefsen (eds.), *The Routledge Handbook of Collective Responsibility* (New York: Routledge: 2020), Parts I and II.
22 Alan Feuer and Frances Robles, "Proud Boys under Growing Scrutiny in Capitol Riot Investigation," *New York Times*, January 26, 2021, updated April 13, 2021, https://www.nytimes.com/2021/01/26/us/proud-boys-capitol-riot.html.
23 Arthur C. Danto, *The Transfiguration of the Commonplace: A Philosophy of Art* (Cambridge, MA: Harvard University Press, 1981), 31–9.
24 This approach seems to be endorsed by Philip Auslander, *In Concert: Performing Musical Persona* (Ann Arbor: University of Michigan Press, 2021), 198–9.
25 This result will not bother those who reject theories that focus on "'encoding' and 'decoding'" meanings, such as Allan F. Moore, "Interpretation: So What?" in *The Ashgate Research Companion to Popular Musicology*, ed. Derek Scott (Farnham: Ashgate, 2009), 419. Among philosophers, the problem of patchwork creativity has supported the view that such projects are multiply authored, not even co-authored; see Gaut, *Philosophy of Cinematic Art*, 116, 132.
26 For arguments both for and against the possibility of a "group mind," see Deborah P. Tollefsen, *Groups as Agents* (Cambridge: Polity, 2015), chap. 4.

27 We might therefore think that producers have assumed the role of auteur in popular music, but that has not, in fact, become the norm. See Tuomas Auvinen, "Creative Communities of Practice: Role Delineation in Record Production in Different Areas and across Different Genres and Production Settings," in *The Bloomsbury Handbook of Music Production*, eds. Andrew Bourbon and Simon Zagorski-Thomas (New York: Bloomsbury Academic 2020), 161–77.

28 Read in this way, I recognize the coherence of the position of critics and fans who regard *Piper* as Barrett's record and who think that Pink Floyd ceased to exist when Barrett left the group. See John Cavanagh, *The Piper at the Gates of Dawn* (33 1/3 series) (New York and London: Continuum, 2003), 122.

29 See Dave Marsh, *Louie Louie: The History and Mythology of the World's Most Famous Rock 'n Roll Song* (New York: Hyperion, 1993).

30 Quoted in Rose, *Which One's Pink?* 43; originally from Nick Sedgewick, "A Rambling Conversation with Roger Waters Concerning All This and That," in n.a., *Wish You Were Here Songbook*, 1975.

31 My discussion is heavily influenced by Robert Stecker, *Interpretation and Construction: Art, Speech, and the Law* (Malden, MA: Blackwell Publishing, 2003), 42–50.

32 One might object that Waters might be bluffing to burnish his persona. But, as I argued in Chapter 3, we need not take a transparent persona at face value, and performer interviews are, or are highly akin to, performances that signal a transparent persona.

33 Deborah Tollefsen, "Organizations as True Believers," *Journal of Social Philosophy* 33 (Fall 2002): 397.

34 See Berys Gaut, *A Philosophy of Cinematic Art* (Cambridge: Cambridge University Press, 2010), 98, 124.

35 The argument that follows is based on David Copp, "On the Agency of Certain Collective Entities: An Argument from 'Normative Autonomy,'" in *Midwest Studies in Philosophy*, eds. French and Wettstein, 194–221 and Deborah Tollefsen, "The Rationality of Collective Guilt," in *Midwest Studies in Philosophy Volume XXX: Shared Intentions and Collective Responsibility*, eds. Peter A. French and Howard K. Wettstein (Oxford: Blackwell, 2006), 222–39.

36 This argument is a paraphrase of Tollefson, *Groups as Agents*, 101–4.

37 This objection might gain traction against Tollefesen's method of cashing out the thesis in greater detail, but the objection does not succeed against a functionalist stance on mental states. For a contrast of the two approaches, see David Strohmaier, "Two Theories of Group Agency," *Philosophical Studies* 177 (2020): 1901–18.

38 See Tollefsen, *Groups as Agents*, chap. 6.

39 Raimo Tuomela, "Actions by Collectives," *Philosophical Perspectives* 3 (1989): 471–96.

40 "Abused by John Lydon: the Jam! Interview," JohnLydon.Com, http://www.johnlydon.com/jamm96.html.

41 Another argument favoring this thesis is that we attribute intentions to minds despite our failure to understand how parts of the brain work together to contribute to intentionality. By analogy, then, our failure to understand exactly *how* a group has intentions is no reason to deny that groups have them. See Copp, "On the Agency of Certain Collective Entities," 194–221. See also Tollefsen, *Groups as Agents*, chap. 5.

Chapter 6

1. Kendall L. Walton, "Categories of Art," *Philosophical Review* 79 (1970): 334–67.
2. My decision to investigate post-punk was serendipitous, although not arbitrary: Aaron Meskin invited me to give a talk at a one-day conference at University of Leeds in 2009, and my ideas took shape knowing that some members of Gang of Four were to be in attendance and would hear my presentation.
3. This point distinguishes what follows from studies that discuss an intermediate kind of context that provides a background to communication, the cultural space that constitutes a musical scene. An excellent introduction to scene theory is Andy Bennett and Ian Rogers, *Popular Music Scenes and Cultural Memory* (London: Palgrave Macmillan, 2016).
4. Clinton Heylin, *From the Velvets to the Voidoids: A Pre-Punk History for a Post-Punk World* (New York: Penguin, 1993).
5. Georges Braque advanced this position; see Anne Ganteführer-Trier, *Cubism* (Köln and London: Taschen, 2004), 32.
6. Plato, "Meno," in *The Dialogues of Plato*, vol. 2. 3rd ed., ed. and trans. Benjamin Jowett (Oxford: Clarendon Press, 1892), 29.
7. Ken Tucker, "New Wave: Britain," in *The Rolling Stone Illustrated History of Rock & Roll*, revised and updated, ed. Jim Miller (New York: Random House/Rolling Stone Press, 1980), 435–9.
8. Greil Marcus, *Ranters & Crowd Pleasers: Punk in Pop* Music, *1977–92* (New York: Doubleday, 1993), 195, 197.
9. Stewart Home, *Cranked Up Really High: An Inside Account of Punk Rock* (London: Codex, 1995), 9.
10. *New Wave*, vinyl and cassette, Vertigo/Phonogram 6300 902 (1977).
11. Richard Meltzer, "St. Stephen Revisited and Beyond," in *The Grateful Dead Reader*, eds. David G. Dodd and Diana Spaulding (Oxford: Oxford University Press, 2002), 117.
12. David Shumway, "Rock & Roll as a Cultural Practice," in *Present Tense: Rock & Roll and Culture*, ed. Anthony DeCurtis (Durham, NC: Duke University Press, 1992), 123.
13. Shumway, "Rock & Roll as a Cultural Practice," 119.
14. As I explain in the book's introduction, a recording should not be confused with a music performance. A post-punk listener's primary access is recorded music, just as it was for Jerry Garcia and most listeners in 1977. Consequently, Wendy Fanarow's principle that "the music performance [is] the unit of analysis" (Fonarow, *Empire of Dirt: The Aesthetics and Rituals of British Indie Music* (Middletown, CT: Wesleyan University Press, 2006), 11) may slant her analysis of British independent rock.
15. Paul Ziff, "On H. P. Grice's Account of Meaning," *Analysis* 28 (1967): 1–28.
16. Ludwig Wittgenstein, *Philosophical Investigations: The English Text of the Third Edition,* trans. G. E. M. Anscombe (New York: Macmillan, 1968), 8.
17. Dave Laing, *One Chord Wonders: Power and Meaning in Punk Rock* (Milton Keynes: Open University Press, 1985), 115.
18. For a philosophical perspective, see Jennifer Judkins, "Style," in *The Routledge Companion to Philosophy and Music*, eds. Theodore Gracyk and Andrew Kania (New York: Routledge, 2011), 134–43.
19. Meyer Schapiro, "Style," in *The Art of Art History, A Critical Anthology*, ed. Donald Preziosi (Oxford: Oxford University Press, 1998), 143.

20 Walton, "Categories of Art," 341.
21 Leonard B. Meyer, *Style and Music: Theory, History, and Ideology* (Chicago: University of Chicago Press, 1996), 3.
22 For purposes of clarity, I am ignoring the ability of many popular musicians to perform in more than one style, and how personal styles feed into, and change, general styles.
23 Stephanie Ross, "Style in Art," in *The Oxford Handbook of Aesthetics*, ed. Jerrold Levinson (Oxford: Oxford University Press, 2003), 228.
24 Richard Wollheim, "Pictorial Style: Two Views," in *The Concept of Style*, ed. Berel Lang (Philadelphia: University of Pennsylvania Press, 1979), 129–45; but see also the criticisms in Jason Gaiger, *Aesthetics and Painting* (London and New York: Continuum, 2008), 99–102, 111–13.
25 E. H. Gombrich, *Art and Illusion* (New York: Pantheon, 1960), 313.
26 Following Walton, we have both a psychological thesis, that expectations about what is standard and contra-standard for a style will affect how the music strikes us, and a normative thesis, that "it is correct to perceive a work in certain categories, and incorrect to perceive it in certain others" (Walton, "Categories of Art," 356).
27 For background on the teddy boy precedent for this cross-modal association, see Dick Hebdige, *Subculture: The Meaning of Style* (London: Routledge, 1979), chap. 5.
28 For an analysis of punk style in the requisite sense, see Laing, *One Chord Wonders*, 59–63, and Allan F. Moore, *Rock: The Primary Text* (Buckingham: Open University Press, 1993), 112–21.
29 I will not expand on the notion of genre here. Arising from marketing distinctions in the music industry, "genre" was previously a matter of classifying an artwork's subject matter (e.g., Shakespeare's histories as opposed to his tragedies). In popular music, genres are "nothing more or less than the names we give to communities of musicians and listeners" (Kelefa Sanneh, *Major Labels: A History of Popular Music in Seven Genres* (New York: Penguin, 2021), xii).
30 For example, the term appears frequently in Robert S. Nelson and Richard Shiff (eds.), *Critical Terms for Art History*, 2nd ed. (Chicago: University of Chicago Press, 2003), but the term itself is not considered a critical term needing attention.
31 The Art History Babes, *An Honest Art Dictionary: A Jovial Trip through Art Jargon* (London: White Lion, 2020), 174.
32 Edward Lucie-Smith, *Movements in Art Since 1945*, 2nd ed. (London: Thames and Hudson, 2020), 37.
33 This is the great lesson of the work of E. H. Gombrich, both in *Art and Illusion* and *Meditations on a Hobby Horse and Other Essays on the Theory of Art* (London: Phaidon, 1963).
34 Simon Reynolds, *Rip It Up and Start Again: Postpunk 1978-1984* (New York: Penguin, 2006).
35 Reynolds, *Rip It Up*, xi, 3–7. Like many historians, Reynolds attempts to locate individual styles within a general style. He generally uses the term "style" to characterize the distinctive features of an individual or band (e.g., Reynolds, *Rip It Up*, 20, 57), but his extended discussion of how various instruments are characteristically employed is an attempt to locate a general post-punk style, one that he regards as significantly influenced by reggae and dub (e.g., Reynolds, *Rip It Up*, 3).
36 Reynolds, *Rip It Up*, 2, 245, and 395.
37 David Summers, "'Form,' Nineteenth-Century Metaphysics, and the Problem of Art Historical Description," in Preziosi, *The Art of Art History*, 133.

38 Theodor W. Adorno, *Introduction to the Sociology of Music*, trans. E. B. Ashton (New York: Seabury, 1976), 31.
39 Reynolds, *Rip It Up*, 116–18.
40 Reynolds, *Rip It Up*, 118. Earlier, in Chapter 4, I challenged this common association of Romanticism and "authenticity." For a discussion of how we might better understand Ian Curtis and authenticity, see Jennifer Otter Bickerdike, *Fandom, Image and Authenticity: Joy Devotion and the Second Lives of Kurt Cobain and Ian Curtis* (Basingstoke: Palgrave Macmillan, 2014), 7–11.
41 Bernard Gendron, *Between Montmartre and the Mudd Club: Popular Music and the Avant-Garde* (Chicago: University of Chicago Press. 2002), 277–8.
42 Simon Frith, *Performing Rites: On the Value of Popular Music* (Cambridge, MA: Harvard University Press, 1996), 57.
43 Immanuel Kant, *Critique of the Power of Judgment*, trans. Paul Guyer and Eric Matthews (Cambridge: Cambridge University Press, 2000), 186–9 (§§44–47).
44 For a longer summary, see Theodore Gracyk, "Genius," in *The Cambridge Kant Lexicon*, ed. Julian Wuerth (Cambridge: Cambridge University Press, 2021), 199–200.
45 Kant, *Critique*, 183 (§43).
46 Kant, *Critique*, 192 (§49).
47 Kant, *Critique*, 203–4 (§53).
48 Kant, *Critique*, 188 (§47).
49 Kant, *Critique*, 191 (§48).
50 Kant, *Critique*, 191 (§48).
51 Kant, *Critique*, 192 (§49).
52 Mary McCloskey, *Kant's Aesthetic* (Albany: State University of New York Press, 1987), 120.
53 Reynolds, *Rip It Up*, 189.
54 Reynolds, *Rip It Up*, 203.
55 David Hesmondhalgh, "Post-Punk's Attempt to Democratise the Music Industry: The Success and Failure of Rough Trade," *Popular Music* 16 (1998): 255.
56 Hesmondhalgh, "Post-Punk's Attempt," 260.
57 Reynolds, *Rip It Up*, 51–2.
58 Kant, *Critique*, 185 (§45).
59 Kant, *Critique*, 186 (§46).
60 King calls it "democratic music, where we don't have a 'star' thing'" (Reynolds, *Rip It Up*, 58).
61 Paraphrase of Kant by Salim Kemal, *Kant's Aesthetic Theory: An Introduction*, 2nd ed. (New York: St. Martin's Press, 1997), 136.

Chapter 7

1 Noël Carroll, *The Philosophy of Mass Art* (Oxford: Clarendon, 1998), 196. I worry, however, that calling it "mass art" is misleading, because it does not matter whether it is art. A similar idea is advanced to explain the popularity of comics in David Carrier, *The Aesthetics of Comics* (The Pennsylvania State University Press, 2000), 84–5. See also David Novitz, "Aesthetics of Popular Art," in *The Oxford Handbook of Aesthetics*, ed. Jerrold Levinson (Oxford: Oxford University Press, 2003), 733–47. However, we must not reduce popular culture to mass art (where the work is distributed through

mass production of identical copies, such as digitalized, streamed music), as some of my critics worry that I have done in the past. See Christopher Bartel, "Rock as a Three-Value Tradition," *Journal of Aesthetics and Art Criticism* 75 (2017): 143–54.
2. "After all, when I spoke of 'untutored audiences,' I did not mean to refer to wolf children" (Carroll, *Mass Art*, 227).
3. The feminist message is more overt with "Pretty Hurts" than "Betty." The latter highlights a narrative about a high school girl who dumps a boyfriend who wronged her. Here, a feminist reading requires understanding that the first-person narrator is male. However, because a woman sings it, some listeners assume the narrator is female and it is about a lesbian relationship. It is only by grasping the song's allusions to two other Swift songs, "Cardigan" and "August," that one can confirm that the "Betty" narrator is male. See Lauren Huff, "Taylor Swift's Teenage Love Triangle Songs on *Folklore* Explained," *Entertainment*, July 29, 2020, https://ew.com/music/taylor-swifts-teenage-love-triangle-songs-folklore-explained/.
4. See, for example, the essays in *Popular Music and the Politics of Hope: Queer and Feminist Interventions*, eds. Susan Fast and Craig Jennex (Abingdon: Routledge, 2019).
5. See Ted Cohen, "High and Low Art, and High and Low Audiences," *Journal of Aesthetics and Art Criticism* 57 (1999): 141.
6. Carroll, *Mass Art*, 100.
7. Ted Cohen makes the point that most jokes work this way, too. Cohen, *Jokes: Philosophical Thoughts on Joking Matters* (Chicago: University of Chicago Press, 1999), 12–21.
8. Carroll, *Mass Art*, 227.
9. See Stacie Friend, "The Real Foundation of Fictional Worlds," *Australasian Journal of Philosophy* 95 (2017): 29–42.
10. The next film, *Matrix Reloaded*, returns to it in the scene where the Oracle offers Neo a red candy.
11. One of my children provided this example to me. When I wrote an early draft of this chapter, I could find no commentary on *The Matrix* acknowledging it. An account was subsequently published by James Lawler, "Only Love Is Real: Heidegger, Plato, and *The Matrix* Trilogy," in *More Matrix and Philosophy: Revolutions and Reloaded Decoded*, ed. William Irwin (Chicago and La Salle: Open Court, 2005), 26–37. Lawler became aware of the allusion when William Irwin (with my permission) shared my in-progress essay with Lawler.
12. I am using "text" in order to emphasize the overlap between two structural types. But since a source text must historically precede and influence an alluding text, the source text is part of the historical context of the alluding text. Following the common practice of using "text" to indicate an abstract structural type and "work" to mean a historically situated type, it should be understood that I am at all times claiming that an alluding utterance refers to a source *work*.
13. William Irwin and J. R. Lombardo, "The Simpsons and Allusion: 'Worst Essay Ever,'" in *The Simpsons and Philosophy: The D'Oh! Of Homer*, eds. William Irwin, Mark T. Conard and Aeon J. Skoble (Chicago and La Salle: Open Court, 2001), 82.
14. William Irwin, "What Is an Allusion?" *The Journal of Aesthetics and Art Criticism* 59 (2001): 294. Although Irwin correctly objects to small details in the definition of allusion defended by Stephanie Ross, Ross provides strong supporting argument for the second and third conditions of Irwin's definition. See Stephanie Ross, "Art and Allusion," *The Journal of Aesthetics and Art Criticism* 40 (1981): 59–70. Following

Ross, we should note that our usage (e.g., "*The Matrix* alludes to *Sylvie and Bruno*") is shorthand for the claim that the author of the former alludes to the latter work (Ross, "Art and Allusion," 69n2).
15 Irwin and Lombardo, "The Simpsons and Allusion," 82.
16 Consistent with what I said in Chapter 2, a fuller statement of this point is that the act of singing it creates a fiction and the direct reference tells auditors what to incorporate into their make-believe.
17 Ross, "Art and Allusion," 59-70.
18 This problem is explored at length by Jeanette Bicknell, "The Problem of Reference in Musical Quotation," *Journal of Aesthetics and Art Criticism* 59 (2001): 185-91.
19 For an analysis of multiple examples of musical quotation as allusion in Zappa's work, see Christopher Smith, "'Broadway the Hard Way:' Techniques of Allusion in Music by Frank Zappa," *College Music Symposium* 35 (1995): 35-60, and Matthew Ferrandino, "What to Listen for in Zappa: Philosophy, Allusion and Structure in Frank Zappa's Music," Master's thesis, University of Oregon, June 2015, https://core.ac.uk/download/pdf/36693175.pdf.
20 This requirement is defended in Marcus Walsh, "Allusion," in *The Oxford Handbook of British Poetry, 1660-1800*, ed. Jack Lynch (Oxford: Oxford University Press, 2016), 649-67.
21 As Irwin puts it, with allusion "we are supposed to make unstated associations, and in this sense the reference is indirect" (Irwin, "What Is an Allusion?" 288).
22 Joseph Pucci, *The Full Knowing Reader: Allusion and the Power of the Reader in the Western Literary Tradition* (New Haven: Yale University Press, 1998), 41.
23 Pucci, *Full Knowing Reader*, 40.
24 Pucci, *Full Knowing Reader*, 43.
25 Pucci, *Full Knowing Reader*, 256.
26 See Robert Stecker, *Artworks: Definition Meaning Value* (University Park, PA: The Pennsylvania State University Press, 1997), 172-3, and *Interpretation and Construction: Art, Speech, and the Law* (Oxford: Blackwell, 2003), 29-50. See also Peter Lamarque, *Fictional Points of View* (Ithaca: Cornell University Press, 1996), 178-80.
27 Monroe C. Beardsley, "Intentions and Interpretations," in *The Aesthetic Point of View: Selected Essays*, eds. Michael J. Wreen and Donald M. Callen (Ithaca: Cornell University Press, 1983), 198.
28 Noël Carroll, "On the Ties That Bind: Characters, the Emotions, and Popular Fiction," in *Philosophy and the Interpretation of Pop Culture*, eds. William Irwin and Jorge J. E. Gracia (Lanham: Rowman & Littlefield, 2007), 100.
29 The classic source on illocutionary and perlocutionary acts is J. L. Austin, *How to Do Things with Words* (Cambridge, MA: Harvard University Press, 1962).
30 See the discussion of the pleasures of games throughout C. Thi Nguyen, *Games: Agency as Art* (Oxford: Oxford University Press, 2020). But Nguyen emphasizes narrative structure, whereas the cognitive satisfactions of crossword puzzles and some allusions are independent of narrative drama.
31 As in Chapter 2, I draw on Kendall L. Walton's well-known position that representational art offers props that mandate imaginings in games of make-believe. See Walton, *Mimesis as Make-believe: On the Foundations of the Representational Arts* (Harvard University Press, 1990), 69-72. In saying that props "mandate imaginings," Walton makes them normative with respect to our imaginings.

32 See Deirdre Wilson and Dan Sperber, *Meaning and Relevance* (Cambridge: Cambridge University Press, 2012), chap. 1.
33 Irwin and Lombardo, "The Simpsons and Allusion," 85.
34 For an extended discussion of other ramifications of this process, see Theodore Gracyk, *I Wanna Be Me: Rock Music and the Politics of Identity* (Philadelphia: Temple University Press, 2001), Part II.
35 Yet it is also the case that popular culture can call attention to and thus encourage learning about a wide variety of specialized information that we would not otherwise encounter. Allusions can be part of this process. See Carolyn Korsmeyer, "Philosophy and the Probable Impossible," in *Philosophy and the Interpretation of Pop Culture*, eds. Irwin and Gracia, 21–40.
36 William Irwin, "The Aesthetics of Allusion," *The Journal of Value Inquiry* 36 (2002): 523. See also Irwin and Lombardo, "The Simpsons and Allusion," 86.
37 Notice Cohen's emphasis on occasions for joke telling; Cohen, *Jokes*, chap. 4.
38 Christopher Ricks, *Dylan's Visions of Sin* (London and New York: Viking, 2003).
39 See also Brandon Polite, "Shared Musical Experiences," *British Journal of Aesthetics* 59 (2019): 429–47.
40 Irwin, "The Aesthetics of Allusion," 528.
41 Irwin is constructing a very close parallel between allusion and joking. Cohen argues that a joke that is not immediately understood cannot generate the intimacy that is intended in joke telling.
42 Irwin suggests a conflict between the two pleasures; Irwin, "The Aesthetics of Allusion," 528–9.
43 Irwin, "What Is an Allusion?" 288. Irwin is responding to Michael Leddy.
44 Jon Caramanica, Joe Coscarelli, Jon Pareles, Ben Sisario and Lindsay Zoladz, "Taylor Swift Remade 'Fearless' as 'Taylor's Version.' Let's Discuss," *New York Times*, April 9, 2021, https://www.nytimes.com/2021/04/09/arts/music/taylor-swift-fearless-taylors-version.html.

Chapter 8

1 See the essays assembled in George Plasketes (ed.), *Play It Again: Cover Songs in Popular Music* (Farnham: Ashgate, 2010). See also Cristyn Magnus, P. D. Magnus, and Christy Mag Uidhir, "Judging Covers," *Journal of Aesthetics and Art Criticism* 71 (2013): 361–70, which distinguishes four types of covers and argues that each type demands distinctive evaluative criteria.
2 George Plasketes, "Introduction: Like a Version," in *Play It Again*, ed. Plasketes, 1.
3 Kurt Mosser, "'Cover Songs': Ambiguity, Multivalence, Polysemy," *Popular Musicology Online* 2 (2008), http://www.popular-musicology-online.com/issues/02/mosser.html. See also Michael Rings, "Doing It Their Way: Rock Covers, Genre, and Appreciation," *Journal of Aesthetics and Art Criticism* 71 (2013): 55–63. An admirable study that implicitly supports my analysis is Michael Awkward, *Soul Covers: Rhythm and Blues Remakes and the Struggle for Artistic Identity* (Durham, NC: Duke University Press, 2007).
4 Deena Weinstein, "Appreciating Cover Songs: Stereopnony," in *Play It Again*, ed. Plasketes, 245. I find much to endorse in her essay except that she does not emphasize performance intentions.

5   As with Elvis and "Hound Dog," a few fans would have realized its remake status and would have compared the two versions, but my point is that cover status is (partly) a matter of intentions. It is hard to see how Björk could have intended her audience to make the connection when she recorded it in 1995. The internet was in its infancy and the information was not readily available. Or we might postulate a category of gnostic covers, where attuned fans will suspect a covering relationship and will hunt down the base version for purposes of comparison.

6   Mosser categorizes tribute bands who mimic famous musicians and bands as "reduplication covers," and he recognizes that this usage pushes on the boundaries of what it is to be a cover (Mosser, "Cover Songs"). This terminology is idiosyncratic, since it is more common to call such performances either "tribute" performances (as in calling a group a "tribute band") or "impersonation" performances (as in, "The hotel was hosting a convention of Cher impersonators"). The audience is expected to evaluate performance details by reference to recordings that are imitated, so this does give them the status of covers.

7   Throughout this chapter, "interpretation" refers exclusively to a performer's interpretation of the music and never to the audience's understanding of what the performer is attempting to communicate.

8   For the idea of aesthetic communication, see Gary Iseminger, *The Aesthetic Function of Art* (Ithaca: Cornell University Press, 2004).

9   As with movies, recorded music tracks are frequently group collaborations. For the reasons explained in Chapter 5, group intentions are consistent with my requirement of an intention to refer.

10 Nothing said here should be understood to discount the importance of the song itself as an element of the communication; see Franklin Bruno, "A Case for Song: Against an (Exclusively) Recording-Centered Ontology of Rock," *Journal of Aesthetics and Art Criticism* 71 (2013): 68–9.

11 On the general topic of mass-distributed popular art, see Noël Carroll, *A Philosophy of Mass Art* (New York: Oxford University Press, 1998), and Theodore Gracyk, *I Wanna Be Me: Rock Music and the Politics of Identity* (Philadelphia: Temple University Press, 2001).

12 See James Dickerson, *Faith Hill: Piece of My Heart* (New York: St. Martin's Press, 2001), 56.

13 An interesting discussion of intertextuality and sampling is Justin A. Williams, "Intertextuality and Lineage in the Game's 'We Ain't' and Kendrick Lamar's 'm.A.A.d. City,'" in *The Pop Palimpsest: Intertextuality in Recorded Popular Music*, eds. Lori Burns and Serge Lacasse (Ann Arbor: University of Michigan Press, 2018), 291–312.

14 For simplicity's sake, I am treating tracks as recorded performances. The Joplin recording might well be spliced together from multiple vocal "takes." However, that detail is not important to the subsequent analysis, in which a virtual performance will be treated as if it were a performance *simpliciter*.

15 For discussion of an interesting case in jazz, see P. D. Magnus, "Kind of Borrowed, Kind of Blue," *Journal of Aesthetics and Art Criticism* 74 (2016): 179–85. Glenn Gould's second recording of Bach's Goldberg Variations, in 1981, *might* be thought of as a cover of his 1955 recording, but few other cases come to mind.

16 See Andrew Kania, "All Play and No Work: An Ontology of Jazz," *Journal of Aesthetics and Art Criticism* 69 (2011): 391–403; Theodore Gracyk, *Rhythm and Noise: An Aesthetics of Rock* (Durham, NC: Duke University Press, 1996), 37–67; and Andrew Kania and T. Theodore Gracyk, "Performances and Recordings," in *The Routledge*

Companion to Philosophy and Music, eds. Theodore Gracyk and Andrew Kania (New York: Routledge, 2011), 80–90.
17   For an analysis distinguishing five types of interpretation in performing a composed musical work, see Stephen Davies, "The Multiple Interpretability of Musical Works," in *Is There a Single Right Interpretation?* ed. Michael Krausz (University Park: Pennsylvania State University Press, 2002), 231–50.
18   Julian Dodd, *Being True to Works of Music* (Oxford: Oxford University Press, 2020), 142.
19   An important recent discussion of this phenomenon is Nemesio García-Carril Puy, "The Ontology of Musical Versions: Introducing the Hypothesis of Nested Types," *Journal of Aesthetics and Art Criticism* 77 (2019): 241–54.
20   This example is even more complex that it initially appears. Eisler worked from a particular published edition of Bruckner's symphonies, and thus we have five potential objects of audience interest and evaluation: the work, the version, the arrangement, the conductor's interpretation, and the orchestra's performance.
21   See Stephen Davies, "The Ontology of Musical Works and the Authenticity of Their Performances," *Noûs* 25 (1991): 21–41.
22   See Stephen Davies, *Musical Works and Performances* (Oxford: Clarendon Press, 2001), 20. An excellent general overview of this topic is Andrew Kania, *Philosophy of Western Music: A Contemporary Introduction* (New York: Routledge, 2020), chap. 7. This is a chapter on authenticity, but using that term in a way seldom used in relation to popular music.
23   For a detailed account of this move away from popular music, see Lee B. Brown, David Goldblatt, and Theodore Gracyk, *Jazz and the Philosophy of Art* (New York: Routledge, 2018), chaps. 1 and 3.
24   I thank an anonymous peer reviewer of the manuscript for getting me to clarify this point.
25   See Gracyk, *I Wanna Be Me*, 13–50.
26   Some "tribute" albums are intended to call attention to neglected songwriters, as with *Sweet Relief: A Benefit for Victoria Williams* (1993) and *The Inner Flame: A Rainer Ptacek Tribute* (1997), and these are not collections of covers as is *The Last Temptation of Elvis*.
27   Nicola Dibben, *Björk* (London: Equinox, 2009), 156.
28   See also William Irwin, "What Is an Allusion?" *Journal of Aesthetics and Art Criticism* 59 (2001): 287–97. Although less common, literature also creates the conditions for extended allusion that is much like covering (e.g., Tom Stoppard's *Rosencrantz and Guildenstern Are Dead* as a cover of Shakespeare's *Hamlet*).
29   Arthur C. Danto "The Artworld," *Journal of Philosophy* 61 (1964): 581.

Chapter 9

1   Lawrence Grossberg, "Same as It Ever Was? Rock Culture. Same as It Ever Was! Rock Theory," in *Stars Don't Stand Still in the Sky: Music and Myth*, eds. Karen Kelly and Evelyn McDonnell (New York: New York University Press, 1999), 106.
2   Tom Carson, "Chrissie Hynde Wants to Be Rock and Roll's Number One Heroine," *Rolling Stone* 1 (October 1, 1981): 93.

3   However, the two topics are not unrelated, as can be seen in Donald Davidson's emphasis on intentions and utterance meaning as a counter to the idea that a system of conventions determines meaning. For example, Donald Davidson, *Inquiries into Truth and Interpretation* (Oxford: Clarendon Press, 1991).
4   Andrew Bennett, *The Author* (London: Routledge, 2004), 13.
5   Terry Eagleton, *Literary Theory: An Introduction*, 3rd ed. (Minneapolis: University of Minnesota Press, 2008), 119.
6   Roland Barthes, *Image—Music—Text*, trans. Stephen Heath (New York: Hill & Wang, 1977), 148. For a cogent analysis of "the death of the author," see Peter Lamarque, "The Death of the Author: An Analytical Autopsy," *British Journal of Aesthetics* 30 (1990): 319–31, and David Davies, *Aesthetics and Literature* (London: Continuum, 2007), 93–7.
7   Nicholas Cook, "Beyond Music: Mashup, Multimedia Mentality, and Intellectual Property," in *The Oxford Handbook of New Audiovisual Aesthetics*, eds. John Richardson, Claudia Gorbman and Carol Vernallis (Oxford: Oxford University Press, 2013), 56.
8   Richard Middleton, *Studying Popular Music* (Milton Keynes: Open University Press, 1990), v.
9   David Shumway, "Rock and Roll as a Cultural Practice," in *Present Tense: Rock & Roll and Culture*, ed. Anthony DeCurtis (Durham, NC: Duke University Press, 1992), 123.
10 Lorraine Ali, "Devil's Haircut," *Rolling Stone* (August 21, 1997): 119. Similarly, Roxy Music becomes its album covers, and we cannot fault this assessment of them by Duran Duran's John Taylor: "In pop music, the photograph is important. By the time Duran Duran made records, videos were even more important… Roxy Music was important to post-'70s English bands because of their album covers." Quoted in Scott Cohen, *Yakety Yak: Midnight Confessions and Revelations of 37 Rock Stars & Legends* (New York: Fireside, 1994), 137.
11 Shumway, "Rock and roll as a Cultural Practice," 115.
12 Shumway, "Rock and roll as a Cultural Practice," 124.
13 John Fiske, *Television Culture*, 2nd ed. (New York: Routledge, 2011), 110. See also Philip Auslander, *In Concert: Performing Musical Persona* (Ann Arbor: University of Michigan Press, 2021).
14 Pamela Wilson, "Mountains of Contradictions: Gender, Class, and Region in the Star Image of Dolly Parton," *South Atlantic Quarterly* 94 (1995): 109–34.
15 See Jonathan Zilberg, "Yes, It's True: Zimbabweans Love Dolly Parton," *Journal of Popular Culture* 29 (1995): 111–25.
16 I attacked this assumption in Chapter 7. See also Theodore Gracyk, *I Wanna Be Me: Rock Music and the Politics of Identity* (Philadelphia: Temple University Press 2001), 58–66.
17 Fiske, *Television Culture*, 109.
18 See Diana Raffman, *Language, Music, and Mind* (Cambridge, MA: MIT Press, 1993).
19 John Shepherd, "Music and the Last Intellectuals," *Journal of Aesthetic Education* 25 (1991): 113.
20 Christopher Peacocke, "Holism," in *A Companion to the Philosophy of Language*, eds. Bob Hale and Crispin Wright (Oxford: Blackwell, 1997), 227. See also Peter Pagin, "Meaning Holism," in *The Oxford Handbook of Philosophy of Language*, eds. Ernest Lepore and Barry Smith (Oxford: Clarendon Press, 2006), 213–32. Jerry Fodor reduces it to "the doctrine that whole theories are units of meaning" and then argues that holism is a "dubious doctrine of skeptical import" that gets most of its support

from confusions with a parallel but different doctrine, epistemic or confirmational holism, which is the idea that isolated propositions cannot be confirmed as true or false except in relation to their place in a "web" of intertwined beliefs (Jerry Fodor, "Banish Discontent," in *Language, Mind and Logic*, ed. Jeremy Butterfield (Cambridge: Cambridge University Press, 1986), 12). Confirmational holism does not secure meaning holism.

21 For a review of several varieties of holism, see Eli Dresner, "Meaning Holism," *Philosophy Compass* 7 (2012): 611–19.

22 In philosophy, an influential defense of meaning holism is W. V. Quine, "Two Dogmas of Empiricism," *Philosophical Review* 60 (1951): 20–43. An important response is Hilary Putnam, *Realism with a Human Face* (Cambridge, MA: Harvard University Press, 1990), 278–302.

23 For an independent defense of local holism, see Akell Bilgrami, "Why Holism Is Harmless and Necessary," in *Philosophical Perspectives 12: Language, Mind and Ontology*, ed. James E. Tomberlin (Malden: Blackwell, 1998), 105–26.

24 Shumway, "Rock and Roll as a Cultural Practice," 124.

25 Quine, "Two Dogmas of Empiricism."

26 Ludwig Wittgenstein, *Philosophical Investigations: The English Text of the Third Edition*, trans. G. E. M. Anscombe (New York: Macmillan, 1968), Remark 32.

27 See Eli Dresner, "Holism, Language Acquisition, and Algebraic Logic," *Linguistics and Philosophy* 25 (2002): 419–52.

28 Gérard Genette, *Palimsests: Literature in the Second Degree*, trans. Channa Newman and Claude Doubinsky (Lincoln, NE: University of Nebraska Press, 1997), 397.

29 Craig Marks, "Zero Worship," *Spin*, June 1996, 56.

30 W. V. Quine, "Two Dogmas in Retrospect," *Canadian Journal of Philosophy* 21 (1991): 268.

31 Genette, *Palimsests*, 1.

32 Genette, *Palimsests*, 5.

33 Vincent Descombes, *The Institutions of Meaning: A Defense of Anthropological Holism*, trans. Stephen Adam Schwartz (Cambridge, MA: Harvard University Press, 2014), xxii.

34 Lawrence Grossberg, *Dancing in Spite of Myself* (Durham, NC: Duke University Press, 1997), 11.

35 Grossberg, *Dancing in Spite of Myself*, 41. Grossberg elaborates that the "rock and roll apparatus" involves three organizing axes: youth as a distinct generation, celebration of bodily pleasure, and post-modernity. He re-examines these in "Reflections of a Disappointed Popular Music Scholar," in *Rock over the Edge: Transformations in Popular Culture*, eds. Roger Beebe, Denise Fulbrook and Ben Saunders (Durham, NC: Duke University Press, 2002), 25–59.

36 Shumway, "Rock & Roll as a Cultural Practice," 118.

37 Lawrence Grossberg, "Another Boring Day in Paradise: Rock and Roll and the Empowerment of Everyday Life," in *Dancing in Spite of Myself: Essays on Popular*, 5, 67.

38 Daniel Silver, Monica Lee and Clayton Childress, "Genre Complexes in Popular Music," *PLoS One* 11 (2016), doi: 10.1371/journal.pone.0155471.

39 The most notable version is the one proposed by George Dickie, *Art and Aesthetic: An Institutional Analysis* (Ithaca: Cornell University Press, 1974), and revised in *The Art Circle: A Theory of Art* (New York: Haven, 1984).

40 For a review of the early response to this theory, see Stephen Davies, *Definitions of Art* (Ithaca: Cornell University Press 1991), 78–114.
41 Shumway therefore reasons that all music played at the original Woodstock festival, "regardless of its formal diversity, is properly identified as rock and roll" (755). But what is true of Woodstock is presumably true of the 1969 Isle of Wight festival, which would make a Miles Davis jazz performance into rock. However, a French phrase does not become English because Labelle sang one in "Lady Marmalade" (1974).
42 Grossberg, *Dancing in Spite of Myself*, 11.
43 As at other points in this book, I defer to Kendall L. Walton, "Categories of Art," *Philosophical Review* 79 (1970): 334–67.
44 Grossberg accepts this point (*Dancing in Spite of Myself*, 17–23). But because he does not conceptualize his project in terms of intertextuality and holism, he does not think of the rock formation as a language system. Thus, his "obsession with the notion that rock is dead" (Grossberg, *Dancing in Spite of Myself*, 17).
45 Roland Barthes, *S/Z*, trans. Richard Howard (New York: Hill and Wang, 1974), 20–1.
46 Paul Willis "The Golden Age," in *On Record: Rock, Pop, and the Written Word*, eds. Simon Frith and Andrew Goodwin (New York: Pantheon, 1990), 50–2.
47 My point is adapted from Davies, *Definitions of Art*, 111. For an illustration of this tendency, see Scott Appelrouth and Crystal Kelly, "Rap, Race and the (Re)production of Boundaries," *Sociological Perspectives* 56 (2013): 301–26.
48 Sandra Mace, Cynthia Wagoner, David Teachout and Donald Hodges, "Genre Identification of Very Brief Musical Excerpts," *Psychology of Music* 40 (2011): 112–28. Notice, in this regard, that I examined post-punk in Chapter 6 as the odd case of a category that defies stylistic unity.
49 Grossberg, *Dancing in Spite of Myself*, 30.
50 Michael Schudson, "The New Validation of Popular Culture: Sense and Sentimentality in Academia," *Critical Studies in Mass Communication* 4 (1987): 64.
51 Wittgenstein, *Philosophical Investigations*, Remark 234.
52 For example, Natachi Onwuamaegbu, "The Unexpected Link between Britney Spears and Olivia Rodrigo Explains So Much about Being a Pop Star Today," *Washington Post*, August 3, 2021, https://www.washingtonpost.com/arts-entertainment/2021/08/03/britney-spears-olivia-rodrigo/.
53 O. K. Bouwsma, "The Expression Theory of Art," in *Aesthetics Today*, ed. Morris Philipson (Cleveland: Meridian Books, 1961), 166.
54 This is not to imply that music apprehension is always individualistic. See Brandon Polite, "Shared Musical Experience," *British Journal of Aesthetics* 59 (2019): 429–47.
55 Thomas R. Roberts, *An Aesthetics of Junk Fiction* (Athens: University of Georgia Press, 1990), 214.
56 Peter Manuel, *Cassette Culture: Popular Music and Technology in North India* (Chicago: University of Chicago Press, 1993), 13.

Bibliography

Abell, Catharine. *Fiction: A Philosophical Analysis*. Oxford: Oxford University Press, 2020.
Abrams, M. H. *The Mirror and the Lamp*. Oxford: Oxford University Press, 1953.
Adorno, Theodor W. *Essays on Music*, edited by Richard Leppert. Berkeley: University of California Press, 2002.
Adorno, Theodor W. *Introduction to the Sociology of Music*, translated by E. B. Ashton. New York: Seabury, 1976.
Agawa, Kofi. *Music as Discourse: Semiotic Adventures in Romantic Music*. Oxford: Oxford University Press, 2009.
Ali, Lorraine. "Devil's Haircut." *Rolling Stone* (August 21, 1997): 29–30, 119.
Ali, S. Omar, and Zehra F. Peynircioğlu. "Songs and Emotions: Are Lyrics and Melodies Equal Partners?" *Psychology of Music* 34 (2006): 511–34.
Anscombe, G. E. M. *Intention*. Cambridge, MA: Harvard University Press, 1963.
Appelrouth, Scott, and Crystal Kelly. "Rap, Race and the (Re)production of Boundaries." *Sociological Perspectives* 56 (2013): 301–26.
Austin, J. L. *How to Do Things with Words*. Cambridge, MA: Harvard University Press, 1962.
Armour-Garb, Bradley, and James A. Woodbridge. *Pretense and Pathology: Philosophical Fictionalism and Its Applications*. Cambridge: Cambridge University Press, 2015.
Art History Babes. *An Honest Art Dictionary: A Jovial Trip through Art Jargon*. London: White Lion, 2020.
Auslander, Philip. *In Concert: Performing Musical Persona*. Ann Arbor: University of Michigan Press, 2021.
Auslander, Philip. *Liveness: Performance in a Mediatized Culture*. London and New York: Routledge, 1999.
Auslander, Philip. *Performing Glam Rock: Gender and Theatricality in Popular Music*. Ann Arbor: University of Michigan Press, 2006.
Auvinen, Tuomas. "Creative Communities of Practice: Role Delineation in Record Production in Different Areas and across Different Genres and Production Settings." In *The Bloomsbury Handbook of Music Production*, edited by Andrew Bourbon and Simon Zagorski-Thomas, 161–77. New York: Bloomsbury Academic 2020.
Awkward, Michael. *Soul Covers: Rhythm and Blues Remakes and the Struggle for Artistic Identity*. Durham, NC: Duke University Press, 2007.
Babbitt, Milton. "Who Cares If You Listen." *High Fidelity* (February 1958): 38–40, 126–7.
Bach, Kent. "Context ex Machina." In *Semantics versus Pragmatics*, edited by Zoltán Gendler Szabó, 15–44. Oxford: Clarendon, 2005.
Bacharach, Sondra. "Toward a Metaphysical Historicism." *Journal of Aesthetics and Art Criticism* 63 (2005): 165–73.
Bacharach, Sondra, and Deborah Tollefsen. "*We Did It*: From Mere Contributors to Co-authors." *Journal of Aesthetics and Art Criticism* 68 (2010): 23–32.
Bangs, Lester. "Swan Dive into the Mung." In *The Bowie Companion*, edited by Elizabeth Thomson and David Gutman, 117–19. New York: Da Capo Press, 1996.

Bazargan-Forward, Saba, and Deborah Tollefsen eds. *The Routledge Handbook of Collective Responsibility*. New York: Routledge, 2020.
Barker, Hugh, and Yuval Taylor. *Faking It: The Quest for Authenticity in Popular Music*. New York: W. W. Norton, 2002.
Barlow, Eve. "Brandi Carlile on Her Song to Subvert the Grammys: 'It's a Call to Action.'" *The Guardian*, February 8, 2019. Available online: https://www.theguardian.com/music/2019/feb/08/brandi-carlile-grammys-country-gay-marriage-cancun.
Barnes, Barry. *Everything I Know about Business I Learned from the Grateful Dead: The Ten Most Innovative Lessons from a Long, Strange Trip*. New York: Business Plus, 2011.
Bartel, Christopher. "Rock as a Three-Value Tradition." *Journal of Aesthetics and Art Criticism* 75 (2017): 143–54.
Barthes, Roland. *Image—Music—Text*, translated by Stephen Heath. New York: Hill and Wang, 1977.
Barthes, Roland. *The Pleasure of the Text*, translated by Richard Miller. New York: Hill and Wang, 1975.
Barthes, Roland. *S/Z*, translated by Richard Howard. New York: Hill and Wang, 1974.
Beardsley, Monroe C. "Intentions and Interpretations." In *The Aesthetic Point of View: Selected Essays*, edited by Michael J. Wreen and Donald M. Callen, 188–207. Ithaca: Cornell University Press, 1983.
Behr, Adam. "Join Together with the Band: Authenticating Collective Creativity in Bands and the Myth of Rock Authenticity Reappraised." *Rock Music Studies* 2 (2015): 1–21.
Behr, Adam. "Tom Petty Stood up for Authentic Rock Music—and He Never Backed Down." *The Conversation*, October 4, 2017. Available online: https://theconversation.com/tom-petty-stood-up-for-authentic-rock-music-and-he-never-backed-down-85187.
Benner, Samantha. "Rock Music Engineering and Production." In *The Bloomsbury Handbook of Rock Music Research*, edited by Allan F. Moore and Paul Carr, 179–93. New York and London: Bloomsbury, 2020.
Bennett, Andrew. *The Author*. London: Routledge, 2004.
Bennett, Andy, and Ian Rogers. *Popular Music Scenes and Cultural Memory*. London: Palgrave Macmillan, 2016.
Bicknell, Jeanette. *Philosophy of Song and Singing: An Introduction*. New York: Routledge, 2015.
Bicknell, Jeanette. "The Problem of Reference in Musical Quotation." *Journal of Aesthetics and Art Criticism* 59 (2001): 185–91.
Bieri, Guido. *Life on the Tracks: Bob Dylan's Songs*. Basel: Moondance, 2008.
Bilgrami, Akeel. "Why Holism Is Harmless and Necessary." In *Philosophical Perspectives 12: Language, Mind and Ontology*, edited by James E. Tomberlin, 105–26. Malden, MA: Blackwell, 1998.
Boden, Margaret. *Creativity & Art: Three Roads to Surprise*. Oxford: Oxford University Press, 2011.
Bordwell, David. *Making Meaning: Inference and Rhetoric in the Interpretation of Cinema*. Cambridge, MA: Harvard University Press, 1989.
Borg, Emma. "Intention-based Semantics." In *The Oxford Handbook of Philosophy of Language*, edited by Ernest Lepore and Barry C. Smith, 250–66. Oxford: Oxford University Press, 2006.
Bourdieu, Pierre. *Distinction: A Social Critique of the Judgement of Taste*, translated by Richard Nice. Cambridge, MA: Harvard University Press, 1984.

Bouwsma, O. K. "The Expression Theory of Art." In *Aesthetics Today*, edited by Morris Philipson, 145–68. Cleveland: Meridian Books, 1961.
Bradley, A. C. *Poetry for Poetry's Sake: An Inaugural Lecture Delivered on June 5, 1901*. Oxford: Clarendon, 1901.
Bratman, Michael. *Intention, Plans, and Practical Reason*. Cambridge: Cambridge University Press, 1999.
Breskin, David. "Voodoo Child." *Rolling Stone* 660/661, July 8/July 22 (1993): 88.
Brown, Lee B., David Goldblatt, and Theodore Gracyk. *Jazz and the Philosophy of Art*. New York: Routledge, 2018.
Brownstein, Carrie. *Hunger Makes Me a Modern Girl: A Memoir*. New York: Riverhead Books, 2015.
Burnett, Robert. *The Global Jukebox: The International Music Industry*. New York: Routledge, 1996.
Bruno, Franklin. "A Case for Song: Against an (Exclusively) Recording-Centered Ontology of Rock." *Journal of Aesthetics and Art Criticism* 71 (2013): 65–74.
Cappelen, Herman. "Semantics and Pragmatics: Some Central Issues." In *Context-Sensitivity and Semantic Minimalism: New Essays on Semantics and Pragmatics*, edited by Gerhard Preyer and Georg Peter, 3–24. Oxford: Oxford University Press, 2007.
Cappelen, Herman, and Ernest Lepore. "A Tall Tale: In Defense of Semantic Minimalism and Speech Act Pluralism." In *New Essays in the Philosophy of Language*, edited by Maite Ezcurdia, Robert J. Stainton, and Christopher Viger, 3–28. Calgary: University of Calgary Press, 2004.
Caramanica, Jon, Joe Coscarelli, Jon Pareles, Ben Sisario, and Lindsay Zoladz. "Taylor Swift Remade 'Fearless' as 'Taylor's Version.' Let's Discuss." *New York Times*, April 9, 2021. Available online: https://www.nytimes.com/2021/04/09/arts/music/taylor-swift-fearless-taylors-version.html.
Carroll, Noël. "Interpretation." In *The Routledge Companion to Philosophy of Literature*, edited by Noël Carroll and John Gibson, 302–12. New York: Routledge, 2016.
Carroll, Noël. "Moderate Moralism." *British Journal of Aesthetics* 36 (1996): 223–38.
Carroll, Noël. "On the Ties That Bind: Characters, the Emotions, and Popular Fiction." In *Philosophy and the Interpretation of Pop Culture*, edited by William Irwin and Jorge J. E. Gracia, 89–116. Lanham: Rowman & Littlefield, 2007.
Carroll, Noël. *A Philosophy of Mass Art*. Oxford: Clarendon Press, 1998.
Carson, Tom. "Chrissie Hynde Wants to be Rock and Roll's Number One Heroine." *Rolling Stone* (October 1, 1981): 93.
Cavanagh, John. *The Piper at the Gates of Dawn* (33 1/3 series). New York and London: Continuum, 2003.
Christgau, Robert. "Popular Music Colliers Encyclopedia." Robert Christgau website. Available online: https://www.robertchristgau.com/xg/music/collier.php. Posting of a publication from 1984.
Clague, Mark. "'This Is America': Jimi Hendrix's Star Spangled Banner Journey as Psychedelic Citizenship." *Journal for the Society for American Music* 4 (2014): 435–78.
Clarke, Eric F. *Ways of Listening: An Ecological Approach to the Perception of Musical Meaning*. Oxford: Oxford University Press, 2005.
Clifford-Napoleone, Amber R. *Queerness in Heavy Metal Music: Metal Bent*. New York: Routledge, 2015.
Cohen, Jonathan. "Indexicality and the Puzzle of the Answering Machine." *Journal of Philosophy* 110 (2013): 5–32.

Cohen, Scott. *Yakety Yak: Midnight Confessions and Revelations of 37 Rock Stars & Legends*. New York: Fireside, 1994.
Cohen, Ted. "High and Low Art, and High and Low Audiences." *Journal of Aesthetics and Art Criticism* 57 (1999): 137–43.
Cohen, Ted. *Jokes: Philosophical Thoughts on Joking Matters*. Chicago: University of Chicago Press, 1999.
Cone, Edward T. *The Composer's Voice*. Berkeley and Los Angeles: University of California Press, 1974.
Cook, Nicholas. "Beyond Music: Mashup, Multimedia Mentality, and Intellectual Property." In *The Oxford Handbook of New Audiovisual Aesthetics*, edited by John Richardson, Claudia Gorbman, and Carol Vernallis, 53–76. Oxford: Oxford University Press, 2013.
Copp, David. "On the Agency of Certain Collective Entities: An Argument from 'Normative Autonomy.'" In *Midwest Studies in Philosophy Volume XXX: Shared Intentions and Collective Responsibility*, edited by Peter A. French and Howard K. Wettstein, 194–221. Oxford: Blackwell, 2006.
Cott, Jonathan ed. *Bob Dylan: The Essential Interviews*. New York: Simon and Schuster, 2017.
Crafts, Susan D., Daniel Cavicchi, Charles Keil et al. *My Music: Explorations of Music in Daily Life*. Middletown, CT: Wesleyan University Press, 1993.
Cray, Wesley C. "Transparent and Opaque Performance Personas." *Journal of Aesthetics of Art Criticism* 77 (2019): 181–91.
Cresswell, Max J. *Logic and Languages*. London: Methuen, 1973.
Currie, Gregory. *The Nature of Fiction*. Cambridge: Cambridge University Press, 1990.
Danto, Arthur C. "The Artworld." *Journal of Philosophy* 61 (1964): 571–84.
Danto, Arthur C. *The Transfiguration of the Commonplace: A Philosophy of Art*. Cambridge, MA: Harvard University Press, 1981.
Davidson, Donald. *Inquiries into Truth and Interpretation*. Oxford: Clarendon Press, 1991.
Davies, David. *Aesthetics and Literature*. London: Continuum, 2007.
Davies, David. "Book Review: *The Performance of Reading: An Essay in the Philosophy of Literature*." *Journal of Aesthetics and Art Criticism* 66 (2008): 89–91.
Davies, David. "Fictive Utterances and the Fictionality of Narratives and Works." *British Journal of Aesthetics* 55 (2015): 49–55.
Davies, David. *Philosophy of the Performing Arts*. Oxford: Blackwell, 2011.
Davies, David. "Semantic Intentions, Utterance Meaning, and Work Meaning." In *Contemporary Readings in the Philosophy of Literature: An Analytic Approach*, edited by David Davies and Carl Matheson, 167–81. Peterborough: Broadview Press, 2008.
Davies, Stephen. "The Aesthetic Relevance of Authors' and Painters Intentions." *Journal of Aesthetics and Art Criticism* 41 (1982): 65–76.
Davies, Stephen. "Artistic Expression and the Hard Case of Pure Music." In *Contemporary Debates in Aesthetics and the Philosophy of Art*, edited by Matthew Kieran, 179–91. Oxford: Oxford University Press, 2006.
Davies, Stephen. *Definitions of Art*. Ithaca: Cornell University Press, 1991.
Davies, Stephen. "Interpreting Contextualities." *Philosophy and Literature* 20 (1996): 20–38.
Davies, Stephen. "John Cage's 4'33": Is It Music?" *Australasian Journal of Philosophy* 75 (1997): 448–62.
Davies, Stephen. "The Multiple Interpretability of Musical Works." In *Is There a Single Right Interpretation?* edited by Michael Krausz, 231–50. University Park: Pennsylvania State University Press, 2002.

Davies, Stephen. "Musical Understanding." In *Musical Understanding: And Other Essays on the Philosophy of Music*, 88–128. Oxford: Oxford University Press, 2011.
Davies, Stephen. *Musical Works and Performances: A Philosophical Exploration.* Oxford: Oxford University Press, 2001.
Davies, Stephen. "The Ontology of Musical Works and the Authenticity of Their Performances." *Noûs* 25:1 (1991): 21–41.
Davies, Stephen, and Constantijn Koopman. "Musical Meaning in a Broader Perspective." In Stephen Davies, *Musical Understanding: And Other Essays on the Philosophy of Music*, 71–87. Oxford: Oxford University Press, 2011.
Davis, Angela Y. *Blues Legacies and Black Feminism: Gertrude "Ma" Rainey, Bessie Smith, and Billie Holiday.* New York: Random House, 1998.
De Clercq, Rafael. "Aesthetic Properties." In *The Routledge Companion to Philosophy and Music*, edited by Theodore Gracyk and Andrew Kania, 144–54. New York: Routledge, 2011.
Dempster, Douglas. "How Does Debussy's Sea Crash? How Can Jimi's Rocket Red Glare?: Kivy's Account of Representation in Music." *Journal of Aesthetics and Art Criticism* 52:4 (1994): 415–28.
Dennis, Andrea L., and Erik Nielson. *Rap on Trial: Race, Lyrics, and Guilt in America.* New York and London: The New Press, 2019.
DeNora, Tia. *Music in Everyday Life.* Cambridge: Cambridge University Press, 2000.
Descombes, Vincent. *The Institutions of Meaning: A Defense of Anthropological Holism*, translated by Stephen Adam Schwartz. Cambridge, MA: Harvard University Press, 2014.
Desler, Anne. "History without Royalty? Queen and the Strata of the Popular Music Canon." *Popular Music* 32 (2013): 385–405.
Diallo, David. "Dr. Dre and Snoop Dogg." In *Icons of Hip Hop" An Encyclopedia of the Movement, Music, and Culture*, edited by Mickey Hess, vol. 2, 317–40. Westport and London: Greenwood Press, 2007.
Dibben, Nicola. *Björk.* London: Equinox, 2009.
Dibben, Nicola. "Vocal Performance and the Projection of Emotional Authenticity." In *The Ashgate Research Companion to Popular Musicology*, edited by Derek Scott, 317–33. Farnham: Ashgate, 2009.
Dickie, George. *Art and Aesthetic: An Institutional Analysis.* Ithaca: Cornell University Press, 1974.
Dickie, George. *The Art Circle: A Theory of Art.* New York: Haven, 1984.
Dissanayake, Ellen. *Homo Aestheticus: Where Art Comes from and Why.* Seattle: University of Washington Press, 1992.
Doherty, Thomas. *Hollywood's Censor: Joseph I. Breen and the Production Code Administration.* New York: Columbia University Press, 2009.
Dutton, Denis. "Artistic Crimes." *British Journal of Aesthetics* 19 (1979): 302–41.
Dresner, Eli. "Holism, Language Acquisition, and Algebraic Logic." *Linguistics and Philosophy* 25 (2002): 419–52.
Dresner, Eli. "Meaning Holism." *Philosophy Compass* 7 (2012): 611–19.
Dyer, Richard. *The Culture of Queers.* New York: Routledge, 2002.
Dylan, Bob. *Writings and Drawings by Bob Dylan.* New York: Knopf, 1973.
D'Zurilla, Christie. "Carly Simon Finally Reveals Who's So Vain in 'You're So Vain.'" *Los Angeles Times*, November 18, 2015. Available online: http://www.latimes.com/entertainment/gossip/la-et-mg-carly-simon-youre-so-vain-about-warren-beatty-partially-20151118-story.html.

Eagleton, Terry. *Literary Theory: An Introduction*, 3rd ed. Minneapolis: University of Minnesota Press, 2008.

Eliot, T. S. *Four Quartets*. New York: Harcourt, 1943.

Fan, Jiayang. "Yuck! The World's Most Disgusting Foods." *The New Yorker* (May 17, 2021): 42–9.

Fast, Susan, and Craig Jennex eds. *Popular Music and the Politics of Hope: Queer and Feminist Interventions*. Abingdon: Routledge, 2019.

Ferber, Michael. *Romanticism: A Very Short Introduction*. Oxford: Oxford University Press, 2010.

Ferrandino, Matthew. "What to Listen for in Zappa: Philosophy, Allusion and Structure in Frank Zappa's Music." Master's thesis, University of Oregon, June 2015. Available online: https://core.ac.uk/download/pdf/36693175.pdf.

Feuer, Alan, and Frances Robles, "Proud Boys under Growing Scrutiny in Capitol Riot Investigation." *New York Times*, January 26, 2021, updated April 13, 2021. Available online: https://www.nytimes.com/2021/01/26/us/proud-boys-capitol-riot.html.

Fine, Kit. "The Non-Identity of a Material Thing and Its Matter." *Mind* 112 (2003): 195–234.

Fisher, John Andrew. 2011. "Popular Music." In *The Routledge Companion to Philosophy and Music*, edited by Theodore Gracyk and Andrew Kania, 405–15. New York: Routledge.

Fiske, John. *Television Culture*, 2nd ed. New York: Routledge, 2011.

Fodor, Jerry. "Banish Discontent." In *Language, Mind and Logic*, edited by Jeremy Butterfield, 1–23. Cambridge: Cambridge University Press, 1986.

Fonarow, Wendy. *Empire of Dirt: The Aesthetics and Rituals of British Indie Music*. Middletown, CT: Wesleyan University Press, 2006.

Fornäs, Johan. "Moving Rock: Youth and Pop in Late Modernity." *Popular Music* 9 (1990): 291–306.

Fouz-Hernández, Santiago, and Freya Jarman-Ivens, *Madonna's Drowned Worlds: New Approaches to her Cultural Transformations, 1983–2003*. Aldershot: Ashgate, 2004.

Fox, Aaron A. *Real Country: Music and Language in Working-Class Culture*. Durham, NC: Duke University Press, 2004.

Frank, Gillian. "Discophobia: Antigay Prejudice and the 1979 Backlash against Disco." *Journal of the History of Sexuality* 15 (2007): 276–306.

Friend, Stacie. "Imagining Fact and Fiction." In *New Waves in Aesthetics*, edited by Kathleen Stock and Katherine Thomson-Jones, 150–69. Basingstoke: Palgrave, 2008.

Friend, Stacie. "The Real Foundation of Fictional Worlds." *Australasian Journal of Philosophy* 95 (2017): 29–42.

Frith, Simon. "Creativity as a Social Fact." In *Musical Imaginations: Multidisciplinary Perspectives on Creativity, Performance and Perception*, edited by David Hargreaves and Dorothy Miell, 62–72. Oxford: Oxford University Press, 2012.

Frith, Simon. *Music for Pleasure: Essays in the Sociology of Pop*. New York: Routledge, 1988.

Frith, Simon. *Performing Rites: On the Value of Popular Music*. Cambridge, MA: Harvard University Press, 1996.

Frith, Simon. *Taking Popular Music Seriously: Selected Essays*. Aldershot: Ashgate, 2007.

Gaiger, Jason. *Aesthetics and Painting*. London and New York: Continuum, 2008.

Gamble, Steven. *How Music Empowers: Listening to Modern Rap and Metal*. New York: Routledge, 2021.

Gantefführer-Trier, Anne. *Cubism*. Köln and London: Taschen, 2004.

Garchik, Leah. "Shocked Show Shut Down over Gay Slur." *SF Gate*, May 18, 2013. Available online: http://www.sfgate.com/entertainment/garchik/article/Shocked-show-shut-down-over-gay-slur-4363898.php.
Gaut, Berys. "Art and Ethics." In *The Routledge Companion to Aesthetics*, 3rd ed., edited by Berys Gaut and Dominic McIver Lopes, 394–403. New York: Routledge, 2013.
Gaut, Berys. *A Philosophy of Cinematic Art*. Cambridge: Cambridge University Press, 2010.
Gelbart, Matthew. *The Invention of "Folk Music" and "Art Music": Emerging Categories from Ossian to Wagner*. Cambridge: Cambridge University Press, 2007.
Gendron, Bernard. *Between Montmartre and the Mudd Club: Popular Music and the Avant-Garde*. Chicago: University of Chicago Press, 2002.
Genette, Gérard. *Palimsests: Literature in the Second Degree*, translated by Channa Newman and Claude Doubinsky. Lincoln, NE: University of Nebraska Press, 1997.
Giddins, Gary, and Scott DeVeaux. *Jazz*. New York: W. W. Norton, 2009.
Gilbert, Jeremy, and Ewan Pearson. *Discographies: Dance Music, Culture and the Politics of Sound*. London and New York: Routledge, 1999.
Gilbert, Margaret. "Concerning Sociality: The Plural Subject as Paradigm." In *The Mark of the Social: Discovery or Invention?* edited by John Greenwood, 17–36. Lanham, MD: Rowman and Littlefield, 1997.
Gioia, Ted. *Healing Songs*. Durham, NC: Duke University Press, 2006.
Gioia, Ted. *Love Songs: The Hidden History*. Oxford: Oxford University Press, 2018.
Gioia, Ted. *Work Songs*. Durham, NC: Duke University Press, 2006.
Godlovitch, Stan. *Musical Performance: A Philosophical Study*. New York: Routledge, 1998.
Goldman, Alan H. "Aesthetic Properties." In *A Companion to Aesthetics*, 2nd ed., edited by Stephen Davies, Kathleen Marie Higgins, Robert Hopkins, Robert Stecker, and David E. Cooper, 124–8. Malden and Oxford: Blackwell, 2009.
Goldman, Alan H. "Interpreting Art and Literature." *Journal of Aesthetics and Art Criticism* 48 (1990): 205–14.
Golson, G. Barry ed. *The Playboy Interviews with John Lennon & Yoko Ono*. New York: Berkley Books, 1982.
Gombrich, E. H. *Art and Illusion*. New York: Pantheon, 1960.
Gombrich, E. H. *Meditations on a Hobby Horse and Other Essays on the Theory of Art*. London: Phaidon, 1963.
Gracyk, Theodore. "Documentation and Transformation in Musical Recordings." In *Recorded Music: Philosophical and Critical Reflections*, edited by Mine Dogantan-Dack, 61–81. Hendon: Middlesex University Press, 2008.
Gracyk, Theodore. "Genius." In *The Cambridge Kant Lexicon*, edited by Julian Wuerth, 199–200. Cambridge: Cambridge University Press, 2021.
Gracyk, Theodore. *I Wanna Be Me: Rock Music and the Politics of Identity*. Philadelphia: Temple University Press, 2001.
Gracyk, Theodore. "Ontological Contextualism." In *A Companion to Aesthetics*, 2nd ed., edited by David Cooper, Stephen Davies, Kathleen Higgins, Robert Hopkins, and Robert Stecker, 449–53. Oxford: Blackwell, 2009.
Gracyk, Theodore. "Popular Music." In *The Oxford Handbook of Western Music and Philosophy*, edited by Tomás McAuley, Nanette Nielsen, Jerrold Levinson, Ariana Phillips-Hutton, 533–53. Oxford: Oxford University Press, 2020.
Gracyk, Theodore. *Rhythm and Noise: An Aesthetics of Rock*. Durham, NC: Duke University Press, 1996.

Grice, H. P. (Paul). "Logic and Conversation." In *Syntax and Semantics, vol. 3, Speech Acts*, edited by Peter Cole and Jerry L. Morgan, 41–58. New York: Academic Press, 1975.
Grice, Paul. *Studies in the Way of Words*. Cambridge, MA: Harvard University Press, 1989.
Grossberg, Lawrence. "Another Boring Day in Paradise: Rock and Roll and the Empowerment of Everyday Life." In *Dancing in Spite of Myself: Essays on Popular Culture*, 29–63. Durham, NC: Duke University Press, 1997.
Grossberg, Lawrence. "The Media Economy of Rock Culture: Cinema, Postmodernity and Authenticity." In *Sound and Vision: The Music Video Reader*, edited by Simon Frith, Andrew Goodwin, and Lawrence Grossberg, 185–209. London and New York: Routledge, 1993.
Grossberg, Lawrence. "Reflections of a Disappointed Popular Music Scholar." In *Rock over the Edge: Transformations in Popular Culture*, edited by Roger Beebe, Denise Fulbrook, and Ben Saunders, 25–59. Durham, NC: Duke University Press, 2002.
Grossberg, Lawrence. "Same as It Ever Was? Rock Culture. Same as It Ever Was! Rock Theory." In *Stars Don't Stand Still in the Sky: Music and Myth*, edited by Karen Kelly and Evelyn McDonnell, 99–121. New York: New York University Press, 1999.
Grossberg, Lawrence. *We Gotta Get Out of This Place: Popular Conservatism and Postmodern Culture*. New York and London: Routledge, 1992.
Gura, Philip F. *Truth's Ragged Edge: The Rise of the American Novel*. New York: Farrar, Straus and Giroux, 2013.
Haberman, Maggie. "Trump Departs Vowing, 'We Will Be Back in Some Form.'" *New York Times*, January 20, 2021. Available online: https://www.nytimes.com/2021/01/20/us/politics/trump-presidency.html.
Hamm, Charles. *Putting Popular Music in Its Place*. Cambridge: Cambridge University Press, 1995.
Hamilton, Jill. "Ani DiFranco." *Rolling Stone* (November 13, 1997): 150.
Hawkins, Stan. "Personas in Rock." In *The Bloomsbury Handbook of Rock Music Research*, edited by Allan F. Moore and Paul Carr, 239–54. New York: Bloomsbury Academic, 2020.
Hawkins, Stan. "'You Have Killed Me'—Tropes of Hyperbole and Sentimentality in Morrissey's Musical Expression." In *Morrissey: Fandom, Representations and Identities*, edited by Eoin Devereux, Aileen Dillane, and Martin Power, 307–23. Bristol: Intellect, 2011.
Hebdige, Dick. *Subculture: The Meaning of Style*. London: Routledge, 1979.
Hedin, Benjamin ed. *Studio A: The Bob Dylan Reader*. New York: W. W. Norton, 2004.
Heiser, Marshall. "Control, Chaos, Power, and Play: Interview with Dr Bill Bruford." *Journal on the Art of Record Production*, May, 2021. Available online: https://www.arpjournal.com/asarpwp/control-chaos-power-and-play-interview-with-dr-bill-bruford/.
Hennessy, Tom. Beyond *Authenticism: New Approaches to Post War Music Culture*. Doctoral thesis, Birkbeck, University of London, 2016.
Hesmondhalgh, David. "Post-Punk's Attempt to Democratise the Music Industry: The Success and Failure of Rough Trade." *Popular Music* 16 (1998): 255–74.
Hesmondhalgh, David, and Leslie M. Meier. "Popular Music, Independence and the Concept of the Alternative in Contemporary Capitalism." In *Media Independence: Working with Freedom or Working for Free?* edited by James Bennett and Niki Strange, 94–116. New York: Routledge, 2014.
Heylin, Clinton. *From the Velvets to the Voidoids: A Pre-Punk History for a Post-Punk World*. New York: Penguin, 1993.

Hirsch, Lily E. "Rap as Threat: The Violent Translation of Music in American Law." *Law, Culture and the Humanities* 14 (2014): 1–19.

Hoffmann, E. T. A. "Beethoven's Instrumental Music." In *E. T. A. Hoffmann's Musical Writings: Kreisleriana, the Poet and the Composer, Music Criticism*, edited by David Charlton, translated by Martyn Clarke, 96–103. Cambridge: Cambridge University Press, 1989.

Home, Stewart. *Cranked Up Really High: An Inside Account of Punk Rock*. London: Codex, 1995.

Horgby, Björn, and Fredrik Nilsson eds. *Rockin' the Borders: Rock Music and Social, Cultural and Political Change*. Cambridge: Cambridge Scholars Publishing, 2010.

Horowitz, Joseph. *Understanding Toscanini: How He Became an American Culture-God and Helped Create a New Audience for Old Music*. New York: Knopf, 1987.

Hoskyns, Barney. *Across the Great Divide: The Band and America*. New York: Hyperion, 1993.

Hoskyns, Barney. *Lowside of the Road: A Life of Tom Waits*. London: Faber and Faber, 2009.

Hsu, Hui-Chieh, and Lily I-wen Su. "Love in Disguise: Incongruity between Text and Music in Song." *Journal of Pragmatics* 62 (2014): 136–50.

Huff, Lauren. "Taylor Swift's Teenage Love Triangle Songs on Folklore Explained." *Entertainment*, July 29, 2020. Available online: https://ew.com/music/taylor-swifts-teenage-love-triangle-songs-folklore-explained/.

Hughes, Walter. "In the Empire of the Beat." In *Microphone Fiends: Youth Music and Youth Culture*, edited by Andrew Ross and Tricia Rose, 147–57. New York: Routledge, 1994.

Irvin, Sherri. "Authors, Intentions and Literary Meaning." *Philosophy Compass* 1 (March 2006): 114–28. Available online, doi:10.1111/j.1747-9991.2006.00016.x.

Irwin, William. "The Aesthetics of Allusion." *Journal of Value Inquiry* 36 (2002): 521–32.

Irwin, William. "What Is an Allusion?" *Journal of Aesthetics and Art Criticism* 59:3 (2001): 287–97.

Irwin, William, and J. R. Lombardo. "The Simpsons and Allusion: 'Worst Essay Ever.'" In *The Simpsons and Philosophy: The D'Oh! Of Homer*, edited by William Irwin, Mark T. Conard, and Aeon J. Skoble, 81–92. Chicago and La Salle: Open Court, 2001.

Iseminger, Gary. *The Aesthetic Function of Art*. Ithaca: Cornell University Press, 2004.

JohnLydon.Com. "Abused by John Lydon: The Jam! Interview." Available online: http://www.johnlydon.com/jamm96.html.

Johnson, Julian. *Who Needs Classical Music? Cultural Choice and Musical Value*. Oxford: Oxford University Press, 2002.

Jones, Gaynor, and Jay Rahn. "Definitions of Popular Music: Recycled." *Journal of Aesthetic Education* 11:4 (1977): 79–92.

Jones, Peter. "Works of Art and Their Availability-for-Use." *British Journal of Aesthetics* 11 (1971): 115–22.

Jonze, Tim. "Bigmouth Strikes Again and Again: Why Morrissey Fans Feel So Betrayed." *The Guardian*, May 30, 2019, https://www.theguardian.com/music/2019/may/30/bigmouth-strikes-again-morrissey-songs-loneliness-shyness-misfits-far-right-party-tonight-show-jimmy-fallon.

Judkins, Jennifer. "Style." In *The Routledge Companion to Philosophy and Music*, edited by Theodore Gracyk and Andrew Kania, 134–43. New York: Routledge, 2011.

Kania, Andrew. "All Play and No Work: An Ontology of Jazz." *Journal of Aesthetics and Art Criticism* 69 (2011): 391–403.
Kania, Andrew. *Philosophy of Western Music: A Contemporary Introduction*. New York: Routledge, 2020.
Kania, Andrew, and T. Theodore Gracyk. "Performances and Recordings." In *The Routledge Companion to Philosophy and Music*, edited by Theodore Gracyk and Andrew Kania, 80–90. New York: Routledge, 2011.
Kant, Immanuel. *Critique of the Power of Judgment*, edited by Paul Guyer, translated by Paul Guyer and Eric Matthews. Cambridge: Cambridge University Press, 2000.
Kearney, Mary Celeste. *Gender and Rock*. Oxford: Oxford University Press, 2017.
Keightley, Keir. "Reconsidering Rock." In *The Cambridge Companion to Pop and Rock*, edited by Simon Frith, Will Straw, and John Street, 109–42. Cambridge: Cambridge University Press, 2001.
Kelly, Michael ed. *The Encyclopedia of Aesthetics*, 2nd ed. Oxford: Oxford University Press, 2014.
Kemal, Salim. *Kant's Aesthetic Theory: An Introduction*, 2nd ed. New York: St. Martin's Press, 1997.
Kendon, Adam. *Gesture: Visible Action as Utterance*. Cambridge: Cambridge University Press, 2004.
Kivy, Peter. *Authenticities: Philosophical Reflections on Musical Performance*. Ithaca, NY: Cornell University Press, 1995.
Kivy, Peter. "Messiah's Message." In *Sounding Off: Eleven Essays in the Philosophy of Music*, 113–30. Oxford: Oxford University Press, 2012.
Kivy, Peter. *The Performance of Reading: An Essay in the Philosophy of Literature*. Oxford: Blackwell, 2006.
Kivy, Peter. *The Possessor and the Possessed: Handel, Mozart, Beethoven, and the Idea of Musical Genius*. New Haven: Yale University Press, 2001.
Korsmeyer, Carolyn. *Making Sense of Taste: Food and Philosophy*. Ithaca and London: Cornell University Press, 1999.
Korsmeyer, Carolyn. "Philosophy and the Probable Impossible." In *Philosophy and the Interpretation of Pop Culture*, edited by William Irwin and Jorge J. E. Gracia, 21–40. Lanham: Rowman & Littlefield, 2007.
Korsmeyer, Carolyn. *Savoring Disgust: The Foul and the Fair in Aesthetics*. Oxford: Oxford University Press, 2011.
Korsmeyer, Carolyn. *Things: In Touch with the Past*. Oxford: Oxford University Press, 2019.
Kripke, Saul. "Speaker's Reference and Semantic Reference." In *Midwest Studies in Philosophy* 2, edited by Peter A. French, Theodore E. Uehling, Jr., and Howard K. Wettstein, 255–76. Morris, MN: University of Minnesota, 1977.
Kuhn, Elisabeth D. "'I Just Want to Make Love to You': Seductive Strategies in Blues Lyrics." *Journal of Pragmatics* 31 (1999): 525–34.
Laing, Dave. *One Chord Wonders: Power and Meaning in Punk Rock*. Milton Keynes: Open University Press, 1985.
Lamarque, Peter. "The Death of the Author: An Analytical Autopsy." *British Journal of Aesthetics* 30 (1990): 319–31.
Lamarque, Peter. *Fictional Points of View*. Ithaca: Cornell University Press, 1996.
Lamarque, Peter. *The Philosophy of Literature*. Oxford: Blackwell, 2009.
Lamarque, Peter. *Work and Object: Explorations in the Metaphysics of Art*. Oxford: Oxford University Press, 2010.

Lawler, James. "Only Love Is Real: Heidegger, Plato, and the Matrix Trilogy." In *More Matrix and Philosophy: Revolutions and Reloaded Decoded*, edited by William Irwin, 26–37. Chicago and La Salle: Open Court, 2005.

Leeds, Jeff. "Deadheads Outraged Over Web Crackdown." *New York Times*, November 30, 2005. Available online: http://www.nytimes.com/2005/11/30/arts/music/deadheads-outraged-over-web-crackdown.html?mcubz=0.

Lena, Jennifer C. *Banding Together: How Communities Create Genres in Popular Music*. Princeton: Princeton University Press, 2012.

Leppert, Richard. "Commentary." In *Theodor W. Adorno, Essays on Music*, edited by Richard Leppert, 327–71. Berkeley: University of California Press, 2002.

Lewis, Randy. "Carly Simon and Taylor Swift Duet on 'You're So Vain.'" *Los Angeles Times*, August 1, 2013. Available online: https://www.latimes.com/entertainment/music/posts/la-et-ms-taylor-swift-carly-simon-duet-youre-so-vain-20130801-story.html.

Levinson, Jerrold. *Music in the Moment*. Ithaca, NY: Cornell University Press, 1997.

Levinson, Jerrold. "What a Musical Work Is." *Journal of Philosophy* 77 (1980): 5–28.

Liao, Shen-Yi, and Aaron Meskin. "Morality and Aesthetics of Food." In *The Oxford Handbook of Food Ethics*, edited by Anne Barnhill, Mark Budolfson, and Tyler Doggett, 658–79. Oxford: Oxford University Press, 2018.

Lindberg, Ulf, Gestur Guomundsson, Morten Michelsen, and Hans Weisethaunet. *Rock Criticism from the Beginning: Amusers, Bruisers, and Cool-headed Cruisers*. New York: Peter Lang, 2005.

Livingston, Paisley. *Art and Intention: A Philosophical Study*. Oxford: Oxford University Press, 2005.

Livingston, Paisley. "Cinematic Authorship." In *Film Theory and Philosophy*, edited by Richard Allen and Murray Smith, 132–48. New York: Oxford University Press, 1997.

Locke, John. *An Essay Concerning Human Understanding*, edited by Peter H. Nidditch. Oxford: Clarendon Press, 1975.

Loder, Kurt. "Bob Dylan." In *The Rolling Stone Interviews: The 1980s*, edited by Sid Holt, 93–104. New York: St. Martin's Press, 1989.

London, Justin. "Metric Entrainment and the Problem(s) of Perception." In *The Philosophy of Rhythm: Aesthetics, Music, Poetics*, edited by Peter Cheyne, Andy Hamilton, and Max Paddison, 171–82. Oxford: Oxford University Press, 2019.

London, Justin. "Musical and Linguistic Speech Acts." *Journal of Aesthetics and Art Criticism* 54:1 (1996): 49–64.

London, Justin. "Third-Party uses of Music and Musical Pragmatics." *Journal of Aesthetics and Art Criticism* 66:3 (2008): 253–64.

Lott, Eric. *Love and Theft: Blackface Minstrelsy and the American Working Class*. Oxford: Oxford University Press, 1993.

Loux, Michael J. "Endurantism and Perdurantism." In *Metaphysics: Contemporary Readings*, edited by Michael J. Loux, 321–7. New York: Routledge, 2001.

Lowe, Kelly Fisher. *The Words and Music of Frank Zappa*. Westport, CT: Praeger, 2006.

Lucie-Smith, Edward. *Movements in Art since 1945*, 2nd ed. London: Thames and Hudson, 2020.

Lycan, William G. *Philosophy of Language: A Contemporary Introduction*, 2nd ed. London and New York: Routledge, 2008.

Mace, Sandra, Cynthia Wagoner, David Teachout, and Donald Hodges. "Genre Identification of Very Brief Musical Excerpts." *Psychology of Music* 40 (2011): 112–28.

Magnus, Cristyn, P. D. Magnus, and Christy Mag Uidhir, "Judging Covers." *Journal of Aesthetics and Art Criticism* 71 (2013): 361–70.

Magnus, P. D. "Kind of Borrowed, Kind of Blue." *Journal of Aesthetics and Art Criticism* 74 (2016): 179–85.
Mann, Brent. *Blinded by the Lyrics: Behind the Lines of Rock and Roll's Most Baffling Songs*. New York: Citadel, 2005.
Mann, Geoff. "Why Does Country Music Sound White? Race and the Voice of Nostalgia." *Race and Ethnic Studies* 31 (2008): 73–100.
Manning, Toby. *The Rough Guide to Pink Floyd*. London: Rough Guides, 2006.
Manuel, Peter. *Cassette Culture: Popular Music and Technology in North India*. Chicago: University of Chicago Press, 1993.
Marcus, Greil. *Bob Dylan by Greil Marcus: Writings 1968–2010*. New York: Public Affairs, 2010.
Marcus, Greil. *Ranters & Crowd Pleasers: Punk in Pop Music, 1977–92*. New York: Doubleday, 1993.
Mark, Thomas Carson. "Philosophy of Piano Playing: Reflections on the Concept of Performance." *Philosophy and Phenomenological Research* 41 (1981): 299–324.
Marks, Craig. "Zero Worship." *Spin* (June 1996): 56.
Marsh, Dave. *Louie Louie: The History and Mythology of the World's Most Famous Rock 'n Roll Song*. New York: Hyperion, 1993.
Martin, Toby. "Historical Silences, Musical Noise: Slim Dusty, Country Music and Aboriginal History." *Popular Music History* 12 (2019): 215–36.
Matravers, Derek. *Fiction and Narrative*. Oxford: Oxford University Press, 2014.
McAuley, Tomás, Nanette Nielsen, Jerrold Levinson, and Ariana Phillips-Hutton eds. *The Oxford Handbook of Western Music and Philosophy*. Oxford: Oxford University Press, 2020.
McCloskey, Mary A. *Kant's Aesthetic*. Albany: State University of New York Press, 1987.
McKinney, Devin. *Magic Circles: The Beatles in Dream and History*. Cambridge, MA: Harvard University Press, 2003.
McLeod, Kembrew. "Between Rock and a Hard Place: Gender and Rock Criticism." In *Pop Music and the Press*, edited by Steve Jones, 93–113. Philadelphia: Temple University Press, 2002.
Meltzer, Richard. "St. Stephen Revisited and Beyond." In *The Grateful Dead Reader*, edited by David G. Dodd and Diana Spaulding, 117–19. Oxford: Oxford University Press, 2002.
Menand, Louis. *American Studies*. New York: Farrar, Straus and Giroux, 2002.
Merricks, Trenton. "Endurance and Indiscernibility." In *Metaphysics: Contemporary Readings*, edited by Michael J. Loux, 364–5. New York: Routledge, 2001.
Meyer Leonard, B. *Style and Music: Theory, History, and Ideology*. Chicago: University of Chicago Press, 1996.
Middleton, Richard. *Studying Popular Music*. Milton Keynes: Open University Press, 1990.
Middleton, Richard. *Voicing the Popular: On the Subjects of Popular Music*. New York: Routledge, 2006.
Millar, Stephen R. "'I Forbid You to Like It:' The Smiths, David Cameron, and the Politics of (Mis)appropriating Popular Culture." *Echo*, 2015. Available online: http://www.echo.ucla.edu/article-millar-i-forbid-you-to-like-it/#fn-1054-9.
Millar, Stephen R. *Sounding Dissent: Rebel Songs, Resistance, and Irish Republicanism*. Ann Arbor: University of Michigan Press, 2020.
Miller, Alex. *Philosophy of Language*, 2nd ed. Milton Park: Routledge, 2007.
Miles, Barry. *The British Invasion*. London and New York: Sterling Publishing, 2009.

Monelle, Raymond. *Linguistics and Semiotics in Music*. London and New York: Routledge, 2014.
Monk, Katherine. *Joni: The Creative Odyssey of Joni Mitchell*. Vancouver: Greystone Books, 2012.
Moore, Allan F. "Authenticity as Authentication." *Popular Music* 2 (2002): 209–23.
Moore, Allan F. *The Beatles: Sgt. Pepper's Lonely Hearts Club Band*. Cambridge: Cambridge University Press, 1997.
Moore, Allan F. "Interpretation: So What?" In *The Ashgate Research Companion to Popular Musicology*, edited by Derek Scott, 411–25. Farnham: Ashgate, 2009.
Moore, Allan F. *Rock: The Primary Text*. Buckingham: Open University Press, 1993.
Moore, Allan F. *Song Means: Analysing and Interpreting Recorded Popular Song*. Farnham: Ashgate, 2012.
Morris, Wesley. "Michael Jackson Cast a Spell. 'Leaving Neverland' Breaks It." *New York Times*, February 28, 2019. Available online: https://www.nytimes.com/2019/02/28/arts/television/michael-jackson-leaving-neverland.html.
Mosser, Kurt. "'Cover Songs': Ambiguity, Multivalence, Polysemy." *Popular Musicology Online* 2 (2008). Available online: http://www.popular-musicology-online.com/issues/02/mosser.html.
Nanay, Bence. *Aesthetics: A Very Short Introduction*. Oxford: Oxford University Press, 2020.
Nelson, Erik, and Andrea L. Dennis. *Rap on Trial: Race, Lyrics, and Guilt in America*. New York and London: The Free Press, 2019.
Nelson Robert, S., and Richard Shiff eds. *Critical Terms for Art History*, 2nd ed. Chicago: University of Chicago Press, 2003.
Nguyen, C. Thi. *Games: Agency as Art*. Oxford: Oxford University Press, 2020.
Nochlin, Linda. *Women, Art, and Power and Other Essays*. London and New York: Routledge, 2018.
Nordheim, Christie. "'Shocking' Revelations from Singer Michelle Shocked." *Outlines* (May 1990): 25.
Novitz, David. "Aesthetics of Popular Art." In *The Oxford Handbook of Aesthetics*, edited by Jerrold Levinson, 733–47. Oxford: Oxford University Press, 2003.
Novitz, David. *The Boundaries of Art*. Philadelphia: Temple University Press, 1992.
Ó Maoilearca, Laura Cull, and Alice Lagaay eds. *The Routledge Companion to Performance Philosophy*. New York: Routledge, 2020.
Onwuamaegbu, Natachi. "The Unexpected Link between Britney Spears and Olivia Rodrigo Explains So Much about Being a Pop Star Today." *Washington Post*, August 3, 2021. Available online: https://www.washingtonpost.com/arts-entertainment/2021/08/03/britney-spears-olivia-rodrigo/.
Orejuela, Fernando, and Stephanie Shonekan eds. *Black Lives Matter and Music: Protest, Intervention, Reflection*. Bloomington: Indiana University Press, 2018.
Osborn, Brad. *Interpreting Music Video in the Post-MTV Era*. New York: Routledge, 2021.
Otter Bickerdike, Jennifer. *Fandom, Image and Authenticity: Joy Devotion and the Second Lives of Kurt Cobain and Ian Curtis*. Basingstoke: Palgrave Macmillan, 2014.
Paddison, Max. "Meaning and Autonomy." In *The Oxford Handbook of Western Music and Philosophy*, edited by Tomás McAuley, Nanette Nielsen, Jerrold Levinson, and Ariana Phillips-Hutton, 5763–83. Oxford: Oxford University Press, 2020.
Paterniti, Michael. "Brad Pitt Talks Divorce, Quitting Drinking, and Becoming a Better Man." *GQ*, May 3, 2017. Available online: https://www.gq.com/story/brad-pitt-gq-style-cover-story.

Pattison, Louis. "Twenty Years after In Utero, Nirvana's Importance Hasn't Diminished." *The Guardian*, August 31, 2013. Available online: https://www.theguardian.com/music/2013/aug/31/nirvana-dave-grohl-krist-novoselic-in-utero.

Pattison, Robert. *The Triumph of Vulgarity: Rock Music in the Mirror of Romanticism*. Oxford: Oxford University Press, 1986.

Peacocke, Christopher. "Holism." In *A Companion to the Philosophy of Language*, edited by Bob Hale and Crispin Wright, 227–47. Oxford: Blackwell.

Penrose, Nerisha. "Anti-Donald Trump Ad Reworks Carly Simon's 'You're So Vain.'" *Billboard*, October 10, 2016. Available online: http://www.billboard.com/articles/news/politics/7534395/donald-trump-ad-carly-simon-youre-so-vain.

Plasketes, George. "Introduction: Like a Version." In *Play It Again: Cover Songs in Popular Music*, edited by George Plasketes, 1–7. Farnham: Ashgate, 2010.

Plato. *The Dialogues of Plato*, 3rd ed., edited and translated by Benjamin Jowett. Oxford: Clarendon Press, 1892.

Polite, Brandon. "Shared Musical Experiences." *British Journal of Aesthetics* 59 (2019): 429–47.

Pucci, Joseph. *The Full Knowing Reader: Allusion and the Power of the Reader in the Western Literary Tradition*. New Haven: Yale University Press, 1998.

Putnam, Hilary. *Realism with a Human Face*. Cambridge, MA: Harvard University Press, 1990.

Puy, Nemesio García-Carril. "The Ontology of Musical Versions: Introducing the Hypothesis of Nested Types." *Journal of Aesthetics and Art Criticism* 77 (2019): 241–54.

Quine, W. V. "Two Dogmas in Retrospect." *Canadian Journal of Philosophy* 21 (1991): 265–74.

Quine, W. V. "Two Dogmas of Empiricism." *Philosophical Review* 60 (1951): 20–43.

Pagin, Peter. "Meaning Holism." In *The Oxford Handbook of Philosophy of Language*, edited by Ernest Lepore and Barry Smith, 213–32. Oxford: Clarendon Press, 2006.

Pattie, David. *Rock Music in Performance*. Basingstoke: Palgrave Macmillan, 2007.

Raffman, Diana. *Language, Music, and Mind*. Cambridge, MA: MIT Press, 1993.

Reed, Katherine. "Rock Hermeneutics." In *The Bloomsbury Handbook of Rock Music Research*, edited by Allan F. Moore and Paul Carr, 255–68. New York and London: Bloomsbury, 2020.

Regev, Motti. *Pop-Rock Music: Aesthetic Cosmopolitanism in Late Modernity*. Cambridge: Polity Press, 2011.

Reynolds, Simon. *Rip It Up and Start Again: Postpunk 1978–1984*. New York: Penguin, 2006.

Ricks, Christopher. *Dylan's Visions of Sin*. London and New York: Viking, 2003.

Ridley, Aaron. "*Persona*, Sometimes *Grata*: On the Appreciation of Expressive Music." In *Philosophers on Music: Experience, Meaning, and Work*, edited by Kathleen Stock, 130–46. Oxford: Oxford University Press, 2007.

Rings, Michael. "Doing It Their Way: Rock Covers, Genre, and Appreciation." *Journal of Aesthetics and Art Criticism* 71 (2013): 55–63.

Roberts, Thomas R. *An Aesthetics of Junk Fiction*. Athens: University of Georgia Press, 1990.

Rose, Phil. *Which One's Pink? An Analysis of the Concept Albums of Roger Waters and Pink Floyd*. Burlington, Ontario: Collector's Guide Publishing, 1998.

Ross, Stephanie. "Art and Allusion." *Journal of Aesthetics and Art Criticism* 40 (1981): 59–70.

Ross, Stephanie. "Style in Art." In *The Oxford Handbook of Aesthetics*, edited by Jerrold Levinson, 228–44. Oxford: Oxford University Press, 2003.
Russell, Bertrand. "On Denoting." *Mind* 14 (1905): 479–93.
Russell, Paul. *The Gay 100: A Ranking of the Most Influential Gay Men and Lesbians, Past and Present*. New York: Carol Publishing, 1995.
Salmon, Nathan. "Two Conceptions of Semantics." In *Semantics versus Pragmatics*, edited by Zoltán Gendler Szabó, 317–28. Oxford: Clarendon Press, 2005.
Sandler, Martin W. *How the Beatles Changed the World*. New York: Bloomsbury, 2014.
Sanneh, Kelefa. *Major Labels: A History of Popular Music in Seven Genres*. New York: Penguin, 2021.
Schellekens, Elisabeth. *Aesthetics and Morality*. London: Continuum, 2007.
Schneider, Joanne. *The Age of Romanticism*. Westport, CT: Greenwwod Press, 2007.
Schudson, Michael. "The New Validation of Popular Culture: Sense and Sentimentality in Academia." *Critical Studies in Mass Communication* 4 (1987): 51–68.
Scott, Derek B. *Sounds of the Metropolis: The 19th Century Popular Music Revolution in London, New York, Paris and Vienna*. Oxford: Oxford University Press, 2011.
Sellors, C. Paul. "Collective Authorship in Film." *Journal of Aesthetics and Art Criticism* 65 (2007): 263–71.
Shelton, Robert. *No Direction Home: The Life and Music of Bob Dylan*. New York: Beech Tree Books, 1986.
Shapiro, Meyer. "Style." In *The Art of Art History, A Critical Anthology*, edited by Donald Preziosi, 143–9. Oxford: Oxford University Press, 1998.
Shepherd, John. "Music and the Last Intellectuals." *Journal of Aesthetic Education* 25:3 (1991): 95–114.
Shteamer, Hank. "Bill Bruford on His Ups and Downs with Yes and King Crimson, Life after Retirement." *Rolling Stone*, 2021. Available online: https://www.rollingstone.com/music/music-features/bill-bruford-yes-band-king-crimson-genesis-earthworks-interview-902501/, 2021.
Shuker, Roy. *Understanding Popular Music*, 2nd ed. London and New York: Routledge, 2001.
Shumway, David. "Rock & Roll as a Cultural Practice." In *Present Tense: Rock & Roll and Culture*, edited by Anthony DeCurtis, 117–34. Durham, NC: Duke University Press, 1992.
Silver, Daniel Monica Lee, and Clayton Childress. "Genre Complexes in Popular Music." *PLoS One* 11 (2016), doi: 10.1371/journal.pone.0155471.
Simon, Carly. *Boys in the Trees: A Memoir*. New York: Flatiron, 2015.
Smith, Christopher. "'Broadway the Hard Way:' Techniques of Allusion in Music by Frank Zappa." *College Music Symposium* 35 (1995): 35–60.
Smith, Patti. "How Does It Feel?" *The New Yorker*. December 14, 2016. Available online: https://www.newyorker.com/culture/cultural-comment/patti-smith-on-singing-at-bob-dylans-nobel-prize-ceremony.
Smith, R. J. *The One: The Life and Music of James Brown*. Garden City, NY: Avery, 2012.
Solender, Andrew "All the Artists Who Have Told Trump to Stop Using Their Songs at His Rallies." *Forbes*, June 28, 2020. Available online: https://www.forbes.com/sites/andrewsolender/2020/06/28/all-the-artists-who-have-told-trump-to-stop-using-their-songs-at-his-rallies/.
Solie, Ruth A. "Whose Life? The Gendered Self in Schumann's *Frauenliebe* Songs." In *Music and Text: Critical Inquiries*, edited by Steven Paul Sher, 219–40. Cambridge: Cambridge University Press, 1992.

Sonvilla-Weiss, Stefan ed. *Mashup Cultures*. Vienna: Springer, 2010.
Sorkin, Andrew Ross, and Jeff Leads. "Music Companies Share in YouTube-Google Deal." *New York Times*, October 19, 2006. Available online: https://www.nytimes.com/2006/10/19/technology/19iht-youtube.3214225.html.
Starbuck, Edwin D. and Frank K. Shuttleworth et al. *Guide to Literature for Character Training: Volume 1 Fairy Tale, Myth, and Legend*. New York: Macmillan, 1928.
Stecker, Robert. *Artworks: Definition Meaning Value*. University Park, PA: The Pennsylvania State University Press, 1997.
Stecker, Robert. "Interpretation." In *The Routledge Companion to Aesthetics*, 3rd ed., edited by Berys Gaut and Dominic McIver Lopes, 309–19. New York: Routledge, 2013.
Stecker, Robert. *Interpretation and Construction: Art, Speech, and the Law*. Malden, MA: Blackwell Publishing, 2003.
Stecker, Robert. "Testing Artistic Value: A Reply to Dodd." *Journal of Aesthetics and Art Criticism* 71 (2013): 288–9.
Stalnaker, Robert. "Pragmatics." *Synthese* 22 (1970): 272–89.
Stokes, Geoffrey. *Star-Making Machinery: Inside the Business of Rock and Roll*. New York: Random House, 1977.
Stone, Alison. *The Value of Popular Music: An Approach from Post-Kantian Aesthetics*. Lancaster: Palgrave Macmillan, 2016.
Storey, John. *Inventing Popular Culture: From Folklore to Globalization*. Malden, MA: Blackwell, 2003.
Stratton, Jon. "Capitalism and Romantic Ideology in the Record Business." *Popular Music* 3 (1983): 143–56.
Strohmaier, David. "Two Theories of Group Agency." *Philosophical Studies* 177 (2020): 1901–18.
Sullivan, Denise. *R.E.M.: Talk about the Passion: An Oral History*, rev. ed. New York: Da Capo, 1998.
Summers, David. "'Form,' Nineteenth-Century Metaphysics, and the Problem of Art Historical Description." In *The Art of Art History, A Critical Anthology*, edited by Donald Preziosi, 127–42. Oxford: Oxford University Press, 1989.
Svedberg, Andrea. "I Am My Words." *Newsweek* (November 4, 1963): 94–5.
Szabó, Zoltán Gendler. "The Distinction between Semantics and Pragmatics." In *The Oxford Handbook of Philosophy of Language*, edited by Ernest LePore and Barry C. Smith, 361–89. Oxford: Oxford University Press, 2006.
Talbot, Margaret. "Reach for the Stars: The Secret Hollywood of 'You Must Remember This.'" *The New Yorker* (July 5, 2021): 66–9.
Taylor, Timothy. *Global Pop: World Music, World Markets*. London and New York: Routledge, 1997.
Thom, Paul. *For an Audience: A Philosophy of the Performing Arts*. Philadelphia: Temple University Press, 1993.
Thornton, Sarah. *Club Cultures: Music, Media, and Subcultural Capital*. Cambridge: Polity, 1995.
Todd, N. P. M. "The Kinematics of Musical Expression." *Journal of the Acoustical Society of America* 97 (1995): 1940–9.
Todd, N. P. M. "Sensory-Motor Theory of Rhythm, Time Perception and Beat Induction." *Journal of New Music Research* 28 (1999): 5–28.
Tollefsen, Deborah Perron. *Groups as Agents*. Cambridge: Polity Press, 2015.
Tollefsen, Deborah. "Organizations as True Believers." *Journal of Social Philosophy* 33 (2002): 395–410.

Tollefsen, Deborah. "The Rationality of Collective Guilt." In *Midwest Studies in Philosophy Volume XXX: Shared Intentions and Collective Responsibility*, edited by Peter A. French and Howard K. Wettstein, 222–39. Oxford: Blackwell, 2006.

Tolstoy, Leo. *What Is Art?* translated by Aylmer Maude. New York: The Liberal Arts Press, 1960.

Toynbee, Jason. *Making Popular Music: Musicians, Creativity and Institutions*. London: Arnold, 2000.

Tucker, Ken. "New Wave: Britain." In *The Rolling Stone Illustrated History of Rock & Roll*, Revised and Updated, edited by Jim Miller, 435–29. New York: Random House/Rolling Stone Press, 1980.

Tuomela, Raimo. "Actions by Collectives." *Philosophical Perspectives* 3 (1989): 471–96.

Unterberger, Richie. *White Light/White Heat: The Velvet Underground Day by Day*. London: Jawbone Press, 2009.

Ventre, Michael. "Hendrix Created Banner Moment at Woodstock." *Today*. August 10, 2009. Available online: https://www.today.com/popculture/hendrix-created-banner-moment-woodstock-2D80555766.

von Appen, Ralf. "Feigning or Feeling? on the Staging of Authenticity on Stage." *Samples* 18 (2020). Available online: www.gfpm-samples.de/Samples18/vonappen.pdf.

Walton, Kendall L. "Categories of Art." *Philosophical Review* 79 (1970): 334–67.

Walton, Kendall L. *Mimesis as Make-believe: On the Foundations of the Representational Arts*. Cambridge, MA: Harvard University Press, 1990.

Walton, Kendall L. "Thoughtwriting—In Poetry and Music." In *Other Shoes: Music, Metaphor, Empathy, Existence*, 54–74. Oxford: Oxford University Press, 2015.

Walser, Robert. *Running with the Devil: Power, Gender, and Madness in Heavy Metal Music*. Middleton, CT: Wesleyan University Press, 1993.

Walsh, Marcus. "Allusion." In *The Oxford Handbook of British Poetry, 1660–1800*, edited by Jack Lynch, 649–67. Oxford: Oxford University Press, 2016.

Wang, Amy X. "Facebook Is Finally Putting Music Back into Social Networking." *Rolling Stone*, June 5, 2018. Available online: https://www.rollingstone.com/pro/news/facebook-is-finally-putting-music-back-into-social-networking-629164/.

Warner, Timothy. *Pop Music—Technology and Creativity: Trevor Horn and the Digital Revolution*. Aldershot: Ashgate, 2003.

Webb, Jimmy. *Tunesmith: Inside the Art of Songwriting*. New York: Hyperion, 1998.

Weinstein, Deena. "Appreciating Cover Songs: Stereopnony." In *Play It Again: Cover Songs in Popular Music*, edited by George Plasketes, 245–52. Farnham: Ashgate, 2010.

Weisethaunet, Hans, and Ulf Lindberg. "Authenticity Revisited: The Rock Critic and the Changing Real." *Popular Music and Society* 33 (2010): 465–85.

Wenner, Jann S. ed. *Lennon Remembers*. San Francisco: Straight Arrow Books, 1971.

Wharton, Tim. *Pragmatics and Non-Verbal Communication*. Cambridge: Cambridge University Press, 2009.

White, Timothy. "Pink Floyd." In *Rock Lives: Profiles and Interviews*, 510 and 520–1. New York: Henry Holt, 1990.

Whiteley, Sheila. *Women and Popular Music: Sexuality, Identity, and Subjectivity*. London and New York: Routledge, 2000.

Wilde, Oscar. *The Picture of Dorian Gray*, edited by Joseph Bristow. Oxford: Oxford University Press, 2006.

Will, Richard. *The Characteristic Symphony in the Age of Haydn and Beethoven*. Cambridge: Cambridge University Press, 2002.

Willard, Mary Beth. *Why It's OK to Enjoy the Work of Immoral Artists*. New York: Routledge 2021.
Williams, Justin A. "Intertextuality and Lineage in the Game's 'We Ain't' and Kendrick Lamar's m.A.A.d. City." In *The Pop Palimpsest: Intertextuality in Recorded Popular Music*, edited by Lori Burns and Serge Lacasse, 291–312. Ann Arbor: University of Michigan Press, 2018.
Willis, Ellen. "Dylan." In *Bob Dylan: A Retrospective*, edited by Craig McGregor, 218–39. New York: William Morrow, 1972.
Willis, Paul. "The Golden Age." In *On Record: Rock, Pop, and the Written Word*, edited by Simon Frith and Andrew Goodwin, 43–55. New York: Pantheon, 1990.
Wilson, Dierdre, and Dan Sperber. *Meaning and Relevance*. Cambridge: Cambridge University Press, 2012.
Wilson, Dierdre, and Dan Sperber. "Relevance Theory." In *The Handbook of Pragmatics*, edited by Laurence R. Horn and Gregory Ward, 607–32. Malden, MA: Blackwell, 2004.
Wimsatt, William, and Monroe C. Beardsley. "The Intentional Fallacy." *Sewanee Review* 54 (1946): 468–88.
Winship, Lyndsey. "Into the Groove: How We Taught Madonna to Krump and Thrust." *The Guardian*, November 24, 2015. Available online: https://www.theguardian.com/stage/2015/nov/24/into-the-groove-how-we-taught-madonna-to-krump-and-thrust.
Wittgenstein, Ludwig. *Philosophical Investigations: The English Text of the Third Edition*, translated by G. E. M. Anscombe. New York: Macmillan, 1968.
Wittgenstein, Ludwig. *Zettel*, edited by G. E. M. Anscombe and G. H. Von Wright, translated by G. E. M. Anscombe. Berkeley: University of California Press, 1970.
Wolff, Francis. *Pourquoi la musique?* Paris: Fayard, 2015.
Wollheim, Richard. *Art and Its Objects*, 2nd ed. Cambridge: Cambridge University Press, 1980.
Wollheim, Richard. "Pictorial Style: Two Views." In *The Concept of Style*, edited by Berel Lang, 129–45. Philadelphia: University of Pennsylvania Press, 1979.
Wolterstorff, Nicholas. *Art Rethought: The Social Practices of Art*. Oxford: Oxford University Press, 2015.
Wolterstorff, Nicholas. "Toward an Ontology of Art Works." *Noûs* 9 (1975): 115–42.
Womack, Kenneth. *Maximum Volume: The Life of Beatles Producer George Martin, The Early Years, 1926–1966*. Chicago: Chicago Review Press, 2017.
Young, James O. *Critique of Pure Music*. Oxford: Oxford University Press, 2014.
Zanes, R. J. Warren. "Too Much Mead? Under the Influence (of Participant-Observation)." In *Reading Rock and Roll: Authenticity, Appropriation, Aesthetics*, edited by Kevin J. H. Dettmar and William Richey, 37–72. New York: Columbia University Press, 1999.
Ziff, Paul. "On H. P. Grice's Account of Meaning." *Analysis* 28 (1967): 1–28.
Zilberg, Jonathan. "Yes, It's True: Zimbabweans Love Dolly Parton." *Journal of Popular Culture* 29 (1995): 111–25.

Index of Songs Cited

3 Hour Drive (Keys) 9
911 is a Joke (Public Enemy) 12

Affectionate Punch (Associates) 119
A Hard Rain's a-Gonna Fall (Dylan)
    Patti Smith 79–80
American Pie (Mclean)
    Madonna 67
American Woman (Guess Who)
    Lenny Kravitz 160
Amphetamine Logic (Sisters of Mercy) 132
Ashes to Ashes (David Bowie) 130, 131

Babe I'm Gonna Leave You (Anne
    Bredon) 143
Baltimore (Newman)
    Nina Simone 116
Betty (Taylor Swift) 127, 157, 204 n.3
Bitter Sweet Symphony (Verve) 145
Blessed Assurance (Knapp) 31
    as This Is My Story, This Is My Song
    (Monk) 31
Blown' in the Wind (Dylan) 64–5, 191 n.35
    Peter, Paul, and Mary 3, 4
Blue Suede Shoes (Perkins) 141–3
    Elvis Presley 141–2
    Lemmy and the Upsetters 141–2
Boredom (Buzzcocks) 118
Brain Damage (Pink Floyd) 96
Bye Bye Blackbird (Henderson and
    Dixon) 151

Ça Plane pour Moi (Plastic Bertrand) 40, 42
Childhood (Michael Jackson) 191 n.37
C Moon (Wings) 174

Da Butt (E.U.) 2
Da Doo Ron Ron (Crystals) 14
Dancevision (Human League) 118

Dazed and Confused (Holmes) 143
    Led Zeppelin 143
    String Quartet Tribute to Led Zeppelin 150
De Do Do Do (The Police) 14
Dear God (XTC) 48
Diamonds Are a Girl's Best Friend (Styne
    and Robin) 167
Diana Parts 1 and 2 (Kantner and Slick) 137
Dizzy Miss Lizzy (Williams) 117
Don't Fence Me In (Fletcher and Porter) 98
Don't Worry Baby (Beach Boys) 81
    Bryan Ferry 81
Dover Beach (Bangles) 132, 135
Dreaming (Blondie) 163
    Smashing Pumpkins 163–4
Dreams (Fleetwood Mac) 2, 5, 15, 37, 38

Everlong (Foo Fighters) 137

Fairytale of New York (Pogues) 15
Farewell Mother Dear (Stephen Foster) 10
F* the Police (Mal and Beaz) 47

Give Ireland Back to the Irish (Wings) 12, 173–4
Go Down, Moses (traditional) 190 n.31
God Save the Queen (Sex Pistols) 73, 92
Good Vibrations (Beach Boys) 9
Goodnight Irene (traditional) 46
Guitar Man (Reed) 139

Hail to the Chief (traditional melody) 131
Hallelujah Chorus (G. F. Handel) 34
Happy Birthday to You 23, 24, 25
Help! (Beatles) 134
Here Comes the Bride (traditional) 46
He's Got the Whole World in His Hands
    (traditional) 3

Index of Songs Cited

He's So Fine (The Chiffons) 131
Hit 'Em Up Style (Oops!) (Cantrell)
 Carolina Chocolate Drops 148
Hurricane (Dylan) 49, 187 n.41
Hurt (Nine Inch Nails) 152, 178 n.32
 Johnny Cash 152, 178 n.32

I am the Walrus (Beatles) 134
I Left my Heart in San Francisco (Cory
 and Cross) 81
I Saw Mommy Kissing Santa Claus
 (Ronettes) 171
I Still Miss Someone (Johnny Cash) 67
I Think We're Alone Now (Cordell) 152–4
 Rubinoos 152, 154
 Tiffany 152–4
I Will Always Love You (Parton)
 Dolly Parton 9, 76
 Whitney Houston 9
Ice Ice Baby (Vanilla Ice) 150
Idiot Wind (Dylan) 65–6
If I Should Fall from Grace with God
 (Pogues) 15–16
I'll Be Home (Newman) 67
In Germany Before the War (Randy
 Newman) 67
In the Navy (Village People) 70
It's Alright Ma (I'm Only Bleeding)
 (Dylan) 27, 32
It's Oh So Quiet (Land and Meder)
 Björk 91–2, 143, 145, 151
 Betty Hutton 91, 143, 145
It Wasn't God Who Made Honky Tonk
 Angels (Miller)
 Kitty Wells 129–30, 157
I've Just Seen a Face (Beatles) 117

Jambalaya (On the Bayou) (Williams) 3
J'avais rêvé du Nord (Peste Noire) 66
The Joke (Carlile) 50
Jolene (Parton) 23

Kidnapper (Blondie) 163

Landslide (Fleetwood Mac)
 Dixie Chicks 98
Last of the Steam-Powered Trains (Kinks)
 137

Lies (Knickerbockers) 151
Like a Rolling Pin (Replacements) 25
Like a Rolling Stone (Dylan) 25
Long Black Veil (Dill and Wilkin) 67
Losing my Religion (R.E.M.) 163
Louie Louie (Berry) 104
Love Thang (First Choice) 116
Lucy in the Sky with Diamonds (Beatles)
 9
Lust for Life (Iggy Pop) 131

Macho Man (Village People) 70
Mack the Knife (Brecht and Weill) 24
Material Girl (Brown and Rans)
 Madonna 160, 162, 167
Me and Bobby McGee (Kristofferson)
 151
Mississippi Goddam (Nina Simone) 89
Modern Love (Bowie)
 Last Town Chorus 24
My Man's Gone Now (Gershwin) 149
My Sweet Lord (Harrison) 131
My Way (François and Revaux)
 Elvis Presley 58
 Frank Sinatra 58
 Sid Vicious 58, 66

Natural's Not in It (Gang of Four) 124–5
No More Auction Block (traditional) 64
North Country Blues (Dylan) 68

Oh! Susanna (Stephen Foster) 42–3, 44,
 49, 106
 Taj Mahal 43
Okie from Muskogee (Haggard) 11
 Grateful Dead 11–14
Old Man (Young) 41
 The Wailin' Jennys 41
Old Man Trump (Guthrie) 89
Old Town Road (Lil Nas X) 104, 165
On the Atchison, Topeka and the Santa Fe
 (Warren and Mercer) 130
O Superman (Anderson) 51
Ouch (Rutles) 134

P.A.'s (Scritti Politti) 119
Peggy Sue (Holly) 130, 139
Peggy Sue Got Married (Holly) 130–1, 139

Piece of My Heart (Ragovoy and Berns)
  Erma Franklin 144–5
  Faith Hill 145, 151, 153
  Janis Joplin 144–5
Piggy in the Middle (Rutles) 134
Pink Moon (Drake) 2–3, 37
Please Please Please (James Brown) 80, 82
Pretty Hurts (Beyoncé) 127, 204 n.3
Purple Haze (Hendrix) 40

Radio Free Europe (R.E.M.) 162, 170
Redondo Beach (Patti Smith) 116
Ring of Fire (Johnny Cash) 67
Roadhouse Blues (Doors) 133

San Francisco (Be Sure to Wear Some Flowers in your Hair) (McKenzie) 130
Scarborough Fair/Canticle (Simon and Garfunkel) 116
See Emily Play (Pink Floyd) 101
Senior Service (Elvis Costello) 137
Shine on You Crazy Diamond (Pink Floyd) 96, 104–6
Short People (Randy Newman) 32, 66–7
Sign o' the Times (Prince) 89
Sluggin' for Jesus (Cabaret Voltaire) 118
Smokestack Lightning (Howlin' Wolf) 137
Someone to Watch over Me (Gershwin) 55–6
Something in the Air (Thunderclap Newman) 51
Somethin' Stupid (Parks) 189 n.4
Space Oddity (Bowie) 130
Spirit in the Sky (Greenbaum) 150
Stayin' Alive (Bee Gees) 116
Strange Fruit (Meeropol) 68
Strawberry Fields Forever (Beatles) 47
Street Fighting Man (Rolling Stones) 8, 10
Sunday Morning Coming Down (Kristofferson) 151
Sun King (Beatles) 76

Taps (traditional) 29–30, 32, 131, 183 n.39
Tell Me Why You Like Roosevelt (Jackson) 39
  Jesse Winchester 39, 41, 47

Terraplane Blues (Robert Johnson) 25
The Fly (U2) 157
The Great Gig in the Sky (Pink Floyd) 92, 99
The Last Time (Rolling Stones) 145–6
The Macarena (Los del Río) 2
The Medium was Tedium (Wigley) 124
The Soldier's Joy (traditional) 60
The Star-Spangled Banner (Key) 27–30, 32, 34, 38, 184 n.3
  Jimi Hendrix 27–34, 38, 39, 43, 44, 80, 131, 183 n.37
The Way You Look Tonight (Kern and Fields) 145
This Flight Tonight (Mitchell)
  Joni Mitchell 57
  Nazareth 57
This May Be the Last Time (Staple Singers) 145–6
Time after Time (Lauper and Hyman) 149
To Anacreon in Heaven (traditional) 29
Train Kept A Rollin (Bradshaw) 137
Train to Nowhere (Savoy Brown) 151
Try a Little Tenderness (Campbell, Connelly, and Woods) 167
Turning Japanese (Vapors) 150
T.V.O.D. (Miller) 114

Us and Them (Pink Floyd) 105

Vision of Johanna (Dylan) 131

Walking Blues (Johnson) 133
Warm Love (Morrison) 3
We Shall Overcome (traditional) 3, 63
Werewolves of London (Zevon, Marinell, and Wachtel) 44, 49, 187 n.45
White Car in Germany (Associates) 118–19
White Rabbit (Jefferson Airplane) 135
Whoomp! (There It Is) (Tag Team) 3
The Wild Side of Life (Hank Thompson) 130
Wish You were Here (Pink Floyd) 103
With a Little Help from My Friends (Beatles) 75
  Joe Cocker 75
Woke up this Morning (King) 133

Wooden Heart (Wise, Weisman, Twomey, and Kaempfert) 139

Yesterday (Beatles) 117
Yes! We Have no Bananas (Silver and Cohn) 65
Y.M.C.A. (Village People) 70
You're So Vain (Simon)
   Carly Simon 41–2, 44–5, 49, 50
   Marilyn Manson 41
   Taylor Swift 5, 43, 50
You'll Never Walk Alone (Rodgers and Hammerstein) 2, 113
In Your Eyes (Peter Gabriel) 38, 43, 49
You've Got a Friend in Me (Randy Newman) 67

General Index

Names of songs are listed in their own dedicated index

Abell, Catharine 186 n.23
accessibility of popular music 7, 30, 118, 123–4, 128–9, 135–6, 152, 168, 171
Adams, Ryan 139
Adorno, Theodor 121
aesthetic ideas 123–5
aesthetic pleasure/rewards 2, 7, 170, 179 n.41
aesthetic properties 32, 46–7, 49, 56–7, 62, 76
   and autonomism 56, 59
   expressive properties 32, 57
   See also disgust, ethicism, expressivity
aesthetic response 58–9
agency 1, 59, 84–5, 91, 153, 159
   atomistic/individual 75, 85, 89, 103, 106
   collective and group 83, 85, 99, 103–7
   display in performance 63
   of movie directors 84–5
   of video directors 197 n.84
allusion 127–39, 152–4
   covert 136–7
   cross-modal 131
   disruptive 136, 139
   as indirect reference 130–2
   as intention-dependent 130, 132–4
   in *The Matrix* 128–30, 131, 133, 135–6, 138, 204 n.11
   prescriptive 134
   saturated 139, 152, 208 n.28
   transitive 130
   See also cover songs
Altamont Speedway concert 9, 168
answer songs 129–30
anti-intentionalism 13–14, 25, 51–2, 104, 132–3, 158
Apodaca, Nathan 2–3, 5, 15, 38

appropriation 7, 38, 40, 58, 76, 77, 82, 142, 143, 146, 150, 151, 174, 185 n.6, 194 n.30, 196 n.70
Associates, The 118
Auslander, Philip 5, 83, 191 n.39, 194 n.39
authentic inauthenticity 78–9
authenticity 73–87, 122
   as ascribed 80–4
   of country music 73, 79, 83
   ideology of 77–9, 86, 195 n.45
   and modernism 74
   postmodern rejection of 77–9
   and Romanticism 75–6
   as perceived 74, 76–7
   socio-historical criterion of 74–7, 87

Bacharach, Sondra 98, 182 n.22
Back to the Future (film) 167
Band, The 83
Bangles 132, 135, 136, 138
Barrett, Sid 90, 92–4, 96, 97–8, 101, 103, 104, 105, 200 n.28
Barthes, Roland 52, 158
Beach Boys, The 11–12, 81
Beatles, The 2, 9, 47, 63–4, 117, 138, 163, 166, 176 n.4
   Ed Sullivan Show 166
   fan behavior 176 n.7
   imitated 151
   parodied 134
   See also names of particular individuals
Bee Gees 70, 116
Beethoven, Ludwig 24, 91, 145, 147
Behr, Adam 80, 83, 85
Bennet, Andrew 157
Bennet, Tony 81
Beyoncé 75, 93, 103, 127

Bicknell, Jeanette 5, 21, 56, 68, 180 n.1
  on singer persona 55, 63–5
Björk 91–2, 143, 145, 146, 207 n.5
Bon Jovi (band) 83
Bordwell, David 197 n.89
Borges, Jorge Luis 102
Bouwsma, O.K. 169
Bowie, David 24, 118, 130–1
  theatricality 78
Bragg, Billy 84
Braque, Georges 112
Brecht, Bertolt 24
Bredon, Anne 143
Brownstein, Carrie 82
Bruford, Bill 199 n.18
Burroughs, William 131
Buzzcocks 118, 122
Byrne, David 119

Cabaret Voltaire (group) 112, 115, 118–19
Carlile, Brandi 40
Carlisle, Belinda 113
Carroll, Lewis
  Alice's Adventures in Wonderland 128–30, 135
  Sylvie and Bruno 129–31, 133, 136, 138
Carroll, Noël 127–8, 133, 178 n.24, 190 n.24, 204 n.2
Cash, Johnny 67, 151, 152, 178 n.32
Cervantes (Miguel de Cervantes Saavedra) 102–3
Chaucer, Geoffrey 133
Christgau, Robert 6
Clash, The 118
classical music 5, 119, 154, 178 n.20, 178 n.25
  autonomy of 114
  composer/work centrality 6, 23–4, 51, 146–8, 168
  performance goal 4, 42, 146–7
  popular, distinguished from 4, 6, 7, 146–8
  posthumous work completion 198 n.4
  See also names of particular individuals
Cobain, Kurt 55, 79
Cohen, Ted 127, 138
collaboration 84–5, 93–5, 98–103, 105–7, 198 n.5, 199 n.18
  weak versus strong 92, 100, 103, 105
  See also group agency, intentions

composer
  as communicative agent 4, 6, 23, 31, 60–1, 114, 147
  intentions of 25–6, 28, 33–4, 42–3, 51
  See also songwriters
context of communication 1–6, 9, 11, 14–15, 26–7, 34–5, 42, 57, 59–62 65–70, 165
  author attitudes as element of 56
  author intentions as element of 25–6, 33–4, 151–4
  musico-historical and cultural 23–4, 26, 77, 85, 114, 116, 135, 146–50, 165, 170
  recontextualization 4, 15, 37–40, 42–4, 50–1, 57, 137
  utterance meaning dependent on 21–2, 27–8, 32–3, 37–40, 42–4, 50–1, 102, 113, 152–5, 174–5
  See also allusion, contextualism, covers, intentions, persona
contextualism 56–7, 59–62, 65, 69, 71, 102, 153
country (genre) 12, 31, 40, 73, 79, 83, 129–30, 145, 151, 165
Corgan, Billy 163–4
cover albums 139, 143, 207 n.15
cover bands 82–3
covers (recordings) 81, 91, 139, 152–5
  cultural conditions for 144, 146–51
  defined 142–4, 151
  remakes distinguished from 141–6, 153–4
  self-covering 139
Cray, Wesley 66–8
cubism 57, 112
Curtis, Ian 122, 203 n.40

Danto, Arthur 56, 103, 153
Dash & Lily (series) 15
Davidson, Donald 209 n.3
Davies, David
  fictive utterance 186 n.33, 187 n.45
Davies, Stephen 29, 46, 181 n.13, 182 n.18, 182 n.19
  levels of intentions 182 n.35
Davis, Angela Y. 5
Davis, Miles 103, 149–50, 211 n.41
  Kind of Blue 150

Del Rey, Lana 75
Deliverance (film) 135–6
Desler, Anne 86
Desperate Bicycles, The 124
Dewey, John 1
Dibben, Nicola 191 n.41
Dickens, Charles 48
Dion, Céline 28
disco (genre) 70, 78, 112–13, 116
disgust 58–9, 61–2, 69–70
Dissanayake, Ellen 46
Dodd, Julian 4
Dr. Dre (Andre Young) 69
Drake, Nick 2–3, 37
Dylan, Bob 27, 32–3, 74, 78, 80, 85–6, 131, 138
　at March on Washington 3, 64
　persona 63–6, 68
　poetic license by 48, 187 n.41
　rejects determinate interpretation 183 n.50

Eliot, T.S. 46, 132–3, 135–6, 138
ethicism 56, 61, 68, 83, 190 n.24
expressivity 16, 31, 45–6, 57–8, 61–2, 65–6, 75, 92, 102–3, 116–17, 164, 173, 186 n.25
　authenticity of 62, 74, 80–1

Fall, The 103, 115, 118, 119, 121
feminism 113, 127, 129, 204 n.3
Ferry, Brian 81
Festival Express (film) 69–70
fictionality 28, 29, 38, 43–5, 47–51
　Abell, Catharine 186 n.23
　Davies, David 186 n.33, 187 n.45
　Friend, Stacie 186 n.33
fictional world 28, 29, 43–4, 49–50, 128–9
First Choice 116
Fiske, John 160, 167
Fitzgerald, Ella 24
Fleetwood Mac 2, 15, 37, 38, 123
Fleetwood, Mick 2
Flying Lizards, The 124
Fodor, Jerry 209 n.20
forgery 62, 64
Foster, David 9
Foster, Stephen 10, 42–3
Fox, Aaron 79
Friend, Stacie 186 n.33

Frith, Simon 76, 115
　on authenticity 74, 76–7, 122

Gang of Four (musical group) 112–14, 125
Garcia, Jerry 11, 14, 69, 113–15, 122, 125
Gartside, Green 119
Gaut, Berys 61, 190 n.25
Gaye, Marvin 37
gender 6–8, 40, 79, 127, 136, 152–3
Gendron, Bernard 122
Genette, Gérard 164
genius 75, 84–6, 122–3
genre classification 5, 60–1, 66, 73–7, 79, 86, 119, 133, 135, 151, 161, 164–7, 169, 170
Germs, The 113, 164
Gershwin, George and Ira 55, 92, 94
Gilbert, Margaret 98
Gilbert and Sullivan 48
Gilmour, David 90, 92–7, 101, 103–5, 107
Gioia, Ted 5
Godlovitch, Stan 63
Go-Go's 113
Gombrich, E.H. 117
Grateful Dead 11–12, 46, 69–70, 132, 138
Grice, Paul 179 n.44, 198 n.1
Grossberg, Lawrence 74, 77–9, 157, 164–5, 168
group agency 69–70, 83, 89–93, 95, 101–7, 116
　See also collaboration
group identity 83, 92–101

Hamm, Charles 7, 9–10
Hardy, Thomas 49
Harrison, George 131
Hawkins, Stan 55
Haydn, Joseph 10, 34, 147–8
Hays Code 60
Hayward, Charles 124
hermeneutics 1–2, 62, 80, 125
Hesmondhalgh, David 124
Heylin, Clinton 112
Hip-hop 47, 79, 165
Hoffmann, E. T. A. 91
Holmes, Jake 143
holism
　See meaning holism

Holly, Buddy 117, 130, 132
Home, Stewart 113
Houston, Whitney 9
Hudson, Rock 70, 192 n.53
Hughes, Walter 70
Human League, The 113–14, 118
Hunter, Meredith 9, 168
Hunter, Robert 132, 135

identity
　criterion of 95–8
　of a musical performance 28–9, 33, 182 n.35
　Leibniz 98
　Locke 95–6, 98
　See also group identity
imaginative engagement 44–9, 67, 123–4, 183 n.41, 186 n.33, 187 n.45
　See also fictionality
Impressionism 111, 115–17, 119
　musical 119
ineffability 16, 123, 160
intentional fallacy 25
intentions 12–14, 26, 59, 85, 132–5, 139, 160, 209 n.3
　collective/group 90, 93, 96, 97, 99, 101–7
　composer/songwriter 23, 25–6, 28, 32–4, 41–52
　defined 13, 89, 102
　hypothetical 104–6
　illocutionary and perlocutionary 134–5
　performers 12–14, 27–8, 32–4, 69, 90, 93, 101–7, 119–20, 142–4, 149, 152–4, 182 n.35, 188 n.1, 207 n.5
　and pragmatics 12, 22, 52, 179 n.44
　utterance context as feature of 25–6, 33–4, 151–4
　See also anti-intentionalism
intertextuality 114, 128, 157–71
　architextuality 164–5
　of cover versions 142–3
　radical, defined 157–8
　See also allusion, covers, genre classification, meaning holism
irony 11–12, 43, 78–9
Isle of Wight festival 211 n.41
Irwin, William 130–1, 135, 138, 205 n.21, 206 n.41

Jackson, Alan 31
Jackson, Michael 119, 191 n.37
Jackson, Otis 39
Jagger, Mick 8–9
　as co-writer with Keith Richards 10, 145
James, William 1
jazz 31, 145, 146–50, 154, 211 n.41
　as popular music 7–8
Johnson, Julian 178 n.21
jokes 41, 78, 130, 133–4, 138, 206 n.41
　musical 32, 131
Joplin, Janis 144–6, 149, 151
Joplin, Scott 7
Joyce, James
　Ulysses 60
Joy Division 115, 121, 203 n.40
　as Romantics 122

Kant, Immanuel 122, 124
Keightley, Keir 75–7
King, Jon 125, 203 n.60
King, Martin Luther, Jr. 2, 64
Kinks, The 137
Kivy, Peter 42, 51
Korean popular culture 137
Korsmeyer, Carolyn 58–9
Kravitz, Lenny 160
Kripke, Saul 21–2
Kristofferson, Kris 152

Lamarque, Peter 62
Larkin, Philip 8
Last Town Chorus, The 24
Leibniz, W. G. 98
Lennon, John 9, 63–4, 76, 174
Levinson, Jerrold 61
Led Zeppelin 143, 150, 163
Lez Zeppelin 143
literature
　See fictionality, poetry and literature
Locke, John 95–6, 98
Longworth, Karina 85
Lycan, William 22

Madonna (Madonna Louise Ciccone) 67, 78
　choreography collaborations 196 n.84
　"Material Girl" video 160, 162, 167
　as textual sign 159

Manson, Charles 2, 138, 176 n.4
Manuel, Peter 170
March on Washington (1963) 2–4, 64–5
Marcus, Greil 74, 78, 113
Mark, Thomas Carson 42
Martin, George 85
M*A*S*H (film) 38
Mason, Nick 90, 92, 94, 97, 101
mass art 144
   defined 127, 178 n.24
Matrix, The (film) 128–31, 133, 135–6, 138
McCartney, Linda 12, 173–4
McCartney, Paul 12, 117, 173–4
meaning
   personal and idiosyncratic 3–4, 114, 160
   of referring expressions 12, 22, 25, 38, 41–2, 44–5, 49–50
   See also hermeneutics, pragmatics, reference, semantics, semiotics, utterance meaning, utterer's meaning
meaning holism 157, 161–4, 166–71, 209 n.20, 211 n.44
   types distinguished 161–2, 169
Middleton, Richard 8–10, 158
Millar, Stephen 82
Miller, Daniel 114–15
Miller, Roger 151
Mitchell, Joni 57
   on Bob Dylan's inauthenticity 74
modernism 75, 112, 117, 121–3, 125
   and Romanticism 75, 122, 125
Mondrian, Piet 117
Monk, Thelonious 31, 145, 149
Moore, Allan F. 4, 5, 75, 177 n.9
   on performer authenticity 79–83, 195 n.52
Morrissey, Steven Patrick 83–4
Mosser, Kurt 142, 207 n.6
movements, artistic and cultural 112–17, 119–22, 125
   distinguished from style 115–17, 119, 125
Mozart, W.A. 24, 32, 95
musical style 12, 14, 17, 25, 30–1, 43, 75–6, 79, 81, 95, 106, 111–13, 115–16, 118, 121–2, 148–9, 167, 169
   appropriation of 142, 150–1, 196 n.70
   fashion, contingent relationship with 117–18
   individual versus general 119, 139, 202 n.35
   as prerequisite for utterance meaning 116–17, 165
   See also movements
music video 2, 5, 15, 38, 50, 67, 70, 85, 127, 137, 143, 157–8, 159, 160, 162, 167, 169, 174, 197 n.84, 209 n.10
mythology, classical 137

Nazareth (band) 57
Newman, Randy 32, 66–8
New Wave (music genre) 113, 115, 118, 150, 163–4
Nicks, Stevie 2, 38
Nirvana (band) 83
Nixon, Richard 27, 32
Nochlin, Linda 84–5
Normal, The 114–15

Oasis 10

Paddison, Max 12
parody 102, 133
Parton, Dolly 7, 9, 23, 76
   persona of 159–60
Pere Ubu 112
performance 3, 11–13, 26–30, 55
   distinguished from recorded track 9
   of classical music 4–5, 6–7, 24, 42, 48–9
   defined 188 n.1
   as sites of utterance meaning 33–4
   of work songs 49
   See also persona
persona 29, 55–71, 73–4, 78, 83–6, 91, 106, 118, 141, 151, 189 n.2, 189 n.4
   of Bon Jovi 83
   defined 55
   of Dolly Parton 159–60
   of John Lennon
   of Madonna 67, 197 n.84
   meaning, bearer of 159
   opaque 66–8, 75, 77
   of Paul McCartney 174

of Randy Newman 66–8, 192 n.45
of R.E.M. 162
transparent 66–9, 75, 81, 83, 200 n.32
See also sincerity
Peste Noire 66
Pet Shop Boys 78
Petty, Tom 79, 195 n.48
Phair, Liz 116
Picasso, Pablo 112
  Guernica 57
Pink Floyd 90–107
  See also names of particular individuals
plagiarism 131
Plaskete, George 142
poetry and literature 26, 33–4, 48, 158, 174
  and songs 46, 51–2, 188 n.48
  See also fictionality
Pop, Iggy 131–2
popular music
  classical music contrasted with 4–7, 146–8
  defined 6–7
  folk music distinct from 177 n.14, 193 n.13
  See also accessibility of popular music
Pogues, The 15–16, 37
post-punk 111–14, 118–25, 163
  lack of stylistic unity in 118–19, 121–5
  as mode of artistic modernism 120–5
pragmatics 1–2
  gesture contributes to 15, 191 n.41
  defined 10–12
  distinguished from hermeneutics 1–2
  distinguished from semantics 12–14, 21–30, 33, 41, 43
  of norms violation 14
  as study of context-dependent meaning 11–13, 21–2, 26, 39, 41–3
  See also context of communication, intentions, relevance principle, utterance meaning
pragmatism 1
Presley, Elvis 58, 139, 141–2, 166
production
  See recording production

punk (genre) 73–8, 111–12, 117–18, 121, 154
  Grossberg on 78

Quine, W. V. 162, 164

Raincoats, The 112–13, 115, 119
Ramones 78
rap
  See hip-hop
recontextualization
  See context of communication (recontextualization)
recording
  See track
recording production 9, 85, 93, 151, 197 n.83, 200 n.27
reference 12, 14, 21–3, 27–9, 38, 41–4, 49, 51, 81, 103, 133–7, 162–3, 174
  indirect 130–2, 135
  in fiction 38–9, 44–7, 49–50, 187 n.45
  See also covers, intertextuality
relevance principle 11, 39, 135, 179 n.44, 198 n.1
R.E.M. (group) 159, 162–3, 169–70
remakes
  See covers
Replacements, The 25, 158
Reynolds, Simon 120–2, 124, 202 n.35
rhythm 7–8, 16, 30–1, 46
  entrainment 46
  style 116
Robeson, Paul 190 n.31
Roches, The 34
Rodriguez, Olivia 169
Rolling Stones, The 8, 10, 131
  musical appropriation by 145–6, 196 n.70
  See also Altamont Speedway concert, *names of particular individuals*
Romanticism 75–6, 121–2, 193 n.23
Ross, Stephanie 131, 204 n.14
Rotten, Johnny (John Lydon) 78, 105–7
Rutles, The 134

Say Anything (film) 37–8, 40, 43, 49
Schapiro, Meyer 115

Schumann, Robert (*Frauenliebe* songs) 6–7
semiotics 176 n.3
Sex Pistols 73, 92, 118, 122
    See also names of particular individuals
Shakespeare, William 27–8, 41
Shocked, Michelle 64, 70
Shumway, David 114, 158–9, 161, 164–5
Simon, Carly 5, 41–2, 44–5, 50
Simon, Paul 76
Simon and Garfunkel 116
Simone, Nina 89, 116
Simpsons, The (television) 130, 135
Sinatra, Frank 55–6, 58
    duet with Nancy Sinatra 189 n.4
sincerity 17, 32, 42, 56, 62–3, 68, 73–4, 76, 80, 83, 86, 122
    See also persona
singing
    as action 8, 13–14, 23, 33–4, 39, 47
    See also performance
Sleater-Kinney 82, 167
Slits, The 113
Smith, Patti 55, 80, 83, 116
Smiths, The 75, 82–3, 163
Snoop Dog (Calvin Broadus Jr.) 79
Socrates 112–13
Song Exploder 9, 178 n.32
song-centered view of meaning 39–44
songs
    as distinct from recorded tracks 8–10, 142–4
    as structures for use 16, 29, 33, 47, 50, 174
    as thin musical works 24, 33, 35, 148–9, 152, 174
    See also work identity
songwriters
    as thoughtwriters 16, 174
Stecker, Robert 3, 26, 33
style
    See musical style
Summer, Donna 112
Summers, David 121
Swift, Taylor 127, 139, 157, 167, 204 n.3
    covering "You're So Vain" 5, 43–4
    rerecording *Fearless* 139

Talking Heads 113, 119
Taylor, Timothy 194 n.30
text
    distinguished from artwork 26, 204 n.12
    writerly 159–60, 162–3, 170
    See also intertextuality, songs
Thom, Paul 55
Throbbing Gristle 118, 121
TikTok 2, 5, 15, 39
Tollefsen, Deborah 98, 105–6
Tolstoy, Leo 190 n.26
track
    song distinguished from 8–10, 38–9, 142–4
    as utterance 38
Trump, Donald 44, 50, 58
Tucker, Moe 83
Turner, Tina 55

Urban, Keith 83
utterance meaning 26–30, 161–3, 168, 170–1, 175, 181 n.6
    of covers 152–4
    of literature 26
    semantic meaning, divergence from 10–14, 21–2, 29–30, 33–5, 66–7
    style as contributing factor in 116–17
    as utterer's meaning 10–14, 26–30
    of videos and recordings 15, 37–40, 43, 49, 67, 104, 114, 174
    See also context of communication, group agency, reference

Velvet Underground, The 7, 83
Vicious, Sid 58, 66
video
    See music video
Village People 70

Waits, Tom 51
Walser, Robert 83
Walton, Kendall 44
    on categories of art 57, 111, 116–17, 202 n.26
    on thoughtwriters/writing 16, 50
Waters, Roger 90, 92–8, 100–7

General Index

Watts, Charlie 10, 131
Webb, Jimmy 46
Weill, Kurt 7, 24
Weinstein, Deena 142
Weir, Bob 69–70
Wells, Kitty 129–30, 157
Who Sell Out, The 77
Wilde, Oscar 56
Willis, Ellen 85
Willis, Victor 70
Wilson, Brian 9
Wilson, Pamela 159
Winchester, Jesse 39, 41
Wittgenstein, Ludwig 115, 162, 169, 173

Woodstock (festival) 9, 27, 44, 75, 159, 169
  See also Hendrix, Jimi
work identity 10, 33, 56–7, 62–3, 165
  classical music 10, 23–4, 146–8
  popular songs 10, 23–4, 29, 148–9
work songs 5, 49, 181 n.12
Wright, Richard 90, 92, 94, 96, 97, 101, 106, 107

Yankovic, "Weird Al" 55–6

Zappa, Frank 32, 131
Ziff, Paul 114
Z'Nuff, Chip 159

www.ingramcontent.com/pod-product-compliance
Lightning Source LLC
Chambersburg PA
CBHW062139300426
44115CB00012BA/1979